Words and Stones

Oxford Studies in Anthropological Linguistics
William Bright, General Editor

Editorial Board

Wallace Chafe, *University of California, Santa Barbara*
Regna Darnell, *University of Western Ontario*
Paul Friedrich, *University of Chicago*
Dell Hymes, *University of Virginia*
Jane Hill, *University of Arizona*
Stephen C. Levinson, *Max Planck Institute, The Netherlands*
Joel Sherzer, *University of Texas, Austin*
David J. Parkin, *University of London*
Andrew Pawley, *Australian National University*
Jef Verschueren, *University of Antwerp*

WORDS AND STONES

The Politics of Language and Identity in Israel

Daniel Lefkowitz

OXFORD
UNIVERSITY PRESS

2004

OXFORD
UNIVERSITY PRESS

Oxford   New York
Auckland   Bangkok   Buenos Aires   Cape Town   Chennai
Dar es Salaam   Delhi   Hong Kong   Istanbul   Karachi   Kolkata
Kuala Lumpur   Madrid   Melbourne   Mexico City   Mumbai   Nairobi
São Paulo   Shanghai   Taipei   Tokyo   Toronto

Copyright © 2004 by Oxford University Press, Inc.

Published by Oxford University Press, Inc.
198 Madison Avenue, New York, New York 10016

www.oup.com

Oxford is a registered trademark of Oxford University Press

All rights reserved. No part of this publication may be reproduced,
stored in a retrieval system, or transmitted, in any form or by any means,
electronic, mechanical, photocopying, recording, or otherwise,
without the prior permission of Oxford University Press.

Library of Congress Cataloging-in-Publication Data
Lefkowitz, Daniel, 1961–
Words and stones : the politics of language and identity in Israel / Daniel Lefkowitz.
   p. cm. — (Oxford studies in anthropological linguistics ; 26)
Includes bibliographical references and index.
ISBN 0-19-512190-2
1. Anthropological linguistics—Israel. 2. Language and culture—Israel
3. Sociolinguistics—Israel. 4. Symbolism in communication. 5. Jews—Israel—Identity
6. Palestinian Arabs—Israel—Ethnic identity. I. Title. II. Series.
P35.5.I75L44 2004
306.44'095694—dc22   2003060956

9 8 7 6 5 4 3 2 1

Printed in the United States of America
on acid-free paper

For
Israel Szabo
and
Jimmy Craig
In Loving Memory

Preface

My title, "*Words and Stones*," interweaves various strands of meaning that are central to my book's content. *Words* stand for "language" in the popular imagination. We use the simplifying metaphor of the word to approximate the unthinkably complex materiality of human language. And though this book focuses on abstract dimensions of language structure, such as phonology, intonation, and discourse, it begins with words.

Stones stand for place and identity in the popular imagination of Israel/Palestine— in short, for struggle. Stones mark Palestinian space within the Jewish State. Homes built of stone pre-date the establishment of Israel, marking neighborhoods within Israeli cities as Palestinian space. Old walls built of stone crisscross newer Israeli forests, marking formerly Palestinian space as they outline vanished villages and homes. Most recently stone represents Palestinian identity through the deployment of stone-throwing as a weapon of insurrection in the *intifada*, the Palestinian national uprising. But stones represent more than just Palestinian presence in Israel. Jewish Israelis also lay claim to the image. While the dominant re-making of urban space in Israel replaced Palestinian stone houses with cinderblock buildings, Jewish Israel has also appropriated the stone tradition. Israel rebuilt the Jewish Quarter of the Old City in Jerusalem with stone homes, stone streets, and stone benches. The most fashionable homes for middle-class Jewish Israelis in Haifa are preserved stone houses that once belonged to Palestinians. Haifa, a city built up a steep mountainside, is now crisscrossed with monumental stone retaining walls, making way for roads, parks, and apartment buildings. Indeed, the most powerful mark of Israel as Jewish space are the enormous stones of the Wailing Wall in Jerusalem. Stones thus symbolize struggle in Israel/Palestine.

Juxtaposing "words" with "stones" also plays on the American childhood proverb, *"sticks and stones will break my bones, but words will never harm me."* My title plays ironically on this proverb, for the book claims the opposite: that "words" have the power to create what even the largest "sticks" cannot destroy. This book examines how language—and especially the deployment of language in actual discourse—both exerts and resists social power. Words are thus seen as an important locus of political struggle.

The many people who have helped me with the research, writing, and publication of this book are far too numerous to list here. Those I would like to single out for special thanks include mentors Joel Sherzer, Anthony Woodbury, Avraham Zilkha, and Tamar Katriel; colleagues Louise Meintjes and Lindsay Hale; relatives Aliyah Dex, Dafnah, Nitzana, and Maya Strauss; editors Peter Ohlin and Mary Brohammer; reviewer Bernard Spolsky; and friends Bethany Dreyfus, Ruti Shapira, Nabila Espanioli, Amir Makhoul, Yaron Shemer, and Pamela Saunders.

Acknowledgments

The author thanks the following for permission to use copyright material:

Lori Grinker and Contact Press Images Inc. for figure 4.1, that appeared on the cover of the 1986 paperback edition of David Shipler's *Arab and Jew*, Penguin.

The publishers of *Yedioth Ahronoth* for: figure 6.1, that appeared in the daily edition of that newspaper on May 25, 1992, p.1; figure 6.2, that appeared on May 25, 1992, p.3; figure 6.3, that appeared on May 25, 1992, p.3; figure 6.4, that appeared on May 25, 1992, p.5; figure 6.5, that appeared on May 25, 1992, p.2; figure 6.6, that appeared on May 25, 1992, p.7; figure 6.7, that appeared on May 25, 1992, p.1; figure 6.8, that appeared on May 25, 1992, p.1 of the "24-Hours" section; figure 6.9, that appeared on May 27, 1992, p.1; figure 6.10, that appeared on May 28, 1992, p.3; figure 6.11, that appeared on May 25, 1992, p.1; figure 6.12, that appeared on May 25, 1992, p.1 of the "24-Hours" section; figure 6.13, that appeared on May 29, 1992, p.23; figure 6.14, that appeared on May 27, 1992, p.3; figure 6.15, that appeared on May 25, 1992, p.6; figure 6.16, that appeared on May 26, 1992, p.1; figure 6.17, that appeared on May 26, 1992, p.3; figure 6.18, that appeared on May 29, 1992, p.1 of the "Friday Supplement" section.

University of Pennsylvania Press for figure 7.1, which is based on William Labov, *Sociolinguistic Patterns*, 1972, p.114.

Contents

Transcription Conventions

All English text (except where specifically indicated otherwise) is the author's translation of Hebrew speech. Translations adhere as closely as possible to the structure of the original Hebrew. Speaker pseudonyms appear on the left margin. The following conventions are observed in representing speech on the written page.

Punctuation marks indicate phrase-level pitch phenomena:

- Commas (",") represent an unmarked boundary of intonational phrasing
- Em-dashes ("—") represent a marked boundary of intonational phrasing—whether due to hesitation, self-repair, or interruption
- Question marks ("?") represent rising intonation, whether the phrase is syntactically or pragmatically a question or not
- Lines of transcribed text correspond to prosodic phrases.

Ellipses are used to represent pauses in the utterance, or conversational material that is omitted from the transcription:

- A two-dot ellipsis (..) represents a short pause in an utterance
- A three-dot ellipsis (…) indicates words left out within an utterance, or an omission of one or more turns at talk.

Parentheses enclose information about speech that is not a direct transcription of the speech, including paraphrased or approximated transcriptions and descriptions of meta-linguistic events, such as laughter:

- Rounded parentheses ( ) enclose the author's best transcription of speech that was difficult to discern
- Double parentheses (( )) enclose descriptions of non-speech events
- Square brackets [ ] enclose material that departs in some way from word-for-word translations of the Hebrew original.

Symbols used in the book to transcribe Hebrew words and names are pronounced as they are in English, with the exception of the following:

- /'/, a glottal stop (also represented as /ʔ/)
- /x/, a voiceless velar fricative
- /ħ/, a voiceless pharyngeal approximant
- /ʕ/, a voiced pharyngeal approximant.

Italicized Hebrew words are broadly phonemic representations. Additional technical linguistic conventions include:

- Angle brackets /a/ enclose phonemes.
- Square brackets [a] enclose phonetic representations.

Words and Stones

1

Negotiations and Identities

Many ethnographies begin with dramatic tales of the anthropologists' first—or last—encounter with "the field." This ethnography of language use in Israel, however, begins with a tale of the ethnographer at home, far from the field.

Far from the Field

I had been home nearly a year when Yasir Arafat, Chairman of the Palestinian Liberation Organization (PLO), and Yitzhak Rabin, Prime Minister of Israel, shook hands on the White House lawn as they signed what became known as the Oslo Peace Accords. This handshake seemed at the time to signal a remarkable watershed, as intractable enemies prepared to work together.

A few days later I received an email from an Israeli anthropologist, who wrote euphorically:

> *I [hope] everything you have to say about Israeli Arabs will have to be modified before you finish your writing — as language catches up with the incredible sociopolitical changes we're witnessing.*

As someone who had lived in Israel, whose relatives still live there, who had seen the terrible effects of violence, I too felt euphoric that peace might break out, at the prospect of a Palestinian state. But as a graduate student, working to finish my dissertation on the negotiation of Palestinian and Jewish identities in Israel, I felt shaken by the potential effect of this turn of events on my thesis. I had spent two eventful years in Israel, witnessing

3

the Gulf War, the Madrid Peace Conference, and the dramatic 1992 Israeli elections.[1] At home in the United States I felt distant from the ever-changing subject of my research—as if it were slipping away from me.

With the benefit of hindsight, I now see my feelings as the typical reaction of the ethnographer, rather than the unique experience of one who writes about the Middle East. Current events appear particularly dramatic in the Middle East—in part because they garner great media attention in the United States. The Middle East is so dynamic and so turbulent that "the present" rapidly becomes "the past." But all societies are constantly changing, and the ethnographic project is best understood as an attempt to capture culture as a process, rather than as an object. Anthropologists have come to recognize that ethnographic descriptions are always provisional, and this realization has coincided with new thinking about ethnographic texts. In abandoning the notions of an isolated and static ethnographic Other, ethnographers have also left behind writing styles that fix this Other by inscribing it in positivist texts.

But it is not only ethnographers who perceive reality as provisional. The provisional nature of identity was a recurrent theme among Palestinian Israelis I interviewed during my fieldwork in Haifa, Israel.[2] Many Palestinians constructed their own identities, for example, as dependent on the political situation. In one such interview, Stella, a Jewish Israeli research assistant, asked a group of three Palestinian Israelis about language use in their homes:[3]

TEXT 1.1.   HEBREW USE IN PALESTINIAN ISRAELI HOMES

Stella	What language do you speak with the children? Hebrew or Arabic?[4]
Lisa	No, only Arabic,
Samir	Never, we don't speak any other language, ...
	They know Hebrew well, very well, English too, ...
	They speak only Arabic, but they know Hebrew,
Rhoda	That is, they don't ... it's as if they don't dare speak, eh—
	...
Stella	What don't they dare speak?
Rhoda	OK, ... my son too, ...
	Television, neighbors,
	But to come and speak [Hebrew] with him instead of Arabic, ...
	He needs to know [Hebrew],
	And it'll take root in him,
	That ... Arabic is his mother-tongue,
	And Hebrew is a language that can—
	It may be that it'll be the language of the street,
	But, not at home,
	OK, good, and all, but not to feel that that— that it's equal, ...
	Maybe, after there is peace, maybe there will be—
	And the Jews, too, will learn [Arabic], ... (193B:2:20–5:20)[5]

Rhoda asserts that Arabic—not Hebrew—represents her own and her children's identity as Palestinians, but she ties these sentiments to the then ongoing official state of war between Israel and Palestinian political organizations. Did Rhoda's ideas about her own identity change dramatically after the signing of the Oslo peace accords? Did her ideas about language change? Did her own use of language change?[6]

Maybe. But social and cultural processes do not change as quickly as do political realities, and the discourse of peace that emerged from the Oslo Accords appeared to make more salient the ethnic, racial, national, and class divisions that comprise Israeli "identity." In the months immediately following the signing of the Israel-PLO agreement, for example, observers speculated that Israeli Arabs (i.e., Palestinian citizens of Israel) and Mizrahi Jews (i.e., Jewish Israelis whose families had emigrated from Arab and Middle Eastern countries) would constitute a cultural bridge between Israel and the Arab world. History unfolded differently, however. Israeli electoral politics were turned upside down by ethnic parties and identity politics (Lefkowitz 1997), and unprecedented numbers of Arabs and Jews were killed in renewed violence between Jewish settlers and Palestinian residents in the Occupied Territories.[7] Arguably, by blurring political and military boundaries, the peace accords pressured marginalized groups to negotiate social boundaries ever more vociferously. The dramatic political negotiations may well change the way in which Israelis negotiate their identities, but the negotiation itself remains central to an understanding of cultural process.

Negotiation

This book examines Israeli national identity, looking at the ways in which it is imagined (Anderson 1991) and at the ways various imaginings are deployed in the semiotics and politics of everyday life. I am interested specifically in the ongoing recreation, redefinition, and reapplication of nationalist imaginings.

This is not a historical study, though the history of identity constructions is crucial background for understanding their semiotics.[8] This study looks at the semiotics of national identity constructions by looking at the contestation over social identity in Israel. While specifically looking at Israel—where this struggle has high visibility and significance—I hope to provide more general insights into social transformation. The configuration of overlapping and inconsistent national, racial, ethnic, and class divisions found in Israel exists also in other parts of the modern world. Language is the lens I use to observe, clarify, and magnify the subtle processes involved in this struggle. I also hope to provide insights into how language itself is structured and how it is transformed.

To study society by studying language is at the same time to study language by studying society. This recursive perspective draws inspiration from the work of Pierre Bourdieu, who defines the *habitus* as "both the generative principle of objectively classifiable judgments and the system of classification ... of these practices" (Bourdieu 1984:170). Actual instances of language use draw upon the meanings inherent in the abstract language system, while at the same time offering the possibility of rearranging those meanings for future use. Such historical recursiveness coincides with a contextual recursiveness, as speech draws on the context of utterance for its meaning, even as utterances contribute to the definition of context (see Briggs and Bauman 1992; Goodwin and Duranti 1992).

To think about these recursive, dialogic relationships I employ the spatial metaphor of a spiral, which captures three key features of sociolinguistic symbols:

- The meaning of a symbol may change over time.

- The meaning of a symbol may differ for various socially positioned speakers.

- The meaning of a symbol at any particular time recalls earlier and differently positioned meanings.

Figure 1.1 represents these ideas schematically. The figure shows a spiral that expands rightward across (historical) time, while oscillating within a space defined by the orthogonal axes, labeled "symbolic value" and "social position." The spiral's rightward expansion represents the change in symbolic meaning over time. The spiral's oscillation within the space of symbolic value/social position represents the semiotic gaps that emerge between old and new meanings of a symbol on the one hand and between the meanings a symbol evokes for differently positioned individuals on the other. The spiral's tendency to return to proximity (though not identity) with earlier states suggests the dialogic connections new meanings retain with old.

These ideas can be explicated through a detailed look at figure 1.1. Figures 1.2–1.4 transform the three-dimensional diagram into two-dimensional images, projecting the spiral onto the plane constituted by the symbolic/social space. These figures present

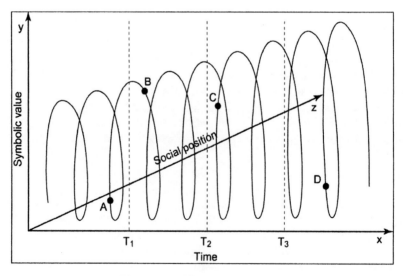

Figure 1.1.   The Discourse Spiral.

cross-sections of the spiral taken at three points in time, T_1, T_2, and T_3. Figure 1.2a illustrates a common semiotic phenomenon, namely a gap in meaning across social space. Here the same symbol encompasses divergent meanings for two social groups. The word *bad* offers a simple example, since it means "not-good" for most White speakers in the United States but can also mean "good" for African-American speakers.[9] Figure 1.2b illustrates another common phenomenon in the social life of symbols, namely a change in meaning. Here the same symbol assumes different meanings over time for the same social group. The word *gay* demonstrates this phenomenon, since it once meant "happy" but has come to mean (also) "homosexual."

Figures 1.1–1.4 can be applied to more complex semiotic processes, such as the debate in the United States over the meaning of the "Confederate battle flag." During the 1990s several southern state legislatures voted to modify state flags so as to remove

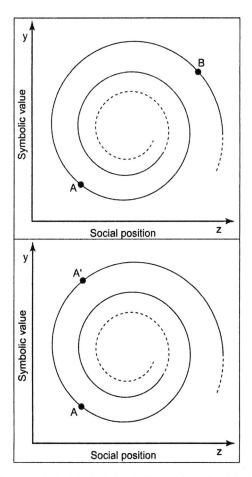

Figure 1.2.   The Discourse Spiral Projected onto the Symbolic/Social Plane at Point T_1.

(or reduce) the Confederate symbols they contained, while other states voted not to make such changes (Webster and Leib 2001). This acrimonious debate hinged on what the flag meant—and to whom. To White Southerners the Confederate flag is a potent symbol of self-reliance and states' rights. To African Americans the Confederate flag is a potent symbol of slavery and hatred. Figure 1.2a can represent this social difference in meaning: the difference in symbolic value between points A ("self-reliance") and B ("discrimination") corresponds to a difference in social positioning (White/Black).

What is often omitted (or obscured) by the debate over symbols of the Confederacy, however, is the symbol's history. The recent debate was precipitated by actions taken in the 1960s, when many southern state legislatures inserted the Confederate symbols as a statement against the civil rights legislation being imposed upon them at the time (Webster and Leib 2001:272). Figure 1.3 schematically represents this meaning space in the 1960s. This cross-section of the spiral from figure 1.1 at time T_2 includes a third point, labeled C. Point C has approximately the same coordinate for "social position" as point A, representing the meaning of the flag for Whites in the 1960s. Point C also has approximately the same coordinate for "symbolic value" as point B, representing a situation in which Whites and Blacks agreed that the flag meant "race."

Finally, figure 1.4 represents the situation in the mid-1990s. This cross-section at time T_3 of the figure 1.1 spiral includes a fourth point, labeled D. Point D represents the meaning of the flag to Whites in the 1990s. Its symbolic value coordinate is close to that of point A, reflecting the fact that the modern deployment of the symbol rhetorically evoked its earlier meanings of "self-reliance" and "states' rights." This dialogism (see Bakhtin 1981) is represented in figure 1.4 by the dotted lines connecting points A and D, as well as points B and D. Discourse often represents such historically separated reincarnations of a symbol (i.e., points A and D) as if they were the same—

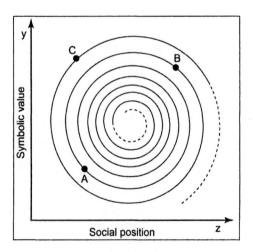

Figure 1.3.   The Discourse Spiral Projected onto the Symbolic/Social Plane at Point T_2.

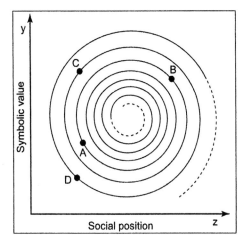

Figure 1.4.   The Discourse Spiral Projected onto the Symbolic/Social Plane at Point T_3.

but they are not identical. Symbolic processes revisit prior meanings without returning to them. Utterances draw on dialogic resonances, both historical and social, while inflecting them with new settings. Current meanings evoke earlier meanings, but are not defined by them. The spiral metaphor helps conceptualize recursiveness as a projection forward in time, in which symbols accumulate layers of historicized meaning as they become richer, more complex, and ever more significant.

The linguistic symbols used in Israeli negotiations of identity behave as if they were points on the spiral in figure 1.1. Old prestigious forms give way to newer vernacular forms in the Jewish community at the same time that they are adopted by Palestinian Israeli speakers of Hebrew. And the multivocal social meanings of the forms adopted by Palestinian Israelis are associated both with the high prestige of standard Israeli Hebrew and with the low prestige Israeli discourse attributes to symbols inflected with Arabness (see chapter 7). The dynamic that drives the dialogic spiral is the negotiation of meaning.

The most prominent division in Israeli society—between Arab and Jew—stands in opposition to a lower-profile division between Ashkenazi and Mizrahi Jews.[10] In turn, the latter division will be explicated with reference to the important dichotomy of Mizrahi Jew and Palestinian Arab. One site of such negotiation is the day-to-day, face-to-face interaction between individual social actors.

THE VISA OFFICE LANGUAGE BALLET

The visa office is in a stately part of town, next to a public park on the flanks of Mount Carmel, with a magnificent view of Haifa harbor and the Mediterranean Sea. The office occupies an old British colonial building, one of many still used more or less in their old capacities. Inside the stateliness ends, supplanted by drab walls and narrow hallways overflowing with impatient petition seekers.

As an American visitor needing only the periodic renewal of my tourist visa, I glide past most of the lines. Interior Ministry buildings all over Israel are packed these days because of the huge influx of Russian immigrants. These recent arrivals need to stand in lines for hours.

My wait is no more than twenty minutes. I watch carefully for my turn, then push through the crowds to get into the office. Inside, three women sit behind cluttered desks, facing computer terminals. Their desks are surrounded by walls of old cardboard files, mountains of old documents. The office suitably represents Israel's awkward position between first and third worlds: the computers lay claim to a modernity that the walls of dusty files contest.

I take a seat at one of the desks but find I am interrupting a Russian man's desperate plea for the official's attention. The official prefers to deal with me and my straightforward visa renewal, but the Russian man is aggressive and insistent. He is also talkative. From our accents it is clear where each of us comes from. Although I have been in Israel for a year and speak Hebrew well, I have not lost my strong American accent. The Russian man has been in Israel only a few months, and he speaks Hebrew haltingly and ungrammatically. The woman official is a native speaker of Hebrew.

As my visa application is processed, a negotiation over language unfolds as a choreographed ballet. I address the Israeli official in Hebrew, and she responds to me in English. The Russian man, apparently pleased to meet an American, starts a conversation with me in English. I answer him in Hebrew, but he returns to English. Meanwhile, the Russian man's dialogue with the Israeli official becomes quite heated. They conduct their struggle in Hebrew, despite his rudimentary skills in that language and his evident preference for English.

These language choices constitute a negotiation of identity, as power is being won and lost in a simple language game. The native-Hebrew-speaking Israeli insists on English with the American and Hebrew with the Russian, while the Russian insists on English with the American and accepts Hebrew with the Israeli. Multiple negotiations are playing out simultaneously: the Russian man is negotiating over the official's attention and assistance; he deploys his English knowledge via a conversation with me, as part of this struggle. I am negotiating a position in Israeli society by insisting on Hebrew despite the eagerness of others to use English (which is an easier language for me). The official is negotiating her authority—as native Israeli, as gatekeeping power broker, and, not insignificantly, as a woman in conversation with two men.

Hebrew is the pride and joy of the (Jewish) Israeli people and the primary socializing force in integrating the Russian immigrants (see chapter 5). The Israeli official must therefore insist on Hebrew, despite the man's displayed preference for English. Yet with the American, the negotiation is over status, not national identity, and competence in English is the key to this contest. The fact that both the Israeli official and the Russian immigrant insist on English with the Hebrew-speaking American tourist reflects a deep-seated linguistic insecurity (see Labov 1982a) that pervades modern Israeli life.

Yet the full extent of this negotiation can be explicated only with respect to a much broader social context. The triangular nature of this language-use struggle stems from the particular social situation in Israel. My ethnographic research coincided with a massive immigration to Israel of Jews from the then Soviet Union. During the latter part of 1990 as many as two thousand immigrants were streaming into Israel each day, taxing the country's material resources for providing housing, employment, and social services (Siegel 1998). Perhaps more crucially, the influx taxed Israel's ideological resources. Israeli socialization efforts converged on the teaching of Hebrew to the incoming Russians.

American Jews, on the other hand, have a different status in Israel. Lumped together with Jews from Britain, South Africa, and other English-speaking countries as *anglo-saksonim*, "Anglo-Saxons," Americans have both a superior symbolic status and a certain irrelevance. High status stems from their relative wealth; their prominence in academic, professional, and business elites; their association with the United States, Israel's major benefactor; and, not least, their mastery of English. Yet they are irrelevant because they are considered nonmainstream Israeli. Indeed, popular stereotypes construct "Anglo-Saxons" as *frayerim*, "suckers," in contrast to the more aggressive Israelis (Bloch 1990). And the Americans' disproportionate association with left-wing, peace-camp politics adds to their marginalization.[11] At one political demonstration, an Israeli-born right-wing protester shouted (in Hebrew) "Learn Hebrew first!" at an American left-wing demonstrator who had lived in Israel for forty years without shedding the telltale accent.[12]

But, so far, this discussion has glossed over an essential part of the story—Arabs and Arabic. The struggle over identity in Israel is most spectacular between Arab and Jew, and yet this struggle is in many ways silenced. Perhaps it is the vehemence of the struggle that silences it, for the struggle between Israelis and Palestinians in the Occupied Territories so dominates Israeli and world attention that the struggle between Jew and Arab within Israel almost is lost in the shuffle.

The Ethnographer

"The Visa Office Language Ballet" also highlights the role I played, as ethnographer, in the processes I was observing. As an American, my interactions with Israelis unavoidably implicated my own identity and brought my language, English, into the negotiation.

A Ship's Chandler

A RESEARCH ASSISTANT AND I WERE INVITED TO THE HOME OF LOUIS, A PALESTINIAN MAN WHO WORKED IN THE HAIFA PORT AS A SHIP'S CHANDLER.

From his stories I gather that Louis enjoys his work, and from the comfort and grace of his home I gather that he does it well. He seems a comfortable man.

His Hebrew is fluent and colloquial, but every so often he misses a word, or pauses to reflect on how to express his thought in this—his third—language. At one point he stumbles over an irregular Hebrew plural. He tries out one form, then another. Finally he looks for help to my Jewish

Israeli research assistant, the only native speaker of Hebrew in the room. She nods her approval to the first form.

Stella, the research assistant, is quiet tonight—more so than usual. In these interviews I present myself as the main researcher, and I usually begin by asking the questions. My strategy, though, is for the research assistant to gradually take the initiative, so that the discussion becomes one between Israelis. With Stella silent, this strategy fails.

Louis seems to be contributing to Stella's silence. When he searches for a word he sometimes provides an English equivalent. At one point, he does this to help me out, when I don't understand the Hebrew word for "chandler." But I'm not familiar with the English word either, so he explains in Hebrew what he does. He frequently switches into English, though, a language that Stella doesn't command.

Louis seems proud of his English. It has a fluent, American sound to it. His English is better than my Hebrew, but aside from up-to-sentence-length fragments—code-switches—he sticks with Hebrew. There is a subtle American coloring to his Hebrew, too. Hard to pinpoint—maybe a retroflex /r/, or a diphthonged vowel.[13] I find myself questioning his sincerity because of his accent.

In this negotiation of identities, Louis combined narrative and style to navigate a complex course among the various currents of social identity available to him. His use of English, his affecting an American accent in Hebrew, even his use of an English first name[14] indicated an orientation that distanced him from his official status as a citizen of Israel.[15] This orientation toward English simultaneously constituted a strong claim for status within the interview context. Since English is a language that he shared with the primary researcher and that excluded the research assistant, he was able to define his status in terms of the primary researcher. Indeed, I interpreted both his accent and much of his searching and stumbling for Hebrew words as a strategic move within the negotiation over status.

But many of the narratives he told during our interview contested the indifference toward Israeli identity that the style of his language expressed. He frequently positioned himself, for example, as a defender of Israeli society and of his position within it. At one point he told us about setting American sailors straight: that although he is an Arab, he doesn't hate Jews.

Social Identity

This book focuses on the strategic manipulation of linguistic variation and the pragmatic effects of such manipulation on social interaction. Language-use can be called strategic in two important senses. First, speakers use language to create—as well as reflect—their social identities. Second, language-use constitutes social action, which has material consequences for social relations.

The idea that language and identity are related has a long pedigree in Western thought. Its origins are conventionally associated with the eighteenth-century German philosopher Johann Gottfried von Herder, who proposed that each folk, or people, had its own set of characteristics, traced ultimately to the influences of geographic location (Berlin 1976; Wilson 1973). Over time, these folk characteristics influenced cultural domains, such as dress, traditions, and—most important—language.

Herder's philosophical writings achieved enormous popularity and influence in his own time (Wilson 1973) and gave rise to several important fields of scholarship, including folklore and historical linguistics.[16] His work buttressed mainstream efforts in eighteenth-century Europe to consolidate nationalities—under the rubric of national language groups. The unification of Germany, for example, was based on the construction of a language, "German," posited to be common to all the peoples encompassed by the proposed territory. The task demanded great feats of abstraction, since dialect diversity was extraordinarily great at that time in middle Europe. A national language was posited as a central tendency, and dialects were posited as variants on this tendency.

This theoretical structure was very useful for the emerging science of linguistics, but it also had wide-ranging political consequences. Herder's ideas gave impetus to the emerging political philosophy we now call romantic nationalism, and they were transformed by some of nationalism's more virulent streams to buttress essentialist political doctrines. Essentialist interpretations of Herder's work are problematic, however, for theories that link language and identity, since the actual relationship is extremely complex (see Lucy 1992a, b). Dell Hymes (1984), for example, argues that since the boundaries for a "language" are as flexible as those for a "people," the relationship between languages and peoples takes on a variety of forms. Whereas linguists see Serbian and Croatian as the same language, Serbs and Croats see them as two different languages.[17] Similarly, Hymes provides examples of languages that are constructed as "the same" by their users, despite significant objective differences.

Although Hymes eloquently deconstructs a deterministic Herderian interpretation of the relationship between language and identity, he does not argue that the connection is unimportant. Rather, he argues that precisely because the relationship between language and identity is indeterminate, variable, and mutable, it is crucial to anthropology. Indeed, the politics of the language/identity nexus is no more determinate than the linguistics. This nexus has been used to buttress resistant ideologies and subaltern identities, even as it is used to reproduce dominant identities. French in Canada, Gaelic in Scotland, and Hebrew in Palestine are prominent examples of political resistances fought with the help of language symbolism (see Handler 1988; Harshav 1993; MacDonald 1997).

Modern approaches to the study of language and identity owe much to the work of William Labov. Labov showed that variable phenomena in language (such as the pronunciation of vowels in New York City) were, in fact, rule governed—the rules made reference to social categories, such as ethnicity, gender, and class (Labov 1982a). His study of language change on the island of Martha's Vineyard, in Massachusetts (Labov 1963), for example, linked changes in dialect form to changes in social identity.

While Labov's work focuses on an analysis of language form and describes language in terms of social structure, John Gumperz (1982b) worked in the opposite direction. Taking linguistic structures as analytic points of departure, Gumperz applies them to help explain social phenomena, such as discrimination, bias, and other forms of social conflict. He studied service encounters in a British airport cafeteria, for example, where most of the servers were female immigrants from India and Pakistan, and most of the patrons were male airline workers born in England (Gumperz 1982a:173–174). A problem arose when customers complained that the servers were "surly and uncooperative" and servers complained of unpleasant working conditions. Gumperz argued that servers and patrons miscommunicated: the intonation contour servers used in asking a question (e.g., "Do you want gravy?") was often interpreted by customers as statement-intonation, leading them to feel that servers were behaving rudely. Because such miscommunication occurred in the context of an encounter with the Other— immigrants in Britain from India and Pakistan—it generated patterned perceptions, or bias (see van Dijk 1984).

Through careful attention to the ethnographic details of face-to-face interactions and a focus on the linguistic cues speakers use to frame and thereby contextualize their utterances, Gumperz and his colleagues have vastly increased our understanding of language and interethnic conflict. One of the important contributions of this work is that Gumperz treats speakers as intentional agents who use language as social action. Yet by assuming that cases of communicative disharmony constitute failures of communication, this approach downplays the degree to which ethnic groups in conflict may, in fact, negotiate to miscommunicate.

Moreover, the work of Labov and Gumperz share a common, or complementary, shortcoming. By assuming either social (Labov) or linguistic (Gumperz) categories as analytic points of departure, these scholars place the dynamic relationship between language and society beyond the scope of their research. The view proposed here entails a strategic approach to social and linguistic categories, in which notions such as class, gender, and ethnicity are seen as resources used in the active construction of social identity, and linguistic structures, such as phonological variables and intonational contours, are creatively deployed in innovative ways.

More recent work in linguistic anthropology has begun to unite these two perspectives within a framework that looks at conversation as a contestation over identity and recognizes that the social construction of both communication and miscommunication need to be studied. Carol Myers-Scotton (1983), for example, has shown that speakers in multilingual communities negotiate their respective rights and obligations through their choice of language. Similarly, Penelope Eckert (1989) has shown that students in an American high school construct the opposed social identities of "jock" and "burnout" by adopting opposing values of phonological variables that are in the process of change (Eckert 1989). These scholars build on the work of Gregory Bateson (1972) and Erving Goffman (1974, 1983) in focusing on the playful or dramaturgical aspects of social interaction.

Concurrently, social theorists have begun to view categories such as class, gender, and ethnicity as themselves socially constructed, and have turned their attention to the processes through which specific identities are created, transformed, and redefined. This focus on process has led to a growing interest in discourse and in how language can structure social interaction, bringing about an intriguing convergence of interests between sociolinguistics and social anthropology.

"NATION, NOT RACE!" 1

In Israel I found myself conducting research on a topic that did not exist. Whichever way I phrased my project, Israelis would fail to recognize some part of it.

I once told two Israelis that I was researching "race" and "ethnicity" in Israel, but they recoiled at the word "race." The Arab-Jewish difference in Israel, they said, is one of "nation," not "race."

When I phrased my topic in terms of "ethnicity," however, Israelis took it to be historical in focus, and my interest in Palestinian Israelis was missed. "Ethnic" differences between Ashkenazi and Mizrahi Jews are widely felt to have disappeared, while Arab Israelis are not thought to participate in "Israeliness" enough to constitute an "ethnicity"—they are officially termed a "minority."

If I phrased my work in terms of "nationhood," Israelis assumed I was looking at Arab-Jewish relations, and my research was instantly politicized and placed beyond the borders of Israel: Real Arab-Jewish relations occur in the Occupied Territories, not in Israel. Again, Palestinian Israelis were rendered invisible.

Finally, when I phrased my project solely as a study of "dialect changes in Israeli Hebrew," it was suggested that I study the Israeli military, whereby both Jewish-Jewish "ethnicity" and Arab-Jewish "nationality" were obscured behind the dimension of age and the vitality of youth culture.

My difficulty in articulating the aims of my research in a way that Israelis understood stems, in part, from a mismatch of terms. The Hebrew words corresponding to "ethnicity," "nation," and "race" have taken on very specific, constrained meanings in Israel. For example, the Hebrew word *eda* (plural: *edot*) is usually translated as "ethnic group," but its application is restricted in actual usage to Mizrahi Jews. Thus, Moroccan Jews and Yemeni Jews are considered *edot*, but parallel groups of Ashkenazi Jews, such as German Jews and Polish Jews, are not. The Hebrew term for "ethnicity" therefore fails to encompass the struggle between Mizrahi and Ashkenazi Jews over Jewish Israeli identity; rather, it refers to a conundrum of Oriental behavior that is ideologically held to have vanished from Jewish Israeli society. Nor is *eda* used to refer to Arabs: *mi'ut* is reserved for this purpose. The literal meaning of *mi'ut* is "minority," but its use is restricted to Palestinian Israelis—not to any of the Jewish groups that might be held to constitute a minority.[18] The Hebrew word for "nation," *l'om*, is used as an official designation on Israeli identification cards, distinguishing *Jew*, *Arab*, and *Druze* as legal categories. Finally, Hebrew *geza*, "race," is rarely applied to Israeli social groups at all, although the derived form *giz'anut*, "racism," is a frequent descriptor for Arab-Jewish relations, and a common, though less frequent, descriptor for Ashkenazi-Mizrahi relations.

Thus the social phenomenon of identity is neither fully determined by the linguistic structures for referring to it nor completely independent of them. Rather, the meaning and consequences of talk about identity are effects of discourse. *Eda* means less than "minority group" because of the constraints on its use; it means more than "minority group" because of the ideological backdrop to its deployment. The gap between *eda* and *mi'ut* signals a parallel gap in the Israeli ideology of identity between discourses of inclusion and discourses of exclusion (see chapter 6). Zionism, the Jewish romantic nationalist movement that emerged in Europe in the latter part of the nineteenth century, sought to supersede traditional Jewish identities by creating a "New Jew" (Almog 2000) in Israel. The model for the new "Israeli" Jew erased vast differences of culture, language, and history among nineteenth-century Jews living in places as disparate as Yemen and Germany. *Eda* includes the ideologically weighted meaning of "heritage," which, in turn, implies anachronism. At the same time that Zionism constructed its discourse of inclusion with respect to Jewish difference, it established a discourse of exclusion with respect to Arab difference. Zionism never theorized the presence of the resident Palestinian (Arab) population in Palestine when it theorized the Jewish return to Palestine. *Mi'ut* therefore includes the ideologically weighted meaning of "absence," which implies irrelevance.

This study draws on recent theorizing of discourse to explore the idea of identity and the component notions, "ethnicity," "nation," and "race," as they represent, and are represented in, Israeli social identity. Drawing on the work of Michel Foucault (1979, 1980), I explore Israeli identity discourse as a historically constituted regime of discourse that controls—through constraint and proliferation—actual speech in Israel. And drawing on the work of Joel Sherzer (1987), I explore the myriad ways individuals use language to manipulate or contest received notions of identity. The play, within the domain of identity, between structured discourse and structuring (speech) practices forms a spiral of discourse and a nexus of power that is both hegemonic and resistant.

Israel

Israel's unique history makes it an ideal place to study the interaction of language and social identity. Language plays a particularly crucial role in Israel because the revival of Hebrew as a spoken language played such a special role in Zionist political philosophy and practical action (see chapter 5). In addition, however, Israel is a place where the joint processes of social dialect and social identity formation can be studied as they emerge because contact between the competing groups—Arabs and Jews—is so recent a phenomenon. Finally, the study of language and identity in Israel/Palestine carries enormous significance because of the corresponding importance of the broader Arab-Israeli conflict in the Middle East.

Three main social groups compete for the emergent Israeli identity: Palestinian Arabs; Mizrahim, or Jews of Middle Eastern heritage; and Ashkenazim, or Jews of European heritage. New patterns of interaction and identity are emerging, following major demographic changes during the past century, and especially following Israeli statehood. Sizable Jewish residence in Israel began little more than a hundred years ago, and large-scale, intensive interactions between Arabs and Jews is as recent as the creation of Israel in 1948. This momentous event led to a sudden change for Palestinians, from majority to minority status; and a gradual change for Ashkenazi Jews, from majority to minority status within the Jewish population, as Mizrahi immigration grew rapidly over the following decade.

The struggle for identity within Israel takes on particular significance through association with the broader Arab-Israeli conflict, yet the issue's complexity has only begun to be explored from an anthropological perspective. Most researchers have looked at Jewish and Arab communities separately, focusing on the complex divisions along religious, class, ethnic, and political lines within each community. Such studies simplify the situation by downplaying the numerous intersecting and overlapping linkages among Jews and Arabs. Thus, Palestinian Arabs and Mizrahi Jews share affinities of socioeconomic class and cultural heritage, while Mizrahi and Ashkenazi Jews share strong religious and national affinities. Scholarship that focuses only on Arab-Jewish or on Mizrahi-Ashkenazi relations, however, places the pivotal processes linking these three groups in a common contestation over Israeli identity beyond the scope of research.

Language plays a central role in the expression of social identities in Israel. Powerful associations tie Hebrew to the Israeli state and Arabic to Arab cultural heritage. The two languages coexist in Israel due to separate residence patterns and education systems. Within each language, subtle differences of social identity and sociopolitical positioning are reflected in language-use. Studies of Palestinian Arabic, for example, have shown that Palestinian national identity is expressed in changing phonological patterns in Palestinian Arabic (e.g., Shorrab 1981). And studies of Hebrew have shown phonological articulations of the "New (Israeli) Jew" (e.g., Blanc 1968). The complexity and importance of language in Israel is clearest, however, when all three groups are taken into account. Griefat and Katriel (1989), for example, compare norms of use for Hebrew and Arabic, arguing that Hebrew-speaking Israelis are far more direct in their speech than are Arabic-speaking Israelis. The uniformity of the Hebrew-speaking Israeli population is brought into question, however, by research that shows retention of historical differences between Mizrahi and Ashkenazi dialects (e.g., Yaeger-Dror 1988). Finally, a study showing that Israeli Palestinians prefer to borrow English, rather than Hebrew words into their Arabic speech (Amara and Spolsky 1986) demonstrates the centrality of language in sociopolitical positioning in Israel.

On Methods

This study of Israeli identity is based upon nearly two years of ethnographic research conducted in Haifa, a city where day-to-day interaction among Ashkenazi, Mizrahi, and Palestinian Israelis is (relatively) common. What counts as "data," however, is often the ethnographer's first problem.

NEWS ON THE BUS

When I arrived in Israel on December 2, 1990, there was a high level of war anxiety. Iraq had occupied Kuwait the previous August; American President George Bush had declared a January 15 ultimatum for Iraq to withdraw; and Iraqi president Saddam Hussein had made no secret of his intent to involve Israel in any war that might break out.

This war-anxiety atmosphere is best represented for me by one memory in particular. When I arrived in Haifa, I noticed that city bus drivers kept their radios tuned to talk shows, with the volume high enough that all passengers could, indeed had to, hear. On the half-hour, the drivers turned the volume even higher for the regular news reports.

At first I mistook these radio-listening practices on Israeli buses for precisely the kind of exotic cultural difference from which ethnographers make their living. When the Gulf War ended, however, and Israeli life had returned to a more normal footing, I realized—not without some disappointment—that the radios had been tuned to news-talk in part because of the extraordinary anxiety over an upcoming war. Later on it struck me that there was indeed something interesting about Israeli attention to news (see chapter 6), but the main lesson I drew from "News on the Bus" was that ethnographic learning does not always end up quite as it was planned.

One reason for the indeterminacy of ethnographic learning is that writing about an Other (in this case Israeli) identity inevitably brings the ethnographer's own identity into question.

"THE GULF WAR IS A CATASTROPHE"

I had been in Israel only a few weeks when embassies began warning their citizens to leave, international airlines stopped flying into and out of Israel, American students in the dormitory where I was living left to return home, and my friends, relatives, and advisers called in a panic, urging me to come home, too.

I didn't go home until twenty-one months later, after I had wrapped up my fieldwork, but my reasons for staying remain an open question. I had professional reasons to stay, to be sure. I had already delayed my trip several months, in the hope that tensions resulting from Iraq's invasion of Kuwait would die down. Moreover, it was clear that war would be a fascinating social drama to observe as an ethnographer. I was already vaguely aware of the benefits, in terms of ethnographer-informant relations, that would accrue to me if I stuck it out and shared the experience: it would be a "way in."[19]

But I suspect that my being Jewish was also a factor. I had been prepared to examine my identity as it related to my research. In writing grant proposals, for example, I had claimed my Jewishness as an advantage: building on my own positioning with respect to the conflict, I argued that I would be able to see clearly how the ethnographer influences the context he studies, thereby avoiding the trap of objectivism.

So I suspect that I stayed out of a sense of identification with the fate of Israel.[20] But I thereby became situated within a certain discourse on Israel. The Israeli press was harshly critical of those who chose to leave Israel in its "time of need."[21] Conversely, staying became a litmus test of national identity. Most strongly criticized were Israeli citizens living abroad who stayed away;[22] most celebrated were American Jews who came to be in Israel during the war.[23] Somewhere in between were Tel Aviv residents who moved to safer regions within Israel, and American Jews who stayed for the duration.

This distinction extended to Palestinians as well. Many left Haifa to be with their families in rural areas, but those who remained (for whatever reason) said so in interviews with a certain pride, or claim to pride. On a live call-in radio program aired during the Gulf War, for example, a Palestinian Israeli man called up to say that, in this war, Arab and Jewish Israelis were in the same boat.

> *"This is a catastrophe for me as an Arab ... in the middle of the night I have to slap my son in order to get him up and get a gas mask on him ... let's just say our opinions on the conflict in the Gulf differ a bit from the national consensus, but as far as our Israeliness is concerned ... [we] are in the same boat with regard to Saddam's missiles...* "[24]

These discourses forced me to negotiate my own positioning. Staying in Israel was a move to avoid the superposition of American identity—so raw in the power of American students to return home, while my (Jewish) Israeli roommate went off to man antiaircraft artillery guns on the Syrian border. But the beneficial insider status it afforded me unavoidably implied a Zionist stance that made me uncomfortable—not only with respect to Palestinian Israelis, for whom the Gulf War was deeply problematic, but also with respect to Jewish Israelis, who insistently argued that Jewish Americans should immigrate to Israel.

I adopted a discourse-centered approach to ethnography in examining social identity in Israel (Sherzer 1983, 1987; Sherzer and Urban 1986). This paradigm proposes that cultural meanings are intimately linked to the forms of discourse through which they are expressed. Though in part I focus on detailed analysis of linguistic structure (see chapters 7 and 8), I also take a broad perspective on discourse, looking to various symbolic systems of meaning and the complex webs of intertextuality that connect them. I pay careful attention to the emergent nature of symbolic meaning and to the ways in which symbolic meaning is situated—meaning different things in varying contexts and to variously positioned conversational participants.

Wartime Spectators

The war started on January 16, in Iraq, in the very early morning hours. In my Israeli dormitory, crowds of students gathered in the commons room, eyes glued to the television, watching the retransmitted CNN broadcasts from Washington and Baghdad. A party atmosphere prevailed through the night. Hour after hour, the reports and pictures of American, British, and French bombs lighting up the Iraqi sky captivated the Israeli students. The crowd around the television swelled; more and more students, awakened by friends, came in wearing robes and nightclothes; bringing chairs and trays of food and coffee.

Among the latter was a young woman student dressed in the modest clothing of Muslim orthodoxy. I was taken aback by the image of a Muslim Arab in Israel appearing to join the celebration of the American demolition of Iraq.

And celebration it was! Israeli students were all but dancing. "We knew it would happen," many said. Praise for American President Bush flowed liberally. American students were slapped on the back and congratulated until even those, like me, for whom the outbreak of war was not unquestionably good, were swept up in the enthusiasm. It felt good to be an American.

And it felt good, I imagine, to be an Israeli—at least, a Jewish Israeli. Reports claimed that all of the missiles aimed at Israel were knocked out, and that the chances of an attack on Israel were rapidly vanishing. For the first time, Israel was being directly defended by its mighty friends. An implacable and dangerous foe of Israel was being devastated militarily and humbled in the eyes of the world. I remember wondering, however, how it felt to be an Arab Israeli, a Palestinian Arab citizen of Israel, at this moment of crisis in the Arab world.

I employ three main theoretical paradigms to address the relationship of language and identity: sociolinguistics, interpretive anthropology, and symbolic interactionism. My focus on the empirical analysis of language-use in natural contexts stems from the work of sociolinguists, such as John Gumperz, Dell Hymes, and William Labov, who have emphasized the social meaning and function of language variation (see Gumperz 1982a, b; Hymes 1974, Labov 1972a, b). Analysis of the situated meaning of linguistic forms, however, depends upon an interpretive understanding of the multiple layers of meaning present in the social context of speech (see Basso 1979, Geertz 1973) as well as an understanding of the way participants actively manipulate symbolic resources in playful, or contested negotiations of social identity, status, and power (see Goffman 1974).

Linguistic data for this study consist of a representative sample of actual speech, and of speakers' evaluations and interpretations of speech. Interviews were conducted with residents of two neighborhoods where ethnicity was particularly salient, and where I was also a participant observer, either through residence or employment. In analyzing the interview data, I looked at the complex relationships between language form and communicative content, paying close attention to narratives—not only as examples of vernacular speech but also as emotionally charged tools in the expression of Self. Participants in the interview are seen as social actors with particular social and political positionings, and the meaning of an utterance is linked to the complex face-to-face interactions that constitute the interview.

AN INTERVIEW WITH SHARON

Nurit stops by my apartment on our way to the interview with Sharon. Usually I meet my research assistants at some convenient bus stop or landmark near the central neighborhood where we do most of our interviewing, but today's interview is with a neighbor and friend of mine.

In the few minutes it takes us to walk to Sharon's apartment, I tell Nurit a little about Sharon and about the topics I think will go over well in today's interview. Nurit is an Israeli university student, one of four I have hired to help me with my research interviews. Being an American, and researching language, I have decided to use native speakers of Hebrew to carry out the bulk of the interviewing.

The interviews are complex, combining both sociolinguistic and ethnographic techniques. The protocol I have developed is long and demanding, and none of my assistants has really mastered it. Nurit, in particular, has found it difficult to carry out the interviews the way I envision them.

In walking from my house to Sharon's, we traverse neighborhoods. I live on the edge of a Jewish working-class neighborhood that borders Haifa's largest Muslim Arab neighborhood. A stark boundary separates the two. Walking downhill, we pass several hundred yards of wreckage—where stone houses once stood, long since demolished, not yet rebuilt. Then come houses that have been sealed, or partially sealed—gray cinderblock walls filling in what had been apartment windows. It is a bleak no-man's land powerfully reminding any who pass of the divisions in Israel between Arab and Jew—and of the ongoing conflict.

As we walk, I tell Nurit about Sharon: that she and I work together at a community center in central Haifa; she is the daughter of Iraqi Jewish immigrants, very involved in Arab-Jewish rapprochement, and an outspoken critic of the treatment of Mizrahim in Israel. I tell Nurit that I am therefore particularly interested in asking Sharon about her reasons for choosing to return to the neighborhood of her childhood, which is now entirely Arab and very poor.

Early in our interview, Sharon tells how her family came to Haifa from Iraq, and about her mixed feelings toward the memory:

TEXT 1.2. "THERE WERE ALMOST NO ARABS"

Sharon	Look, most of the neighborhood here,	
	is actually— uh,	(1)
	Made up of people who came to Haifa	
	from villages,	(2)
	They were mostly young couples,	
	or something like that,	(3)
	Who didn't have any place to live in the village,	(4)
	Or that they had work in the city, here in Haifa,	(5)
	And they came to live here,	(6)
	When I lived here— uh, that is till 1970— uh,	(7)
	The whole area, all the way up to the mosque,	
	there were almost no Arabs,	(8)
Nurit	Mmhm,	(9)
Sharon	That is, before, before '48, only Arabs lived here,	(10)
	But after '48, they— th— we—	(11)
	We always heard about stories that—	(12)
	People just came to—	(13)
	Entered houses, went into houses,	
	and lived there, eh— in the house,	(14)
	Several families together,	(15)
	There was— a common toilet,	
	a common kitchen,	(16)
	And afterwards there started to be	
	more separation,	(17)
	Things were more ordered,	(18)

	I mean people split up,	(19)
	They didn't like it,	
	several families living together,	(20)
	Anyone who could leave left,	(21)
	And so it started to be one-family residences,	(22)
	And then anyone who succeeded, somehow,	
	in bettering himself, left the neighborhood,	(23)
	Like my family, for example,	(24)
	For a long time they uh— waited for—	(25)
	They told them,	(26)
	They'll resettle you out,	(27)
	They'll resettle you out,	(28)
	And when they saw that—	
	they're not resettling them... ((laughs))	(29)
Nurit	Where's your family from?	(30)
Sharon	Iraq, when they saw that no one would	
	resettle them, they bought the apartment...	(31)
	Most of the people who had lived here	
	did pretty much the same thing,	(32)
	And in their place came—	(33)
	I mean we left in order to move up in standing,	(34)
	People came in who didn't have so much choice,	(35)
	And they came here... (40A: 10:10)	(36)

AFTER SOME DIGRESSION, WE RETURN SHARON TO HER
STORY:

Nurit	From the stories you heard from your parents,	
	what was their immigration like?	(37)
Sharon	Eh, not like for Arabs,	(38)
	I mean Arabs, they're here, it's not— ((laughs))	(39)
	My parents, they really went through	
	everything that Iraqis went through,	(40)
	Eh, most Iraqis, they came in '51,	(41)
	When they told them—	(42)
	I mean they were rich families in—	(43)
Nurit	Mmhm	(44)
Sharon	In Iraq,	(45)
	And they came to Israel when	
	they were telling them, eh—	(46)
	You should emigrate now,	(47)
	Because if you don't come now, then eh—	(48)
	We don't know what will happen,	(49)
	I mean the borders will be closed,	(50)
	And you'll be stuck here,	(51)
	Now eh— because their lives were very eh—	(52)
	Life was good there, very good and all that,	(53)
	But eh— they didn't feel that they belonged,	(54)
	I guess, like they entirely belonged,	(55)
	I mean they were— in Jewish groups,	
	of communists and that,	(56)

	So that every time there were uprisings,	
	they would harass them,	(57)
Nurit	Mmhm,	(58)
Sharon	And it's true that there were also Arabs who—	
	who defended them,	(59)
	There were— I guess— the kind that took them	
	to their homes in times of— uh— uh— (),	(60)
	But no one liked being in a situation like that,	(61)
	So they uh— were afraid,	(62)
	When they tell you eh—	(63)
	When you— when you know that something bad	
	is liable to happen,	(64)
	When you know eh— things like that,	(65)
	And they come and tell you,	(66)
	Now they're going to close you off,	(67)
	And if you don't emigrate that's it, you're stuck,	(68)
	So they preferred taking their things	
	and coming here,	(69)
	Now at that time they weren't allowed to take	
	any of their possessions,	(70)
	And they came here,	(71)
	And they weren't Zionist, in the sense of eh—	(72)
	They were dying to eh—	
	to come to the Land of Israel,	(73)
	Because of its being the Holy Land,	(74)
	And all these stories of people	
	coming in such a situation,	(75)
	I can see that it's sort of similar to the	
	Russian immigration, ...	(76)

(40A:18:56–21:05)

In this short segment of interview speech, Sharon weaves a complex subjectivity from the warp of informative answers to our interview questions and the weft of narratives of personal experience. The eloquence with which Sharon constructs this identity is striking. As Livia Polanyi (1985:12) puts it, "upon close examination, a story told in a conversation reveals itself to be as formally constructed as any carefully worked out acknowledged piece of literary verbal art." Polanyi's comparison of everyday conversation to poetic writing reframes the comparison made earlier between choice of language in a visa office to a choreographed ballet.

In the interview with Sharon, as in "The Visa Office Language Ballet," identities are being negotiated through language, but in this case all participants are speaking the same language—Hebrew. The subtle negotiations effected through language depend upon creative manipulation of the rhetorical structure of discourse (Woodbury 1987b). Conversation is a highly structured cultural practice, in which meaning is conveyed at multiple levels of linguistic structure. Indeed, messages conveyed by different dimensions of the linguistic sign may overlap or conflict, generating second-level messages through their interaction. Such enjambment, as Woodbury (1987b) points out, is another way in which conversation is like poetry. In poetry, enjambment occurs when syntax and meter clash, leaving a line to end before (or after) a natural break in the sentence structure. Often poets use enjambment in order to call attention to particular ideas, making the reader think twice about their meaning. So too for conversational enjambments: the literal meaning of a speaker's words often clashes with the way the words are uttered, calling attention to additional, or alternative meanings.

Western ideologies of language grant priority to the lexical and syntactic levels of meaning (Woolard and Schieffelin 1994), but much of the meaning actually communicated in conversation is of another type altogether. It is this second kind of message that often carries the social import. In analyzing instances of talk in this book, such as Sharon's narrative, presented here, I focus on several additional levels of rhetorical structure that convey social meaning. Speech takes on meaning by virtue of the physical setting in which it is uttered (Hymes 1967). Speech takes on meaning by virtue of the identity of the speaker—or the identity that the speaker provisionally negotiates by means of his/her speech (Gumperz 1982b). Speech takes on meaning by virtue of the participants to the interaction—who utters it, who hears it, and who overhears it (Goffman 1983). And speech takes on meaning by virtue of the language, dialect, style, or genre used (Hymes 1967). Who can speak what to whom has to do with the languages people learn—in school, from their parents, in places of work, or through social interaction (Fishman 1971). Speech takes on meaning by virtue of its intertextual references to images and ideas from the media (see Bakhtin 1981). Speech takes on meaning by virtue of the subtle distinctions of sound that (provisionally) identify a speaker as male or female, relaxed or formal, from "here" or from "there" (Labov 1972a). And speech takes on meaning by virtue of the myriad paralinguistic devices—pauses or hesitations, disfluencies or emphases, rhythms or tunes—by which speakers routinely comment upon their own speech (see Kristeva 1980). Spirals of meaning emanate from the complex interactions between such levels of rhetorical structure.

Speakers use such indirect means to communicate their messages for two main reasons, one aesthetic and one political. Speakers use aesthetically (rhetorically, poetically) structured language because it communicates emotion. Affect is an enormously important part of what we communicate when we converse, but it is not thought to reduce completely to words. Speakers also use indirect means of communication in order to negotiate power. As James Scott (1985) has cogently described, indirection in language often serves as a "weapon of the weak," providing a means for resisting power while putting on a plausible show of accepting it.

More will be said about these theoretical issues in chapter 3; for now, I would like to operationalize the approach through a brief analysis of Sharon's narrative of place and identity, presented as text 1.2. While Sharon's speech appears to be about neighborhoods, at a deeper level it addresses nothing less than being Israeli. Spirals of meaning take us from neighborhood to identity and back. Sharon's emphasis on place provides an illustration. Sharon contrasts the "here" of her neighborhood to several spatial and temporal instances of "there"—villages in Israel from which Palestinian Israelis came to the neighborhood (lines 1–6), previous eras in the neighborhood's history (lines 7–11), upscale Haifa neighborhoods to which her family and their neighbors moved (lines 17–23), and cities in Iraq from which her parents arrived (lines 53–57).

Sharon's discourse on place takes on meaning with respect to Israeli claims to belonging in Israel/Palestine. Sharon has moved back, as a middle-aged adult, to the neighborhood in which she grew up. She has done so, in part, because she believes in coexistence between Jewish and Palestinian Israelis, and breaking down the stark patterns of residential segregation is important to her. The historical parallels in her narrative, though, are striking. Forty years ago her family moved into a neighborhood that had been Arab (part of a phenomenon that displaced the resident Palestinian population). By narrating her parents' arrival in Haifa as a displacement (from Iraq, where they were comfortable, rich, etc.; see lines 40–45), Sharon legitimizes her parents' displacement of Palestinians. Indeed, Sharon notes that many of her current Palestinian neighbors also came to the neighborhood from elsewhere (lines 1–6), implicitly drawing the link between her family's plight and that of her Arab neighbors.

But Sharon draws back from complete identification with Palestinian Israelis. When we ask her about her neighborhood, there is a telling shift in pronoun usage from "we" to "they" (line 3), as she alternately elides and constructs the boundary between herself and her Palestinian neighbors. At this point in her narrative, her speech becomes disfluent, as she starts and restarts utterances (see lines 7–14). Sharon backtracks to correct an earlier statement that there were no Palestinians in the neighborhood when she was growing up (line 10). She hedges again when she begins her narrative of her parents' immigration by saying "it wasn't like being Arab" (line 38).

Of course, Sharon is not speaking to Palestinians, but to an American Jewish researcher, whom she knows, and to a research assistant, whom she assumes is an Ashkenazi Israeli. Sharon constructs distance between herself and Ashkenazi Israel. In sharp contrast to dominant interpretations of Israeli history, she represents her Mizrahi parents as having been unwilling Zionists who had been well off and friendly with Arabs in Iraq (e.g. line 43), and who were intimidated into leaving Iraq through promises of resettlement in Israel (lines 46–49) that turned out to be false (lines 24–31). In this way, she also links her position with that of Palestinian Israelis.

Sharon's use of (forms of) the verb *l'fanot* carries interesting resonances. The verb has a range of meanings, including "to vacate, empty, evacuate, remove, or evict." One resonance is thus the displacement of the Palestinians—both in the general sense of having been displaced by the Jewish return to Palestine, and the specific sense of Sharon's Haifa neighborhood having been cleared of its Palestinian residents in the aftermath of the 1948 warfare. Sharon, however, uses *l'fanot* in two other contexts: first that the Israeli authorities had told her parents and their neighbors that they would be "evacuated" from the slum to better housing (lines 24–31); and second, that the Zionist agents had earlier urged the "evacuation" of the Jewish community of Iraq (lines 66–69). In Sharon's narrative neither of these evacuations benefits her family. Indeed, the word resonates with the harsh treatment meted out to Mizrahi Jews in general (see chapter 2) and constitutes part of Sharon's negotiation of her identity with respect to Nurit, the interviewer Sharon assumes to be Ashkenazi.

The notion of "evacuation" forms an aesthetic nexus for Sharon's narrative speech in part because it is an ideological nexus for Israeli discourses of identity, place, and history. In schools, in books, in films, in all manner of public discourse, Israelis are represented as (Ashkenazi) Jewish victims who needed to be rescued from "there," and whose presence "here," in Palestine, benefited the local population. It is not just Palestinian Israelis who must narrate against this image, but Mizrahi Jewish Israelis, as well.

Language style also contributes to the message Sharon's narrative communicates. The dialect of Hebrew that Sharon uses in this interview contains traces of a complex negotiation of identity: Sharon claims mainstream Israeli identity by avoiding the stigmatized Mizrahi dialect of Hebrew associated with Iraqi immigrants. Nonetheless, she peppers her speech with prosodic tunes typical of Mizrahi Israelis, thereby negotiating an identity distinct from that which she attributes to her Israeli interlocutor, Nurit.[25] At a broader level, language choice constrains the set of identities Sharon can negotiate. The flexible boundaries that she verbally constructs and elides between herself and her (current) Palestinian neighbors find their limit. Elsewhere in the interview, for example, Sharon tells us of her efforts to teach her son Arabic, the language of the neighborhood (see "Not Learning Iraqi Jewish Arabic" in chapter 5). While Sharon's parents were speakers of Arabic—and learners of Hebrew—Sharon herself only "understands" Arabic. She must arrange for her son to be tutored so that he can interact with other neighborhood children. The desire to speak Arabic—as a gesture of coexistence and a claim of belonging—is common among politically liberal Israelis, but the ability to speak it fluently is rare. Thus, in conversation with her Palestinian neighbors, whatever relationship she would like to claim, she must do so in Hebrew.

Overview of the Chapters

Two analytic themes recur throughout this study: the dialogic nature of symbolic forms, and the spiral recycling of symbolic meanings. Identities, I argue, are constructed in dynamic opposition to other copresent groups. Symbols linked to Jewish Israeli identity can be transformed into symbols that claim Palestinian identity, and vice versa. Symbols that historically evoked Arab identity can be revived in the present as Jewish symbols.

Negotiations of identity occur within historically specific contexts. Accordingly, chapter 2 introduces the study by tracing strands of the current discourse of modern Israel and Palestine back to their historical antecedents. This narrative approximates a genealogy of everyday interactions in Haifa—interactions that draw meaning from the history of settlement and resettlement. The daily physical, political, and discursive contestations over identity are traced out as they are played out across urban space—buildings being razed; streets being renamed; wealth moving uphill; Arabs replacing Jews replacing Arabs in downtown neighborhoods. These struggles over space generate spatial symbols of identity—from the appearance of homes to the language of newspapers—and mirror, constitute, and constrain the negotiation of identity.

Chapter 3 theorizes several metaphors—negotiation, hybridity, and resistance—that are featured in my discussion of identity. This chapter argues for a theoretical convergence around a notion of *discourse* that links linguistic analysis of language as it is actually used in contexts of face-to-face interaction to anthropological analysis of the deployment of power in the interplay between structure and agency in social process.

Chapter 4 seeks to operationalize the theoretical perspective described in chapter 3, through a discussion of the relationship between theory and methods. This study relies heavily on technical analyses of linguistic detail, and on a set of methodological procedures that are, by their very design, intended to play a role in the work of interpretation. Chapter 4 therefore situates me, the ethnographer, as an active agent in the negotiations of identity under study. Characterizing myself as "an active agent" implies more than an introspective and responsible consciousness of the authority my textualization calls forth. "Active" presence also goes beyond seeing the ethnographer as one who influences the processes he wants to study. This conceptualization sees the ethnographer as a full—if unique—participant in the negotiation of identity. Narrative forms a theme that weaves together the disparate strands of this chapter: the narrative (text) produced by the ethnographer is linked to the narratives (of personal experience) told in the course of ethnographic interviews and interpreted in the course of linguistic analysis, which, in turn, are linked to the narratives constituted by the semiotics of everyday life.

Language-use, whether in face-to-face talk or in the anonymous discourse of public culture, unfolds within a social context, and chapter 5 conveys an ethnographic understanding of the contexts for speech and communication in Israeli society by discussing the learning (and unlearning) of languages in Israel. I focus on the three languages primarily implicated in the negotiation of Arab and Jewish identities in Israel, Hebrew, Arabic, and English, and I argue that the social contexts of language learning produce and constrain the configuration of contexts for language use observable in everyday social practice.

The dynamic tension between the control of historically constituted regimes of discourse and the resistance of voices of individual actors is the subject of chapter 6. An examination of public representations of identity in media discourse probes the role of public culture in constructing identity in Israel. Identities may be negotiated in face-to-face talk interactions, but these negotiations occur within an overarching discursive framework. This regime of discourse controls the negotiation through conjoint processes of proliferation and constraint. Chapter 6 thus explores Israeli public discourse to reveal the rules by which individuals negotiate their own identities.

In contrast, chapters 7 and 8 look at the negotiation of identity from the perspective of the resistant voices of individual actors. Chapter 7 argues that the three-way nature of the struggle over Israeli identity is especially clear in the ambivalent and contradictory meanings associated with two phonological variables in Hebrew, which combine both high and low status. Analysis of the social distribution of variable forms in the speech of Haifa residents, combined with an interpretive analysis of the meaning of these forms, shows how old and stigmatized usages, stereotypically associated with Mizrahi Jews, are being adopted (and thereby recycled) by Palestinian Israelis in constituting a Palestinian Israeli social dialect of Hebrew.

Chapter 8 focuses on a different level of linguistic structure (intonation) and on different dimension of the three-way identity struggle, emphasizing the role of Jewish ethnicity in Israeli national identity. While Mizrahim have abandoned some of the stereotyped (linguistic) markers of their ethnicity, they continue to represent identity

2

Negotiations of Memory
and Space

My first—and last—encounter with "the field" came at Israel's airport. In 1990, when I traveled to Haifa to begin fieldwork, Israel had only one major airport, the Ben-Gurion International Airport,[1] and so most visitors encountered Israel first through the adjacent city of Lod. Or Lydda.

The British built the airport in the 1920s while they were the mandated colonial government in Palestine. The airport was located near the Arab town of Lydda, which was conveniently central in Palestine—roughly half-way between Tel Aviv (or Jaffa)[2] in the east, Jerusalem in the west, the Galilee in the north, and the Negev in the south (see fig. 2.2).

Lod is the Hebrew name given to the (formerly) Arab town of Lydda. Hundreds of places in Israel/Palestine have been renamed by the Jewish immigrants and Israeli authorities.[3] In some cases the Hebrew names revive Biblical names, but in most cases the older Arabic names were merely hebraicized—changed slightly to conform to the sound patterns of Hebrew. I don't know which case Lod/Lydda falls under, but the dual place names recall this process.

What was long known as The Lydda International Airport was renamed the Ben-Gurion International Airport, after Israel's first prime minister, David Ben-Gurion. The (formerly) Arab town of Lydda has receded even further.

Lod/Lydda was a vital strategic nexus in the conflict between Jews and Arabs from 1947 to 1949—a conflict that Israelis now call *milxemet ha-shixrur*, "The War of Independence," and which Palestinians call *an-nakba*,[4] "The Defeat." In July 1948, the Israeli military commander Moshe Dayan

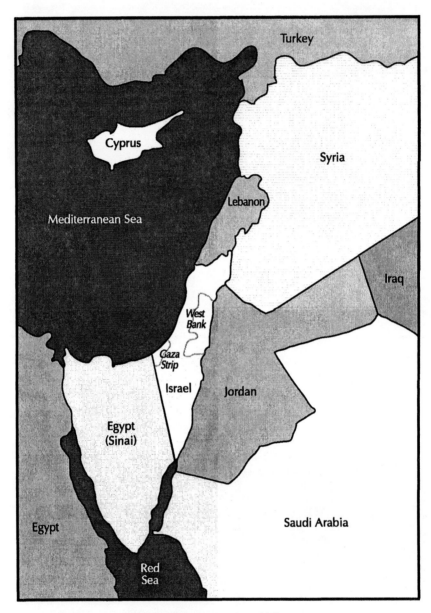

Figure 2.1. Israel in the Middle East.

captured the airport, as well as nearby (Arab) towns, for the Israelis (Sachar 1989:331). As part of these military actions nearly 100,000 of the local (Arab) inhabitants were encouraged to leave their towns and villages (Sachar 1989:334).

Much of the property owned by Palestinian residents of Lydda was essentially confiscated, and in the early 1950s, when hundreds of thousands of Jewish immigrants arrived in Israel from the Arab and Muslim countries of the Middle East, many were settled in "abandoned" homes of Lydda/ Lod.

Today the Lydda/Lod/Ben-Gurion International Airport is a place of great discomfort for Palestinian Israelis.

TEXT 2.1.   AIRPORT HASSLES

FROM AN INTERVIEW WITH SAMIR AND HIS WIFE, LISA, AND
THEIR FRIEND, RHODA, THREE PALESTINIAN RESIDENTS OF
HAIFA.

Lisa   If you want to say whether I manage as an Arab,
        A Haifa resident, in Israel,
        And I'm optimistic, I would say "no",
Dan   Mmhm,
Lisa   I went abroad, last year,
        And I was just about humiliated,
        Because I'm an Arab,
        They just didn't—
        They didn't want to humiliate me,
        I'm not— I don't have any feelings of inferiority in this,
        But they— they humiliated me,
        As an Arab,
        Even if it was not intentional,
        Because— It's their system,
        Not to humiliate Arabs—
        To examine Arabs, to the— in-depth,
Samir   Before you get on the airplane,
Rhoda   At the airport,
Lisa   At the airport...
        (That's) where you feel the discrimination ...
        (193B:29:41–30:24)

This was a story I heard many times from Palestinians I interviewed: Arabs in Israel feel discrimination most when they leave the country—at the airport. Israel claims to provide equal treatment to all of its citizens, but the issue of "security" severely tests this doctrine. At the airport extraordinary security precautions are taken to prevent hijackings. All luggage is thoroughly searched, and all travelers are interviewed. Jewish Israelis, as well as Americans with Jewish-sounding names (like me), pass through relatively quickly, but Palestinians, other Arabs, and even swarthy or dark-haired tourists who happen to look Arab, are often subjected to very different treatment.[5]

I did not perceive the many resonances of the Ben-Gurion Airport when I arrived there in December 1990. I was exhausted, weighted down by a bulky computer and an enormous box of blank cassette tapes, and I was desperately hoping that I would recognize, after ten years, the uncle who had promised to pick me up. But with the benefit of hindsight—the kind of hindsight that comes from two years of participating in and observing Israeli life, from interviewing Israeli people, from reading Israeli newspapers, and from learning Israeli languages—I have come to think of the image of the airport as representing well the frame within which Israelis negotiate identity.

The acquisition of this hindsight is the craft of the ethnographer. Its textualization is the craft of the anthropologist. Much has been written recently about anthropologists' descriptions of their first encounter with "the field." As Mary Louise Pratt (1986:31–32) puts it,

> opening narratives commonly recount the writer's arrival at the field site, for instance, the initial reception by the inhabitants, the slow, agonizing process of learning the language and overcoming rejection, the anguish and loss at leaving. ... They play the crucial role of anchoring that description in the intense and authority-giving personal experience of fieldwork. Symbolically and ideologically rich, they often turn out to be the most memorable segments of an ethnographic work. ... Always they are responsible for setting up the initial positionings of the subjects of the ethnographic text: the ethnographer, the native, and the reader.

In the years since James Clifford, George Marcus, and other critics of "ethnographic authority" helped revolutionize the writing of ethnographies (see Clifford and Marcus 1986; Marcus and Fischer 1986), anthropologists have made major changes in the tropes they use to introduce, and ground, their work. Such experiments may underestimate, though, the parallels between the visiting anthropologist's representation (in the text) of his/her primal encounter with the "native" and the resident "native's" representation of his/her own primal encounter with the ethnographer. Opening scenes are memorable because they stand for something important. It goes without saying that these tropes stand—in the text—for something different from what they represented at the time.

The ethnographic project—both as encounter and as textualization—involves a negotiation of meaning in "space" from the structures and practices of "place." As visitor, the ethnographer seeks both to learn the meanings attached to particular places and to communicate those meanings to others. But everyday life too involves a negotiation of meaning in "space" from the structures and practices of "place." People structure spaces through their symbolic practices, and spaces structure peoples' sense of identity by insisting upon a particular frame within which symbolic practice unfolds. Such recursive narratives of space-making accumulate over time, generating dialogic webs of reference and comprising a community's historical memory.

In Israel/Palestine this dynamic of space and place implicates a struggle over historical memory and the very definition of history and is central to the production of and contestation over identity. The negotiation of identities in everyday Israeli life is critically influenced by the place within which it occurs. Zionist imaginings of homeland were based on narratives of place (Herzl 1988 [1896]), but Israeli constructions of nation are heavily tied to the making and remaking of spaces, through such practices as architectural construction and archeological excavation (Abu El-Haj 1997). Palestinian imaginings of home are similarly rooted in the narrativization of place, and the struggle over constructing Arab space is deeply inscribed in Palestinian towns, villages, and neighborhoods. Historical memory is not solely the history of the Self, but rather is constructed out of the Self's relation to the Other. Israelis use the ideas, images, and terms of history in their face-to-face struggles over identity. And these struggles are inscribed onto the physical terrain, in Israeli places. The dialectic of space and place, with its emphasis on narrative as collective memory, provides a way to understand the importance both of historical memory and of urban geographies in the negotiation of identities in Haifa, Israel.

Approaching Haifa

During my stay in Israel I often spent weekends with my aunt and uncle on their citrus farm in the central part of the country. After the visit I would take a long bus ride from their *moshav*[6] to Haifa (see fig. 2.2), where my research was based, and where I shared a small apartment with two Israeli college students. I loved this ride from Bnai Zion to Haifa. I never tired of watching the physical beauty of the landscape as it flowed past the bus window. And I was always fascinated to watch the physical markers of Israeli history and social structure as they flew past the window as my bus traveled north.

From central Israel, where my relatives' moshav was located, the bus passed through a fertile belt of citrus farm: acre after acre of orange groves with their deep green leaves, broken only momentarily by fields of vegetables or roads to small towns. This is the Sharon Valley, the agricultural heartland of Israel, one manifestation of the Zionist dream of "making the desert bloom."

> In the 1880s European Jews began "returning" to Palestine. The Jewish romantic nationalist movement, called *Zionism*, was gaining adherents throughout eastern Europe, as Jews suffered discrimination and repression. The notorious Dreyfus Affair in France added fuel to the fire—ironically because France had been the most progressive of European countries in granting Jews citizenship, liberties, and belonging (Hertzberg 1959).
>
> In moving from Europe—where most had been landless—to Palestine, Jews began to buy land (Sachar 1989). Theodor Herzl, who was to become the most important spokesman for the new Zionist philosophy, called the movement a "return," evoking Biblical times when Jews had lived there. Herzl thought of Palestine as "a land without people for a people without land" (see Herzl 1988 [1896]).
>
> But of course there were people already living in Palestine toward the end of the nineteenth century. Clearly Herzl did not think that Palestine was literally uninhabited—but rather that Palestine was, like many non-European places, underinhabited. This is a view that he shared with many Europeans of his time.[7] Colonies were thought of as places where European

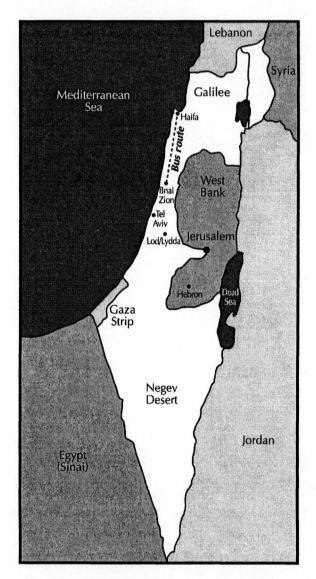

Figure 2.2. Map of Israel, Showing Bus Route from Bnai Zion to Haifa.

technology and industriousness could improve both land and people—if the latter were willing. When Zionist pioneers looked at the swampy valleys, rocky hills, and sand-swept plains of nineteenth-century Palestine, they envisioned land that could be remade into productive farmland.

The land looked prosperous and fertile, but appearances can fool. Here and there in the midst of a sea of luscious green were blotches of brown—plots of land where the citrus trees were no longer being irrigated. During my stay in Israel I watched these brown flecks grow and multiply, as the "bloom" returned to desert. The escalating price of water had long overtaken the profitability of exporting fruit, and in the early 1990s few would have grown oranges if not for government subsidies.

My uncle was one such citrus farmer (see fig. 2.3). For thirty years he cultivated ten acres of oranges along the Haifa road, but during my stay in Israel, the family decided to sell their farm and move to a city apartment. A wealthy businessman bought their house, and my uncle anticipated that he would turn much of the orchard into a swimming pool.[8]

The Sharon Valley is the narrow "neck" of Israel (see fig. 2.2). At Ra'anana Junction only ten miles of Israel separate the Mediterranean Sea from the West Bank—I walked most of the way across Israel one afternoon after getting on the wrong bus by mistake. Road signs here point in one direction to the Israeli cities of Ra'anana and Netanya, and in the opposite direction to the West Bank cities of Qalqilya and Tulkarm. Israelis old enough to remember the "Six Day War" in 1967 recall fearing that the invading Jordanian army would cut the country in half at this point. To Israeli Jews this narrow neck symbolizes vulnerability, but as an American I did not feel vulnerable.

Closer to Haifa the main road hugs the coast, and through the bus window I saw salt marshes and sand dunes. At one point the road comes very close to an Arab village. From the bus I saw unpaved streets, open sewers, and crumbling buildings—telltale signs of poverty and victimization that reminded me how Israel's creation as a Jewish state came at the expense of Palestinians.

> For Palestinians, Zionism was an intrusion. As Jewish pioneers came to Palestine and began to buy up land, many rural and poor Palestinians were displaced. In a common scenario, Jews purchased parcels of land from wealthy Palestinians who owned the land but did not themselves farm it. For centuries, Palestinian farmers had worked land owned by others.
>
> The displacement was caused in part by a strange articulation with Jewish history. Zionism sought to escape the stigma and oppression that had accompanied Jews in Europe by creating a brand-new Jewish identity. This "New Jew" would "return" to productive, manual labor, tilling the soil, operating factories, and fighting wars. The phrase *kibush ha-avoda*, "conquest of labor," encapsulates this core Zionist ideal, and the fabulously successful communal farms known as *kibbutzim* were a direct result.
>
> An indirect result was that as Jews gained ownership of land, the *fellahin*, the Arab peasantry, were unable to continue to work the land. Such displacement led on the one hand to a growing proletarianization of the Palestinian peasantry (Rosenfeld 1978) and on the other hand to growing resentment and conflict.

Figure 2.3.   The Author Picking Oranges at Bnai Zion Moshav.

At the outskirts of Haifa natural beauty overwhelms the eye. Long stretches of beach divide the placid blue of the Mediterranean Sea from the magnificent escarpment of Mount Carmel. White cliffs and bands of rock jut out toward the sea. A cable car leads up sheer cliffs to a Carmelite monastery that commands spectacular views of the Mediterranean. Midway up the cliff face lie Elijah's Caves, biblical places holy to Jews and Moslems. A bit further down the road lie the gardens of the Bahai Temple. Haifa is one of three world centers of the Bahai religion.

This, too, is Haifa, is Israel, is the Holy Land, but Haifa is neither a particularly ancient nor a particularly holy city—at least not in the context of the Holy Land. Although Haifa was built on a natural harbor (see fig. 2.4), other towns were much more prominent historically. Acre and Caesaria, for example, coastal towns twenty miles north and south of Haifa, respectively, were strongholds for successive empires: Roman, Arab, Crusader, and Ottoman. Haifa, in contrast, grew up in this century, becoming an important center of trade, industry, and culture during the British Mandate.

> The territory called Palestine was part of the Ottoman Turkish Empire for hundreds of years before the British arrived. This empire collapsed, however, in the wake of World War I, and France and England divvied up the spoils. England took Palestine. The League of Nations granted England a mandate to govern Palestine in 1917.
>
> While in power, the British constructed a port, oil terminal, and refinery at Haifa, and eventually constructed a railway line that connected oil fields in Iraq with the Haifa industrial facilities. Haifa grew steadily during the

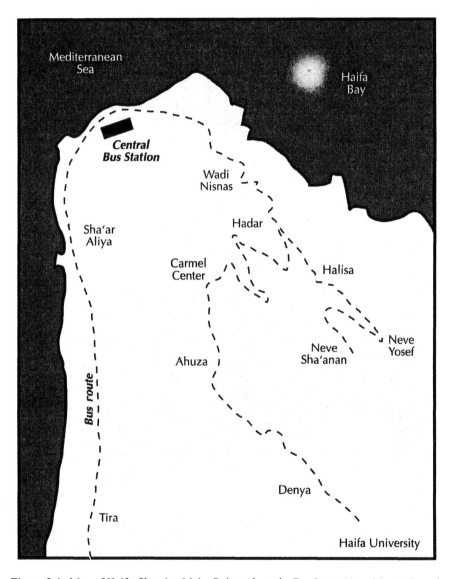

Figure 2.4. Map of Haifa, Showing Major Points Along the Bus Route(s) up Mount Carmel.

mandate period. Heavy Jewish immigration brought new businesses, and the development also attracted Palestinians to the city seeking employment. By 1948 there were more than 100,000 residents in Haifa, half Palestinian and half Jewish (Sachar 1989:332).

The British era was a stormy one. Jewish immigration increased, as did Arab resistance. In 1914 the British issued the Balfour Declaration, which put Britain on record as advocating the creation of a Jewish homeland in Palestine. Subsequent administrative actions and policy declarations, however, vacillated between support for Jewish immigration and support for Arab control. Sectarian violence broke out in the 1920s and again, much worse, in the mid 1930s. By the end of World War II, the British were relieved to abandon the Holy Land to the Jews and the Palestinians.

Sha'ar Aliya

At the approach to Haifa, the bus passed the neighborhood of Sha'ar Aliya (see fig. 2.4). Out the window I saw blocks of modern but lifeless apartment buildings. The neighborhoods resembled a parking lot, with three- to four-story apartment buildings lined up on grids facing each other, separated by neglected semicourtyards, presenting their backsides to the road. The buildings are cinderblock and ugly. No one seems to tend the exteriors or the communal areas. Ironically, these apartments were built in keeping with the communal spirit of Israeli socialism—pragmatic, robust, egalitarian— but these values didn't show up well in architecture.

> Zionism was a European movement, and from the beginning of the "return" in the 1880s to the formation of the State of Israel in 1948, the vast majority of immigrants to Palestine came from Europe. In the wake of the 1948 wars, however, hundreds of thousands of Jews from the Middle East— from Morocco, Iraq, Syria, Egypt, Turkey, and other places—flooded into Israel. During the decade from 1948 to 1958 the Jewish population of Israel doubled, and most of the new immigrants came from the Middle East.
>
> European Zionists were as unprepared for the encounter with Mizrahi Jews as they had been for the encounter with Palestinian Arabs, but the Israeli establishment took a very different approach to the Middle Eastern Jews. While Ashkenazi Jewish immigrants (including the hundreds of thousands of refugees from the Holocaust) were settled in the growing cities of Tel Aviv, Haifa, and Jerusalem, Mizrahi Jews were disproportionately settled in *ayarot pituax*, "development towns," in rural areas, often along the borders with Arab states, and in *ma'abarot*, "transition camps," on the margins of the cities. The Mizrahim entered Israel as a working class, subordinated to the entrenched Ashkenazi elite.

Sha'ar Aliya was once a ma'abara. The *blokim*, "blocks," as the apartment complexes are called,[9] are the reminders of the Jewish Other in Israel—the residues of the ma'abarot, where immigrants of the 1950s were housed in tents (sometimes for years) until permanent housing could be found. In many cases it is as if the walls of the tents were merely solidified into the brick walls of the blokim. Many of the camps are now neighborhoods in which ethnic inequality within the Jewish community is played out. This neighborhood's name, Sha'ar Aliya, means either "Gate of Ascent," or "Immigrant Portal." The Hebrew word for "ascent," *aliya*, is used metaphorically to mean "immigration to Israel," an ironic usage in the context of these neighborhoods at the very bottom of Haifa's mountain, which formed dead-ends, rather than portals, for so many of Israel's immigrants from Middle Eastern countries.

Just beyond Sha'ar Aliya is downtown Haifa.

Ascending Mount Carmel

Haifa is like an archeological site embossed on Mount Carmel: the steep slopes, from the Mediterranean Sea at its base to the Druze villages Isfiyya and Daliat Ha-Carmel[10] at its top, traverse historical periods of settlement and social strata of status, wealth, and identity. Topography is interwoven with history and social structure, as the slopes provide the physical, historical, and social framework upon which ideas of "Haifa" and "Haifans" are constructed.

Just a hundred yards or so from the shores of the Mediterranean lies downtown Haifa. From there the city spreads out and up the steep flanks of Mount Carmel. From any particular point in the city one perceives only a small portion of the whole mountain, but from almost everywhere one sees the steepness. Neighborhoods cling precariously to the slope. Houses are perched on pockets hewn from the rock. Roads are scratched onto the sides, curling up and around outcrops, dangling over sheer cliffs. The slope is so steep that street level on two sides of an apartment building may differ by three or four stories.

Walls are everywhere. Made of rough-cut stone, they hold back the mountain to make way for roads and building (see fig. 2.5). In many places the slope is so severe that stairways replace sidewalks (see fig. 2.6), and the quickest pedestrian route threads its way between homes, back doors, laundry lines, playgrounds, olive trees. Built of yellow stone and equipped with blue handrails, the stairways are everywhere the same, and everywhere unique. Unlike the massive streets, which rip apart Haifa's natural beauty, the poetic stairways merge with the landscape and the neighborhoods they bisect. One hundred and twelve stairs separated the entrance to my apartment building from the bus stop I used to go to work each day.

> Haifa is Israel's third largest metropolitan area, but it differs from the larger cities of Tel Aviv and Jerusalem. Tel Aviv is the bustling fashion and nightlife center of Israel (sometimes called "The Big Orange," in joking comparison to New York), and Jerusalem is the intellectual and spiritual center, with its government institutions, prestigious university, and hallowed religious sites. Haifa, in contrast, is known as a "family city." Many people, and especially the upwardly mobile, leave Haifa for more exciting places while they are young, only to return to the city to raise a family.
>
> Haifa is a working-class city with a strong tradition of labor-oriented government. It is Israel's old port city and the site of much of the country's heavy industry. Noise from the heavy machinery at the port wafted up the

Figure 2.5.   The Walls of Haifa.

hill and intruded insistently into my apartment; the smoke stacks of an enormous factory dominated the view from my window.

Three openings cut into the mountain's slope, and it was on these landings, Hadar, Carmel, and Ahuza,[11] that successive waves of residential and commercial development occurred. At the top of the mountain is the University of Haifa, recognizable by its monumental forty-story office tower protruding from the ridgeline like the proverbial sore thumb. And beyond the university, further along the Carmel ridge, are Druze villages: Isfiyya, Daliat Ha-Carmel, and others.

Wadi Nisnas

Rounding a downtown corner, the bus turned briefly onto a magnificent boulevard lined with stately cedar trees—Ben-Gurion Street—then continued upward, toward Wadi Nisnas, a large valley that leads up to Hadar, the first of the three landings. Wadi Nisnas is Haifa's largest and most important Arab neighborhood.[12]

> Ben-Gurion Street is the name given to a beautiful, tree-lined avenue with a stately view of the Mediterranean Sea in one direction and the slopes of Mount Carmel in the other.
> Israeli street names—like Ben-Gurion Street—seemed oddly national-istic to me. As an American I was used to the kind of bland, systematic street names Israel never uses: Israeli cities do not have a "Main Street,"

Figure 2.6. Stairways Connecting Neighborhoods in Haifa.

nor do they have sequentially numbered streets, or streets named after trees and flowers. Growing up in the United States I was so accustomed to the recurrence of such names in city after city that it had come to seem natural. In Israel, though, I was amused that every town and city seemed to have streets named after famous men from Zionist history like: Trumpeldor, Balfour, Tschernikofsky, Sprintzak, Arlozoroff, Herzl—and, of course, Ben-Gurion. And every town and city seemed to have streets named after Zionist concepts, like *atzma'ut* (freedom), *halutz* (Zionist pioneering), *ma'apilim* (another kind of Zionist pioneering), and *Tziyonut* (Zionism).

Tziyonut Street was particularly interesting, and I often thought of it as the bus passed into the Wadi Nisnas neighborhood. One of my favorite restaurants was located on Tziyonut Street, just where the bus makes a big turn. It is an Arab restaurant frequented by tourists, Israeli Jews, and Palestinian residents of Wadi Nisnas. Its name, "UN Restaurant," intrigued me, but it was the blue-and-white décor that really puzzled me, since those are the colors of the Israeli flag.[13]

I later found out that the road I knew as *Tziyonut*, "Zionism," was earlier called "UN Street," in celebration of the United Nations' 1947 proclamation establishing the Jewish state of Israel. In 1975, however, the United Nations passed a declaration strongly condemning Israel (by equating Zionism with racism), and Israel renamed the street "Zionism" in defiance. The Arab restaurant therefore carries the original name of the street it is on, and, in the context of the subsequent renaming, now constitutes a poignant (and pointed) opposition to the hegemony of Israeli symbolism. The reversal in symbolic associations is an interesting example of the spiraling struggle over memory and place.

The power of this naming is palpable. I noticed, for example, that one young Palestinian friend, whose family happened to live on Tziyonut Street, seemed uncomfortable when pronouncing his address out loud. Perhaps he felt the irony himself, or perhaps he feared that others would feel the irony of a Palestinian living on Zionism Street. I was reminded of my own region of central Texas, where the large, and historically prior Hispanic population had to pronounce the town "Llano" as [læno], rather than [yano]—at least in English.

The bus turned off Tziyonut Street and entered Khouri Street, a steep uphill that traverses the Wadi Nisnas neighborhood on its way to Hadar. Wadi Nisnas is a crowded neighborhood, with narrow winding streets and few open spaces—the kind of neighborhood not made for cars. The three- and four-story houses are built of yellow stone block, in an old, established Arab style. The buildings look dusty, in need of cleaning or repair, but sturdy and solid.

Shops line both sides of the main streets. Restaurants and bakeries dominate the lower part of Khouri Street, while clothing boutiques and electronics stores are located higher up. Entering the neighborhood, one encounters the pleasant aroma of roasting coffee. Further in, straddling the boundary between formal and informal markets, the mall opens out into a vegetable market, where old women in black clothing sit in front of their shops shucking beans or selling leeks.

The streets and sidewalks are filled with pedestrians.

As an American Jew, one aspect of Israeli life that I really appreciated was having my own religious holidays be the nationally recognized holidays. I especially noticed this on Yom Kippur. The most important of the Jewish holidays, and one of the few that I regularly observed, Yom Kippur is also one of the most difficult to fit into a Christian (or secular) work schedule. In Israel—for once—I was not faced with the awkward choice between requesting time off from work and observing my religious holiday.

So it came as quite a surprise to me that in Israel I felt nostalgia for home most intensely during a walk through Wadi Nisnas in December. For the first time in two years I heard the familiar Christmas songs as I walked along the streets, and I saw decorated Christmas trees in shop windows. An intense wave of homesickness swept over me, and my eyes welled up with tears. The nostalgia had more to do with a season I missed, I'm sure, than with the Christmas holiday itself. Nonetheless, the experience served to underscore the degree to which symbols of Arab identity are repressed in Haifa, for the music was played softly and the trees displayed modestly, and this was the only place I saw such trappings. I recognized the situation of being a small and different minority combating the cultural onslaught of the majority.

Further still into the Wadi Nisnas neighborhood is a new pedestrian walk, not quite finished, with pleasant amenities like stone benches and a little fountain. A gleaming school and community center have been built recently in the middle of the neighborhood. Nearby is a lighted and fenced soccer field and playground—among the nicest such facilities in Haifa. Part of an effort to encourage the merchants, perhaps, or to entice more Jewish shoppers, or to repay campaign debts. In the center of the mall is the Communist Party headquarters with its own recreation facilities nearby. The Communist Party was a significant center of Arab community when I arrived in Israel, but it was much less prominent by the time I left.[14]

This area is a popular shopping place on most days, but on Saturdays it is absolutely packed. Nonreligious ("secular") Israeli Jews (who comprise the vast majority of Jews in Israel) come here to shop on the Sabbath, when most Jewish stores (even those owned by secular Jews) are closed. Christian butchers also do a brisk business selling *basar lavan*, literally "white meat," which is Israeli euphemistic slang for "pork," which both Jewish and Muslim dietary laws forbid.

> Walking in one of Haifa's "mixed" neighborhoods—where both Jews and Arabs reside—I stopped by a small kiosk to buy an Arabic-language newspaper. A huge assortment of newspapers in Hebrew and Russian were prominently displayed on the sidewalk outside the kiosk, but no Arabic papers were in evidence. I asked the owner, but he told me he didn't sell them. I asked if he knew where I could get one, and he said he didn't know.
>
> Crossing the street and walking uphill a few yards, I came to another, very similar kiosk, this one owned by a Palestinian man. In a corner, against an inside wall were stacks of the two Arabic-language weeklies: *Kul Al-'Arab* and *Al-Sinnara*. I wondered why the first kiosk owner had not suggested I buy an Arabic newspaper from his Palestinian neighbor.[15]

Russians comprised a smaller proportion of the Haifa population than Palestinians, yet every kiosk sold five or six Russian-language daily papers. But only in Arab neighborhoods could one buy an Arabic newspaper.

Wadi Nisnas is a place where one can buy Arabic papers.

Hadar

At the end of the steep climb up through Wadi Nisnas the bus emerged at Hadar, the first of the three major terraces, or landings, on Mount Carmel. Hadar is Haifa's commercial, cultural, and municipal center. The streets are jammed all day with traffic that is maddeningly slow, in part because just about every Haifa bus line converges there.

The bus enters Hadar on Herzl Street, which is lined with small, owner-operated shops selling clothing, household goods, newspapers, candy, lotto tickets, and the like. Prices are reasonable on Herzl Street, a solidly middle-class shopping district. One street above Herzl is Nordau Street,[16] a fashionable pedestrian mall lined with travel agencies and expensive restaurants and boutiques. One street below Herzl is Halutz Street, a low-end shopping area. One end of Halutz Street is dominated by falafel vendors and bakeries selling pita bread. The other end is Shuk Talpiyot, "Talpiyot Market," Haifa's main open-air fruit and vegetable market.

Hadar Elyon, "Upper Hadar," is a crowded residential quarter just above the commercial hub. In the 1930s this was Haifa's most elegant neighborhood.[17] A street aptly named Emek Ha-Zeitim, "Valley of the Olive Trees," winds its way uphill. About half of the houses here are built in the old stone style; half are newer, more modest stucco. Balconies look out over courtyards, and elegant entranceways are shaded by magnificent olive trees (see fig. 2.7). Hadar is one of the few neighborhoods in Haifa where these beautiful trees can still be seen.

But Hadar has changed. The once picturesque streets are now choked with automobile traffic—dangerous for crossing and impossible for parking. The old stone houses are in disrepair, and the aesthetics of the fancy stone entrances were ruined in 1967, when, in the months before the "Six Day War," massive cement walls were built in front of each entrance as protection in case of house-to-house fighting.

Each war between the Jews and the Arabs of Israel/Palestine has brought about dramatic changes in the physical and social shape of neighborhoods, as one longtime resident of Hadar recalled:

TEXT 2.2.   "WE'RE NOT ARABS, WE'RE JEWS"

IT IS TOWARD THE MIDDLE OF MY INTERVIEW WITH RUTI, AN ELDERLY WOMAN WHO HAS LIVED IN HADAR ELYON SINCE THE 1940S. I ASKED HER ABOUT THE 1992 GULF WAR, BUT HER THOUGHTS QUICKLY TURNED TO HER MEMORIES OF THE 1947 "WAR OF INDEPENDENCE."

Ruti: ((My mother said to our Arab neighbor)),
         "Even if, God forbid, there will be a war,

Figure 2.7. House with Olive Tree on Emek Ha-Zeitim Street in Hadar, Haifa.

You live here, you are like us, ...
Don't be afraid, no one will break in",
And she [says]...
"Jews kill, they kill children",
I said to her,
"I swear, you live here, you were born here,
Did you ever hear of a Jew grabbing a child and killing
        him?
Just say so",
So she says to me,
"No, but..."...
I said to her,
"If there will be war, war is on the front, not in the city,
        not within the State,
We're not Arabs, we're Jews,
And don't worry, there won't be anything",
        ...
They really were afraid of that,
That if God forbid there is war,
That Jews will attack them,
        ...
Me, in the War of Independence, I lived in the same
        building with Arabs,
Near Shuk Talpiyot,
It was a wonderful area, [with] a courtyard,
And everyone had their [space],
When the war began, uh, the Hagana[18] began to come,
Because I [had] a window, right in front of the road,

Dan: Mmhm
Ruti: So the guys came,
And took the room,
They said,
"[Ruti], we want this room, this direction",
And the neighbors, two flights up, the young woman, she
        says to my mother,
"I heard lots of young men at your place",
[My mother] says,
"They're friends of my son,
Is he forbidden from bringing friends over?"
((The neighbor says)),
"No, we heard it,
Listen, eh— Ruhama,
If Arabs come we'll say that we're all Arab,
But if the Jews come, so eh— say that we're all Jews",
[My mother] says,
"God forbid, there won't be anything here,
        don't worry",
        ...
And I was so mad,
I can't believe in (them),

Because the Arabs killed my father,
He was his partner,
And he killed him,
I have no faith in (them),
    …
[The neighbor's] husband came,
And she says to him,
"We're leaving",
"Why?"
"[Ruti] told me… , if there's a war, [Ruti] will come in
        and kill us",
I told her,
"You're stupid, me kill?
I don't even know how to kill,
You want to go, go!"
    …
And they really did leave,
They left and—
And then it started,
The situation got worse,
So eh— they began eh— the Jews began to move up
        higher,
The Arabs began to flee,
And my uncl— my cousin,
That picture there, that's her daughter,

Dan: Mmhm,
Ruti: She was in the middle,
They fled in the middle,
So she left,
She wanted to take the children and leave,
She started to— to pack, and to move,
She came to take eh—
Killed her on the spot,
By the time the men managed to drag her away,
There was— she was killed,
And they dragged her away,
And— at night, the guys, infiltrated,
And they went down,
And they blew up the house,
But one of the boys was killed,
A wonderful boy,
    …
But my poor aunt,
Three or four children, small ones,
((pointing at the picture))
That one was two years old,
Two of the little girls were in their mother's arms,
She came to take them,
They saw the tragedy,
    …

> And then we all moved away,
> Because the situation had deteriorated,
> ...
> So we moved up higher,
> After two months, we get a notice,
> My cousin, a soldier, was killed in Safed, in the invasion
>   of Safed,
> Him, killed,
> So enough already,
> We had all had enough,
> And it was already such a scene,
> So we started to move higher up,
> And more and more and more,
> ...
> I don't know, I don't know,
> We wanted a state,
> We fought for the state,
> Isn't that— it's a box of matches, this state, by God,
> Such a small state,
> And it's wonderful,
> And to give her away, not that, something— I don't know,
>   ... (136A:34:16–40:49)

Wadi Salib

From the bustle of Hadar's main square the bus continued south and east, traversing the mountain. Just past Shuk Talpiyot is Wadi Salib. Or was Wadi Salib. Now a huge field of rubble. Here and there a lone building remains standing. The most prominent of these is a beautiful church with a graceful dome. At first I assumed I was looking at the remains of an Arab neighborhood—and once it had been an Arab neighborhood—but more recently it had been a Moroccan Jewish immigrant neighborhood. The historian of Israel Howard Sachar (1989:422) recounts a critical moment in shaping this place:

> July 9, 1959 ... a sordid barroom brawl in Wadi Salib, one of the shabbier slums of the formerly Arab section of Haifa. With its ramshackle tenements and narrow winding alleys, its overcrowded one- and two-room apartments opening onto dilapidated courtyards, Wadi Salib bore all the lineaments of a classical Near Eastern mellah.[19] Nearly all of its 15,000 inhabitants were Orientals,[20] and a third of these were Moroccans. As the brawl developed, police were called to the scene. In the ensuing melee a drunken Moroccan was shot and wounded resisting arrest. He was taken immediately to a hospital, where his condition was described as serious but not dangerous. Nevertheless, the rumor quickly circulated that he had died, the victim of "police brutality."
>
> Early the next morning a large crowd of Moroccan immigrants surrounded the Wadi Salib police station, demanding "revenge." At first the police allowed the demonstration, but unrest continued sporadically throughout the day. Shortly before 6:00 PM, therefore, a police task force

stormed and dispersed the crowd. By then thirteen policemen and two civilians were injured, most of them by stones thrown from roofs. Thirty-two persons were arrested. Extensive damage was caused to property in the lower slum areas of the city. Parked cars were burned, twenty shops and cafes wrecked; a *Mapai* club and the *Histadrut*[21] club were completely gutted. An account of the riots appeared on the front pages of all of Israel's newspapers. It was quite apparent that some sort of mass protest was being registered by the Oriental community, with implications far deeper than a barroom fracas.

In the late 1960s, grand schemes were laid for rebuilding old and impoverished slum neighborhoods like Wadi Salib, and for integrating Mizrahi and Ashkenazi Jews. As a first step, the Israeli and Haifa authorities encouraged, and then forced, the residents of Wadi Salib to move out. Low-cost housing was built in other areas of the city, and preferential purchase terms were offered as incentives. Many jumped at this opportunity, but for others leaving the Wadi Salib community was not attractive. For the government had split up families and friends in its eagerness to integrate evacuees into wealthier neighborhoods.

After the evacuation the buildings were torn down. Included in the government's scheme were redevelopment plans for the area, but that part has not been carried out. It was hard for me to understand why this land wasn't built on, given the severe and persistent housing crisis in the early 1990s and the huge influx of Russian immigrants.

Halisa

Herzl Street ends in a steep and winding hill down to, and over, an ancient bridge across a deep canyon. As the bus crossed this precarious bridge I could look up and see the Neve Sha'anan and Carmel Center neighborhoods on opposite sides of the gully. It is a majestic view.

Just ahead, though, the bus approached a much less majestic view: Halisa, a depressed and stigmatized neighborhood. The bus stopped at a modest cluster of shops near a dreary lawn. There is a rehabilitation clinic at this corner, which explains the concentration of drunks, junkies, and down-and-out people at this bus stop. Most people would avoid the place if not for its post office branch, the only one in the area.

A steep hill leads up into Halisa. Near its top stands a mosque.

> There are two main Arab neighborhoods in Haifa—Wadi Nisnas, which is largely Christian, and Halisa, which is largely Muslim. This division of neighborhoods parallels more general cleavages among Palestinian Israelis. Most of the Palestinians who live in cities, for example, are Christian, while most of the Palestinians who live in towns and villages are Muslim.[22] This difference has socioeconomic parallels as well, as Christian Arabs are wealthier and better educated, on average, than Muslim Arabs.
>
> The Israeli government does everything possible to reinforce this distinction. While I lived in Israel, for example, the military attempted to enlist Christian, but not Muslim, Palestinians.[23]

No bus actually enters Halisa. A bus stop at the bottom of the hill services the neighborhood, but from the bus stop to where most people live is a long and steep climb. For some I think it would have been easier to come down from the top. High up the mountain is Neve Sha'anan, a spiffy middle-class neighborhood that is served by many bus lines. But to get to Halisa from Neve Sha'anan one has to find a dirt trail that begins behind a parking lot and follow it around a basketball court and down through prickly pear cactus plants. It is a scenic walk (see fig. 2.8), but most Halisa residents walked up from the bottom.

TEXT 2.3.   "OR THEY WERE MADE TO LEAVE"

FROM AN INTERVIEW WITH NABIL, A YOUNG PALESTINIAN
RESIDENT OF HALISA.

Nabil: There are houses here,
There— there— ((pointing)) if you go into the wadi,
There's a wadi here called "Rosh Emir",
It's nice to take walks in there,
One of the nicest spots in Haifa,
And there are houses in there,
And a real nice neighborhood could develop there,
There are houses—
That is, people left them because—
They haven't put money into this neighborhood,
So uh, people couldn't deal with that,

Figure 2-8.   View of Hadar from Above Halisa, Showing Prickly Pear Cactus Plants Growing Around Halisa.

And up above, above the mosque,
If you keep going up the mountain, below Neve
      Sha'anan,
There are houses, on the mountain, really very nice ones,
I go there often to walk,
And here too,
They left here too,
Because the conditions aren't right,

Nurit: They left recently?

Nabil: Mm, in the fifties, after the establishment of the State,
Uh, it's like the story of ... refugees,
They fled of their own accord,
Or they were made to leave,
That is uh— p— people can say,
"We didn't— we didn't say to each one,
      'Leave your home' ",
But what you produce causes them to scram,

Dan: Can I ask what happened to your family in—
You must have heard stories about— the forties—
The time of the—

Nabil: Yes, I told you already,
I'm from a family not from— not from Rami,[24]
eh— a village that's called Iqrit,
It's well known,
One of the villages—
"The Iqrit Affair"—
You hear about it,
   ...

Nurit: Where is it?

Nabil: Near the border,
Where Ilon is,
If you continue in the direction of Shomera, north,[25]
Well it's there,
What remains of it is a church,
It's a Christian village,
It was a Christian village, that—
Well, it's a long story,
I'll tell it,
I'll try to say— like general things,
   ...
You'll know David Grossman, the writer,
He met me,
In connection with this,
On this matter,
So eh— he is writing a book now on the Arabs inside
      Israel,[26]
At the time he was writing *The Yellow Wind* about the
      West Bank,
Now (),

So eh— he met people from here,
Israeli Arabs,
And one of the people is, was me,
He came to my village,
Met my father too,

...

Anyway, eh— in '48 eh—
The army entered,
The Israeli army,
Got to Iqrit,
In Iqrit the people eh— they didn't fight,
eh— they even received the army nicely,
That is, the people,
It's a little village,
And— and people wanted to survive,
They thought, I guess, that the best way was to receive it
    nicely,
And not to become (),
Not a village that struggled,
So eh, they received the army,
And what I—
The village took in the army for two weeks,
Hosted them even, in their homes, ate, drank,
After two weeks, the army commander came,
Asked the people to evacuate the village,
Eh— to Rami village,
Because it was on the border,
Lebanon,
And there was still a war going on,
It was still the 1948 war, that—
And— the situation was— danger—

...

They asked the people to leave for Rami village,
Until it was quiet,
So... the old people, the women, the children left,
And the men left too,
One man from each family stayed,
One person, who stood watch over his house,
Like guards inside the village, sixty people,
And— after two weeks, they extended it for another two
    weeks,
And another two weeks it continued,
After six months,

...

Up to then the houses had remained as they were,
I mean with— with all their [belongings],
People just— left the houses,
Went to live in the houses of refugees in Rami village,
Find families in Rami,

And they wait—

...

After six months they evacuated the sixty too,

Those that had stayed,

So the people began to feel that eh—

There was an attempt to keep them from returning,

...

After some time, people eh— decided to go to Bagatz,[27]

To petition to Bagatz,

And so there was a trial, in '51,

In July of '51 there was— there was a decision to return
the people to their village, ...

There was no reason to prevent them from returning,

So people started to dance,

They were happy, satisfied, in Rami,

They tried to return,

It was— they had to return on animals, on donkeys and
on horseback,

Because there weren't any vehicles,

They had brought them with army vehicles,

So eh— people began to get organized,

In the evening,

The same evening,

That very evening a guy arrived called eh— commander
of the region, with orders,

And announced that the area, that Iqrit was a closed
military area,

That— and no— and anyone who goes there—

...

He's responsible for his own fate, ...

And that was it,

The happiness turned to sadness, and frustration,

And that same year, in '51, on the 25th of December, on
Christmas Eve,

The village was bombed,

eh— what remained there was just the church, ...

Nabil: They claimed that—

Ben-Gurion[28] said at the time—

That it was— that it was a mistake,

That it was because it was an abandoned village and all,

But eh— that it happened on Christmas Eve,

That the whole village was Christian,

It's a combination of circumstances that's very uh—

So that's it,

People since then eh— have struggled,

I mean to return,

All the time,

They formed a committee,

Organized protests very eh— since then, to return,

My father (happens to be) chairman of the committee,
I mean eh— so I've lived it a lot, you know,
But I—
Dan: Have you visited—?
Nabil: Yes, of course,
We always visit,
Till today we visit,
I mean whenever I get the chance,
I go with friends of mine, ...
The church is closed,
They renovated it,
Still under renovation,
We can go there any time,
Open it up and sit inside,
In general it's a nice place,
So we usually go there,
Sleep out there,
(Entertain) families,
A week ago, all sorts of events, you go there, visit eh—
Usually I go with my friends,
Stay there,
Take walks there,
Picnic,
We have a cemetery there,
And till today we still bury there,
I mean it's— it's a social tradition that—
That developed after the—
That everyone who dies eh— is buried there, ...
(34A:36:25–46:18)

The story of Nabil's family during 1948 is by no means unusual. Most of the Palestinians I spoke with told similar histories. Hundreds of villages were obliterated. The prickly pear cactus, which traditionally marked the boundaries of Arab villages, forms a poignant reminder of the dislocation of Arab life. In many places where Israeli forests were planted over the remains of an Arab village (see fig. 2.8), the long-lived and stubborn cactus plants can still be seen (Swedenburg 1995). A well-known story by A. B. Yehoshua tells of an old Arab man who works as caretaker of such a forest; the man sets fire to the forest, thereby revealing the outlines of the village where he had lived (Yehoshua 1991).[29]

In 1948 the British Mandate in Palestine came to an end when the United Nations called for a partition of mandatory Palestine into a Jewish and an Arab State. The Zionist leadership accepted partition; the Palestinian Arab leadership did not accept the partition. In the ensuing war, Zionist forces occupied much of the land slated to have become a Palestinian state, as well as maintaining control of the area originally allotted to them.

Of greater significance than the territorial gain was the fate that befell the Palestinian population. Of roughly 900,000 Palestinians living in the territory that became Israel, 700,000 ended up outside its borders and became refugees. Urban populations were hardest hit. In Haifa, for example, where prewar Jewish and Arab populations were about equal (50,000), nearly 95 percent of the Arab population left. Or was forced out.

Indeed the Palestinian population of Haifa is only now back to its prewar level of 50,000, and this recent increase is due to significant in-migration from towns and villages. Nakhleh and Zureik (1980) note that prior to 1948 Jews owned only 8 to 9 percent of the land, but by the 1970s Jewish ownership was listed for over 90 percent. After "independence" in 1948, Israel decreed that land owned by absentee landlords would become state property. But the symbolic dispossession is as powerful as the material, physical dispossession: Israeli domination of its Arab "minority" is critically accomplished by remaking the land, the space, the language into an Israeli, if not Jewish, form.

A "Mixed" City

From the bus stop at the post office below Halisa, the bus turned onto a steep and winding road, Yad la-Banim, that quickly passed what little could be seen of the Arab neighborhood of Halisa and moved into the Jewish neighborhood of Tel Amal. The neighborhoods border one another, and the transition between them is abrupt.

Haifa is said to be the best example of what Israelis call a "mixed" city. Haifa's population is largely Jewish. Most are Ashkenazi, but significant numbers of Palestinians and Mizrahim live in the city as well. In this sense, Haifa is a typical Israeli city. The cities are, in general, Jewish places, since the Palestinian population that remained in Israel after the 1948 fighting was largely rural, the urban population having left in disproportionate numbers. The cities are also, in general, Ashkenazi places, since Mizrahim were disproportionately settled either in rural frontier settlements on the periphery of Israel or in ma'abarot on the margins of cities (Swirski 1989).

But by calling Haifa a "mixed" city, Israelis are referring to the Palestinian population: Haifa is a place where Arabs and Jews live within the same municipal boundaries.

> Before going to Israel, while still preparing my research project, I asked a number of Israelis where I should do my fieldwork. They all insisted that I go to Haifa because of the "good relations" between Arabs and Jews there.[30] I took their advice, but as my research evolved this discourse of "good relations" became increasingly problematic. Despite widespread agreement on the description—both Arabs and Jews described Haifa that way—people differed as to what they meant by it.

Haifa is about 15 percent Arab and 85 percent Jewish. This proportion is roughly comparable to the proportion of Arabs and Jews in Israel as a whole.[31] Yet the two groups are quite separate.

When I first arrived in Israel to begin my fieldwork, I lived in the student dormitories at the University of Haifa in order to improve my language skills while I looked for a more permanent place to live, ideally in a neighborhood suitable for my research.

I was looking for an integrated neighborhood, where there was natural contact and communication between Arabs and Jews. I noticed some census data showing a neighborhood called "Halisa" about 50 percent Arab and 50 percent Jewish. This seemed ideal, but when I visited the neighborhood, I saw two distinct neighborhoods—one Jewish and one Palestinian—conflated by a census unit. Between these neighborhoods was a physical boundary as stark as any I saw in Israel.

Several times I heard Jewish Israelis joke that the most significant point of contact and communication between Arabs and Jews in Israel, and the one domain in which true equality reigns, is in the drug trade and the crime world.

Eventually I moved into an apartment at the edge of Tel Amal, the Jewish neighborhood that borders Halisa, the Palestinian neighborhood. A stark no-man's-land divides the two. Halisa had been Arab and Muslim until 1948, when its population was evacuated to a different location in Haifa for the duration of the war. After the war, immigrants from Middle Eastern countries, in particular Iraq, were housed in the "abandoned" Arab homes (see text 1.2). More recently, the neighborhood has returned to being a Muslim place, as Jewish families have moved "up" the mountain and Muslim families have moved back. Now, the mosque high on the hill looks like it belongs, while the synagogues at the bottom of the hill seem out of place.

The struggle over place and identity presented itself clearly when I walked from my apartment in Tel Amal to Halisa. The route went uphill to a height-of-land, then downhill into the Arab neighborhood. The pavement implied continuity between Tel Amal and Halisa, but the streets defined discontinuity and an unmistakable boundary. At the crest of the hill the street in front of my apartment building, David Raziel Street (named after a Zionist hero), changed abruptly from a one-way street to a two-way street. As a result, cars coming from Halisa encountered a dead end. The buses that rumbled through Tel Amal once an hour turned sharply around a 180-degree hairpin curve, vaulting from David Raziel Street to Pe'er Street, which took them from the brink of Halisa safely back into Tel Amal.

Across the divide formed at the height-of-land by the traffic patterns is a rocky hillside where children sometimes played and sheep sometimes grazed. The hillside is littered with partially destroyed cement foundations, brick stairwells, and rusting iron rods. Just beyond this wasteland are several old stone homes, in which most of the windows have been sealed with cinderblocks and cement. In a four-story building, for example, only one floor still had functioning windows. Walking along this street toward the heart of Halisa seemed like traveling back in time: successive buildings showed greater habitation, but I knew that these buildings would soon meet the same fate as the ones that once stood on the hillside behind me. The municipal government condemned these buildings, and, though legal rulings prevent the eviction of current residents, no new residents could move in. As acts of resistance, Palestinian families steadfastly remain in their apartments, sometimes living for decades as the only occupants in a building the authorities want to demolish.[32]

If Haifa is the place where relations between Jews and Arabs are "good"—and agreement on that is striking—still, the referent of "good relations" is quite different, as two narratives of personal memory, quite possibly referring to the same Haifa neighborhood, make clear.

> Sasson Somekh, a Jewish professor of Arabic literature who was born in Iraq, recalls that his family moved to Israel in the 1950s, when he was a young boy. His first impression of Haifa was bewildering and disorienting, and he spent a long time wandering around the strange streets, not understanding a word of the strange language spoken there (Hebrew). He didn't begin feeling comfortable, he says, until he wandered by chance into Wadi Nisnas, an Arab neighborhood, and into Arab shops, where he heard Arabic spoken by people who welcomed him.[33]
>
> Anton Shammas, a Palestinian novelist who grew up in Haifa, recalls being sent as a young boy on an errand to buy something from a Jewish-owned store in the neighborhood. His mother prepared him with all the Hebrew words he would need for the transaction, words which he carefully memorized and practiced, but the storekeeper asked him a question that exceeded young Shammas' repertoire. A Mizrahi woman, who spoke Arabic, came to his rescue, but Shammas vividly remembers that she then chided him for failing to recognize the Hebrew word for "salt," which is very similar to the Arabic word.[34]

Common to these two narratives is the idea of the Mizrahi Israeli as a bridge between Palestinian (Arab) and European (Jew): the experience of the Oriental Jewish immigrant who feels uncomfortable and unwelcome among Ashkenazi Jews, and is more comfortable among Arabs, who, though not Jewish, speak his language and act his culture. And the experience of Palestinians, who, thrust into contact with the foreign Hebrew society, are helped by the link to Mizrahi Jews, but whose experience of this contact is subordinating. This idea lies deep within Israeli discourses of identity, but its failure to be manifested in the physical environment of lived spaces in Israel contests its message.

Neve Yosef

The bus crawled up the steep hill of Yad La-Banim Street, a busy thoroughfare with heavy car traffic and so many bus lines that it seems as if there is always at least one bus noisily laboring up the incline. At the first hairpin all but one of these lines continue upward, rounding the 180-degree turn that encloses a tiny park and playground, hurrying on to the middle-class neighborhood of Neve Sha'anan, above.

A mammoth stone wall (see fig. 2.5) demarcates the boundary between Neve Sha'anan, above, and Neve Yosef, below. The latter neighborhood is little known, lying to the side of Haifa, the very definition of marginalization. Few Haifans recognize the name, and fewer still know where it is. And those who do hold strong prejudices. One resident told me that a merchant once refused to accept her check because she lived in Neve Yosef.

> The Ashkenazi Jewish character of Israeli cities is augmented by the fact that both Palestinian and Mizrahi urban populations tend to be concentrated in socially marginal neighborhoods on the geographic periphery of the cities. In Haifa, as in Israel generally, Arab-Jewish residence patterns are almost completely segregated, with Palestinians living primarily in two or three neighborhoods where very few Jews live. While there is considerable residential integration of Ashkenazi and Mizrahi Jews, there is in Haifa, as in Israel generally, an ethnic segregation that takes the form of differentiation between rich and poor neighborhoods.

Neve Yosef comes off at the apex of the hairpin curve in Yad La-Banim Street. Crossing the street here is a truly hair-raising undertaking, since there is no point at which pedestrians can be seen by cars coming both from above and from below. A school for religious girls and a shiny new community center—the pride of the neighborhood—grace the upbeat entrance to the neighborhood. A row of shops and modern, attractive apartment buildings round out the nicer section of Neve Yosef— what residents call *l'mala*, "above." A few blocks' walk brings one to *bifnim*, "inside," where the cement high-rise *blokim* take over. The main street ends in a huge cul-de-sac that the one bus line that comes into the neighborhood uses to turn around and exit from Neve Yosef. Neighborhood boys use the cul-de-sac for soccer games. Beyond the pavement is a railing, which marks the boundary of the neighborhood, and beyond the railing is a steep and rocky slope, covered with brush, empty land. Far below lies Checkpost, a shopping, entertainment, and transportation hub, and the gateway to the eastern suburbs called the Krayot.[35] Most Neve Yosef residents have friends or relatives who live in the Krayot, and, as the crow flies, it's not far, but there is no road that connects Neve Yosef with Checkpost or the Krayot. In fact, there is no road leading out of Neve Yosef at all.

Neve Yosef is a Moroccan neighborhood. In the beginning it was planned as a place to settle Palmach veterans,[36] but plans were quickly changed, and in the early 1960s the *blokim* were built to house *m'funim*, "evacuees," from Wadi Salib. Recently many new Russian immigrants have moved in, following earlier waves of immigration, but the neighborhood somehow retains its Moroccan majority and character.

TEXT 2.4. DISCRIMINATION

FROM AN INTERVIEW WITH SHARON, A MIDDLE-AGED IRAQI JEWISH WOMAN WHO LIVES IN THE HALISA NEIGHBORHOOD: WE HAD BEEN TALKING ABOUT RELATIONS BETWEEN ARABS AND JEWS WHEN I ASKED HER WHETHER THERE ARE STILL DIFFERENCES BETWEEN SEPHARDIM AND ASHKENAZIM.

Sharon: Sure there are, I mean eh—
          I— it's a little eh—
          People often ask me that question,
              "Does that exist?",

It's— there are a couple of indicators that are so eh—
    simple,
Go to a neighborhood, Neve Yosef,
What will you find there?
Who lives there?
What does he do?
What's his living ((laughs)) standard?
So you see it explicitly,
They're Mizrahim,
eh— tough economic situation, etc.,
I mean, eh— people don't need to search too far,
And for some reason, they still ask themselves,
    "Does this really—"
eh—
    "Is there really such a thing as this?"
It's awfully clear,
They went and did all those tests of schools,
Or even without doing the tests,
There's the whole issue of *t'une tipuax*,[37]
What is this *t'un tipuax*?
People don't quite know what *t'un tipuax* is,
t'un tipuax, its definition in the Ministry of Education,
That's not my definition,
It depends on the number of children in the home,
eh— the financial situation,
And ethnicity,
That means, eh—
There are components, such that it can't— almost can't
    be an Ashkenazi,
Unless, eh—
It's a family of ten children with a really bad financial
    situation, and he's Ashkenazi,
So what's the whole deal of *t'un tipuax*?
It means they take neighborhoods,
Let's say, take Neve Yosef,
Take Kishon School, near Neve Yosef,
All the children that go there, most of the students there,
They're defined, as *t'une tipuax*,
The school becomes *t'un tipuax*,
And you, as people who deal with sociology and all that,
    know,
And this matter has already been investigated,
That the son of a laborer usually believes that he will be a
    laborer,
Or his dreams, they're pretty realistic,
Son of a doctor, knows that he has a good chance of being
    a doctor,
Son of a laborer, doesn't think he has much chance of
    being a (doctor)—

Now it's also the parents that think this way,
It's also the teachers that think this way,
It's also the kids that think this way,
And it's a little hard to escape from this catch,
I mean you're in this situation,
And then afterwards suddenly to make of yourself some
    kind of professor, that's—
That's not so easy,

Dan: You spoke about limits that people place on themselves,
    is there also discrimination?

Sharon: There is discrimination,
Look, people even today still say, let's say,
    "Today that doesn't exist anymore",
I, today I met with a group that I meet with in Tira,[38]
I— and I say that I do a group for consciousness-raising
    for women,
For Mizrahi women,
So they say to me,
    "What, how can you speak this way?
    That's not nice, in our time to speak this way,
    You don't do—"
I don't go and say, eh—
    "I really want to do this with Mizrahi women,"
Now when I get to the group,
At the community center, in Tira,
I don't say eh—
    "Just give me Mizrahi women,
    Because I'll only work with them",
But the chance that there will be Ashkenazi women
    there—
It's not that if they were in this group it wouldn't interest
    me,
It's definitely so,
I mean, she would definitely be accepted,
But eh— the biggest likelihood, that— eh— most of the
    group, will be, Mizrahi,
And almost all— and every group in Tira is Mizrahi,
And my whole group in Acre is Mizrahi,[39]
In Acre there is one Ashkenaz—
Because that's the way they live in the neighborhoods,
I mean it's not— it's not a fabrication of mine,
It's— I didn't choose the group,
I didn't say
    "I want her and her and her to be in the group",
And the people didn't choose either,
They signed up for the group in the community center,
eh— I mean they came to the session, to the club, to Isha
    L'Isha,[40]
And they arrived,

And the whole group was Mizrahi,
I mean, what I mean is, if I go, to—
If there's a community center, I don't know, but no
    difference, for some eh—
Community center in the Carmel,[41]
So there maybe there would be a different ratio,

Nurit: Mmhm
Sharon: Most of it Ashkenazi, maybe,
I mean there would be Mizrahi women there too,
But if I go to a neighborhood like Neve Yosef,
And Tira, or places like those,
Shxunat Ha-Tikvah in Tel Aviv,
Neve David here,
eh— all kinds of neighborhoods like that,
Most of the women are Mizrahi,
…

And— within the Mizrahi group, someone told me, this
    week,
eh— something interesting,
She's a young woman,
Twenty-five years old, married, children, from Tira,
She said that she eh—
They accepted her to work eh— in— during the summer
    holidays,
And when— … when she had come to work as a
    substitute,
During the summer break,
And there was, eh— eh— an Ashkenazi secretary,
You notice about her [the secretary] that she's one of
    those with self-confidence, you know,
And she [the secretary] asked her what her ethnicity is,
So eh— she said to her [the secretary],
    "Yemenite",
So then she [the secretary] says to her,
    "Oh, the Yemenites they're very nice",
And so on,
And suddenly, she gets a grip on herself,
And she (thought),
"Why did she say— why did she say she was Yemenite?
She's not Yemenite, she's a Moroccan,
So why did she say she was Yemenite?"
She said Yemenite because she knows that between—
That she looks Mizrahi,
And among Mizrahi ethnicities, the Yemenites, they're
    the nicest,
They, you know, make the nicest impression on them,
So she suddenly got mad at herself,
    "Why does she [the secretary] suddenly say that?"
And that woman [the secretary], she started to praise her,

So she said to her [the secretary],
        "No, I'm not Yemeni,
        I'm a Moroccan",
So eh— she says that that woman really eh— she really
        didn't like that,
eh— I mean she [the secretary] didn't like ((laughs)) that
        she was a Moroccan,
And she didn't like—
Now we don't live in—
I don't know where we live today, in the year eh— '91,
That things like that happen,
And that's women who try hard,
eh— they're always saying—
I mean they really try to say "this thing doesn't exist in
        their lives",
        "We've gotten past that already",
Because they too hope that their children won't go
        through this,
Through this whole deal again,
But eh… (40B:01:32–8:20)

Carmel Center

Winding its way up the mountain, high above the neighborhoods of Hadar, Halisa, and Neve Yosef, the bus approached Carmel Center, the second of Mount Carmel's three landings.[42] The road that leads to Carmel Center is appropriately named Yefe Nof, "Beautiful View," since the houses on this street have a truly beautiful view of downtown Haifa, the Mediterranean Sea, and many points north and south. Wealthy Palestinians of an earlier era built mansions along Yefe Nof, and Herzl's utopian novel, Altneuland, extols the virtues of this street (Herzl 1960 [1902]). A row of nightclubs from a more recent era sizzle and scream with excitement and bulge with teenagers on Saturday nights. Carmel Center is home to skyscraping hotels, sidewalk cafes, Italian restaurants, and fashionable stores. The sidewalks are packed with children. This is where the good ice cream is sold, where movie theaters and concert halls are, where Israeli teens come for a night out.

Off the main drag are residential neighborhoods with low-rise, three- and four-story apartment buildings built in the 1950s. These buildings face the street and have yards in front. Effort has gone into their design and aesthetics.

Language, too, is different higher up the mountain. Arabic is rarely heard—and rarely seen. Gone are the trilingual street signs that grace many of the streets in the older Hadar neighborhood.[43] Whereas in Hadar one sometimes hears older people speaking Yiddish, here one often hears German. And everywhere, English and Russian. American sailors from the Sixth Fleet, which takes shore leave in Haifa, flood the restaurants and clubs every few weeks.

TEXT 2.5. THE SCHWEITZER CAFE

FROM AN INTERVIEW WITH YA'EL, A MIDDLE-AGED
ASHKENAZI JEWISH WOMAN WHO LIVES IN THE HADAR
NEIGHBORHOOD: I HAVE ASKED WHAT IT WAS LIKE LIVING IN
HADAR IN THE 1930s, WHEN JEWS WERE A SMALL MINORITY
THERE.

Ya'el: Yes, I'll tell you something else,
        The— the Jews also eh—
        There was Wadi Nisnas,
Dan: Mmhm,
Ya'el: ... there were a lot of Jews I don't [know] what the
        proportions were,
Dan: Mmhm
Ya'el: I didn't feel like a Jewish minority,
        And— eh— I know that— people also concentrated
        themselves in Hadar,
        My father worked at— Eged, on Atzma'ut Street,[44]
        ...
        And my mother at that time wanted to move to live in the
        Carmel,
        Because she saw things in terms of property values,
        My father wanted to live close to his work,
        And also, no one was living there,
        Who lived in Carmel?
        At the price of an apartment these days, you could have
        gotten some fantastic land there,
Dan: Mmhm
Ya'el: And beautiful houses,
        But no one wanted to live there,
        Just a very few, began to move up,
        And— in truth I don't remember Arab friends during
        childhood,
        I mean, because they weren't—
        I remember relations with Arabs through my father's
        work,
        Because my father was a member of Eged,
        And he had contacts with Arabs,
        And— in particular Druze,
Dan: Mmhm
Ya'el: In particular Druze,
        They were very very good friends,
        Went eh— we went to visit them many times,
        I remember that there was "City High School A" in
        Kiryat Eliezer,
        I think that it was mixed,
        Even then it was Arab-Jewish, like today,[45]
        ...
        eh— I didn't have, I mean I didn't have any Arab friends,

But eh— it's not just that,
There was also a class difference within the— among
　　　Jews themselves,
Afterwards, I'm speaking already about my own time, that
　　　I was already alive,
I was already eh— an elementary school student,
There were huge differences, between us and the
　　　Carmelistim,
Those who lived in the Carmel,
We lived—
Those who were in Hadar, with relatively speaking a
　　　lower economic class position,
And those who lived in the Carmel,
They had relatively speaking a higher economic class
　　　position,
And there were huge differences,

Dan:　Mmhm
Ya'el:　Snobbism, and— and— really very sharp class
　　　differences, and— eh—
Dan:　() discrimination?
Ya'el:　No, I don't know if I ever felt discriminated against,
Because our financial situation at home was excellent,
Because my father was an Eged member,
And at that time it was good money,
And— what I dreamed of at night I got in the morning,
And I was also an only daughter,
And— we also lived— the street was also a beautiful
　　　street,
Masada Street, it was an aristocratic street,
The whole area was beautiful,
We also lived in a house built by Eged members,
And till today it's one of the nicest houses in the area,
　　　Masada 7 ...
　　　It's a great house,
And I didn't feel any discrimination,
No, not at home,
And not away from home,
I don't think that anyone felt discrimination,
What we did feel, we felt eh— big differences,
Dan:　Mmhm
Ya'el:　Between the— the status eh— of them,
Afterwards at that time, I went to High School up there,
　　　in the Carmel
Dan:　Mmhm
Ya'el:　And— but again not feelings of discrimination,
But I remember the differences eh—
I always had friends from there and from here,
So I always moved betw— ...
But the— there was a difference in terms of () one
　　　another,

eh— where he is from, where you came from,
Differences of eh— money, of course,
That's what creates these differences in the final analysis,
...
I think that— the level of education too,
They were— look, they got here, many— many eh—
    after the war,

Dan: Mmhm

Ya'el: A class came with— from a high status,
I mean in terms of eh— eh— profession...
Professional people,
Some of them began to get payments,
The [reparations] payments from Germany,[46]
And that immediately sprang... them economically,
And— OK I'm already talking about a stage when I was
    eleven or twelve years old,
Eh— that's already '51, toward the end of the fifties,
Near the beginning of the sixties,
And they had already begun—
The building had already begun in the Carmel,
They were already living in the Carmel,
Denya wasn't even around yet, ...
But the Carmel did exist,
And we would go up,
My parents for example and me,
Every Saturday to Cafe Pe'er,
That was the aristocratic cafe,
We went up there to drink coffee, in a cafe,
Even though I remember that there was a cafe at Bet Ha-
    Kranot,[47]
Something, huge,
That a Yugoslavian couple—
I think they were killed later in an airplane accident in
    Yugoslavia or on some trip,
There were— I mean you're an American, you don't—
    you're not familiar with the European culture,
The classical culture of the nineteenth century,
Beginning of the twentieth century,
So there was this cafe in the style of Schweitzer ...
If I'm not mistaken built of wood,
With big mirrors,
It was huge,
You went there for strudel, for cake, with a cup of tea, a
    cup of coffee,
And newspapers, imported, ...
Who ever saw foreign newspapers?
Magazines, as they were called,
I remember that because I really loved it, ...
(67A:13:35–19:46)

Ahuza

Above Carmel Center the bus traveled along wide, four-lane avenues named Moria and Horev. At Ahuza the city was widening the street, paving the median strips with patterned brickwork, and landscaping the traffic circles with flowerbeds. At Denya a new subdivision was being built (fig. 2.9). The building boom was spurred by the Russian immigration, but these houses were high up the hill—they were not the low-rent units that immigrants would occupy. These were the houses that veteran Israelis would move up into when new immigrants moved into their old houses lower down.

Haifa leans back along the Carmel ridge at this point, still rising, but now more gradually. Moriah Street runs along the crest of the knife-edged ridge, and neighborhoods fall away dramatically to both sides. To the west established neighborhoods were being augmented; to the east new neighborhoods were being built. Deep, forested gorges swoop down from ridge crest to sea. The Israeli Nature Protection Society built trails down several of these gorges, allowing one to hike from shopping center to beach.

Daliat Ha-Carmel

Just past Denya, at the very top of Mount Carmel, my bus arrived at its final destination: Haifa University. The campus commands spectacular views in all directions, and borders

Figure 2.9.   New Construction in Haifa.

the Carmel Forest National Park with its many hiking trails and picnic sites. Clashing with the natural beauty of its surroundings, the campus itself is a clump of ugly buildings tossed along the ridge top. The university was built as the last bulwark of Jewish Haifa, constituting (pushing) the border between Haifa and the Druze towns and villages that extend south and east from Haifa along the Carmel Range.

> The Druze appear to be a classic ethnic group. In Israel, Lebanon, and Syria they constitute minority populations that are residentially concentrated and socially isolated. Historically, the Druze stem from a religious split in the Muslim community, and since about the turn of the first millennium they have survived as a surprisingly influential religious minority among more numerous and more-powerful Christian and Muslim Arab communities. The comparison to Jews comes readily to mind.
>
> Arabic is the language of Druze homes in Israel—as it is in Syria and Lebanon—but historical forces have conspired with the Israeli Druze to create for them a complex position in the Israeli identity structure. For centuries the Druze had conflictual relations with Muslim Ottoman authorities and with Muslim neighbors. In the Galilee region of Palestine, which became Israel, residential segregation was high, and most Druze lived either in all-Druze villages or in villages shared with Christian communities. In the 1940s when the Jewish settlers were vying with the British and the Palestinian Arabs for control over Palestine, an informal alliance was forged between the Jews and the Druze.
>
> Since 1948 the differences between the Druze and other Palestinian, Arabic-speaking communities have been magnified by Israeli policies. For example, Druze men must serve in the Israeli military, while neither Muslim nor Christian Arab men are required to do so. Indeed, a relatively high percentage of Druze make a career of service in various branches of the Israeli security apparatus.

TEXT 2.6.   LIVING-ROOM TALK AND SHOWER TALK

> FROM AN INTERVIEW WITH SALMAN, A MIDDLE-AGED DRUZE WRITER WHO LIVES IN DALIAT HA-CARMEL: I HAVE ASKED HIM ABOUT HEBREW KNOWLEDGE IN THE DRUZE VILLAGE.

Salman: Look, good Hebrew—
They start learning Hebrew from first grade in school,
I think that maybe that is different from Arab villages,
Other, the— because of the proximity to Haifa,
Because of the nature of the work people here do,
Because of the army,
All of that,
It has an influence,
Definitely, eh— Israeli culture is— is closer in Dalia,
Than it is farther up in other towns in the Galilee,
...

Dan: You define yourself as Druze?
Salman: Yes,
Dan: Do you define yourself as a Druze writer?

Salman: No, I— I'm Druze, but a Palestinian writer,
Dan: Are there Druze writers?
Salman: Yes, there are Druze writers, but eh—
Dan: What distinguishes you from the others?
Salman: eh— I— eh— as—
         There's no definition of a Druze writer,
         I mean there's no— when a writer belongs to a certain
                 literature,
         (To the literature of his mother tongue),
         The same topics, the same—
         The Druze don't have any other language,
         The Arabic language is the language of the Druze,
         The mother tongue,
         They think in— in Arabic,
         They eh— so this distinction, Druze writer or not a Druze
                 writer, it doesn't exist,
         I— I don't— many Druze writers will say,
         "I'm a Druze,
         (I'm) a writer born to Druze ethnicity,
         He was born that way,
         He belongs to that ethnic group, like me",
         But me— in my writing, my work is part of Palestinian
                 literature,
         That is written in Israel,
         And in the Territories,
         And outside this region,
         If you define that as a person, as a citizen, as a member of
                 a certain ethnicity,
         Yes, I'm Druze,
         I () of all the people who are in the village,
         The behavior, the customs, eh— origin, everything,
         I am part of the society,
         But my writing,
         I— I— I'm a Palestinian writer,
         Good, bad, well liked, it's not important,
         But eh— no, it's a matter of fact,
         It's part of that same Palestinian literature that's written
                 here, there, and in other places,
                 …
Dan: Could you tell me a bit about the book?
                 …
Salman: It's something interesting,
         I mean eh— interesting in its conception,
         And also— also the style I think,
         I wanted to give—
         To investigate, in Bet She'an, two years ago, (two
                 things),[48]
         One and the principle thing, that's if the people there are
                 really racist,

...

Because all the time people write in the newspapers that
    Bet She'an is you know a symbol of the Israeli
    racism—
Sephardi racism, yes?
Of the Sephardi Jews,
And I always had this notion,
"It can't be, that someone, from Arab origins,
Because he still has the Arab culture,
He can't be so anti-Arab",
He can be anti-Arab,
But so anti-Arab, as they describe him,
Because after all the culture is— it— represents the
    character of the person,
What can't be, it's not possible that— that—
That a group like that disconnected so completely from
    the culture,
From its roots,
And became anti-this that and the other,
No, I always thought about that, that can't be,

Dan: Mmhm,
Salman: Something's not quite right,
And— I set out to take a look at the matter,
I also wanted to look at the background of eh— David
    Levi,[49]

...

I'm not interested in his (politics),
I'm interested in the society he grew up in,
Where he lives, what— where he might lead,
And the best way is to go to— to his village,
Because he's very tied to Bet She'an,
To go to his village,
To hear, to make impressions,

...

And— and third, eh— there was a certain coincidence,
A writer from there,
That I wrote about,
And also— the first guy that I got to know from Bet
    She'an,
He eh— eh— he has an interesting story,
I included him in— in the book,
He once was in Gush Emunim,[50]
There was some tragic incident,
He— that he saw, suddenly he changed,
Became eh— someone who grasped the Palestinian issue,
In favor of peace,
And so on,

...

So also— eh— after this acquaintance, with this guy, I
     said,
"There's some— there's material here,
There's a— there's something interesting,
That I should go look at",
And I went, I—
During two months time I would go there twice, three
     times weekly,
And the first guy that I got to know there,
After that young man,
Was the editor of the local paper, of Bet She'an,
And on the first day, when I arrived there, he met me,
So he included an article,
He said to me,
That he wanted to publicize,
That I had come to write a book and all,
I said to him,
"Listen,
If you're going to publicize,
Don't say that I'm Druze,
Please, write, 'Palestinian writer,'
Because then I want to know,
If they'll accept me as a Palestinian,
Because it's no big deal to be accepted in Bet She'an as a
     Druze,
That's not— I have no problem,
But as a Palestinian, that's the problem,
I want to go straight to the— to this problem,
So if you write, write 'Palestinian writer' ",
And he really did publish,
That I'm a Palestinian writer,
So people knew that I existed,
And— already from the first day I discovered that people
     were waiting for me,
I mean, they wanted, to— to know, eh— no—
There wasn't any hostility at all,
Every time I went to people's homes,
They knew my name of course,
I would present myself,
"Ahlan, Shalom, how are you?[51]
How's the book coming?"
People didn't reject— that I was Palestinian,
That's— that was very very () for me,
And— I left— during that period,
That is not a population that has any deep hatred,
Not for the Palestinian people,
And not for Arabs in general,
In my book I called it,
"The Man in the Living Room", and "The Man in the
     Shower",

When a man's in the living room, so he's in the living
    room,
He is all buttoned-up, and nice, and ordered,
And recites all the slogans,
And all the— the words that flatter,
And all the you know official things,
Because the position requires it,
When he's in the shower, he's naked, he's closed the
    thing,
And under the water,
Then he sings all sorts of songs,
And goes wild,
And he can do something,
He can allow himself to do what he wants in the shower,
And then I () go, eh— to reach the man in the shower in
    Bet She'an,
Not in the living room,
I don't want people of the living room,
It's people who will tell me their inner truth,
Not— not the platform of the Likud, and not of
    Moledet,[52]
And not of Labor,
  …

We've already been to that movie a bunch of times,
But we haven't been in the shower yet,
I want to get to the shower,
  …

And people really cooperated with me a lot,
That's how it happened with each person I met,
That there was the "guy in the shower" and the "guy in
    the living room",
At first, all the stuff from the living room, they sent me,
I mean,
"Land of Israel, Land of our Fathers,
Eh— Jerusalem more—
Hebron is more important than Jerusalem,
And God gave us this piece of land,
And Arabs screwed us, and murdered us,
And and and",
I let the people you know say all this,
And then, after all that was finished—
The sentences, there were sentences that I would hear in
    each place,
After that was over, that battery finished,
Then they would speak differently,
Usually I'd ask what they listen to, what kind of music,
And then he starts talking about Farid Al-Atrash, and
    Umm Kulthum,[53]
  …

Dan: By the way, did you speak Arabic with the people?

Salman: Arabic? eh—
Dan: Do some speak Arabic?
Salman: Almost all of them, speak Arabic,
But Arabic that I don't understand... (66A:14:42–16:37)

In Daliat Ha-Carmel I was able to buy a Hebrew newspaper—but not an Arabic paper.

3

Theoretical Frameworks for Linguistic Negotiations of Identity

In chapter 2 I showed how Israel inscribes, and reinscribes, identity on geographical terrain. A bus trip through Haifa, ascending Mt. Carmel from the narrow streets of old, downtown neighborhoods to the wide avenues of lofty suburban quarters, re-presents past and present struggles over the construction and interpretation of place. Fragmented and contradictory narratives of history and locale show an ongoing process of negotiation that is simultaneously structured and structuring. Israeli renaming of streets after Zionist ideas and heroes constructs Jewish space by inscribing Israeli history as a narrative of place. An Arab restaurant, named simply for the street on which it is located, participates in this negotiation of place, as it profits from an Israeli act of reinscription. When Israel renames the street, the restaurant's retention of its earlier name becomes a claim to Palestinian space, a narrative of Palestinian place, and therefore a resource for Palestinian resistance.

This negotiation of identity takes form as a play of signifiers. At the level of semiotics and discourse, the alternation of names and partially forgotten meanings can be seen as humorous. Linked to social structure, however, this symbolic struggle generates material consequences for relations of power. Negotiation of symbolic identities is therefore both playful and serious. Israeli (re)naming of streets is an attempt to impose hegemony, in the face of which a restaurant's name assumes resistant meaning. The play signals an underlying negotiation of structure and agency.

Such negotiations take place continuously, dispersed across space and time. Discourse offers individuals ready-made identities that individuals adopt, adapt, reject, and deny in their symbolic expressions. Learned in school, accepted by parents, represented on television, textualized in newspapers, inscribed in the stone and plaster of urban environments, discourse interpellates subjects into ratified identities. Discourse becomes the site of struggle, but the struggle also emerges in and through discourse. Such a negotiation spirals back upon itself, for in adapting a ready-made subjectivity to the pragmatic demands of situated discourse, individuals call into existence signifiers—symbols—that challenge and bend the ratified identities. Like the restaurant that steadfastly retains its name when caught up in dislocations beyond its control, individuals engage with master narratives of identity by negotiating the meanings of everyday symbols: the clothes they wear, the homes they live in, the politics they support, and the languages they speak.

Play

The notion of "play" encapsulates many of the meanings behind terms such as "negotiation," "struggle," and "dialogism."[1] Play captures ideas of indeterminacy, creativity, and strategy in human behavior, while juxtaposing these notions to a framework of rule-based behavior. At first glance, "play" seems a simple word, but a review of its common-sense meanings indicates its complexity. "Play" can mean:

- A space in which something can move, as the play in a joint
- Acts in fun, recreation, nonserious activity, as in children's play
- A dramatic composition or performance, as a Shakespeare play

Play is a space, a gap. The play in a steering wheel, for example, is a space of free movement. Within the range of play in the steering column, small changes in the steering wheel do not turn the car. The play in discourse is a similar space of free movement. All languages provide different ways of "saying the same thing." The words "chew" and "masticate," for example, refer to the same activity, and they are said to have the same *referential meaning*. In discourse, however, in situated use, "chew" and "masticate" are separated by a gap of formality, authority, erudition, and history. In an actual context of speech, a speaker's choice of one or the other conveys—alongside the referential meaning—a social or affective meaning. Variation in language provides the symbolic resources with which speakers play on, and play with their messages, thereby negotiating social relationships.[2]

Play is also a game, a recreation. Children's play, for example, is fun, imaginative, and nonserious behavior. A "play on words" is recreational language-use. We think of language as a rational, scientific code for directly communicating information, but much of what is actually communicated through language is communicated indirectly.

The apparent contradiction stems from a powerful ideology of language that privileges the rational over the creative or the aesthetic in language.

Even in poetry we focus on the information content, despite recognizing the importance of rhyme and meter. Edgar Allen Poe's poem "The Raven," for example, tells a powerful story of love and loss, but, as Roman Jakobson (1960) has pointed out, the poem's fame stems from an exquisite pattern of sound. The memorable line

> Quoth the Raven, "Nevermore,"

draws its power from the play of sounds, including the rhyming of the final syllable with previous lines, the rhythmic pattern of dactylic feet followed by trochaic feet, and most subtly but most significantly, the symmetrical opposition of the recurring sounds r, v, and n, in RaVeN NeVeRmore. Jakobson (1960) argues that Poe's playfulness with sound in "The Raven" calls attention to alternative, or additional meanings. The parallelism of repeating the line "Quoth the Raven, 'Nevermore,'" at the end of many stanzas, and of repeating the sounds r-v-n within this line, establishes the raven as a symbol, as an index of something beyond itself, as more than just a word that refers to a bird.

Poetic symbols, like Poe's raven, are specialized forms of indirect communication, but indirection—and the play involved—is fundamental to the way everyday conversations work as well. For example: A boss stares at an empty coffee pot and says to her assistant,

> "The coffee pot is empty."

Here the boss has communicated much more than she has said. The boss is doing much more than stating her observation about the world (coffee pot ➜ empty). She is requesting that the employee make more coffee—but she is doing this indirectly. This too is play with language, since there are many other ways the boss might have phrased her request. She might have said "Make some more coffee," for example. We recognize in the boss's indirect formulation that she was trying to be polite, considerate, or modest. In other words, her choice of language form was embedded in a negotiation of situationally relevant identities.

Such dramaturgical use of language suggests the third meaning of play: a dramatic composition or performance. A Shakespearean play is both the script that underlies the performance and the performance itself. In the first sense, it is the set of rules that guides the actors' behavior. In the second sense, it is the way reality emerges from the scripted interactions of the individual actors.

Erving Goffman (1959) has suggested viewing social life in general as a play in which members of society are actors performing (more-or-less) scripted roles. Building on the work of George Herbert Mead (1962 [1934]) and Gregory Bateson (1972), Goffman's dramaturgical model of symbolic interaction looks to the nuances of face-to-face encounters to reveal the rules underlying social interaction. Though Goffman begins with the notion of the script, his interest is actually closer to ad-libbing. Actors follow their scripts, but they are also aware that they are acting, representing, and constructing identities, and that they are interacting with individuals who are similarly aware of the multiple levels of interactional structure.

The play within the play provides room to maneuver. Actors come out of role; they take on new roles; they dispute the roles of others. Social reality, in Goffman's world, is both up for grabs and created on the fly as it emerges from the details of face-to-face social interaction. In the coffee pot example, boss and assistant perform a loosely scripted scene, using the play in language to negotiate their roles.[3]

The metaphor of play helps to explicate the idea of the linguistic negotiation of identity, but the full range of meanings of play must be taken into account. Identity is a freedom of maneuver within a field of power. Individuals receive their identities prescripted, but they may perform their roles in various ways.

Identity

Identity is a complex field of ideas. As Richard Handler (1994) has pointed out, a paradox attends the common use of "identity" in referring to social group membership. "Identity" implies complete equivalence, as in the related word "identical," but social scientists conceptualize a person's "social identity" as meaning the opposite, namely the ways in which a person differs from other individuals. Moreover, "identity" in its mathematical meaning of "equation" implies an eternal equivalence, whereas recent studies of identity focus on the ways that individuals may be constituted differently depending upon the context.

Identity is conceptualized in this book as a discourse phenomenon, as a rhetorical device, as a field of play. I refer to "identities," plural, to emphasize their multiplicity and situated provisionality. I metaphorize identities as something that can be haggled over, or negotiated, in order to emphasize that they are subject to contestation and the source of conflict. This formulation never loses sight of the real power that is won and lost as identities are fixed—and refixed—by culture, by ideologies, and by individuals in their everyday speaking practices.

"THE ISRAELI KID"

The summer of 1992 was an exciting time for Israelis, as two athletes brought home medals from the Olympic Games in Barcelona—a first for Israel. In the midst of this celebration of Israeli nationhood; however, a young man from Nazareth stole the show.

The Olympic medals came in the obscure sport of judo. Ya'el Arad, a world champion in her weight class and the odds-on favorite to garner the first Israeli medal, won a silver medal. Then, a complete unknown turned in a once-in-a-lifetime performance, and he too won a silver medal. Both athletes were native-born, classically attractive emblems of Israeli society, and they instantly became media darlings.

As Israelis were celebrating their heroes' second-place medals, a young boxer from Nazareth took a first-place medal. This latter event (a professional boxing world championship) received much less attention, but it was featured on the popular Friday night television news magazine, and it was written up in the weekend newspapers. In a complex web of significations, the news report showed a tearful Palestinian man calling himself "The Israeli Kid," draping himself in the blue-and-white Israeli flag, and crying with emotion at the playing of "Ha-Tikva," the Israeli national anthem.

The reporter, the regular United States correspondent for Israeli television, whose flawless, if accented, English was heard each night interviewing American politicians, now interviewed the boxer in Hebrew. The young man's Hebrew was halting and stilted—rusty, it seemed. He had been living in the United States for several years, trying to make it as a boxer. His Hebrew was from high school, and I sensed that he was embarrassed. Toward the end of the interview the reporter allowed him to say hello to his mother, and the contrasting fluency of his Arabic highlighted the disfluency of his Hebrew.

This play of symbols plays with identities. The boxer was claiming an Israeli national identity that was consistent with the norms of international sport, but striking for a Palestinian man in Israel. Organized spectator sports have long been associated with constructions of national identity (see Appadurai 1996:97–105; Oriard 1993; Pope 1993), and global events, such as the quadrennial Olympics or World Cup soccer championship, call special attention to a phenomenon that is extraordinarily widespread. By emblazoning his white boxing robe with the blue label "The Israeli Kid," this boxer was participating in the hyped-up style of international boxing, in which nicknames and stage personas contribute to a uniqueness of media identity critical to success (see Barthes 1972). But the reference to national identity stems from the nation-state foundation of international sport, in which individuals must compete as part of nationally organized and supported teams. The link between competition and nation, and the patriotism involved in spectatorship, are reinforced by the public playing of the victor's national anthem.

This public display of national identity was a striking play on identity in the Israeli context because it claimed Israeliness for a Palestinian Arab Self. At one level the play stems from "Israeli" including "Palestinian" within its scope of reference. At another level the play is reversed, stemming not from the suggestion that "Israeli" could stand for "Arab," but that a Palestinian would stand for being labeled "Israeli." Israel is so closely associated with its majority population, Jews, and so vividly opposed to its neighbors, Arabs, that the embrace of Palestinian and Israeli symbols calls poetic attention to itself. In so doing the play calls attention to deep ambiguities and contradictions in Israeli society: What does it mean to be "Israeli"? Does Israeli citizenship imply Israeli nationality? However, by embracing these ambiguities, the young boxer appears to efface his Palestinian identity. His play was thus either audacious, in claiming mainstream status, or politically suspect, in wanting to.

Discourse

There is nothing simple about the play of symbols in "The Israeli Kid" as described here. They are enmeshed in webs of signification that lead outward in many directions.

To understand what such signification means and does, I approach it from a discourse perspective, according to which cultural meanings are generated in the communicative forms through which they are expressed (Sherzer 1987; Urban 1991). Symbols are meaningful by virtue of their deployment in situated contexts of communication, and their meaning emerges from such use, rather than inhering in the symbols themselves. This discourse approach depends upon a crucial reflexivity, which I conceptualize as a spiral (see chapter 1). Symbols are deployed in discourse as meaningful elements; they bring particular meanings to the discourse. But the meaning of any particular deployment of a symbol depends upon emergent characteristics of the discourse context. Moreover, discourse has history, in the sense that subsequent uses of symbols bear the traces of earlier deployments. The gap between a symbol's (historical) meaning potential and its emergent meaning in discourse is a source of play. Discourse is thus simultaneously structured, by the historical meanings of symbols, and structuring, as it re-sets trajectories for subsequent meanings (see Bourdieu 1977).

The idea of discourse, as it is used here, draws on three threads of meaning. Formal linguists tend to use discourse to refer to levels of linguistic structure larger than the sentence. Linguistic anthropologists use discourse to refer to "instances and types of language use" (Urban and Sherzer 1988:284). And cultural anthropologists use discourse in the Foucaultian sense of forms of power that work by limiting and constraining what can be said (see Foucault 1972, 1980). These strands are usefully different in their focus, and complementary in their implementation. The methodological focus on studying signs in actual use (in conversation, in media representations, etc.) necessitates attention both to the syntagmatic structuring of discourse in relations of cohesion between a given utterance and previous utterances, and to the social structuring of discourse in relations of power between speakers and recipients.

The discourse approach to language and culture is based upon an ethnography of speaking (see Gumperz 1968; Hymes 1967) that attends to the social structuring of contexts within which communication occurs, as well as to the consequences such structuring entails for discourse, as it unfolds. For example, an ethnography of speaking approach helps to unpack the complexity of the "Israeli Kid" discourse by focusing on the multiple layers of mediation. At its core is a boxing match that took place in a sports arena in an American city. Israeli television reported on the match, assigning its international news correspondent to cover the sporting event, and editing the report to include footage of the boxing match as well as direct transmission of the interview conversation. Israeli audiences of various kinds watched the televised report. Thus what appeared as a simple conversation between news reporter and boxer unfolds as a complex communicative phenomenon. The signifier "The Israeli Kid" takes on disparate meanings for different recipients of the signification, such as: the spectators in the boxing arena, the broader American public, Israeli Jews, and Israeli Palestinians. Moreover, the meaning to Israeli Palestinians of the boxer's signification is not independent of its potential meaning to, for example, Israeli Jews and the American public. The discourse approach views situated utterances as spiral relations among meanings that are always both emergent and provisional.

Dialogue

Meanings that emerge from discourse are provisional, but they are not necessarily vague. The specificity of discourse meaning stems from their dialogism, their reference to other, well-established meanings. The playing of the Israeli national anthem after the boxer's victory—and its replaying in the Israeli television's reporting on the boxer—provides a good example of dialogic meaning.

The idea that utterances are (inherently) dialogic stems from Bakhtin's work on reported speech and novelistic discourse (Bakhtin 1981; Vološinov 1973).[4] The development of the novel as a form of artistic expression signals, for Bakhtin, the crystallization in written discourse of the dialogic nature of everyday speech. By "dialogic" Bakhtin means that the words represented on the page resonate with multiple voices, and that the meaning or interpretation of the words must take the several voices into account. By looking at the use of indirect, or quoted, speech in novels, Bakhtin elegantly demonstrates a simple example of what he argues is a pervasive, indeed quintessential, aspect of discourse. Indirect speech is speech of one individual as retold by another and, therefore, retold from the perspective of that other. Since novelists frequently embed the speech of their actors at many nested levels, dialogism is seen to be recursive. Speech is embedded not just in the voice of another character (or the narrator, etc.), but in a series of embeddings that introduce multiple perspectives, or "multivocality."

Bakhtin's study of indirect speech sets up a foil: what is clearly true in the simple case is then convincingly argued to be true for progressively more subtle cases. If a narrating voice can report the words of a character, thereby imparting his/her own perspective or interpretation to the other's words, then the narrator too can speak in the manner of that other character, tingeing his own words with the character's accent, style, or perspective. In this way Bakhtin shows all discourse to be inherently dialogic and multivocal. Dialogic because the speech of the Self refers to and takes on meanings from an Other, and multivocal because both the Self and the Other are, in fact, complex objects that signify at multiple levels. As Bakhtin puts it in "Discourse in the Novel,"

> the authentic environment of an utterance ... is dialogized heteroglossia, anonymous and social as language, but simultaneously concrete, filled with specific content and accented as an individual utterance ... imagine the work as a rejoinder in a given dialogue, whose style is determined by its interrelationship with other rejoinders in the same dialogue (in the totality of the conversation). ... The dialogic orientation of a word among other words (of all kinds and degrees of otherness) creates new and significant potential in discourse ... which has found its fullest and deepest expression in the novel. (Bakhtin 1981:272–275)

Building upon Bakhtin's notions of dialogism and multivocality, Julia Kristeva (1980) pointed out that speech is intertextual, inescapably interwoven with the dialogic meanings other voices contribute. Kristeva's observation deconstructs received notions of stable meaning and subjectivity, for if reference is always and constantly intertextual, partaking of meaning from the complex of (con)texts implicated by the discourse, then no object can have a stable, immanent meaning, and no voice a stable and immanent subjectivity.

National anthems are played as a routine formality preceding and following some athletic events. In the Olympics and international boxing the anthem of the victorious competitor is played as the trophy is awarded. In such contexts the anthems are usually played as music—without the lyrics. In the case of "The Israeli Kid," the music to the Israeli national anthem, "Ha-Tikvah," was played to the American spectating audience. To the American audience the playing of the anthem was a simple symbol of nationhood, but when replayed on Israeli television as part of the report on the Israeli boxer, the anthem took on additional meanings.

Anthems are so commonly played that we take the lyrics for granted. I am vaguely aware, for example, that the American national anthem refers to a military victory, but when I sing (or hear) "The Star-Spangled Banner," I do so by rote and do not think about the meaning of the words.

So too, I am sure, for Israelis. The Israeli national anthem, called "Ha-Tikvah," "The Hope," puts a Zionist poem to music:

"HA-TIKVAH," "THE HOPE"

So long as still within our breasts
The Jewish heart beats true,
So long as still towards the East,
To Zion, looks the Jew,
So long our hopes are not yet lost—
Two thousand years we cherished them—
To live in freedom in the Land
Of Zion and Jerusalem.[5]

The lyrics of the anthem highlight the Jewish nature of the state of Israel and erase the Palestinian presence by equating the "we" with Jews and by recapitulating the Israeli master narrative of legitimacy, including the two-thousand-year displacement from "home." Though taken for granted, the meaning of the lyrics is evoked by the play in the signification. "The Israeli Kid" refers dialogically to whole sets of practices and discourses that privilege Jews in Israel and subordinate Arabs. The dialogic nature of discourse establishes a relation of intertextuality, in which the meanings of one text (e.g., the boxing match) are linked to the meanings of another text (e.g., Zionism).

Other texts are referenced by "The Israeli Kid" as well. The sport of boxing generates a certain irony that was highlighted in an Israeli newspaper feature story. Growing up in Nazareth, the boxer had trained with, and often fought against, Jewish boys. Such matches, in the political and social tension that permeates Israeli society, are unavoidably fraught with overtones. Boxing, it seems, often provides an outlet for a society's repressed classes, and the symbolic retribution is not lost on the practitioners.

Viewed with respect to the various sources of intertextuality, the boxer's play on identity takes on parodic meaning. The social identities in play in this media representation refuse neat categorization and thereby provoke a rethinking of categories. A Palestinian calling himself *the* Israeli Kid crosses the boundaries between established identities, thereby blurring the distinction between them. Such play manipulated symbolic forms, such as the Israeli flag, colors, and anthem, and recontextualized them. Such a new use of old symbolic forms becomes a parodic counteruse, for no Israeli could miss the situation's irony. New, ironic, parodic, resistant meanings emerged from the play, and such emergent use of symbols constitutes a renegotiation of their meaning.

The boxer's play involves, further, the relation between subjectively felt identities, public media images, and situated enactments of identity. The media's juxtaposition of the celebration of mainstream Israeli identity (the Olympian heroes) to the boxer's challenge from the margins of Israeli identity highlights the way that the media constructs, disciplines, and maintains identity boundaries. At the same time, however, it points to the media's potential as a venue for transgression. Symbolic play is political, but its valence is up for grabs. This particular media play was deeply ambivalent. Did the boxer's use of Israeli symbols resist dominant Israeli articulations of identity? Or was his own subjectivity coopted? The Nazareth boxer's play with identity flouts taken-for-granted aspects of the Israeli discourse of identity by violating (and thereby challenging) the idea that "Arabs" are not "Israelis."

By challenging this idea the boxer exposes contradictions in the Israeli discourse of identity, which posits two mutually inconsistent metaphors for identity: nationality and ethnicity. The metaphor of nationality applies to the opposition between Arabs and Jews in Israel. The metaphor of ethnicity applies to the opposition between Ashkenazi and Mizrahi.[6]

Power

The two metaphors—nationality and ethnicity—are mutually incompatible. They are also insufficient, since neither concept adequately represents the full range of identity processes in Israel. Race and class are concepts familiar in the social sciences but largely silenced within Israeli discourses of identity.

"NATION, NOT RACE!" 2

Not long after I arrived in Israel to begin my research—and while I was still getting my bearings—I described my project to two University of Haifa linguistics professors over lunch. They understood my interest in studying dialects of Hebrew, including the use of Hebrew by Palestinian Israelis in Haifa, but they were mystified—and a little shocked—by my description of the project as distinguishing between ethnic and racial processes in Israeli discourses of identity. One assured me in a polite but firm tone of voice that "The Arab-Jewish difference in Israel is one of nationality, not race!" And with that the topic was changed.

If Israeli identity discourses are conceptually confused, so too are social scientific discourses on identity. Scholars have long debated the scope, reference, and utility of terms like *nation, ethnicity, race,* and *class,* which are used in overlapping and mutually inconsistent ways. Accordingly, in order to clarify the phenomenon under investigation, I will begin by reviewing Israeli (emic) and social scientific (etic) discourses of identity.

Israeli Ideologies of Identity

Theorizing identity is crucial to an understanding of Israel because Israeli identity discourses hold enormous power. Israeli identity discourses are ideological in that they tend to mystify social practice so as to justify the dominant social order. One way that the Israeli discourse of identity supports the dominant social order is by obscuring dimensions of social injustice. Constructing identity in Israel as either "national" or "ethnic," for example, erases potential allegiances between Mizrahim and Palestinians based on shared socioeconomic class position. Constructing identity in Israel as simultaneously "national" and "ethnic" establishes a categorical difference between Jews and Arabs that naturalizes the boundary between groups, while obscuring its racialized rigidity. The erasure of "class" serves ideological purposes in Israel, which was founded in the socialist spirit of classlessness. The erasure of "race" masks the hardness of identity boundaries. Casting the racialized division between Arab and Jew in Israel in terms of "nation" supports Israeli discourses of legitimacy by rendering the imposition of Jewish presence on Arab soil less visible.

The opposition of Jew to Arab is constructed as an opposition of *l'om*, "nation." The term *l'om* is an official designation in Israel, represented, for example, on the identification card every Israeli citizen carries (see text 5.4). Each Israeli citizen is thus officially designated "Jew" or "Arab."[7] Neither of these terms, however, identifies a national group unproblematically. "Jew," for example, more conventionally applies to a religious group. The attribution of nationhood to Jews was one of the major innovations of the Zionist movement. "Arab" applies to people living in a number of different nation-states—Egypt, Morocco, Iraq, and others, in addition to Palestinian. Parallel to Jewish nationhood, Arab nationhood is also the result of a political project. Various pan-Arab nationalist discourses have gained prominence in Middle East politics since the 1960s, harking back to a long and storied heritage of Arabness constructed through the notion of *umma*, "nation," though these discourses—again intriguingly parallel to the case of Jews—are more intimately tied to Islamic religious identity than to normative notions of nationhood.

Zionism argued that the revival of a common language (Hebrew) and the re-populating of an ancestral territory (Palestine) could create nationhood for a people scattered among the nations of the world. Nation building remains a prominent process in Israel, partly due to its creation (or recreation) and immigrant character, and partly due to its isolation in a historically hostile environment. Tremendous ideological energy has gone into constructing what it is to be Israeli and in producing actual Israelis, as seen for example, in the revival of Hebrew (see Blau 1981b; Fellman 1973a; see also chapters 5 and 7) or the construction and planning of Israeli national observances (Dominguez 1989; Zerubavel 1995). Calling Jews a nation thus serves political ends for Zionism. The same Zionist political ends are served by calling Arabs (as opposed to Palestinians) a nation.[8]

But if Jews and Arabs comprise separate nations, then the reference of "Israeli" is unclear. Indeed, the boundaries of "Israeli" are inherently unstable, as the dominant construction of the Israeli nation extends potential Israeliness to all Jews throughout the world. The Israeli "Law of the Return" grants immediate citizenship to any Jew who chooses to immigrate to Israel, whereas obtaining Israeli citizenship is quite difficult for nonJews. The idea of the Jewish nation is thus unbounded in two important senses. Membership in the Jewish nation is, as a practical matter, limitless, since the number of Jews around the world (and thus the number of potential Israelis) is far greater than the number of actual Israelis. The idea of the Jewish nation is also unbounded in the sense that it is nonreciprocal: diaspora Jews do not consider themselves to be "Israeli" in quite the way that Israelis consider them to be. The Israeli discourse of Arab nationhood is similarly problematic. Neither Jews nor Arabs imagine "Israeli" to encompass "Arab." Both Jewish and Palestinian Israelis, for example, sometimes use the words "Arab" and "Israeli" to distinguish between Palestinian and Jewish Israelis.

"Ethnicity" is a complementary identity term in Israel, and it is similarly complex. In scholarly discourse, the loan word, *etniyut*, is used for "ethnicity," but in everyday speech the Hebrew word *eda*, "ethnic group," is used. The derived term, *adatiyut*, "ethnicity," is attributed primarily to Jews in Israel, and in particular, to Mizrahi Jews. The phrase *edot ha-mizrax*, "ethnic groups of the East," for example, refers to "Oriental Jews," or Mizrahim, but no parallel term is commonly used to mean "Ashkenazi Jews." Mizrahi Jews, whose families came to Israel one generation ago from places like Morocco or Iraq or Yemen, are "ethnic"; but Ashkenazi Jews, whose families arrived at the same time from Germany, Poland, or Russia, are not. Having "ethnicity" in Israel means being Mizrahi, and the term *eda* has taken on a strongly negative stigma.

Thus the Israeli ideology of identity constitutes Palestinians as inherently national, Mizrahim as inherently ethnic, and only Ashkenazim as "Israelis." This ideology over-values "nation" and "ethnicity," making them signify more than they mean, and under-values "class" and "race," making these terms signify less than they mean. The ideas of "social class" and "race" do not commonly occur in everyday discussions of identity in Israeli Hebrew, which is why my phrasing of my research questions often raised eyebrows (if not hackles). This raises the question of why I felt it important to think about identity in Israel with terms that (Jewish) Israelis rejected, and I turn now from a discussion of Israeli ways of thinking identity to a discussion of social scientific discourses on identity.

Social Scientific Discourses on Identity

Identity is an overused and undertheorized term in anthropology, as Richard Handler (1994) has pointed out. Identity is either (or both) too hard or too soft a concept. When viewed as an essentialized primordial category ("the Zulu are X," or "Italians do Y"), the concept lacks intellectual rigor. When viewed as the way people make sense of their lives, it lacks specificity. Bouncing between these poles, identity has remained fuzzy in its conceptualization.

The too-hard conceptualization stems from an earlier era when anthropologists studied isolated and small-scale societies whose members were very different from the researcher, and whose economies did not overlap with the modern, technological world. In such studies, the Self/Other characterization was uncomplicated, from the standpoint of both the researcher and the native. Anthropologists treated native identity as primordial—a straightforward matter of birth and socialization to a particular culture. This view of the native was buttressed by constructions of the native's own view. Emic worldviews were constructed as uniform and unified, epitomized by cases in which a people's name for themselves appeared to be glossable only as "people" or "humanity." In this way anthropologists attributed to the objects of ethnographic description an emic discourse of total ethnocentrism.

This anthropological discourse of aboriginal identity, centered on its prototypical concept, the "tribe," was deeply embedded in the political projects of colonialism. Nineteenth-century colonialism spawned both the anthropological project and the political doctrine of race. As Brackette Williams (1989:431) notes, "the current proto-typical features of the races of mankind were invented, transferred, and institutionalized during colonial maneuvers to justify conquest, slavery, genocide, and other forms of social oppression."

As a corrective to essentialized notions of identity bound up in the service of oppressive political projects, Franz Boas and his students pioneered the concept of culture at the turn of the century. Boas focused on language and history, showing that biological and genetic notions of race did not correlate with cultural development. Linguistic history, for example, showed the effects of contact, adaptation, and borrowing. Similarly for cultural inventories, whether they be folklore repertoires or pottery styles. This historicization of culture discredited essentialized and deterministic models of the relationship between bodies and social organization. Identity became much more complex—and more interesting—when it was historicized.

The idea of identity as "ethnicity" took hold in the postcolonial world of the 1960s. The world that anthropologists were describing had changed markedly, and many of the groups formerly considered "tribal" were now competing for economic position among nation-states. As recently liberated "tribal" groups of the Third World came to resemble "ethnic" groups of the First World, social sciences advanced to treat them as such. By the early 1970s, Abner Cohen, a prominent ethnicity theorist, wrote, "the traditional subject matter of anthropology—tribes, villages, bands, and isolated communities—was being transformed into ethnic groupings, making ethnicity a 'ubiquitous phenomenon' that anthropology could not afford, heuristically or theoretically, to ignore" (Cohen 1974, cited in Williams 1989:402).

But the turn from "tribe" to "ethnic group" also reflected a theoretical relocation driven by changed attitudes in the social scientific community. The airtight formulation of island tribal groups isolated from contact with other groups left little room either for historical change or for politics. The shift to ethnicity reflected a growing interest in studying societies by studying how they change and interact, rather than how they stay the same. Fredrik Barth's (1972 [1964]) landmark study of shifting patterns of ethnic identification among the Pathans along the border between Afghanistan and Pakistan moved anthropology away from static views of identity and toward a processual model. Barth argued that individuals selected an identity strategically, based upon competition over material resources.

Barth also prefigured the important distinction between ideology of identity and identity practices discussed earlier. He noted, for example, that while Pathan identity practices were in fact fluid and situational; Pathans spoke about identity in absolute and durable terms.

The play between "ethnicity" and "nation" is a crucial gap, as international boundaries take on increasingly prominent roles in social identity processes—and are increasingly attended to in scholarship on identity. Barth's study of Pathan "ethnicity," however, curiously ignored the international boundary between Afghanistan and Pakistan, which bisected the Pathan region his research addressed. Similarly, Abner Cohen's work on ethnic groups defined the ethnic group in terms of its relations with other groups within the overarching context of a nation-state, but left "nation" relatively untheorized.

In the 1980s, however, anthropological interest focused on nationalisms—their essence and historical development (Gellner 1983; Handler 1988). In doing so, anthropologists drew heavily on work in other fields by such scholars as: Tom Nairn (1977), Benedict Anderson (1991), Eric Hobsbawm (1992), and Hugh Seton-Watson (1977). The interest generated by this form of identity stems from the paradoxical combination of the intellectual poverty of the idea of "nation" and its enormous practical influence. Benedict Anderson's work has been seminal in this regard. Nationalisms, Benedict Anderson (1983:5) has noted, paradoxically posit the most ancient of pedigrees in order to justify what are patently modern phenomena. In so doing, Anderson focused attention on the discourse of nationalism, and in particular on the role written discourse—novels and newspapers, for example—played in the emergence of this new form of identity (Anderson 1991). Anderson describes the nation as "imagined," placing national identity within the domain of negotiated identities.

Two persistent problems in social analysis frustrate the popularity of concepts such as tribe, culture, ethnicity, and nation: discrimination and hierarchy. Theories of social class and race maintain their centrality in anthropological work, as Brackette Williams (1989) has noted, because of the persistent failure of other concepts to explain systems of domination. Indeed, in many cases it is precisely the discourse of ethnic or cultural difference that obscures systematic patterns of economic subordination and exploitation.

The legitimacy of ethnic differences coinciding with socioeconomic differences is reduced. When linked to race, however, this legitimacy is often buttressed. Racial difference crucially links social groups to behavioral patterns by way of biological characteristics. Such links have powerful discursive and social effects because they naturalize difference, making it both legitimate and eternal. The concept of race helps to explain the distinction between "melting" and "nonmelting" identity groups (see Ogbu 1978). It has long been observed, for example, that many immigrant groups to the United States participated in the assimilatory processes that led to economic and social success along with the disappearance of cultural distinctiveness, while other groups failed to rise socioeconomically. It is striking that the groups in the former category, Irish and Italians, for example, tend to come from Europe, while the groups in the latter category, notably African Americans and Native Americans, are constructed as racially different. Social science thus distinguishes between the racialized divide between blacks and whites in the United States, and the ethnic divisions among white groups.

The core concepts—race, class, ethnicity, and nationality—merge one into another, however. Intermediate groups, like Jews in nineteenth-century Europe, Hispanics in the twentieth-century United States, or Mizrahi Jews in modern Israel, blur these lines and decenter the underlying distinctions. Groups can be intermediate because they are "hybrid," like American Hispanics, who are characterized both as an ethnic group and as a racial group, or because their classification changes over time, like Jews (Brodkin 1998).

Scholars, like activists, have misrecognized the symbols and rhetoric of identity as things, rather than projects. "Instead of focusing on nations as real groups," Rogers Brubaker (1996:7) has written, "we should focus on nationhood and nationness, on 'nation' as practical category, institutionalized form, and contingent event. 'Nation' is a category of practice, not (in the first instance) a category of analysis." Michael Omi and Howard Winant (1994:54–55) echo Brubaker's claim, while phrasing it in terms of race:

> There is a continuous temptation to think of race as an *essence*, as something fixed, concrete, objective. And there is also an opposite temptation: to imagine race as a mere *illusion*, a purely ideological construct that some ideal non-racist social order would eliminate. It is necessary to challenge both these positions ... we should think of race as an element of social structure rather than as an irregularity within it; we should see race as a dimension of human representation rather than an illusion.

Indeed, identity itself needs to be theorized as a set of organizing principles for social projects, rather than as entities. Scientific racism may have been discredited in Boasian times, but race as a political concept maintains its influence to this day. The theorization of identity thus must keep pace with its political applications.

The Rhetoric of Israeli Identity:
From *Kibbutznik* to *Palestinian*

In Israel, too, the notions of "class" and "race" are important—despite their lack of popularity. Israel is a class-stratified society, in which speaking of class goes against the grain, and a racialized society, in which speaking of race is taboo. The absence of "class" in Israeli discourse has historical roots. Early Zionist settlements in Palestine were based on socialist ideals imported from revolutionary Russia in the early part of the twentieth century. Many early state institutions (like the national labor union, called *histadrut*) have a socialist heritage and maintain a powerful discursive tradition of a classless society, even though Israel is by no means a socialist state now. The ideology of classlessness retains its rhetorical power despite a growing material reality of privatization of state industries, increasing wealth differentials, and growing disparities between posh suburbs and poor slums.

Maintaining the notion of a classless society is predicated in part on the image of the kibbutz, a prominent symbol of communal, socialist life. Two important mythologies of Israeli society derive their power from the kibbutz image: *kibush ha-avoda*, "the conquest of labor," and *kibutz galuyot*, "ingathering of exiles." The latter phrase refers to the return of Jews from all corners of the globe to Israel, a place where few of them had ever been, and where all of them would be remade both as Jews and as Israelis. The Ulpan experience, in which doctor, merchant, and peasant alike learned the new language, Hebrew, was a central acculturating influence. Kibbutzim are known to this day as centers of Ulpan-style language teaching (see chapter 5). The idea of the conquest of labor held that Jewish/Israeli redemption lay in a return to the land, to manual labor, and especially to a farming way of life. This ideology purported to treat all immigrants equally, despite enormous disparities in their wealth, skills, and education. Doctors as well as beggars remade their lives as farmers and manual laborers, abandoning class differentiation. The kibbutz was the center of manual labor and agricultural production in the early years of the Israeli state.

In Israel consciousness of class remains low—despite significant class differences—in part because differences of socioeconomic class are obscured by being rhetorically inscribed onto differences of *eda*, "ethnicity." In the 1950s waves of immigrants came to Israel from Middle Eastern countries, such as Iraq, Egypt, Morocco, and others. Included in this immigration were many indigent, illiterate, or unskilled Jews, and the Mizrahim were incorporated into the Israeli economy as manual labor in factories and on farms (Swirski 1989).

The Mizrahi immigration also included many wealthy, educated, and highly trained Jews (Beinin 1998), but Mizrahim were discursively represented as illiterate and poverty-stricken nonetheless, a representation that has since become a stereotype. Indeed, the poverty of some of the Mizrahi immigrants was compounded by specific Israeli policies, such as settling Mizrahi immigrants in remote *ayarot pituax*, "development towns," along the frontiers with Arab countries, or housing them in the temporary *ma'abarot*, "transition camps," where they were doomed to failure.

The gap between the discourse of the Mizrahi immigration and the material reality of the Mizrahi immigration can be seen in a comparison to Ashkenazi immigration at the same time. During the 1950s, in the first decade of Israel's existence as a state, massive waves of immigration nearly doubled its population. In 1949 there were just over one million Jews in what became Israel. By 1961 this number had grown to just under two million (Government of Israel 2000:2–7).[9] Huge numbers of Jews came to Israel from Middle Eastern countries, but a nearly equal number of Jews came to Israel from post-Holocaust Europe. According to official Israeli statistics, in 1948 Ashkenazim comprised 88 percent of Jews in Israel, but by 1961 they comprised only 56 percent (Goldscheider 2002:31). This means that the Mizrahi population skyrocketed from 12 percent of the Jewish population in 1948 to 44 percent in 1961. At the same time that some 700,000 Mizrahi immigrants arrived in Israel, over 450,000 Ashkenazi immigrants came as well. Despite the comparable representation of Mizrahi and Ashkenazi Jews in this massive influx, the immigration is conceptualized as a Mizrahi immigration.[10] Ashkenazi immigrants—refugees from the Holocaust—were as destitute and needy as the Mizrahi immigrants, but immigrant absorption and trauma are nonetheless disproportionately constructed as Mizrahi problems.[11] In modern, colloquial Hebrew many words or phrases index, or indirectly refer to, social class—such as *shxunot oni*, "slums"; *shxunot*, "neighborhoods"; *ayarot pituax*, "development towns"; *mishpaxot m'rubot y'ladim*, "multichild families" (see text 2.4)—but the phrase that directly, literally, means "social class," *ma'amad xevrati*, is rarely heard in everyday conversations. This term lies outside the quotidian vocabulary of Israeli identity.

If Israel is a class-structured society, in which speaking of "class" goes against the grain, it is also a racialized society, in which speaking of "race" is taboo. The Arab/ Jewish divide is heavily racialized. In Israel the social categories "Arab" and "Jew" are absolute, categorical, inalienable, and official. Each Israeli citizen carries an identification card on which his/her *l'om*, "nationality," is inscribed. These cards can be demanded by gatekeepers of various kinds (see text 5.4), making identity a very public matter in Israel. Israelis are born into their l'om, a fact that racializes Israeli identity by linking it to the genetic body.[12] The social/political distinction is constructed in part by reference to body types, as both Arab and Jew carry ideological and stereotypical associations of physical and mental differences. Such biological differences constitute organizing principles for social subordination. Barriers to intermarriage between the groups are nearly absolute, while intragroup marriages are ideologically and legally encouraged. Institutional forms of segregation are far-reaching, as Jews and Arabs have separate schools (with different curricula), separate social service institutions, separate governmental oversight ministries, separate television and radio broadcasting systems, and so on. Systematic forms of discrimination are officially sanctioned and permanently installed, including most dramatically, restrictions on serving in the military service—and therefore, on receiving benefits from such service.

The term "race" itself, however, is rarely heard in everyday conversations. Hebrew words for "racism" (*giz'anut*) and "racist" (*giz'ani*) do occur in colloquial speech, but these refer to individual behaviors, or to political stances. The word for "race" (*geza*) is almost never applied to Israeli social groupings. Israelis substitute "nation."

It is therefore important to distinguish between identity on the one hand and discourses of identity on the other. Identity itself is abstract, provisional, internal, and individual. Discourses of identity, on the other hand, are concrete, durable, overt, and public. What being Palestinian in Israel means to an individual is a very different matter than what "Palestinian" stands for in Israeli discourse. Identity is a process; discourses of identity are projects. As projects, these discourses are material in several senses: they provide material sentential frames for talking about identity; they generate material patterns of representation for identities in newspapers, television advertisements, films, and novels; they generate deeply felt stereotypes that lead to material disadvantage.

A discourse approach looks at identity from two perspectives simultaneously: structural and agentive. Identities constitute a structured set of signifiers that (partially) determine subjectively felt meanings. But identity signifiers are simultaneously semiotic resources with which individual agents can play. Figure 3.1 is a partial representation of the structured set of identity signifiers in Israel.[13] The words on the diagram are placed in quotation marks to indicate that they stand for signifiers, rather than people. In figure 3.1 Israeli identity is represented as a continuum that varies simultaneously along two dimensions of meaning: Israeliness and Easternness, which are intended as ideal-typical poles of identification. The identity words in figure 3.1 are also arrayed hierarchically, top to bottom, reflecting the different status and power indexed by the various signifiers.

Maximal Israeliness corresponds to the mythological attributes of the New Jew, as imagined by Zionist literature and as nostalgically recalled by modern Israeli discourse. Easternness, on the other hand, is the Israeli instantiation of alterity, of otherness; it is the opposite of Israeliness. Israeli alterity mimics Western Orientalist discourses (see Said 1979), projecting such qualities as irrationality, backwardness, primitivity, laziness,

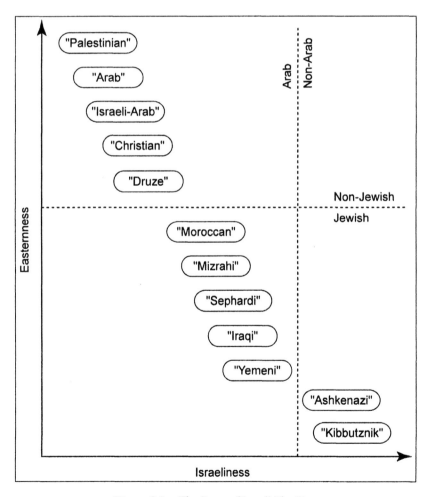

Figure 3.1. The Space of Israeli Identity.

and emotionality onto cultural Others—the Palestinian Other, as well as the Mizrahi Jewish Other (Shohat 1989). Figure 3.1 thus represents graphically Israel's self-concept as a Western European island in the midst of Oriental geography and demography (Shohat 1989).

Israeliness, however, does not completely coincide with Jewish identities in figure 3.1, nor does Easternness completely coincide with Arab identities. Gaps permeate the continuum, leaving space for semiotic play. A dotted horizontal line separates Jewish identities, above, from non-Jewish identities, below. All Arab groups are located above this dividing line, of course, but as Dominguez (1989) and others have argued, discourse at times attributes to several of the non-Jewish categories strikingly Israeli qualities. A dotted vertical line separates Arab identities, on the right, from non-Arab identities, on the left. All Palestinian identities are located to the right of this division, but many of the Jewish (Mizrahi) identities are inscribed with Eastern attributes.

Figure 3.1 also shows a proliferation of subidentities. As kinds of "Palestinian" we find "Palestinian" itself, in addition to "Arab," "Israeli-Arab," "Christian," and "Druze," among others. As kinds of "Mizrahi" we find "Moroccan," "Mizrahi," "Sephardi," "Iraqi," and "Yemeni," among others. These proliferations show the tendency of hegemonic discourses toward structured subdivision (Gal 1994). But the proliferation recapitulates the hierarchy: subaltern identities proliferate in their specificity, but the dominant group is seen as an undifferentiated whole. While "Palestinian" and "Mizrahi" identities splinter almost endlessly, the dominant, Ashkenazi, identity remains relatively unified. As pointed out earlier, there is no common Hebrew usage *edot ha-ashkenaz*, "Ashkenazi ethnicities," parallel to *edot ha-mizrax*, "Oriental ethnicities." "Ashkenazi" just does not subdivide into "Polish-Ashkenazim," "German-Ashkenazim," and so on, the way that "Mizrahi" splinters into "Moroccan," "Yemenite," and "Iraqi."

Within each domain the subcategories are organized hierarchically. For example, the signifier "Palestinian" itself is maximally opposed to the signifier "Israeli." Thus in colloquial Israeli Hebrew, the word *falastinai*, "Palestinian," refers unambiguously to noncitizen residents of the Occupied Territories—that is, non-Israelis even in the legalistic sense of citizenship (see "Arabic and Soldiers" in chapter 5). Within the domain of "Palestinian," the terms "Arab" and "Christian" occupy ranked positions in a hierarchy. In a door-to-door neighborhood survey in Hadar Elyon, for example, a Jewish Israeli woman was asked whether she had any "Arab" neighbors (i.e., whether any Palestinian families occupied apartments in her building). The woman responded, "No, two Christian families live on the first floor, but there are no Arabs living in the building." Her response (which was clearly intended to be cooperative) meant that two Palestinian families lived in her building, and that they were Christian by religion, not Muslim. Following common—if not quite standard—Israeli usage, the woman had used the Hebrew word *aravi*, "Arab," to mean "Muslim (Palestinian) Israeli," expressing what to her was a salient (and ranked) distinction between Christian and Muslim Palestinian Israelis.

Relative to "Palestinian," other terms for Arab groups take on increasingly Israeli character. Dominguez (1989) describes the striking parallels that the Israeli media drew between Lebanese (non-Palestinian) populations and Israelis during the early stages of the Israeli invasion of Lebanon in 1982. The Israeli press, for example, referred to Lebanese social groups as *edot*, parallel to the Israeli usage for relatively internal out-groups, such as Mizrahi Jews and, sometimes, Druze (Dominguez 1989:178–183). Dominguez argues that Israelis accord peoplehood—on a par with themselves—to citizens of other Arab states, such as Egyptians, Syrians, and Lebanese, but not to Palestinians. The term *Arab*, inasmuch as it sometimes refers to (Arab) citizens of other states, thus gains in Israeliness.

The domain of "Mizrahi" identity shows similarly structured subdivision, as in the contrast between "Moroccan" and "Yemenite" (see text 2.4). Israelis of Moroccan heritage are singled out for unfavorable rhetorical treatment. Moroccans are associated with nonconformity to mainstream Israeli culture. Slums and urban protest movements, for example, are conventionally associated with Moroccan Israelis. In dramatic contrast, Yemenite immigrants are singled out for favorable rhetorical treatment. Several ethnographies portray immigrants from Yemen in a particularly positive light (e.g., Gilad 1989; Lewis 1989). They are characterized as dedicated Zionists, willing assimilators, and model Israelis. Yemenite crafts, especially needlework and silver metalwork, have long been very popular. Yemenite food became popular more recently. In the early 1990s a chain of fast-food restaurants called Nargila enjoyed tremendous success. This chain built upon positive stereotypes of Yemenite identity, including the slogan *kef temani*, "Yemenite fun," a décor that featured enormous posters of the owner's mother in "traditional costume," and, of course, the traditional food.[14] Moroccan cultural practices are treated quite differently. Mimuna, for example, is the traditional Moroccan celebration of the final day of the Jewish Passover festival. Many cities, like Haifa, put on large Mimuna celebrations that are advertised citywide and often attended by city officials. These events are located in Moroccan neighborhoods (one was held in Neve Yosef), though, and they are attended mostly by Moroccans and other Mizrahim—but not by large numbers of Ashkenazim.

The two terms "Mizrahi" and "Sephardi" are also ordered hierarchically, despite being essentially synonymous. The terms differ in affective polarity and semiotic associations. *Mizrax* is the Hebrew word for "East," and the derived adjectival noun, *mizraxi*, literally means "Easterner."[15] As a term of identity, Mizrahi evokes the range of stigmatized meanings associated—in English—with the word "Oriental." Stigmatized words and phrases derived from this root include *edot ha-mizrax*, "Orientals"; *mizraxiyut*, "oriental nature"; *mizraxan*, "Orientalist"; *muzika mizraxit*, "Oriental music"; and so on. *Sfarad*, on the other hand, is the standard Hebrew word for the country "Spain," and the derived form, *sfaradi* (plural: *sfaradim*), literally means "Spaniard." *Sfaradim* came to be a term of Israeli identity because it refers to descendants of Jews who were expelled from Spain as part of the 1492 Spanish Inquisition. As such, the term evokes a range of high-status associations: the modern, European country of Spain; the proud heritage of the Golden Age of Jewish culture and letters in medieval Spain (see Sachar 1994); and the fact that some Sephardi refugees made their way to Palestine centuries before the emergence of Zionism. In the context of Zionism's struggle with Palestinian nationhood, those individuals who can point to generations of Israeli heritage do so with pride. They can claim to be the first Zionists—and such people are often referred to as *sfaradim*.

The gaps between "Moroccan" and "Yemenite," "Mizrahi" and "Sephardi," provide room for play. On the one hand there is the play of stereotype and discrimination. On the other hand there is the play of resistance. Smadar Lavie, a Mizrahi scholar, writes:

> the Mizrahim (literally meaning "Orientals"—in Hebrew) ... constitute 68 per cent of the Jewish population and 54 per cent of the total population of Israel. ... The official government term for them is "descendants from Asia-Africa" (yotzei Asia-Africa [sic]), or in short, "Edot Hamizrah," the "bands of the Orient" ... [their] apolitical term for themselves is Sephardim ... but "Mizrahim," or "Arab-Jews" are the terms they use when advocating their rights before the ruling minority, the 28 per cent of Israeli Jewry called Ashkenazim. (Lavie 1992:85–86)

Lavie's claim to the term "Arab-Jew" coopts the negative stereotype into a positive symbol. Reclaiming the signifier of the Arab-Jew for political purposes reflects the flexibility of boundaries of the Israeli Self/Other distinction represented in figure 3.1. The same flexibility, however, is also reflected in the pejorative ways the Self/Other boundary can be negotiated. For many Ashkenazi Israelis the external (Palestinian) Other is closer to the Self than is the internal (Mizrahi) Other (see, for example, text 5.6).

Resistance

The concept of resistance is crucial to any discussion of identity and power. Theorizing resistant, or oppositional, power depends upon the identification of oppositional behaviors that are powerful. While the language of subaltern Israelis may contest hegemonic discourses, ultimately the power of these symbolic deployments depends upon the change they bring about. Eternal opposition is too close to cooptation to be called resistant.

Stereotype and resistance exist in an uncomfortable and unstable equilibrium, merging one into the other. Stereotypical images are often deployed parodically as resistances, for example.

OF PAINTING AND PICTURES

In colloquial Israeli Hebrew, Jews sometimes modify nouns with the adjective "Arab" in order to express a complex of strongly negative attitudes. *Ta'am aravi*, "Arab taste," for example, refers to bad, gauche, or inappropriate taste, as in clothing styles. *Avoda aravit*, "Arab work" refers either to dirty work, as in street sweeping, or work done lazily or sloppily.

The painting of interiors of buildings and homes fascinated me in Israel. Most walls seemed to me to have been painted cheaply, sloppily, or amateurishly. Baseboards, for example, were often smeared with paint that had dripped from the wall. Having spent summers supporting myself in college by painting houses, I was appalled to see so many blemishes that could have been avoided or corrected.

One day, waiting outside my advisor's office high up in the forty-story skyscraper that is Haifa University's signature building, I was struck by a particularly sloppy paint job that had left a different color paint behind a picture hung on a nail in the wall. This wall had been painted so quickly that the painters hadn't even bothered to move the picture.

In a sudden epiphany, I was reminded of James Scott's (1985, 1990) work on modes of everyday resistance. Since painting in Israel is done, by and large, by Palestinians, I suddenly saw in this unpainted shadow of a picture frame an emergence of the subaltern voice into the consciousness of dominant Israel—into the consciousness, that is, of anyone who bothers to look behind the pictures.

Throughout my stay in Israel I saw the blotches and drips of white paint on the tile baseboards of Israeli homes and offices as an "everyday form of resistance" (Scott 1985). James Scott highlights the role of language when the powerless contest the power of the powerful, especially in what he refers to as the "hidden transcript" (Scott 1990). In distinguishing hidden from public transcripts, or, roughly, private from public speech styles, Scott notes that the stark differences between what is said behind the back of power, as it were, and the deference paid to power in public performance, constitute resistant practice. These discourses of the hidden transcript often explode upon the public scene, much as pressurized gas bursts from an overloaded bottle (Scott 1990). Drawing on Bakhtin's (1984) description of carnivalesque celebrations of reversals in the social order, Scott likens the discourse of the hidden transcript to Saturnalias.

James Scott's work leaves unaddressed, however, the important issue of how powerful hidden transcripts really are. Nor does he address how this power is exercised, or witnessed. Foucault (1979) has convincingly argued that in the modern world power is increasingly produced and enforced discursively, rather than coercively, and that these procedures are increasingly dispersed, rather than centralized. Scholars have taken from Foucault's work the notion that resistance too must take discursive and dispersed forms. Everyday infiltrations of the hidden transcript into the public transcript have thus become a site for investigation, leading to a growing interest in the mechanisms of speech and the meanings of language. I found that in Israel irruptions of the hidden transcript into public discourse were both commonplace and powerful, and that they contest the nature of public space itself. Indeed, in conversational interactions it may not be clear which transcript is rolling.

Negotiation

Negotiation is my metaphor for the ways in which social practices—and specifically practices of language-use—mediate between structure and agency. Identity, then, can be seen as a metaphor for the language used in such negotiation.

AN UNTAPED INTERVIEW

Shoshana was in her late thirties when we interviewed her. She had shoulder-length hair that was streaked gray-and-white in a style that was popular then among some Moroccan Israeli women. We conducted this interview in a cramped and noisy office of the Shutafut Community Center, where I worked as organizer of the center's youth soccer team. We conducted most of these interviews in the interviewee's home—but only because interviewees tended to extend the invitation.

The interview began as usual. I introduced Nurit, my Israeli research assistant. We engaged in some small talk. Then I briefly explained the goals of my project and the format of the interview—while assembling the tape recorder and unpacking the microphone. My remarks were synchronized with the setup, enabling me to segue seamlessly into a request to record the interview. The interview with Shoshana occurred well into my research. I had interviewed dozens of people before her, and by this time my routine was well established. No one had yet refused to be recorded, and my request had become perfunctory, presupposing acceptance. This time, however, as I reached across the coffee table to hand Shoshana the clip-on lavaliere microphone, I was brought up short by a firm refusal.[16]

Nurit and I urged Shoshana to allow us to tape-record the interview, but she remained adamant. The interview continued. Nurit posed the questions, and I struggled to record her responses in a tiny spiral notebook. After twenty minutes we again asked to record, pointing to the importance of her words, and repeating our promise to keep her identity confidential. Shoshana explained: "It's not that I'd need my husband's permission, but ..." We continued the interview without taping.

As the interview progressed, the interaction between Nurit and Shoshana became more intimate and more intense. Our questions about Mizrahi identity in Israel, and about the relation between Mizrahi and Arab identity, struck a chord. Shoshana had strong feelings about her Mizrahi identity and about the treatment Ashkenazi Israel metes out to its Jewish Other. Nurit, whose mother was born in Tunisia, began to pose our interview questions from the perspective of one who shared Shoshana's Mizrahi identity. She identified with the experiences Shoshana narrated.

At one point we asked Shoshana how her current experience living in a mixed (Arab and Jewish) neighborhood compared to her previous experience living in a neighborhood that was mostly Mizrahi Jewish. Shoshana replied that the "mixed" neighborhood felt less "Jewish," because it included many Russian Jews, who were not observant—not because of her non-Jewish Arab neighbors ...

Nurit   Can you identify a Russian immigrant?
Shoshana   Immediately.
Nurit   How about Arabs?
Shoshana   Used to be able to, but not anymore.
Nurit   Mizrahim?
Shoshana   Not by the way they look, but as soon as they speak I can. Also, they have different jobs. Unfortunately, Ashkenazim have the important jobs. My daughter, for example, has really blue eyes, but people know she's Mizrahi.
Nurit   I look Ashkenazi, but I'm Sephardi ...

As the interview came to a close, we returned—as often happened at the end of a successful interview—to introductions and small talk. Shoshana asked me more about my research, and she asked Nurit more about herself. We exchanged full names. Upon hearing Nurit's family name—which sounds Ashkenazi—Shoshana became enraged. Struggling to repair the damage, Nurit explained that her Tunisian mother had married an Ashkenazi man, but Shoshana did not appear reconciled. The discussion broke up soon thereafter, and I was left thinking that any satisfaction Shoshana might have derived from the interview had been dissipated by her perception of insincerity on our part.

A negotiation of identity emerged quite suddenly during this interview and turned into a real conflict. Shoshana's angry reaction to Nurit's play with identity was extreme—but understandable. Our research interviews constituted an exchange, in which the researcher obtained information, the research assistants received a salary, and the interviewees (who were not paid for their time) benefited if they derived pleasure from having their story heard. In this case, the good hearing was compromised when the interviewee thought the interviewer was being insincere. The terms of the exchange had therefore been violated. The strength of Shoshana's reaction stems from the great importance identity plays in her life, and from the interview we know that this identity as a Moroccan, a Mizrahi, a Jew, an Israeli is both important and problematic. Images of identity—in this case Jewish Israeli "ethnic" identity—appear uniform, definite, specific, and stable, even though the underlying identities are negotiable and suspect. Negotiable because they can be claimed or denied (as Nurit did in the interview) and suspect because of the power at stake.

Hybridity

In the example just given, Shoshana appeared to be guarding an absolutist notion of what it means to be Mizrahi. Her negotiation with Nurit over possession of "Mizrahi" identity became a zero-sum game, in which Shoshana and Nurit either counted or did not count as "Mizrahi." While politics often pushes identity negotiations into these categorical alternations, a subtler form of negotiation may have more influence on the historical trajectories of identity discourses.

The paradigm case comes from the postcolonial world, where strict dichotomies of colonial/other break down. Frantz Fanon (1967), for example, describes a postcolonial Caribbean world, in which Caribbean (colonized) and European (colonizer) cultures hybridize in mutual influence. The postcolonial subject embodies an amalgam of cultural influences, including the nativistic, the European, and a conjoint of the two. Fanon's own biography—educated Caribbean black native who lived and worked as a physician in French colonial North Africa—dramatically demonstrates this view of culture, of cultural production, and of social identity.

In many places—like Israel—the hybridization of culture and identity is even more complex. Kobena Mercer, for example, argues that the modern black Caribbean experience is better described with reference to three poles of identity, not just two. Referring to these as the "African Presence," the "European Presence," and the "American Presence," Mercer notes that there is a

> critical difference between a *monologic* tendency in black film which tends
> to homogenise and totalise the black experience in Britain and a *dialogic*
> tendency which is responsive to the diverse and complex qualities of our
> black Britishness and British blackness—our differentiated specificity as a
> diaspora people. ... There is no escape from the fact that, as a diaspora
> people ... our blackness is thoroughly imbricated in Western modes and
> codes. ... What is in question is not the expression of some lost origin or
> some uncontaminated essence in black film language, but the adoption of
> a critical voice that promotes consciousness of the collision of cultures and
> histories that constitute our very conditions of existence. (Mercer 1994:62–
> 63)

One such place of cultural contact, of hegemonic domination, and of discursive
resistance is the complex (colonial) encounter between Hispanic, Native American
(Indio) and Anglo-American cultures and peoples along the Mexico/United States
border zone. Gloria Anzaldua (1987) describes the identity processes of the Tejanas:
the intimate incorporation/appropriation of Indian identity in the Mestiza identity of
Hispanic Americans in their conflict and struggle with mainstream culture in the United
States. Anzaldua presents this mixture of identities as seamless, invisible, almost
etymological. Her image for the point of contact between cultures—Mexico and the
United States—is the shifting, chaotic boundary between a body of water and its banks
(Anzaldua 1987:1–3).

Hybridization metaphorizes identity processes by linking disparate components of
particular identities and emphasizing flexibility. Attention is therefore focused on
symbolic processes of discursive elaboration. Kobena Mercer specifically points to
language-use as the best site of hybrid identity construction, which he describes as

> a powerfully *syncretic* dynamic which critically appropriates elements from
> the master-codes of the dominant culture and *creolizes* them, disarticulating
> given signs and rearticulating their symbolic meanings otherwise. The
> subversive force of this hybridising tendency is most apparent at the level
> of language itself where creoles, patois and Black English decenter,
> destabilise and carnivalise the linguistic domination of "English"—the
> nation-language of master-discourse—through strategic inflections, reaccen-
> tuations and other performative moves in semantic, syntactic and lexical
> codes. ... Creolising practices of counterappropriation exemplify the critical
> process of *dialogism*. (Mercer 1994:63–64)

While Mercer's notion of "language" oversimplifies an intricate, complex system
that is better conceived as "discourse," his focus on language/discourse does much to
correct the relatively passive focus of hybrid identity theory. Theories of hybrid identity
capture the complexity, indeterminacy, and mutuality of social identities, but the process
is conceptualized as a passive one. Terms like "hybrid," "creole," and "border" imply
displacement of agency in worlds where blurred identities happen upon individual
actors. In contrast, focusing on the discursive construction of identities conceptualized
as a negotiation highlights agentive processes, in which individuals actively construct
their own identities through a range of encounters—face-to-face interactions, as well
as encounters with institutional discourses.

A discursive approach to hybrid identities also avoids a danger of the hybrid metaphor: losing sight of the role of power. Gloria Anzaldua, for example, appropriates Indio identity into her Mexicana/Chicana/Tejana identity only by eliding important facts—like the marks of a historical people's passing—thereby erasing the sutures, the marks of her appropriation. Indeed, interest in hybridization took hold in academic circles during an era of exploding (ethnic) nationalisms. Ethnicity's emergence as a dominant force in social change decreased its utility as an analytic tool. The West's inability to develop a coherent political position with respect to local conflagrations that are organized around political notions of identity (e.g., the conflict between Bosnians and Serbs in the former Yugoslavia, or between Hutu and Tutsi in Rwanda) has been a powerful stimulus to the development of more complex notions of identity.

This project deconstructs the binary image of dichotomous struggles into a three-way negotiation. By focusing on the intersecting and overlapping linkages between the two oppositions, the dichotomous struggles can be resolved into a common negotiation over a hybrid identity, Israeliness. Evidence for the crystallization of a hybrid Israeli culture derives both from increased participation by Palestinians in the mainstream economic, political, and cultural life of Israel, and from ongoing destabilization of the Western, Ashkenazi cultural hegemony. The affiliations of social class position and cultural heritage that Mizrahim share with Palestinians, for example, crosscut and decenter dominant constructions of identity in Israel.[17]

Expressions of identities that blur or challenge the lines of demarcation between named social identities are commonplace in Israeli media, in everyday conversation, and in the taped interviews conducted during my field research. Blurred identities challenge categorization. A particularly interesting case involves the Druze minority in Israel. Druze identity forms a signifier intermediate between "Arab" and "Jew" in Israel, since it represents an Arab cultural identity that supports the Israeli state politically. For this reason, an intense struggle rages in the press and in everyday discourse over the meaning of "Druze" identity. Druze serve in the Israeli military— the same as Jews, but in contrast to other Arabs.[18] In a media culture in which a picture of each soldier who dies in service is printed on the front page of every national newspaper, the occasion of a Druze soldier falling in action takes on particular meaning. The sacrifice of a Druze life for the (Jewish) state highlights the paradox of Druze identity, yet Israeli (Hebrew) media usually focus on Druze "loyalty." Such representations claim legitimacy from this "Arab" support for Israel, as well as from the Palestinian/Druze antagonisms the representations themselves fuel. Such paradoxes are particularly strong when, as happened several times in the early 1990s, a Druze Israeli falls victim to Palestinian violence connected with the Intifada. The Israeli government milked such events for their symbolic capital, sending high-ranking government and military officials to attend the funerals. On the other hand, Israeli Jews do not always include Druze in the collective as eagerly as these media representations imply. In 1992, for example, a Druze student was elected president of the nationwide University Student Council, but conservative students and government officials objected vociferously.[19]

Identities that are blurred because they are intermediate between received categories are not unique to the Arab/Jewish dimension, but are characteristic also of Jewish ethnic identity in Israel. The central signifier of this blurred identity is the mixed marriage. Most Jewish Israeli interviewees thought that Ashkenazi/Mizrahi cultural differences would soon disappear because there was so much intermarriage. This response biologizes the notion of cultural difference, implying that the absence of biological purity portends the disappearance of ethnic practices.

Dominant Israeli discourse simultaneously dichotomizes (exaggerates) Arab/Jewish difference while it erases (minimizes) Jewish/Jewish difference. Indeed, expression of dichotomized Jewish identities, either strongly Ashkenazi or strongly Mizrahi, is taboo in Israel. The twin processes—discursive proliferation (of Arab/Jewish difference) and discursive silencing (of Jewish/Jewish difference)—interact through the image of the Mizrahi "Arab Jew/Jewish Arab," symbolically linking the Arab and Jew in a complex signification.

Performance

The metaphor of performance is a way of thinking about the relationship between structure and agency. Like the performance of a play, this metaphor suggests an evanescent articulation between an underlying script and an emergent practice. A performance can never unfold "just as it was scripted," because it would lose its emergent character. Nor can a performance ever be completely "unscripted," because it would lose its meaning. Rather, a performance is an articulation of the scripted and the unscripted. Its meanings are negotiations of the script and the nonscript. In this sense they are "hybrid" meanings. Its meanings inhere in the moments of actual performance, and in that sense they are transitory. The script perdures; the performance vanishes. But, as Chris Weedon (1987) has argued, the semipermanent articulations that emerge from performance have material consequences.

The effects of transitory articulations of script and nonscript relate to the spiral of discourse meaning. Momentary articulations of meaning provide the ground from which subsequent signification draws its meaning. The work of Richard Bauman and Charles Briggs does much to illuminate such abstract social processes (Bauman and Briggs 1990; Briggs and Bauman 1992). Working from the disciplinary perspective of folklore, Bauman and Briggs retheorize the "text" as a dynamic set of processes. Canonically thought of as the inscribed script of a centuries-old document (such as the Bible), the text becomes, for Bauman and Briggs, a much more expansive notion, incorporating, for example, Geertz's (1973) idea of social ritual as a "text." Crucially, texts emerge in discourse, at the intersection of two opposed processes that Bauman and Briggs call "recontextualization" and "entextualization." Speakers recontextualize a text when they perform a canonical text (script) in social interaction. Such a performance draws meaning dialogically from the text and applies the meaning to the here-and-now of the speech event—a novel (and emergent) context of interaction. "The Israeli Kid," the Palestinian Israeli boxer discussed at the outset of this chapter, is deeply engaged in recontextualization. Drawing on Israeli cultural symbols that are deeply imbued with meaning (Israel's national anthem, called "The Hope," for example), the boxer recontextualized the symbols in performance, articulating an emergent, hybrid, and potentially resistant meaning.

On the other hand, the complex signification behind "The Israeli Kid" was powerful because of the "entextualization" involved. Bauman and Briggs describe this latter process as the tendency to textualize unscripted performance through semiotic techniques. Entextualization addresses the linguistic (and other semiotic) structuring of symbols. As Roman Jakobson (1960) has pointed out, the efficacy of discourse depends upon form as well as content. Entextualization is, in effect, the reverse of re-contextualization, but in actual discourse the two processes are intertwined, and they feed off one another. The Israeli national anthem is in and of itself a powerful symbol, but its deployment during a Palestinian Israeli's boxing triumph entextualizes it. The entextualization stems from the embedding of the symbol in another ongoing script (a championship boxing match). Playing the anthem belongs to the boxing script; commenting on Palestinian Israeli identity (by the boxer's playing up of the Israeli anthem theme) entextualizes the anthem. By doing so the boxer evoked dialogic resonances, transformed a paradigm onto a syntagm, and played with both symbols and identity. Entextualization inscribes textuality onto emergent interaction, allowing a speaker to claim for his unscripted action the pedigree of script. This is the everyday practice of narrativization.

Language

Socially variable aspects of language entextualize speech. Narrative, for example, the culturally valued ways of relating objective events, embeds speech in cultural discourses, pragmatic interaction, and affective relations (see chapter 4). In so doing, the structures of language—in this case of narrative—structure speaking practice. Other structural aspects of language-use structure speaking practices. Media discourse, for example, entextualizes particular ways of thinking about identity through the structuring practices of headlining, illustrating, and narrating news (see chapter 6). And dialect entextualizes speech by making automatic and unreflecting the variations born of specific interactions, or specific encounters (see chapters 7 and 8).

Close attention to the details of spoken language, as it is used in face-to-face talk interactions, can illuminate important processes of cultural determination and contestation. Ethnography represents not only the Other, but also the Self. In conducting interviews for this research my own identity—as researcher and, more generally, as an American (Jew) in Israel—was very much at stake. In carrying out my research I played upon flexible and overlapping aspects of my own identity, at times emphasizing my American, at times my Jewish identity. While my accent pointed to an American background, it did not completely specify my identity with respect to the Israeli discourse of identity. On the one hand, American immigrants to Israel comprise a prominent component of Israeli society (see Bloch 1990), and on the other hand, both Jewish and non-Jewish Americans have powerful stakes and interests in Israel (see Dominguez 1989; Swedenburg 1995). Although I did not specifically identify myself as Jewish, Israeli Jews assumed that I was. Palestinians, on the other hand, did not always make this assumption, and the ideas they formed of my identity affected the interviews in complex ways.

TEXT 3.1.   ON FOREIGN AND OTHER ACCENTS 1

DURING OUR INTERVIEW WITH NAJIB, A YOUNG PALESTINIAN
MAN LIVING IN THE HADAR NEIGHBORHOOD, WE ASKED
ABOUT PALESTINIANS' FEELINGS ABOUT USING HEBREW,
THEIR ACCENT, THEIR ACCEPTANCE IN ISRAELI SOCIETY, AND
THEIR BEING ABLE TO PASS AS JEWISH:

Najib   Usually I laugh, I don't care what they say,
         Because I really don't sound Arab,
         I know how an Arab sounds when he's speaking
              [Hebrew],
         And I also know how an American sounds when he's
              speaking () American— er— Hebrew,
         And if you spoke Hebrew a bit better I'd be able to tell
              you you don't sound American at all,
         And that wouldn't insult you at all,
         But to say that you don't look Arab—
         'Cuz how— what's looking Arab?
         Or that you look Jewish, so what?
         Do you stereotype Jews? Or to Arabs …
Dan   Yea,
Najib   All of a sudden you're someone that—
Dan   In the States it's— as if you would— I would hear, for
              example, in the US, that I don't look Jewish,
         That would be—
Najib   Uh, you really don't look Jewish, really,
         ((All laugh))
Najib   Are you really Jewish?
Dan   Yes,
Najib   You don't look it,
         And you also sound American,
Dan   American, yes,
Najib   Eh, so you grew up in America?
Dan   American Jew, … (117A:39:40–40:50)

TEXT 3.2.   ON FOREIGN AND OTHER ACCENTS 2

OUR INTERVIEW WITH HANI AND HIS WIFE, FARHA, A YOUNG
PALESTINIAN ISRAELI COUPLE, LASTED SEVERAL HOURS.
WHEN I HAD COME TO THE END OF MY QUESTIONS, THE TALK
BECAME MUCH LESS FORMAL. FARHA ASKED ME ABOUT MY
WORK IN HAIFA:

Farha   How do you know Hebrew so well?
Dan   Thanks, really I feel more limited than—
Farha   ((laughs))
Dan   No, it's from here,

	I had a little preparation,
	I'm Jewish,
	Don't know if that was clear,
Hani	There's no—
Dan	—Almost every Jew gets Jewish education after—
Farha	Yes, but do you study the language?
Hani	Better that I ()—
Dan	((laughs))
Hani	When I made the joke about Jews, about misers,
Farha	((laughs))
Hani	I did so under the assumption that you were Jewish,
Farha	((laughs))
Hani	Don't think that now I'm feeling some kind of "What-
	have-I-done-now" feeling,
Farha	((laughs))
Dan	I'll write that in my dissertation, "Israeli Arabs are racist,
	anti-Semitic"
	((All laugh))
Farha	But you learned Hebrew when you were young? ...
	(206A:06:14–07:01)

In these interviews the dimensions of my own identity—American as opposed to Israeli, and Jewish as opposed to non-Jewish—was a critical, and suspect, aspect of the ongoing negotiation. In these two cases, it was the cause of some mutual embarrassment, but more generally it played a much subtler role, influencing the politics of Self- and Other-representation that comprised the flow of question and answer in the interviews. The important point here, though, is not to provide a detailed exegesis of any particular case of misunderstanding, but to recognize the pervasive role that the identity of the interviewer/ethnographer plays in the process he or she is studying. In chapter 4 I turn to an analysis of the structuring of narrative as a way of understanding the dynamics of sociolinguistic research on identity.

4

Narrating the Crosscultural Encounter

A picture is worth a thousand words, as the saying goes, and the cover of David Shipler's book *Arab and Jew: Wounded Spirits in a Promised Land* narrates an interesting tale about Jews and Arabs in Israel. The cover of the 1986 edition of *Arab and Jew* features a photograph of two men engaged in what appears to be a friendly conversation (see fig. 4.1). The image seems simple, but it encapsulates a complex story. In particular, it relates one version of the Israeli-Arab story—the story of a peaceful coexistence, of a Zionist dream unhindered by the presence of Palestinians. This version approximates the dominant Israeli narrative and departs from Palestinian narratives of identity.

We guess that the two elderly men sitting on a stone bench are an Arab and a Jew because of the title and because each bears badges of ethnicity. One wears a *kipa,* the small skullcap worn by religiously observant Jewish men;[1] one wears a red-and-white checked *kufiya*, the headscarf worn by traditional Palestinian men. The setting appears to be Jerusalem. Enormous stone blocks form an ancient-looking wall behind the men, and the bench they are sitting on is made of the yellow stone, often called "Jerusalem Stone," that is a favorite building material in the city. The reader's thoughts turn to Jerusalem also because the term "Promised Land" in the subtitle links the Israeli/Arab conflict to biblical stories in which Jerusalem is featured. The men appear to be engaged with each other: the Jewish man is looking across at the Palestinian man, with arm extended as if to touch him, or, perhaps, gesturing to make a point. They appear to be engaged with each other also because of certain parallels: they seem about the same

Figure 4.1. Image Appearing on the Cover of David Shipler's *Arab and Jew*. (Photograph by Lori Grinker. Reprinted by permission of Contact Press Images Inc.)

age (mid-sixties, perhaps); they wear similar clothing (dress pants and jacket); and they sit in similar poses (right leg crossed over left).

The positive affect narrated by the picture stands in subtle contradiction to the negative affect conveyed by the words "wounded spirits" in the book's subtitle. The picture cannot be interpreted as showing conflict, or wounded spirits, for several reasons. The men are older (not of combatants' age). They are leaning away from each other. The Arab man appears to be smiling. And a yellow light gently bathes the two in warmth. Thus, the visual characteristics of the image enforce a reading of the cover that opposes the message of the title. Perhaps the photo suggests the "promise" behind the conflict, the spirits that got wounded, the ideal whose realization has been impeded.

Shipler's book is, in fact, a relatively evenhanded journalist's account of Israel/ Palestine in the mid-1980s. But the cover picture narrates a myth that serves Jewish, rather than Palestinian interests: it supports an ideology according to which Israel is a place where cultural, religious, and national pluralism reigns; Jews are engaged with their Arab cocitizens; and Arabs benefit (smile that implies happiness) from the edifying presence of the Jews.[2] These narrative points are ideological because they tend to justify Jewish presence in Israel. They are important because they show that narratives have political implications—whether intended or not.[3]

The picture on Shipler's book is ideological also because there is a *falseness* about the reality it represents (see Eagleton 1991): it suggests a reality very different from the one I encountered in Israel. My project to investigate the use of language to negotiate social identities in Israel was predicated upon studying crosscultural interaction in precisely the kind of everyday encounters Shipler's book cover represents. The more I looked for such encounters, however, the less common they appeared to be, and I ultimately concluded that the primary locus of Arab-Jewish interaction is to be found not in face-to-face encounters, but in the abstract domain of discourse. This chapter traces the evolution of a methodology for studying interaction that is simultaneously deeply felt to be present and desperately difficult to locate. The methodology that emerged involves reading narrative—visual and spoken—for its assertions about identity.

In Search of Interaction

My search for crosscultural interaction generated a paradox: The dominant discourse on identity in Israel overestimated the amount of interaction between Arabs and Jews, which was in fact rare, and underestimated the amount of interaction between Mizrahim and Ashkenazim, which was in fact common. Jewish Israelis were conscious of the presence of Palestinians, often pointing to specific places where "relations are good."[4] Jewish Israelis tended to overrepresent the amount of contact they had with Palestinian Israelis—in part, I believe, because of a pervasive presupposition that little Arab-Jewish interaction was to be expected. In "The Jewish State" any interaction at all with Palestinian Israelis was noteworthy.

Jewish interviewees did not have comfortable responses to questions about their first encounters with Palestinian Israelis. Many vaguely recalled experiences of working with, or hiring Arabs; others referred to nostalgic and perhaps mythic friendships that their fathers or other relatives had had with Arab colleagues or neighbors (see text 2.5). In general, however, the oft-repeated formula "good relations with Arabs" referred to lack of contact, interaction, and knowledge.

For example, in the course of my research in Israel I worked with four different Jewish Israeli research assistants, all of whom held fairly typical ideas about Arab-Jewish interaction. Before hiring the assistants I interviewed them, explaining in great detail the nature of my research and the purpose of the interviews they would need to help with. In these thirty-minute job interviews not one of the four assistants mentioned that they had never actually spoken to a Palestinian. Nonetheless, for each of these Jewish Israelis our first interview with an Arab interviewee constituted their first face-to-face encounter with a Palestinian. While all four assistants had expressed fascinated interest initially (at their first such encounters), most quickly tired of the threat posed to their own sense of identity by the Palestinian narratives and opinions brought out in our interviews (see text 2.3). Only one assistant—the one I refer to as Stella—was ever sufficiently interested by the topic to discuss it with me outside of an interview (see "A Family Connection" in chapter 5).

A diametrically opposed ideological presupposition obtains for Ashkenazi-Mizrahi interaction. The dominant discourse on identity in Israel generates the presupposition that relations between Ashkenazi and Mizrahi Jews are fluid and frequent, leading Israeli Jews to underrepresent their actual interaction. Since Ashkenazi-Mizrahi interaction was held to be ubiquitous, actual interactions became invisible. For Ashkenazi Israelis, the fact that their first encounter with Mizrahim might come only in adulthood is a rich topic for narrativization. For example, Gabi, an Ashkenazi computer programmer in his early thirties, related this story from his military duty, during which he did social service work in a (Mizrahi) development town in northern Israel.

TEXT 4.1. "THE SECOND ISRAEL"

Gabi   We had a leader from the group that had preceded us ...
And they looked for families that would adopt us ...
And they asked us ... if we wanted a family with a
    background similar to the home we came from,
Because there are some there,
There are lots of doctors and all kinds of people went
    there for all sorts of reasons ...
Or whether we wanted a family that it's essentially
    representative of the population,
Usually families that they're below the poverty line,[5]
Troubled families with many children,
Amidar apartments that are neglected,[6]
No need to go into details on this,
This is familiar,
That's it,
And I chose the second possibility,
And I've never regretted it for a minute,
My parents still continue to speak with me,[7]
That's it,

Dan   Why was this such a good experience?

Gabi   It was—I can almost say—
It was the first time that I really seriously got to know the
    other Israel,
That I after all grew up in a home that lacked for nothing,
No, except for the fact that they said that there's a
    problem like this that's called "the ethnic gap,"
    distress, and poverty,
And I mean that I knew about them—
From the books that there was a problem like this,
But I had never encountered it in such an intensive way,
... (42A:23:15–25:14)

Gabi's encounter with the Mizrahi Other during his military service impressed him deeply, but it did not significantly change his social circumstances. At the time of our interview, Gabi's friendship circle in Haifa approximated once again the homogeneous Ashkenazi community he describes growing up in.

In order to study ethnographically the kind of crosscultural encounters my research assistants experienced interviewing Palestinian Haifans, or that Gabi had experienced with his military unit, I sought out places where such interactions might be concentrated: mixed neighborhoods, civic institutions, and encounter groups.

A "Mixed" City: Three Neighborhoods

I situated my research in Haifa because Israelis had told me that Arab-Jewish relations there were "good" (see chapter 2). Within Haifa, I situated my ethnography in three neighborhoods—Hadar Elyon, Tel Amal/Halisa, and Neve Yosef—that were demographically "mixed" because I assumed that intergroup interactions would occur there naturally.

Hadar Elyon

Hadar is Haifa's hub. It is the transportation nexus for buses and taxis, a shopping area, a cultural center, and home to many of the municipal administrative offices. People from all walks of life ride together on buses, shop together in markets, and wait together in lines.

Above the shopping district of Hadar lie several residential neighborhoods. Hadar Elyon, "Upper Hadar," consists of a half-dozen parallel streets climbing a very steep hill. Originally built in a grand Middle Eastern style, Hadar Elyon's narrow and winding streets are lined with elegant stone houses. Graceful stairways lead up the steep hill, forming alleys and public spaces between the apartment buildings (see fig. 2.5). Magnificent olive trees beautify the neighborhood (see fig. 2.6).

In the 1930s, Hadar Elyon was a prestigious place to live, as many long time residents recalled in interview narratives (see text 2.5). Now, however, it is rundown. The old stone houses are in need of repair, and city services are badly neglected. During winter rainstorms, rivers of water gush unchecked down the stone stairways. These days Hadar Elyon is home to an aging population. Many of the Ashkenazi Jews who moved in when it was elegant remain for sentimental reasons—or because they cannot afford to move. But their children have most likely migrated up the hill. Neighborhood veterans are joined by students and young couples looking for affordable housing, and by recent immigrants to Israel. While I was doing my fieldwork, Russian Jews comprised about 20 percent of the neighborhood's population.[8]

Hadar Elyon borders on Haifa's largest Palestinian neighborhood, Wadi Nisnas. Because the primarily Christian Arab population of Wadi Nisnas had been growing rapidly in recent years, apartments were difficult to find there. Many young Palestinian families therefore sought housing in Hadar Elyon, which was a convenient place for them to live, since they remained close to such Arab institutions as schools, churches, stores, community centers—and newspaper vendors. At the time of my fieldwork Palestinians comprised about 15 percent of Hadar Elyon's population.

A small community center, called Shutafut in Hebrew, or Musharika in Arabic (both of which mean "partnership" in English), operated in Hadar Elyon, seeking to bring Jewish and Palestinian residents together in joint activities of community improvement. Daycare and after-school activities for children were set up in a rented house. Community buildings were painted, and a neighborhood park was refurbished. Activists from the community center also lobbied the city for improved services. During my stay in Haifa I volunteered at Shutafut and spent my time organizing a soccer team for

Arab and Jewish boys in the neighborhood. My work for Shutafut gave me many insights into the nature of Arab-Jewish interaction in Israel. For example, although the neighborhood school had a spacious soccer field that was little used in the afternoons, administrators balked at granting Shutafut permission to use it. Although both Jewish and Arab children in the neighborhood longed for a soccer team to play on, only Palestinian boys ended up participating. Although Palestinians and Jews were neighbors in Hadar Elyon, often residing in the same apartment buildings, there was little interaction.

Tel Amal/Halisa

As a hub of transportation and commerce, Hadar was a place of encounter—but not of interaction. As a neighborhood with both Jewish and Palestinian residents, Hadar Elyon was "mixed"—but not integrated. But Hadar Elyon was newly "mixed," and the Palestinian population there was a small minority that looked to Wadi Nisnas for schools, neighbors, and newspapers. I therefore looked for neighborhoods that were more evenly divided between Jews and Palestinians, and in "Halisa" I thought I had found one. As noted in chapter 2, census data indicated that a region called Halisa was 50 percent Arab and 50 percent Jewish by population, but on the ground I found two homogeneous and starkly divided neighborhoods—Palestinian Halisa and Jewish Tel Amal.

During much of my stay in Haifa I lived in an apartment that was perched on the boundary between these two neighborhoods. Both neighborhoods climb a steep hillside from the older downtown region below to the newer Neve Sha'anan neighborhood, high above. A major road, Yad la-Banim, winds its way up these slopes, carving out boundaries between neighborhoods. In its wide sweep up the mountain, the road defines an arc within which both Tel Amal and Halisa are nestled. My apartment was on David Raziel Street—one of the many streets in Haifa that are named after Zionist heroes. Past my building, David Raziel Street rises to the crest of a ridge that forms the boundary between the Jewish and Arab neighborhoods. The street suddenly veers, switching back on itself to return to the Jewish neighborhood. Had David Raziel Street continued along its original trajectory, it would have entered the Palestinian neighborhood, and Jewish Tel Amal would have been linked with Arab Halisa. Instead, this straight stretch of pavement constructed two different streets. While the Tel Amal side of David Raziel Street turned uphill to become Pe'er Street,[9] the Halisa side of David Raziel Street headed downhill to enter a zone of demolished houses and abandoned lots.

The street looks different in Halisa. In Tel Amal, houses are modern, stucco, Israeli. In Halisa, buildings are old, stone, Arab, and—at least in this part of Halisa—condemned. Only the barest outlines of former buildings remain—a cement stoop, dangling steel rods, a fragment of a staircase—above huge piles of brick, stone, glass, refuse, and other rubble from a vanished home. In the right light these remains seem to merge back into the mountainside. Indeed, shepherds sometimes grazed their sheep on the grassy slopes. But mostly, the empty lots served as a barrier. I was one of the very few who regularly crossed this no-man's-land, walking from above (where I lived) to below (where I visited), against the grain.

Beyond the zone of demolition, a number of houses—old, stately, multiple-story stone homes—are in the process of being condemned. Enormous trucks park in front of these homes, whose residents earn their livings as truck drivers, contractors, mechanics, and dealers in secondhand goods. Workspaces spill out into yards and streets. As a pedestrian I often had to step aside to avoid the ongoing overhaul of a car engine. As long as one of the apartments in a building remained occupied, the building remained standing. As each family vacated their apartment, however, the city sealed the doors and windows with cinderblocks and mortar. As soon as the last family moved out, the building was demolished.[10] In several houses along this part of Halisa's David Raziel Street, most of the windows were already sealed.

Halisa was notorious as the center of the Haifa drug trade. It was also the site of the only mosque still active in Haifa. On Friday evenings, the muezzin and the Shabbat siren, calling Muslims and Jews, respectively, to prayer, are often heard at about the same time. This simultaneity reflects the simultaneity of cultures in this complex neighborhood. In the years immediately after statehood (the 1950s), immigrant Jews moved into homes in Halisa (see text 1.2). The homes had been (temporarily) abandoned because the Israeli army concentrated all Palestinians in the Wadi Nisnas neighborhood during the 1948 war (Sachar 1989). Although by the early 1990s few Jews lived in the heart of Halisa, evidence of their earlier presence remained in the form of synagogues that dotted the otherwise entirely Arab neighborhood.[11]

The Halisa neighborhood takes on an Arab feel by virtue of the Arabic-language newspapers sold in the corner stores, the Arabic conversation heard in shops and on the street, the Arabic lettering on election posters, and the halting, accented Hebrew of the shop owners. Halisa is Palestinian enough that the passage of an American draws curious glances and stares from young children playing in the alleys. It is Palestinian enough that in 1987, at the beginning of the Intifada (the Palestinian popular revolt against Israeli occupation in the West Bank and Gaza), one of the synagogues was bombed.

Despite being a focal point of Arab residence and culture in Haifa, Halisa is also a site of Jewish state-building symbolism. Haifa was the first city the Jewish forces conquered during the 1948 war, and Halisa was a major site of Palestinian resistance in that battle (Sachar 1989:307). Israel has inscribed this history onto the landscape of Halisa through (re)naming: R'xov ha-Giburim, "Street of the Heroes," and Gesher G'dud 24, "Battalion 24 Bridge," cross the ravine separating Halisa from Hadar. Actually two bridges span this gorge. One bridge is an ancient concrete-and-stone edifice. During my stay a large section of this bridge fell out, leaving a yawning hole in the road. The other bridge is an impressive, modern, high-rise bridge built of steel and concrete, that dominates the landscape. The new bridge is named for heroic Jewish fighters (Battalion 24) who fought in a crucial battle of the 1948 war.

"TOURING" HALISA

One day when I was walking through Halisa toward the post office, I saw something unusual: tourists. They were standing in the midst of the border zone of demolished and semiabandoned buildings. An elderly guide wearing a Xevra l'Haganat ha-Teva, "Nature Protection Society," t-shirt was pointing to something in Halisa. Lower down the hill there were other groups, who turned out to be school children participating in special activities to commemorate Israel's Independence Day. Halisa's central square was a beehive of activity. Large groups of students were being herded into, and out of, the small plaza in front of the post office. Uniformed soldiers and Nature Protection Society guides were using loudspeakers and huge display boards to recount the drama of the siege of Halisa.

A very old Palestinian woman wandered by, confused by the commotion and not understanding what was going on. She too became grist for the nation-building mill, as the speaker incorporated her into his narrative in an off-color way, while encouraging her to move on—out of the picture he was carefully constructing.

At no other time did I see so many Jewish Israelis in Halisa. The group of Jewish students "touring" Halisa thus constituted a hyperpresence: the sudden presence of Jewish Israelis in Halisa signaled a more enduring absence.

Israelis often told me that Haifa was where Arab-Jewish relations were "good," but I failed to find neighborhoods where such good relations took the shape of neighborly interaction. Like Hadar Elyon, Halisa/Tel Amal was a place of mixture statistically, but not interpersonally. Indeed, I perceived the most enduring aspect of Arab-Jewish interaction in Halisa/Tel Amal to be the chance simultaneity of the Friday evening call of the muezzin and the Shabbat siren, calling Muslims and Jews to separate but parallel prayer. Here, at least, symbols placed interaction in the discourse.

Neve Yosef

In contrast to the way that (Jewish) Israelis thought about Arab-Jewish interaction, the question of where to find Mizrahi/Ashkenazi interaction rarely generated a response at all. Israelis did not know how to answer this question. They did not think of Jewish neighborhoods as "mixed" in the way that they thought of some Arab neighborhoods as "mixed." Instead, I was often directed to one of the many neighborhoods that were considered slums.

Neve Yosef is located off to the side of Mount Carmel. Yad la-Banim, the main road that leads up the hill toward Neve Sha'anan, sheds Neve Yosef at a hairpin curve. Neve Yosef, like Hadar Elyon, is a working-class neighborhood that is rarely touched by city services. Here too an ambitious—though minimally successful—renewal project reaches out to residents. Unlike Hadar Elyon, however, Neve Yosef is not central to anything: it is physically and culturally marginal. Only one road leads into the neighborhood—and it dead-ends there.

Modern high-rise apartment buildings mark the entrance to the neighborhood. At the far end are blokim—drab, old, rundown tenement blocks that give rise to the neighborhood's rough reputation. Neve Yosef was built in the 1950s, conceived as a community for retiring veterans of Israel's army, most of whom were Ashkenazi. In the 1960s, however, the cheap blokim were built to settle new Mizrahi immigrants, and to resettle the Mizrahi *m'funim*, "evacuees," from slums like Wadi Salib (see chapter 2; see also text 1.2). Today the main motivation for people to move to Neve Yosef is government-subsidized Amidar housing (see text 4.1), which enables low-income families to own their apartments.

Neve Yosef is an entirely residential neighborhood, like Hadar Elyon, but is not close to any commercial center. For even such basic needs as grocery shopping, postal or banking services, and entertainment, residents need to take a bus either up to Neve Sha'anan or down to Halisa or Hadar. Residents complain that their neighborhood carries a stigma. One woman reported that a downtown store owner refused to accept her check when he realized she lived in Neve Yosef. Indeed the stigma exists internally as well as externally. Many of the Neve Yosef residents I interviewed distinguished between the outer, upper, "better" part of the neighborhood near its entrance, and what was called *bifnim* or *pnima*, "inside." This "interior" was described with open disdain as the location of *m'funim*, "evacuees," *primitivim*, "primitives," *narkomanim*, "drug addicts," *mishpaxot m'rubot y'ladim*, "families with many children," and other epitaphs. The "interior" formed the locus of all of the undesirable qualities of a stigmatized neighborhood—qualities that parallel the negative stereotype of Mizrahim in general (see text 4.1 or text 2.4). Many residents of Neve Yosef are Mizrahi.

A beautiful community center is situated at the entrance. Built in part with funds donated by the Jewish community of an American "sister city," the center provides daycare and tutoring for children; clubs, dances, and sports for teenagers; card playing, lectures, and movies for adults. Here too I volunteered my services, but when they heard I was associated with the Arab-Jewish organization Shutafut, the Neve Yosef community center was not interested in my working there. Such were the politics of everyday life in this "mixed" city. Discussions of life in Neve Yosef focused on the experience of being Mizrahi—of discrimination, of struggles to get children into better schools, of attempts to move out of the neighborhood.

Thus my search for crossgroup interaction in residential neighborhoods returned me to the paradox of Israeli identity: Israelis held the "site" of Arab-Jewish interaction in Haifa to be the boundary of two homogeneous and separate neighborhoods, and the "site" of Ashkenazi/Mizrahi interaction to be a Mizrahi neighborhood isolated from the rest of the city. Haifa may be a mixed city, but its neighborhoods are not sites of crosscultural interaction. Some, like Tel Amal/Halisa, are separate neighborhoods juxtaposed geographically. Others, like Hadar Elyon, are neighborhoods in transition, with Jews moving out, Palestinians moving in, and (Jewish) immigrants moving through. And the rest, like Denya, Neve Yosef, or Wadi Nisnas, are uniformly one or the other—Ashkenazi, Mizrahi, and Palestinian, respectively. To find interaction among Palestinians, Ashkenazim, and Mizrahim that I could study ethnographically, I therefore turned to institutional sites of public encounter.

Institutional Sites of Interaction

Drawing on a rich tradition of studying language and identity in institutional encounters (e.g., Gumperz 1982b; Scollon and Scollon 1981, 1995), I looked to schools, hospitals, government offices, and stores as possible sites for ethnography. At public institutions, however, I faced a dilemma: the triadic interaction I sought resolved into a choice of dyads: Arab/Jewish or Ashkenazi/Mizrahi.

Israeli schools bring Mizrahi and Ashkenazi Jews together, but forcefully segregate Jews from Arabs.[12] In principle, any public school in Israel is open to any pupil, but in practice, very few Arab children attend Hebrew-language schools, and virtually no Jewish children attend Arabic-language schools. Israeli education has been characterized by separate school systems for Arabic- and Hebrew-language instruction since before the formation of the state (Lustick 1980). The third track of public education, government religious schools, extends the segregatory effect. Since the beginning of the state, the Israeli government has provided a parallel track of religious public schools. These schools inadvertently contributed to Mizrahi/Ashkenazi segregation, since the number of observant Mizrahi Israelis (who would send their children to religious schools) is much greater than the number of observant Ashkenazi Israelis. The recent popularity of religious schools associated with Shas, the Sephardi Orthodox political movement, has augmented this effect. Indeed, the struggles of mothers to get their children into better schools, usually higher up the Haifa hill, was a rich conversation topic in our interviews. In Israel, as in the United States, neighborhood-based public schools have reinforced the patterns of residential segregation by wealth level.

Israel's universities may be the institution that integrates Ashkenazim, Mizrahim, and Palestinians most. At one point I thought the student dormitories at Haifa University would make an ideal site for my research. Haifa University has a diverse student body, and the dormitory population concentrates this diversity.[13] However, my stay in a Haifa University dormitory suite (for several months while beginning my fieldwork) showed that even there contact between groups was limited and constrained.

The organization of the dormitory space, for example, counteracted the remarkable diversity of its residents. Residence was arranged in six-person suites, but these were segregated by national group, as well as by sex.[14] The physical layout of the buildings further constrained interaction among the residents. The dormitory spanned three separate towers connected by ramps at offset levels. Individual suites were relatively isolated, connected more directly by stairwells within each tower than by the ramps joining them.

Many university functions were segregated—informally. Recreational activities at the dormitories, for example, were remarkably self-segregating. While living in the dorms, I participated in weekly basketball and soccer games. Almost all of the basketball players were Palestinian. Soccer attracted both Arab and Jewish players, but these pickup games invariably pitted all-Jewish teams against all-Arab teams. Classes, too, served to segregate, rather than to integrate, the student body at Haifa University. Many math and science courses, for example, were (as a practical matter) off-limits to Palestinian students, who would be unable to land jobs in technical fields because employers routinely required military experience. Not surprisingly, friendship circles were largely confined to one national group or the other.

Since patterns of (self-)segregation at the university minimized the kind of inter-group interaction mythologized on Shipler's cover, I looked to hospitals as a public and institutional site where bureaucratic structures would bring people of all backgrounds together in focused interactions. Accordingly, I spent several months observing doctor-patient interaction in an emergency ward at a major Haifa hospital. At this public hospital, located in an old section of downtown Haifa, a diverse professional staff served a diverse clientele.[15] Palestinians were particularly well represented among the emergency room doctors.[16]

The downtown emergency room was a site of much crosscultural talk, but the hospital turned out to be a site for a very different kind of negotiation. Institutional norms for speech behavior largely determined individual practices in the hospital. Interactions in such a highly structured environment were scripted, and individual actors were constrained in the roles and relationships they could negotiate. For example, the emergency room was one of the very few settings where I witnessed code switching between Arabic and Hebrew. Palestinian doctors frequently switched between Hebrew and Arabic in their casual conversations among themselves (see "Arabic-Hebrew Code-Switching 2" in chapter 5). The professional, medical context created a domain of language-use at the hospital that so powerfully favored Hebrew as the appropriate language that even the private conversations among native speakers of Arabic were conducted partially in Hebrew. Similarly, the hospital was the one place in Israel where even high-status professionals, who spoke fluent English, addressed me, an American, in Hebrew (see "Three Israeli Games of Language Choice" in chapter 5). In these service encounters the roles of caregiver and client largely determined the form of talk in the interaction. Studies of intercultural communication in institutions clarify our understanding of those institutions, but they fail to address the more general circulation of identities and their symbols.

Encounter Groups and Interaction

Half jokingly, friends, colleagues, and acquaintances recommended that I study the criminal underworld, where Arab-Jewish cooperation was rumored to be extensive.[17] More soberly, they recommended the many programs specifically established to bring Palestinians and Jews face to face. The Hebrew word for such encounters is *hafgasha* (plural: *hafgashot*). Grammatically, *hafgasha* is a verbal noun derived from the causative form of the common verb *lifgosh*, "to meet." Hafgasha therefore means "to cause to meet" or "to bring together." Progressive groups throughout Israel organize hafgashot of all kinds in the hope that familiarity will give rise to mutual understanding.

The best known and most ambitious of the hafgasha programs is Neve Shalom, a planned community based on the premise of Arabs and Jews living together in a semi-communal, cooperative settlement.[18] Formed in 1978, on land donated by a Palestinian diocese, the community consists of twenty Palestinian and twenty Jewish families. Decision-making authority in school boards, city councils, and other administrative bodies is scrupulously shared by Arabs and Jews. Children attend school together, learning both Hebrew and Arabic (Abu-Nimer 1999). Despite these efforts, however, language keeps the groups apart. At times of political conflict in the country as a whole, Palestinian community members complain that Jewish members never actually learn Arabic (Friedman 2001).

Another ambitious hafgasha program is the Arab-Jewish youth group Re'ut.[19] Youth groups are prominent in Israeli—especially Jewish Israeli—society. The largest youth groups are similar to scouting organizations in the United States. Nearly all children join a group during their elementary school years. Sometimes entire classes join the same youth group together. Israelis consider leadership roles in childhood youth groups to be significant experiences. Many of the university students I met had served as *madrixim* (singular: *madrix*), "leaders," of their respective youth groups. Each of the assistants I hired to work with me on my research, for example, mentioned having been a madrix when interviewing for the job.

Re'ut was formed in the early 1980s to further peace and to increase contact and understanding among Palestinian and Jewish high school students. Many of the branches bring together teenagers from different towns. Haifa is one of the few places where members come to meetings from the same city. Even in Haifa, though, children live quite far from each other because of segregation by neighborhood. Activities included weekly meetings, national seminars, and group trips. Meetings were planned and led by peer leaders, and they usually involved a creative attempt to draw members into discussions of issues related to the Arab-Jewish conflict. Some of the most highly charged political issues, such as military service for Arabs and Jews, became topics for lively discussion.

I participated in the Haifa Re'ut group's activities for a full year. Language was indeed a critical resource in active negotiations of identity among participants (see "The Youth Group Called Re'ut," "A Form of Broken Hebrew," and "Using Language as a Tool," in chapter 5), but Re'ut shared with Neve Shalom the characteristic that participants were a very select group of individuals who went out of their way to encounter (particular) Others.

A more representative sample of Israelis engaged in hafgasha encounters through school programs. One such program was called Yami, or "Children Teaching Children."[20] Many of the Arab-Jewish encounter programs focused on schools because it was thought that if Arabs and Jews were introduced to each other as children there was a greater chance to influence their ideas, attitudes, and identities. The Yami program brought children together so they could teach each other about cultural identity and difference, and it organized this instruction around the most prominent of differences: having Arabic or Hebrew as native language.

I followed one pair of schools as they progressed through a full year of the program. The schools planned to bring students together throughout the school year in a series of Arab-Jewish meetings (called *du-le'umi*, "binational") that would alternate with lessons each school completed on its own (called *xad-le'umi*, "uninational").[21] The accompanying teachers (three from each school) met regularly to prepare these activities.

The plan, however, did not come to fruition. The pair of schools I observed utterly failed to implement the project. The initial meeting of students exploded into a major conflict, which students from both schools found uncomfortable and distasteful. As the year progressed it became clear that the only Arab-Jewish contact to come from this hafgasha program was the near-weekly meetings of the teachers in charge of organizing the student encounters. These teacher meetings became (and were at times acknowledged to be) a mini-Yami. Talk among the teachers was much less self-consciously Arab-Jewish talk, since the teachers maintained the fiction that they were working together, rather than being brought together. Indeed, language was a creative resource for negotiating identity in these small-group discussions among teachers (see "A Reversal at Yami" in chapter 5).

But the very problems that caused the blowup among the students were played out among the teachers, and the outcome of a year's worth of hafgasha for these two schools, for these two groups of teachers, was embitterment and frustration. Hafgasha programs exist in Israel because Israelis feel that Arab-Jewish interaction ought to occur—in neighborhoods, in schools, in hospitals, in government offices, in stores, and so on—but doesn't.

My search for an ethnographic research site showed me that what was significant about the struggle over Israeli identity, linking Palestinian, Ashkenazi, and Mizrahi Israelis in a common negotiation, did not occur in face-to-face interactions so much as it occurred in discourse. To learn about Shipler's "wounded spirits" we must sample its discourse. The placement of the picture shown in figure 4.1 on the cover of a book about Israel/Palestine tells us about relations between Palestinians and Jews in the "Promised Land" more than any actual conversation between a Palestinian and a Jew. To learn about Gabi's interaction with the Mizrahi Other (see text 4.1), we must hear about it. Gabi's narrative of his remembered encounter speaks volumes about Israeli identity, but it does so indirectly. These encounters are powerful, salient, and influential, but they cannot be observed directly.

An abstract Other is constructed through discourse—and interacted with in discourse. Absent realities are a specialty of language. Linguists fondly point out that a defining feature of human language is the ability to talk about things that are not in fact encountered in reality. We can use the word *unicorn* to refer to an animal that does not exist; we can use future tense to refer to events that have not (yet) occurred; and we can use negation to refer to events that never occur. The importance of language that refers to nonphysical reality is that it constructs such entities as social (if not sensual) reality. Unicorns are powerful social symbols, even if we can never pet them.

An Observer's Paradox

Gabi's narrative of encounter (text 4.1) presented a methodological paradox similar to what William Labov has called the "observer's paradox." The paradox for the sociolinguist, as Labov (1972a:209) describes it, is that "the aim of linguistic research in the community must be to find out how people talk when they are not being systematically observed; yet we can only obtain these data by systematic observation." A similar paradox applies to the anthropological study of identity. Identity is very real as a process, but it vanishes when considered as an object. Identity is a conflation of many overlapping and intersecting concepts, including nationalism, religion, ethnicity, gender, and race. When asked direct questions about their identity, people generally give programmed responses in formal tones, but when asked indirectly, the same individuals may respond in ways that demonstrate enormous concern with such issues. Paradoxically, then, identity is unapproachable (directly) through talk, even though conversation is full of talk-about-identity.

The "mixed" neighborhoods in Haifa (Hadar Elyon, Tel Amal/Halisa, and Neve Yosef) turned out not to be places where Palestinians and Jews interacted (or where Mizrahi and Ashkenazi Jews perceived themselves to be in interaction), but they were places where identity difference was part of the discourse. The encounter with the Other was symbolically salient in these three Haifa neighborhoods, and the conflict of identities was therefore a rich topic for conversation with residents. My project had shifted from the observation of interaction to the analysis of discourse about interaction, and therefore I developed a methodology that built on the tension between two opposites: to investigate natural interaction I set up artificial scenes of encounter (i.e., interviews), and to investigate interpersonal negotiation I examined narratives of personal experience.

An Ethnographic Approach to Sociolinguistic Fieldwork

Relying on the notion of "discourse" as the abstract and emergent nexus between identity and language (see Sherzer 1987), I articulate ethnographic and linguistic approaches to the study of identity negotiation. This articulation takes advantage of parallax: an ethnographic approach to sociolinguistic fieldwork that becomes a discourse approach to ethnographic research, and vice versa. Thus the traditional tools of sociolinguistic research—the neighborhood-based sampling of a speech community and the sociolinguistic interview—keep their place methodologically, but they take on different analytic roles. Neighborhood communities are not the object of study but the place where discourse is studied.[22] Interviews are not the source of language data but the vehicle through which language-use is generated. And linguistic data are not merely counted and classified but also interpreted and read "against the grain" (see Barthes 1977).

I adopted the standard sociolinguistic interview, as developed by William Labov (1978), but I adapted it in several ways. Specific questions were designed to elicit information about participants' sense of social identity, and the sequencing of topics was designed to facilitate discussion around these questions. Identity is a difficult topic to think and talk about directly without resorting to platitudes, truisms, or stereotypes. Direct questions about individuals' feelings of social identity are therefore neither efficient nor sufficient ways to gather information. To overcome such difficulties, the neighborhoods were used as topics for (indirect) discussion of identity. Similarly, interviewees' feelings about their identities were probed indirectly, by eliciting narratives of personal experience and carefully interpreting the stories they chose to tell. The choice of "mixed" neighborhoods as sites in which to study discourse determined that responses to questions about the neighborhood would reflect feelings about social identity.

The Interviews

Interviews were designed to elicit both a range of speech styles and a range of ideas and feelings about identity. My assistants and I conducted seventy interviews in all, involving over one hundred residents of Haifa. Interviewees (i.e., "speakers") were evenly divided among Palestinian, Ashkenazi, and Mizrahi Israelis, as table 4.1 shows. In locating interview participants, I adopted a modified social network approach (Milroy 1980). Contacts made at the Hadar Elyon and Neve Yosef community centers led to some initial interviews in those neighborhoods. As each interview drew to a close, we asked participants to refer us to neighbors who might agree to be interviewed. In this way, we branched out from a relatively homogeneous group of community center activists to a more representative sample of the neighborhoods as a whole.[23] Figure 4.2 shows the distribution of interviews by research neighborhood, and figure 4.3 shows the distribution of interviews by contact generation.

Whenever possible, interviews were arranged as small-group interactions. Respondents who agreed to be interviewed were encouraged to include their spouse, children, friends, or neighbors in the conversation, and many did. Figure 4.4 shows that while most of the interviews involved just a single interviewee, over a quarter involved two interviewees, and a tenth involved a larger group.[24] This strategy generated a relatively conversational and informal atmosphere, and some of the most "natural" exchanges occurred when interviewees interacted chiefly among themselves. Indeed, in our most successful interviews, the interviewers often found it difficult to get a word in edgewise.

Table 4.1. Distribution of Speakers by Social Group, Sex, and Age.

Social Group	Sex	Age				Total
		<19	19–30	31–45	>45	
Ashkenazi	M	0	5	1	1	7
	F	0	3	6	1	15
Mizrahi	M	3	2	1	0	6
	F	4	3	3	1	11
Palestinian	M	0	13	10	1	24
	F	0	8	6	0	14
Ashkenazi/Mizrahi	M	0	0	0	0	0
	F	0	2	0	0	2
Born in Europe/America	M	0	1	0	4	5
	F	0	0	0	4	4
Born in Asia/Africa	M	0	0	3	6	9
	F	0	0	4	4	8
Total	**M**	3	21	15	12	51
	F	4	21	19	10	54

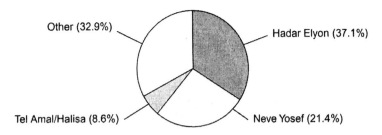

Figure 4.2. Research Interviews by Neighborhood.

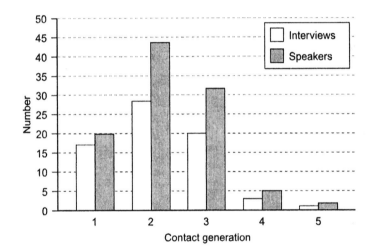

Figure 4.3. Research Interviews by Contact Generation.

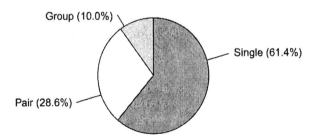

Figure 4.4. Research Interviews by Participant Group Size.

Participation in the interviews was arranged so as to maximize the extent to which the interview itself constituted an encounter in which identities needed negotiation. Participation was diversified most effectively by working with several different research assistants/interviewers. Four Jewish Israeli university students worked as interviewers.[25] Of these, one was Mizrahi, one was Ashkenazi, and two represented themselves as both Mizrahi and Ashkenazi.[26] Ultimately, about 60 percent of the interviews could be considered crosscultural interactions—either Palestinian/Jewish or Mizrahi/Ashkenazi.

Interviews joined the quantitative sociolinguistic techniques developed by William Labov (1984) to the open-ended interview used in ethnographic fieldwork. In joining these methodologies I was also joining two diverse analytic perspectives. In ethnographic interviewing the data generally consist of the content of the interviewee's responses, and ethnographers rarely attend to the subtleties of the linguistic form in which the content is articulated. In sociolinguistic interviewing, on the other hand, the data generally consist of the form of the interviewee's responses, and sociolinguists rarely attend to the content of what is said. The linguistic anthropologist, however, is neither interested in "what is said" alone nor in "how it is said" alone. Rather, it is precisely the relationship between content and form that is the basis of linguistic anthropological analysis.

In the interviews conducted for this research, questions of an ethnographic nature— about family, work, neighborhoods, schools, and so on—were grouped into thematic modules. Each module included several "transition questions," the responses to which were expected to lead naturally into other topics. Figure 4.5 represents the structure of these interviews schematically in the form of a flow chart (modeled after charts in Labov 1984). Topic domains are represented by circles, and lines of likely topic shifts connect these modules in a complex web.[27] All interviews began with the module on personal background and concluded with an explicit discussion of language. In between, discussion meandered along the general themes of neighborhoods, social relations, and personal identity.

This methodology explicitly theorizes the role of the interviewers. At most interviews I was joined by an Israeli research assistant. As joint "interviewers," we coordinated our participation so as to transform the interview from relatively formal talk between Israelis and a foreigner (the ethnographer) to a more casual conversation among Israelis (involving the research assistant).[28] My protocol called for me to begin interviews asking formal questions from the "Personal Background" module (see fig. 4.5) and for the research assistant to gradually take over the posing of the questions. In this way, as we progressed through the protocol, successful interviews became freewheeling conversations among Israelis. The conversations, in turn, became negotiations of identity precisely because of the interviewers' participation—not despite it.

Interviewers encouraged shifts between topics in an exploration for rich topics about which the participants were eager to talk (Labov 1984). Several modules on historical memory, for example, helped create a comfortable atmosphere in the interview context. This was particularly important in interviews with Palestinian Israelis, who were faced with a Jewish American[29] and a Jewish Israeli, both complete strangers, asking questions that were potentially sensitive both politically and personally. For example, early on in our interviews with Palestinian Israelis we asked what had

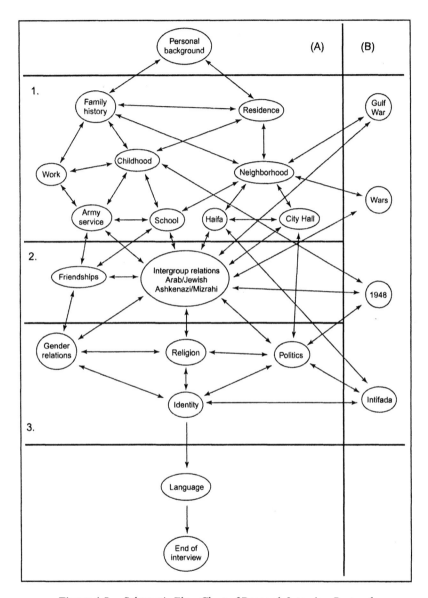

Figure 4.5. Schematic Flow Chart of Research Interview Protocol.

happened to the interviewee's family during 1948.[30] Asking this question helped define the interview as one in which threatening, angry, and resistant feelings could be expressed, and would be heard.[31]

Narrating Identity

Narrative plays a central role in this analysis of linguistic negotiation of Israeli identity—as it does in much of sociolinguistic and linguistic anthropological practice. Narrative forms for me, as it does for Labov, the way around the "observer's paradox." Labov's solution to the sociolinguist's paradox is bound up with the theory of the "vernacular." Linguists define the vernacular as the maximally systematic form of a language as it is spoken by a native speaker unencumbered by contextual influences. This definition depends upon several component ideas. For example, linguists distinguish "native speakers," who "acquire" a language in early childhood, from nonnative speakers, who "learn" a language later in life. The theory of the vernacular holds that only children acquire a mother tongue perfectly. Accordingly, linguists interested in the underlying structure of languages must study the vernacular, the most perfect instantiation of a language.

A second component of Labov's approach to the vernacular involves the idea of contextual variation. It is common knowledge that people speak differently in different contexts—speaking to one's boss, for example, as opposed to speaking to one's closest friend. Context can be approximated as a continuum of formality. A job interview is a formal context, while a friendly chat is an informal context. Labov showed, however, that—contrary to widespread assumption—the more formal one's speech (as in conversation with an authority figure), the less systematic the language. Speakers trying to affect a formal register, for example, often become erratic, using words in unconventional ways (such as conflating "conscious" with "conscientious"), for example, or making inconsistent case assignments (in phrases like "He saw Johnny and I/me at the store"), and so on. Therefore, linguists interested in the underlying structure of languages must study the vernacular—that idealized form of a language that emerges when a speaker is least influenced by context to modify his/her speech.[32] Labov's observer's paradox, thus, says that while the vernacular occurs when the context is least formal, the act of observation unavoidably formalizes the context.

Labov's work linked vernacular to narrative methodologically. He argued that the speech used during the emotional retelling of a narrative of personal experience is relatively devoid of the self-conscious monitoring of speech found in formal contexts of speech—and unavoidably recreated in tape-recorded interviews. Indeed, Labov shows convincingly that Americans shift dramatically into less formal speech styles when retelling dramatic events from memory. Labov argued that speakers use their most informal style in narrative speech because they relive the narrated experiences so vividly. For Labov, then, narrative speech is important because it best approximates the vernacular within the constraints of a research setting.

Labov's insights into the structure and function of oral narrative provide invaluable tools for a discourse-based ethnography. Narrative speech avoids the parallel observer's paradox of the ethnographic investigation of identity because it constitutes affectively charged expressions of Self. Personal involvement in the telling of narratives (pointed to by Labov as the surface reflex of vernacular speech) is not an abstract feature of narrative form, but the side effect of a crux in the negotiation of Self and Other in the context of talk interaction. The greater the speaker's involvement in his/her own speech, the more focused the expression of Self, the more the Self is put on the line, and the more strategic the language use.

Interview settings that affect the context of speech—that is, create contexts for the negotiation of identity—are precisely the desired research tool for studying identity and its negotiation. By viewing the sociolinguistic interview as a negotiation of Self and Other involving both interviewees and researchers, by specifically focusing on narratives of personal experience as emotionally charged expressions of Self, and by giving interpretive depth to the layers of meaning evoked in conversation, the nexus of speech form, speech content, and social context can become a particularly valuable tool in the study of personal, political, and ethnic identities in conflict.

Narrative is so pervasive in everyday life that we take its characteristics for granted. Defined minimally as a telling of events that are ordered in time (Labov and Waletzky 1967), narrative is embellished and elaborated in myriad ways to encompass much of what we do in our symbolic lives. A narrative tells a story—but it often does so indirectly. Narratives are allegorical: the literal story may not be the narrative's ultimate message. Narratives are told for a purpose: they are strategic and embedded in politics. Narratives are creative: they provide a rich environment for play in language. And, perhaps most important, narratives are affectively charged expressions of Self.

In interpreting a narrative's meaning (and the meaning of the speech used in its telling), one must ask "What did the narrator communicate by telling this story in this way?"

TEXT 4.2. "THE UGLIEST LAZY SUSAN"

STORY TOLD AT A JULY 4 PICNIC IN PHILADELPHIA, PENNSYLVANIA:

Narrator:	(One of the) presents we got when,	(1)
	We got married,	(2)
	It was,	(3)
	The ugliest,	(4)
	Lazy susan,	(5)
	I have ever seen in my life,	(6)
	...	
	It—it was green and pink, you know,	
	my favorite colors, it was,	(7)
	And I don't even remember what it was shaped as,	(8)
	We left it on my mother's dining room table,	(9)
	And people would walk in and go, "huuuhhh",	(10)
	And it came with a box from a very jazzy store	
	in San Francisco,	(11)
	So my sister says,	(12)
	"I'm going into town,	(13)

	I'll get you a credit for it",	(14)
	The store said,	(15)
	"It's not ours",	(16)
	We went through every store in the town,	(17)
Interlocutor:	They put it in another box,	(18)
	...	
Narrator:	I finally gave it to Goodwill,	(19)
	I—I put it back in the box, hhhhh,	(20)

This simple story demonstrates many of the crucial characteristics of narrative as a social practice. The story was told by an older woman to a group of college-aged people, who were milling about the food table at a July 4 party in a suburb of a major American city.[33] The narrator performs her story with an eloquence that is difficult to convey on paper. Nonetheless, the transcription does reveal an elegant structure. The core events that are reported in this narrative can be identified as:

- My sister says, "I'm going into town ..."

- The store said, "It's not ours"

- We went through every store in the town.

These events are related in the middle of the narrative (lines 12–17), using short, succinct phrases, in which the action verbs are in the simple past tense ("said" and "went").[34] Several orientation clauses (lines 1–11) precede these main narrative clauses, setting the stage, providing background information, and introducing the characters for the narrative. Here the narrator informs us that the story-events occurred at the time of her wedding and describes the particular gift that becomes the focus of the narrative action. Following the main narrative clauses is a terse resolution section (lines 18–20), in which the narrator brings the story—and her telling of it—to a conclusion. Her resolution remakes the narrative into a humorous story as the minor fraud that forms the theme of the narrative is extended: the narrator also gives (to Goodwill) a cheap serving dish enclosed in a fancy box.[35]

What is actually communicated by the telling of this story becomes a matter for negotiation between narrator and audience (see Polanyi 1985:63–74). One of the listeners interrupts early on, for example, to explain (to those in the audience who might not know) what a lazy susan is. This interjection (omitted from the transcript for the sake of brevity) becomes part of the narrative's orientation section (it occurs in the space of the ellipsis between lines 6 and 7 in the transcript)—even though the narrator herself clearly hadn't intended to include it. More dramatically, toward the end of the narrative, it is a member of the audience who provides the punch line "They put it in another box" (line 18). The narrator builds on this line in her resolution, incorporating it seamlessly into her own narrative. Indeed, by the time the narrative ends, it seems that the point of the story was the "other box" all the time—though, of course, we cannot know what the narrator's original intention was.

This simple story is actually quite powerful. Part of its power comes from the fact that it deals with important cultural concepts, such as marriage, wealth, generosity, honesty, and charity. The narrative is "tellable" (see Labov and Waletzky 1967) because it is funny, to be sure, but its tellability stems also from its significance. By playing with important cultural values, this story presents to the listeners an enactment of cultural belonging. Giving wedding presents is an accepted custom in our society—indeed one that we have strong feelings about. People invited to the wedding of a friend or relative feel obliged to provide a gift, sometimes an expensive gift. On the other hand, every couple has a story about the undesirable wedding gifts they received, and they joyously exchange these stories for the rest of their lives. Indeed, it is in this spirit that the narrator embarked on the story presented as text 4.2.

The twist in this "wedding gift" story, however, is that the lazy susan arrived wrapped in a box that made a cheap gift appear to be an expensive gift. At first the story appears to be about social class and symbolic capital (Bourdieu 1984), as the narrator juxtaposes criticism of how tasteless the object was with its provenance from "a very jazzy store in San Francisco." Once it is revealed that the wrapping was misleading, however, the story is transformed into a tale of uncharitable gift giving. It is not coincidental, then, that the narrator juxtaposes her own charitability—in giving the lazy susan to Goodwill—to the lack of generosity of her wedding guest.[36]

Indeed, it is this turning-of-the-tables that dramatically shows the strategic aspect of narratives, as they are told in conversation. The message communicated by the telling of the literal story involves the narrator's own identity. She is negotiating an identity by positioning herself as a person with culturally valued characteristics—good taste and charitability, among others (see Polanyi 1985). The communicative value of telling the narrative involves the indirect message: by telling this story about receiving a wedding gift, I can assert that I am a good person.

Why speakers use indirection to claim an identity is a question for philosophy, but how such claims are accomplished is a question for linguistic analysis. Rhetorical efficacy depends upon verbal dexterity, the ability to use language in accordance with culturally valued aesthetic rules. A well-told story argues the teller's (indirect) point well; a poorly told story leaves the point unmade—though both may relate the same manifest events. Even in the fairly ordinary narrative analyzed here, we can identify instances of verbal dexterity. The narrator spends a great deal of time and effort, for example, elaborating on a basic point: the lazy susan was ugly. One of her most effective devices is the argument that other people also deemed it ugly. Rather than just asserting, "All our guests thought the lazy susan was ugly," she condenses this expression into the paralinguistic sign of a sharp intake of breath (transcribed above as *huuuhhh*) that she puts into the voices of the guests (line 10). Indeed, the effect of this evaluation is heightened by the context "people would walk in and go," whereby the guests' expression of disgust is constructed as escaping from their mouths instinctively, almost unavoidably. Having spent the first several lines of her narrative describing how ugly the object is, the narrator's very next line constructs the opposite (line 11). By juxtaposing the fancy box to the ugly object, the narrator sets up the initial tension in the narrative. By doing this in adjoining lines, the narrator utilizes a narrative device that William Labov has called "minimax," whereby a minimal amount of language effects a maximal change in meaning (Labov 1972b:349). It is worth pointing out that the narrator ends her story with a similar juxtaposition of contrasting images: putting the gift back in the deceptive box / giving the gift to Goodwill (lines 19–20).

William Labov's (1972c) work on narrative structure focuses on what he calls "evaluation." Much of the content of narrative speech not directly addressed to the core events, he argues, functions evaluatively. Some narrators provide explicitly evaluative comments, such as when a narrator might say "I was scared," or "I was angry." Most often, however, evaluation is achieved indirectly. In text 4.2 the narrator skillfully embeds evaluative content deeply into her text. While she provides the explicit evaluation "It was the ugliest lazy susan I have ever seen ..." in lines 3–6, she also gives implicit evaluation when she argues, in line 10, that others came to the same conclusion: "And people would walk in and go, 'huuuhhh.'" As Labov noted (1972c), there are many elaborate means for embedding evaluation in a narrative, and the deeper the linguistic embedding, the more powerful its effect. Deeply embedding evaluation requires great verbal dexterity and is a sign of great narrative skill.

As Labov (1972c) argues, evaluation is key to narrative. Labov points to the tellability of a narrative as determining its success or failure as rhetoric. Evaluation makes a story tellable because, in general, Americans care about how events affect people, not about isolated events themselves—no matter how dramatic. Evaluation introduces affect by providing information about the speaker's stance with respect to the topic, the characters, and the events in the narrative. Since narratives deployed in conversational interactions are strategic (part of negotiations of identity and difference), evaluation also provides information about the affective relations obtaining between narrator and audience.

The introduction of affect makes narrative powerful, and affect is most powerful when it is hidden, or veiled. As the historian Hayden White (1980) notes, narrative inserts ideology into discourse through its deployments of affect. White's landmark essay, "The Value of Narrativity in the Representation of Reality," compares annals, chronicles, and histories proper as modes of historiographic writing. The great difference between annals and chronicles on the one hand and histories proper on the other, White argues, is the centering of the latter about a moral point of view (White 1980). Histories are stories, or narratives, with a teleology, a direction, a reference point, that is formed by the ideological structures of society. At base this teleology is an ordering of events according to desirability—an affective evaluation.

Labov's insights on spoken narrative and White's insights on historical narrative suggest a methodology for studying identity processes by linking the abstract discourse of identity negotiations to the concrete discourse of interview conversations. This link involves the emotion in everyday life. A brief comparison of two narrative segments from a single interview will demonstrate how careful attention to the linguistic details of narrative embedded in ongoing social interaction—the dialect, intonation, style, and poetics of narrative speech—illuminates everyday negotiations of identity.

TEXT 4.3.   AN-NAKBA

Dan	What happened to your family in 1948?[37]	(1)
Samir	OK,	(2)
	I was in my mother's womb at that time,	(3)
	I— my mother was pregnant,	(4)
	I— and they eh— at that time—	(5)

I'm speaking about my village,   (6)
I mean they— according to what they tell me,   (7)
And this I've heard from several people,   (8)
Eh— they came— OK,   (9)
First of all there were some who—   (10)
They heard about the slaughter in other places,   (11)
You know— you understand?   (12)
Slaughter, so (),   (13)
That's what they say,   (14)
That they came,   (15)
They put young people in— in one line,   (16)
My father was among them,   (17)
And there was—   (18)
I have an uncle who was a doctor,   (19)
And at that time that was really a big deal,   (20)
I mean, in '48 you know,   (21)
So they put them in a line,   (22)
Including the doctor,   (23)
Someone said that there was—
    that the doctor should be excluded,   (24)
One of the elders there,   (25)
So they took him out,   (26)
Afterward they were going to shoot them,   (27)
That's how they felt,   (28)
So then the MP arrived, my dad said ...   (29)
And stopped them,   (30)
So that's what I know,   (31)
And they didn't shoot them,   (32)
Afterwards, all of them—
    all the people in my village,   (33)
Except for the Druze,   (34)
Because the Druze (),   (35)
Because there are Druze and Christians there,   (36)
They fled,   (37)
They told them to leave,   (38)
And they left for some village,   (39)
They call it Piki'in, Piki'in,   (40)
They walked by foot, to the village,
    that's far away,   (41)
A quarter hour by car,   (42)
By foot maybe eh— hours,   (43)
And they stayed there several days,   (44)
And after that they returned to the village,   (45)
And then my father was in— here in Atlit,   (46)
Sheva Prison they call it,   (47)
With several people from the village,   (48)
Prisoners— they took them prisoner,   (49)
I was born and my father didn't see me,   (50)
He saw me maybe after a year, ...
    I've forgotten by now,   (51)

	He was always in detention,	(52)
	He didn't do anything really,	(53)
	They put young men from the village in jail,	(54)
	That's what was in '48,	(55)
	And my mother returned with the grandfather and grandmother,	(56)
	The other women,	(57)
	That was in my village, ... (193B:12:07–14:35)	(58)

Later in the same interview, we asked Samir and his wife about their experiences in the Gulf War:[38]

TEXT 4.4.   THE GULF WAR

Lisa	No— I— on that night—((laughs))	(1)
	I was against that whole war, you know,	(2)
	I didn't know— I—	(3)
	When he shot a missile at Tel Aviv,	(4)
	It was really painful for me,	(5)
	That— it hurt me all the time from the whole Western world,	(6)
	When they threw bombs there on the people,	(7)
	And it really angered me,	(8)
	But the— I felt that this was the problem of their leader,	(9)
	And— but they didn't deserve what they got,	(10)
	A blow like that was very hard on them,	(11)
	I felt more eh—	(12)
Samir	People don't deserve blows—	(13)
	This is political now ... (194A:00:31–01:08)	(14)

After a few minutes, I return to my question about their experiences in the Gulf War:

TEXT 4.5.   THE GULF WAR (CONTINUED)

Dan	And you, did you stay here in Haifa during the war?	(1)
Samir	Yes, a few times we left,	(2)
Lisa	Yes,	(3)
Samir	We sort of fled,	(4)
	We escaped one night,	(5)
	When we heard the Patriot [missiles]	(6)
	And right here there's—	(7)
	We don't want to leave,	(8)
	Until we heard it,	(9)
	We thought that it was a Scud [missile],	(10)
	It's right above our house,	(11)
	Even though it's— the whole neighborhood heard it,	(12)
	And then at exactly 1:00 a.m.,	(13)
	So we put the children into the car and we went,	(14)
	Even though my car was broken,	(15)

That was pretty frightening,	(16)

Lisa   ((laughs)) ...   (17)

That was pretty frightening,   (16)

Lisa   ((laughs)) ...   (17)

We were afraid all the time,   (18)

Samir   That's it, we felt it,   (19)

There the people— began—   (20)

In the beginning, you know, in the beginning,   (21)

They sat in the sealed room,   (22)

And put on [gas] masks,   (23)

After a little while,   (24)

They began to go outside to watch the—(),   (25)

We know () to see,   (26)

But we never—   (27)

I never saw one, for example,   (28)

Not even in the village,   (29)

   ...

Samir   But here it was more frightening,   (30)

You hear the siren, live,   (31)

There in the village you don't hear the siren,   (32)

You listen to the radio,   (33)

Or the siren in Carmiel,   (34)

Here you hear it right here, here from the port,   (35)

And it's very strong,   (36)

Here the siren's frightening,   (37)

That's the feeling,   (38)

What's frightening is the siren,   (39)

After seven minutes you know
        that everything's passed,   (40)

   ...

Lisa   But we love it so much here,   (41)

That we didn't want to leave even in a war,   (42)

And it really was a war for us,   (43)

Stella   Did it ever happen that you were outside
        when the sirens went off?   (44)

   ...

Samir   Today we were reminded,   (45)

We were just talking,   (46)

We were at the sea and we were talking,   (47)

One time there was a missile, it was (),   (48)

If you remember the war,   (49)

He sent one to Saudi Arabia,   (50)

And then here,   (51)

It was always at the same time,   (52)

Stella   Yes,   (53)

Lisa   So my son went down to the street,   (54)

This was in the evening,   (55)

So I call to him,   (56)

"Come upstairs, he's sent one to Saudi Arabia",   (57)
((laughs))

I didn't want... (194A:03:46–07:04)   (58)

These three segments of interview discourse (texts 4.3, 4.4, and 4.5 are presented here in the order they occurred in the interview) show how subtle negotiations of identity can be discerned in the details of linguistic style. I will begin with text 4.4. In keeping with the interview strategy described earlier, the interviewers brought up the topic of the Gulf War well into the interview (in this case it was after we had been talking for ninety minutes). We hoped the question would prompt a narrative of personal experience. In Jewish Israeli homes this question often elicited a lively narrative about how frightened or foolish people had felt during the first days of Scud missile attacks. In such cases the "Gulf War narratives" often had the effect of relaxing the interview atmosphere, relieving some of its formality. For example, at this point interviewees sometimes turned the tables, asking the interviewers questions, since many were interested in my own experiences in Israel during the Gulf War. In Palestinian homes this topic worked differently, but nonetheless we usually posed the question.[39]

It is therefore interesting that we ask the question twice—once just before the segment transcribed as text 4.4, and again a few minutes later (leading to text 4.5).[40] Their first response is very different linguistically from their second response. The first response is characteristic of what Labov has called "soapbox" style. Soapbox style is careful speech used for relatively formal utterances, for declamations. Indeed, Samir interrupts his own train of thought to say "This is political now" (text 4.4, line 14). In doing so, he is saying explicitly what he has already made clear implicitly through the content and style of his speech. His phrases are long and grammatically complex. His speech rate is slow. And his intonation is ponderous and repetitive, beginning low, rising to a crescendo toward the end of each phrase, then falling to a low tone at each phrase boundary. When we rephrase our question (text 4.5, line 1), a narrative of personal experience suddenly emerges. Stylistic differences are striking. In telling about the night his family fled the city in a broken-down car, Samir uses short phrases, animated voice quality, intonational rises at the ends of phrases—and many more hallmarks of the speech of narratives of personal experience.

The influence of the interview context on the form of speech elicited can be seen in disfluency patterns. Disfluent speech characterizes the early part of the An-Nakba narrative (text 4.3), for example. After joking about how young he was at the time ("I was in my mother's womb") in line 3, Samir requires more than twenty lines (5–27) to say that Jewish soldiers lined up the Palestinian men in the village and threatened to shoot them. Moreover, these lines are filled with starts, stops, hesitations, hedges, and backtrackings. A similar disfluency occurs later, at the beginning of the Gulf War story. These segments of disfluent speech contrast dramatically with the subsequent fluency of the narrative of their flight to their home village.

The source of disfluency is clear in both cases: the political sensitivity of the topics being discussed and of the positions being taken. With respect to the story of 1948, a complex negotiation of feelings and positions emerges around each telling. On the one hand, such stories constitute a great silence in the dominant narrative of Israel's formation (see text 2.3). On the other hand, they are a source of great personal regret and sadness for the tellers. Mainstream Israeli discourse insists on a single dominant version of the story of 1948—one that excludes evidence of the victimization of

Palestinian inhabitants of the land that became Israel. The dominant myth asserts that Palestinians fled from their villages, intending to return after the victorious Arab armies had pushed the Jews into the sea (Flapan 1987). As such, Israel owes little to the refugees displaced by the war. More recently, however, a revisionist historiography in Israel has rewritten this story, pointing to the many intentional actions by the Jews and the Israeli army to encourage, even force, Palestinians to leave their homes. According to this version, Israel owes a great deal to the refugee Palestinian population. This difference in historical documentation and interpretation is no idle academic debate. Rather, it has immense consequences for identity and for politics in current Israel. And very strong feelings hinge on nuanced differences between certain words, certain stories.

Thus, in the context of our interview, in which I and my young Jewish Israeli research assistant have been entertained in the home of a Palestinian family, the questions we ask—and the answers we receive—are intensely political. In the early 1990s, voicing the question itself—"What happened to your family in 1948?"—was unusual, and the opportunity for Palestinians to tell a Jewish Israeli woman that Israel had mistreated their families was uncharted territory. Thus it is out of hospitality and politeness that these narratives begin disfluently, but it is the relationship between words and context that generate the message communicated, and—disfluent or not—this story (and others told at this interview) was, I think, deeply shocking to my Jewish Israeli assistant.

Much more will be said about specific narratives in subsequent chapters (see especially chapter 8). The point here is to show how identity is negotiated in narrative form. To see this, the texts must be read "against the grain" (Barthes 1977), interpreting what is communicated, rather than relying on what is literally said. It is the strategic, indirect communication of these narratives that reveals what is at stake in conversation in Israel.

Telling the "An-Nakba" narrative (text 4.3) negotiates a Palestinian Self that was victimized by circumstances beyond one's own control, but it does so in a way that presents the Self as noble and the Other as reasonable. Victimization is powerfully represented in the story through the images of men being lined up (line 22); villagers being forced to walk a long distance to a neighboring town (line 41); and the narrator's father being held in jail and missing his son's birth and infancy, despite having done nothing wrong (lines 50–54). This characterization is strengthened by some less prominent images, such as a pregnant woman (his mother) being forced to walk long distances (see line 4), and discriminatory treatment of Christian Palestinians as opposed to Druze (line 34). In contrast, the village is presented in a noble light: a place where an educated man, his uncle, the doctor, is treated with great respect. The villagers are also presented as noble and reasonable in their response to the soldiers' presence in the village: they did not resist the Jewish occupation. While such a response might count as cowardice, the narrator justifies it with reference to the "slaughter" that villagers had heard about happening elsewhere. There is also a strikingly benign treatment of the Jewish occupiers. The narrative is told with little evaluative comment, little emotion directed toward Jews. Indeed, Jews are constructed as compassionate both in exempting the respected doctor from the fate of the young men (lines 24–26) and in halting the threat of assassinations (lines 29–30).

We can read the "Gulf War" narrative in a similar way. As a fresher historical event—and one that everyone present had lived through, rather than merely read or heard about—the politics are even more acute. The use of the word "flee" stands out in this narrative of a family leaving Haifa during the first night of bombing. This word resonates with several powerful discourses. "Flee" evokes the idea of Palestinians fleeing in 1948—which, as I have shown, forms the nexus of a contentious struggle over symbols (see text 2.3). The word also evokes prominent discourses tied to the Gulf War. The flight of visitors out of Israel at the time of the Gulf War was a prominent image that evoked sadness among (Jewish) Israelis. Most foreigners left Israel before the war broke out, and few tourists came during the war, crippling the economically crucial and symbolically central tourism industry. More important, though, were images of (Jewish) Israelis leaving, which evoked general anger. In particular, television news was filled with stories of ultraorthodox families boarding planes for the United States early in the war, and later on by stories of Israelis "fleeing" the two largest Jewish cities, Tel Aviv and Haifa, which were the main targets of Iraqi missiles, for safer places, such as Jerusalem and smaller towns in the Israeli hinterland. Such images angered many Jewish Israelis, for whom the appropriate response to threat was to stay and fight (see chapter 6). The Tel Aviv mayor gained notoriety by labeling those who left the city "deserters."

Thus the telling of this Palestinian "Gulf War" story constitutes a complex negotiation of identity. Having a Gulf War story enacts participation in mainstream Israeli identity. Indeed, Samir prefaced the narrative presented in text 4.5 by saying "It was for us just like for Jews."[41] In part, this is a narrative of Israeliness, as Samir's narrativization of life in the (Arab) village during the war suggests. Reports in the mainstream Israeli media repeatedly showed Palestinians in the Occupied Territories (and in Jordan and other Arab countries) celebrating the Scud missile attacks on Israel. The phrase used was "dancing on the roofs." Samir begins to say that in the village people at first put on gas masks and stayed in their sealed rooms, but then began to go outside during alarms to watch the missiles come in (lines 24–25). At this point in his narrative he catches himself and abruptly changes course (lines 25–28), noting that they themselves never saw (i.e., never watched for?) a missile. Indeed, Samir continues after this self-correction to argue that it was more dangerous for the Arabs in villages, since they had no alarms to warn of incoming missiles (line 32).[42]

Strategic and Nonstrategic Ambiguities

As I pore over the recording and transcript of these narrative segments from this particular interview, I am struck by the limitations to analysis imposed by the limited fluency of the speakers. These middle-aged Palestinian Israelis speak Hebrew effectively, it seems to me, but not comfortably. Their Hebrew is idiomatic but heavily accented, and it is sprinkled with errors of grammar and word choice that would embarrass them if they heard the tape.

Some ambiguities in the text are especially intriguing. Near the beginning of "The Gulf War" (text 4.4), for example, Lisa appears to be arguing that the Western alliance was punishing the Iraqi people (by the heavy bombings) when it was only Saddam Hussein's leadership that was at fault (for the occupation of Kuwait). She says:

TEXT 4.4.   THE GULF WAR (EXCERPT)

Lisa   But the— I felt that this was the problem
                of their leader,   (9)
           And— but they didn't deserve what they got,   (10)

Lisa's phrasing in Hebrew is a bit awkward. She says *hem lo hayu tz'rixim l'kabel et ze*, which translates as "they didn't need to get this." She uses the verb *l'kabel*, which can mean either "to receive (get)" or "to accept." In the context of Western and Israeli discourses that held out hope that the Iraqi people would rise up and rid themselves of Saddam Hussein's dictatorial leadership, Lisa's utterance is surely more ambiguous than she had intended. Indeed, it is clear from her next phrase, "A blow like that was very hard on them" (line 11 in text 4.4), that she meant the "get" sense of *l'kabel* (thus the translation in text 4.4). To make absolutely certain of an adequate interpretation, her husband, Samir, interrupts her at this point to reiterate the message "People don't deserve blows ..." (line 13 in text 4.4). Here, Samir has used the more idiomatic (and less ambiguous) phrase *lo magia l'anashim*, "people don't deserve"—which his wife had undoubtedly meant to use. The example points to the fact, however, that one's dexterity in using language to negotiate identity depends, in part, on the ways in which language is learned. It is to this topic that I turn now.

5

The Social Organization
of Language Learning
in Israel

Imperfect mastery of a language, such as was discussed at the end of chapter 4, is often attributed to an individual's failure to adequately learn that language. Such a focus on individual ability and failure stems from a particular ideology of language that strictly opposes "mother tongue" to "second language." This view of language erases the social context within which language is produced, thereby erasing also the social meaning situated speech generates. A full appreciation of the social use of language depends on an understanding of how a society structures language learning. This chapter contributes to an ethnography of language acquisition in Israel by examining the varied contexts in which languages are learned and the social conditions underlying those contexts. Such an ethnography of language acquisition facilitates a deeper understanding of the linguistic negotiation of Israeli identities.

To understand the social meaning of language learning we must acknowledge that language learning implies also its opposite: language unlearning. "Language Shift" is the term linguists give to the common process in which a community's norms of language-use change over time (Fishman 1991; Kulick 1992). Susan Gal (1979), for example, found that Austrian towns, where Hungarian had once been the dominant community language, had shifted to become almost entirely German speaking. Similarly, in the American Southwest the use of Spanish was once much more widespread than it is now.

Richard Rodriguez's autobiographical novel *Hunger of Memory* (1982) provides an eloquent articulation of the social structuring and cultural meaning of language learning. Rodriguez describes growing up in a Spanish-speaking family in the American Southwest and confronting a painful choice when he entered school: adopt English or face ostracism from his (Anglo) peers. The young Rodriguez chose English, thereby embarking on a process of actively unlearning his "native" Spanish. Rodriguez achieved the longed-for sense of belonging in the mainstream of his American school cohort, but he paid a painful price. In the process of learning to speak English as a "native," he found that he had unlearned Spanish, such that he could no longer speak to his beloved grandmother, who understood only Spanish (Rodriguez 1982:37).[1] Among bilingual Chicanos in the American Southwest today, switching from English to Spanish evokes meanings derived from the poignant choice Rodriguez describes (see Anzaldua 1987).

Rodriguez's description of learning and unlearning English and Spanish in the American Southwest typifies the uneven and unequal ways in which languages are learned more generally. Some languages are more highly valued than others. Societies place unequal value on the various languages (or language varieties) used in a particular community, and individuals have unequal access to learning the languages.

An Ideology of Language Learning

A mother tongue (also called "native language" or "vernacular") is the language a child "acquires"; all other languages are relegated to the status of second languages—and these must be "learned." Linguistic science has long contrasted the idea of "acquisition" to that of "learning" in order to emphasize the independence of grammar from politics. Since all children acquire a language (i.e., their mother tongue) in essentially the same time and to essentially the same level of mastery, linguists dismiss politicized claims that some languages are illogical, or that some speakers are deficient (see Labov 1969). One result of this celebration of acquisition, however, has been the marginalization of learning, seen, for example, in the marginalization of the study of second-language acquisition as a cultural process. Sociolinguists in particular have shown limited interest in the social life of second languages.

Language acquisition has been conceptualized as a natural process that unfolds in early childhood and that involves only mother and child, but these are limiting assumptions. To be sure, research on first-language acquisition has shown it to be a wondrously complex process, but language continues to be learned throughout the lifespan. The core phonological and syntactic structures of one's mother tongue are learned in early childhood, but many other crucial aspects of language and its use are learned later in life. Children acquire the pronunciation of the sounds of their language early on, but it is only later that they learn how to vary these pronunciations so as to sound formal, friendly, authoritative, or angry. Children acquire the complex grammatical structures of their language early on, but it is only later that children master the conventions for turn-taking that allow them to enter conversations appropriately. In many communities, second—or even third and fourth—languages are used, and these languages are learned in a variety of ways.

Unfortunately, while ethnographic studies of language use and ethnographic studies of language acquisition abound, few studies have looked at the articulation between these two domains. Ethnographic studies of socially meaningful language-use have generally avoided situations of language learning. Even studies of bilingual communities tend to assume (at least tacitly) the presence of two mother tongues, thus discarding issues of learning a second language. Scholars, like John Gumperz (1982b), who have looked at language-use in contexts of imperfect mastery of a second language pay little attention to the social and cultural conditions of acquiring the second language. Similarly, ethnographic studies of language acquisition have addressed language and identity primarily from an individualistic perspective that is far removed from issues of social politics and struggle. Elinor Ochs and Bambi Schieffelin, for example, pioneered the field of child language socialization by showing that (first) language acquisition is inseparable from the process whereby children acquire cultural, gender, age, and status identities (Ochs 1988; Schieffelin 1990; Schieffelin and Ochs 1986), but research on second language acquisition, by focusing on practical issues of learning languages of wider communication, has ignored the ways in which learning particular second languages implicates broader social and political struggles over identity.

Western theories of language have long posited an intimate connection between one's identity and one's mother tongue. From Herderian romanticism that linked folk character to folk language (see Wilson 1973) to Kristevan structuralism that ties the onset of intersubjective awareness to the infant's mastery of grammar (Kristeva 1980), acquiring language has been seen to form and shape identity in a particularly strong way. Such a perspective, however, privileges the mother tongue as a unique site for identity formation, thereby constraining the discovery of the actual relations between language and identity. Studies of language contact (Gal 1979; Myers-Scotton 1983; among others), for example, point to the negotiation (or clash) of identities that results from the contact between languages, but such studies tend to treat the two languages (and identities) as undifferentiated units, paying little attention to processes of acquisition.

Yet there are good reasons for studies of language and identity to focus on language learning. If we take seriously the proposition that "language" and "identity" are independently emergent qualities of social interaction, the distinction between language use and language learning evaporates. For in some sense each instance of discourse is a novel, creative use of language—and thus a context of language learning. Discourse thus becomes the nexus linking structures of language, acts of speaking, and ideas of identity (Sherzer 1987) in a trajectory of structured objects and structuring tendencies. Language-use embedded in social life takes it place in the "habitus" (Bourdieu 1977), deconstructing received notions of mother tongue in order to perceive language styles as emergent from contexts, contexts as emergent from the practice of everyday life, and everyday practices as ever-changing. Throughout the lifespan, languages (or language varieties) are learned, relearned, and unlearned.

Learning Languages in Israel

In Israel the negotiation of identity crucially involves the learning and unlearning (and perhaps relearning) of three primary languages: Hebrew, Arabic, and English. The learning of Hebrew comes first to mind. Learning Hebrew is historically linked with Zionism, the Jewish nationalist movement, and it remains central to the socialization of newcomers to Israel—including ethnographers. Equally important—though not as quick to mind—is the learning of Arabic. The fundamental expression of Palestinian identity in Israel, where the idea of a Palestinian native speaker of Hebrew is all but unthinkable, is the maintenance of Arabic as the language of home, nation, and politics.[2] On the other hand, the not-learning, or the unlearning, of Arabic also plays an important role, as Mizrahi children of Arabic-speaking Jewish Israelis actively unlearn their parents' mother tongue.[3] Finally, an aspect of Israeli language learning that is quite important, though it rarely comes to mind, is the learning of English. English is a language that all Israelis must learn, but its learning powerfully re-creates hierarchical relations among Ashkenazi, Mizrahi, and Palestinian groups in Israel.

Learning Hebrew

The learning of Hebrew is quintessentially Israeli. The nation itself was formed through the revitalization of the Hebrew language (Harshav 1993), and a rich mythology has grown up around this language revival (Fellman 1973a). Israel is famous for its innovative language teaching methods, referred to as "Hebrew in Hebrew" (Spolsky and Shohamy 1999:96–100),[4] as well as for its language schools, called *ulpanim*, that teach Hebrew to immigrants, visitors, and tourists.[5] Still a nation of immigrants, Israel continually reconstitutes itself through acts of learning Hebrew.

Learning Hebrew as a Nation

Israeli culture romanticizes the learning of Hebrew.[6] Popular jokes celebrate the special relationship between Israeli identity and learning Hebrew. Hebrew is often described, for example, as "the one mother tongue that mothers learn from their children." At one level this joke celebrates the immigrant, melting-pot nature of Israeli society, in which only the children of immigrants become native speakers of the language. At another level, however, the joke also refers to Israel as an original "mother" that learned its mother tongue from its native sons. As a revitalized language, Hebrew was like a creole language, "a language in search of native speakers" (see Sankoff and Laberge 1980). But Israelis do not view Hebrew the way linguists view creoles—as a pastiche language formed at the intersection of social conflicts and upheavals. Rather, Israelis view Modern Hebrew as the product of conscious effort and constant devotion. Central to this view of Hebrew is the rich mythology that has been cultivated about the romantic figure of Eliezer Ben-Yehuda, the individual usually credited with bringing about the revival of Hebrew (see Fellman 1973a). Ben-Yehuda is recalled as a brilliant autodidact, a selfless zealot, a tragic hero who dedicated his life to reviving the Hebrew language (see Fellman 1973a; Harshav 1993; see also chapter 7). And central to the mythology of Eliezer Ben-Yehuda is the almost certainly apocryphal story that he raised his son to be the first native speaker of Hebrew in two thousand years by insisting that only Hebrew could be spoken to the infant, despite the fact that his wife, the child's mother, knew very little Hebrew (Fellman 1973a:34).[7]

Learning Hebrew is further romanticized by the story of Israel's "national poet," Haim Nahman Bialik. Born in the Ukraine in the mid–nineteenth century, Bialik grew up speaking Yiddish (as well as other European languages), but he adopted Hebrew for his poetry. Bialik's Hebrew poetry became the literary centerpiece of Zionist imagining of Self. He wrote in an archaic and elaborate Hebrew dramatically different from—and even contradictory in spirit to—modern Israeli aesthetics of language-use (Alter 1994:10), yet his poetry is held up as the symbol of modern Israeli nationhood. For many years, Bialik was required reading in Israeli schools, but by the early 1990s this difficult poetry had declined in pedagogical importance in Hebrew-language schools. While Israel had needed to learn Hebrew in order to acquire its national poet, a nation of native speakers was no longer challenged by Bialik.

AWED TO SPEAK HEBREW

As an American Jew, I was deeply impressed by the revival of Hebrew.

I had grown up learning Hebrew as a badge of identity and as a vehicle for spirituality. In the large Jewish community of Cleveland, Ohio, Hebrew was used in religious observation and taught in religious schools. Like most students, I had rebelled against the imposition of afternoon school, the out-of-date teaching methods, the difficult script, the irrelevance to my everyday life of sports, television, and dating. In Cleveland, Ohio, it was decidedly uncool to speak Hebrew.

When I arrived in Israel, however, I was awed by people speaking Hebrew. I was amazed that people spoke Hebrew even in their most private moments; that young children learned Hebrew before any other language; that it was not just the religious and cultured individuals who spoke Hebrew, but the garbage collectors and high-school toughs as well. The aura of Hebrew as a learned language had gotten through to me. Indeed, I never did lose the slight sense of awe that I was actually speaking Hebrew—even as it became routine and familiar.

Hadas, an Israeli colleague, once said to me: "I'm proud of my Hebrew." At the time I found this a curious statement. I compared my colleague's sentiments to feelings I might have about my own language, but I couldn't think of any context in which I would say, "I am proud of my English."[8] Later on, however, I came to understand what Hadas meant. Hadas, who had been a frequent companion early on in my fieldwork, and whom I counted as a good friend, was one of the few Israelis who spoke to me in Hebrew at a time when I was still struggling with the language—when communication would have been easier in English. Though born in Israel, and therefore a native speaker of Hebrew, Hadas spoke English fluently because her parents were American. Her comment was thus part of the negotiation of identity between us: she was saying that she would overlook my disrespect for her status—by insisting on a halting Hebrew instead of acknowledging her ability to communicate more effectively in English. In part, too, Hadas was explaining something more specific about her identity as an Israeli. Carrying American citizenship (because of her parentage), and having lived in the United States for several years as a young adult, Hadas had the opportunity to live elsewhere but had made the decision to return to Israel.[9] Her pride in Hebrew was her way of expressing identification with Israeliness. Hadas was also interested in helping me to learn Hebrew, as came out in later conversations, in which she praised my advances with a sincerity distinctly absent from other Israelis, whose praise of my Hebrew stemmed in part from an assumption that Americans wouldn't learn Hebrew well at all.

Israelis take great pride in their language. Israelis express pride in the Biblical origins of Hebrew, in the rules of Hebrew's language academy, in the successful revival of a "dead language," and in the spunk and vitality of a new language filled with innovative slang and expressive borrowings. Conversational Hebrew is replete with biblical resonances even in its most streetwise forms, but the use of biblical phrases, idioms, references, and allusions comprises one well-honored mode of linguistic virtuosity in Israeli Hebrew. Israelis are also particularly conscious of notions of correctness in language. The term *ivrit tiknit*, "standard Hebrew," refers to the rules established—and constantly updated, revised, and revisited— by the Israeli language academy for official Hebrew. Though in casual conversation Israelis honor the academy's rules most by their breach, the idea that a correct form exists is widely accepted. During the early 1990s a weekly prime-time television show was devoted to discussion of the meaning and history of Hebrew words. Israelis were fond of pointing out the existence of "official" Hebrew words for the thousands of concepts and things for which loans from European languages are routinely used. An Israeli linguist once told me about her work creating etymologically Hebrew words for car parts. She told this story with great pride, even though such "official" words are rarely used in everyday conversation (see Alloni-Fainberg 1974). Words for "brakes" provide a typical example. The language academy developed an etymologically authentic Hebrew word, *balamim*, for the car part, but the borrowing from English, *breksim*, is used much more frequently.[10] Indeed, even when Israelis say "car," they are as likely to use the borrowing *oto* (from the English word "auto"), as they are to use the etymologically Hebrew word *m'xonit* (from a Semitic root meaning "machine"). One night some Israeli students had some fun at the expense of their American friends, challenging them to come up with the academy's official terms for common borrowings like *kaseta*, *televizia*, and *telefon*.[11]

Learning Hebrew as a "Native"

Israelis also express pride in the vitality of Modern Hebrew, which they articulate through the distinction between *ivrit* and *yisra'elit*, "Hebrew" and "Israeli" (language). Hebrew is the formal language of newspapers, oratory, and the grand tradition, while Israeli is the vernacular language of the streets. In the decades since Hebrew's revival as a spoken vernacular, a lively slang has emerged that has long been associated with youth culture and the military. In the 1950s, when Israeli nation building was at its height, the creative linguistic innovations of the native-speaking Israelis—as heard in conversations, as celebrated in novels and plays, as commented upon in newspapers— constituted a vital symbolic expression of nation (Almog 2000:9–10).

When I told Israelis about my project to study language and identity, many suggested I look at the military, where style, newness, and linguistic vitality are thought to originate, and to flourish.[12] A passage in a recent novel situated in Israel, *From a Sealed Room*, captures the atmosphere well. Dov, a young Israeli soldier, is visiting his parents on weekend leave. His mother, Tami, reflects on her joy at his visit and her melancholy at the changes wrought in her now not-so-innocent boy:

> Dov would be at home. He had arrived in Jerusalem the previous afternoon on a bus from the north, toting his soldier's bag and his gun. His face was sunburnt, slower to change expression, marked from too much coffee, too many cigarettes, too little sleep. He was thinner too, and hoarse, and fa- vored his right leg when he walked. When he spoke it was in a vocabulary of acronyms and slang. Even [his father] had to ask him what he meant by some of the phrases he threw about as casually as he dropped [his rifle] on his bed. (Kadish 1998:21)

Learning Hebrew as an Immigrant

It is no coincidence that the military too is a context of (language) learning. The novel *From a Sealed Room* shows the native Israeli relearning his own Hebrew when he learns the military jargon, but the army is also a place where immigrants learn Hebrew for the first time. One man I interviewed, who had come to Israel from Argentina years earlier, and who spoke a fluent but strongly accented Hebrew, told me he regretted not having done military service because it would have given him a more native-sounding Hebrew.

The emphasis on learning Hebrew is represented best by the institution known simply as *ulpan*. A popular way for American Jews to visit Israel is to spend a summer "doing an ulpan," which usually means living on a kibbutz, working in the fields, and studying Hebrew intensively. For these Jews, learning Hebrew is an important part of exploring and expressing their Jewish identity as Americans. The *ulpanim* (plural of *ulpan*) are famous for their innovative teaching style and their efficient results. Students are taught immersion style by energetic and dedicated teachers.

On another level, the encounter between European and Oriental Jewry was mediated by the learning of the language, and the context of the ulpan. These schools were important centers of socialization and resocialization, instilling not only language skills but literacy, Western ideology, and Sabra mentality (Rosenbaum 1983). The role of the kibbutz movement in providing language schooling had a major effect on the subsequent relations between Ashkenazi and Mizrahi communities, as many Mizrahim recall highly chauvinist and arrogant behavior toward them at the hands of the Ashkenazi teachers. An especially painful aspect of this clash involved religious observance, as the relatively traditional and observant Jews from Morocco and elsewhere in the Middle East confronted the stridently secular ideology of the kibbutz.

The pattern of this interaction persists, as each new wave of immigrants is remade into Israelis through language learning. The system was being stretched, however, in the early 1990s, as Russian immigrants filled ulpanim to capacity. Veteran Israelis expressed frustration that these newcomers—as opposed to other, earlier immigrants—had little interest in learning Hebrew, in becoming Israeli.

A TENSE ULPAN CLASS

When I arrived in Israel I joined an ulpan class of about twenty Russian immigrants—young men and women of high-school and college age who aimed to study at an Israeli university.[13] I thought the instruction in these classes was terrific, but many of my classmates did not share these feelings. Friction between the veteran Israeli teachers and the immigrant Russian students reflected an underlying struggle over identity.

The ulpan curriculum included a heavy dose of lessons on Israeli and Jewish identity. Students were taken on field trips to military bases and parliament buildings, for example. The Russian immigrants were feted at the military base, preparing them for the military service many of the boys would soon begin, and which the State wanted all to desire. Students came back excited by this introduction to the army, and several happily showed me snapshots taken of them holding a machine gun or riding a tank. By the end of my fieldwork many of the men from my class had already entered the military.

Another field trip brought the ulpan students to Jerusalem to visit the Knesset (the Israeli parliament) and Yad va-Shem, Israel's memorial and museum to the Holocaust. These visits reflected the ulpan's desire to teach the Russian newcomers Israeli values of democracy and Jewish identity. The Knesset symbolizes to Israelis a tradition of democratic government that Israelis use to construct their identity in opposition to the autocratic forms of government in the surrounding Arab Middle East.[14] Israelis felt that Russian immigrants, coming from a communist background, also needed to be educated in democratic ideals. This feeling came out in class, as teachers frequently engaged in heated debates with students over the meaning of democracy, capitalism, and other concepts the Israeli teachers took to be uniquely Israeli.

The visit to Yad va-Shem was intended to instill in the Russian immigrants a proper orientation to Jewish heritage. Teachers felt that these immigrants had come to Israel without sufficient sense of Jewish identity. The intensity of the ulpan's socialization message was revealed to me one day in class when a teacher became enraged at Marina, a particularly attentive student. Marina had raised the teacher's ire by asserting that she already had a sense of Jewish heritage.[15]

Teachers and students vented their frustration. Students felt frustration over not being taught vocabulary for their university entrance exams. Teachers were frustrated because the Russian students appeared to reject the ulpan's language-immersion pedagogical structure. Students chattered in Russian throughout class periods and often interrupted language drills to confer among themselves (in Russian) to come up with a correct answer. They also displayed great interest in discussing topics the Israeli instructors found unacceptable: Russia, Russians, Russian language, and Russian military service. Indeed, the only time the Russian students engaged in Hebrew conversation was when they chatted with me during breaks—they and I shared no other common language.

The Russian students' behavior constituted a resistance to the highhanded attitude of the ulpan teachers. Russian students were indeed very adept at vocabulary, and in the final analysis the students knew their own best interest, since the university entrance exams tested vocabulary, not conversational or ideological skills.[16] As it turned out, many of my classmates failed their exams and were unable to pursue career paths similar to those they had left behind in Russia.[17]

Learning Hebrew as a Palestinian Israeli

Palestinian Israelis also learn Hebrew, but they do so under very different conditions. Palestinians always learn Hebrew as a second language: there are no Palestinian native speakers of Hebrew.[18]

TEXT 5.1.   HEBREW USE IN PALESTINIAN ISRAELI HOMES

STELLA, A RESEARCH ASSISTANT, AND I INTERVIEWED SAMIR AND HIS WIFE, LISA, IN THEIR HOME IN HAIFA. TOWARD THE END OF THE INTERVIEW THEIR FRIEND, RHODA, JOINED THE CONVERSATION. SAMIR AND LISA BOTH TEACH IN ARABIC-LANGUAGE SCHOOLS. SAMIR TEACHES IN HAIFA, AND LISA TEACHES IN A PALESTINIAN VILLAGE JUST OUTSIDE OF HAIFA.[19]

Stella	What language do you speak with the children?	(1)
	Hebrew or Arabic?	(2)
Lisa	No, only Arabic,	(3)
Samir	Never, we don't speak any other language,	(4)
	...	
	They know Hebrew well, very well,	(5)
	English too,	(6)
Stella	Do you make an effort to speak Arabic with them?	(7)
Samir	Effort? It's very natural,	(8)
	I don't try, it's very natural,	(9)
	I don't feel— ...	(10)
	It never occurred to me to teach them Hebrew at all,	(11)
	Nor do I speak— ...	(12)
	Let's say even if no one spoke Arabic in Israel, didn't speak it at all,	(13)
	I still wouldn't do that,	(14)
	I speak in— in— that's my mother tongue,	(15)
	Where— where were you born?	(16)

Stella	Me? ... In Netanya,	(17)
Samir	Eh, can you imagine sp—	
	speaking with your parents—	(18)
	Maybe your— I don't know—	(19)
Lisa	No, but there it was different,	(20)
	In—the Jews were from somewhere else,	(21)
	Eh—that's a different case,	(22)
Samir	It's not a matter of eh—of racism,	(23)
	This is my mother tongue,	(24)
	So I pass it on exactly ()— ...	(25)
	We have an Armenian neighbor,	(26)
	I— I was amazed, I've forgotten already,	(27)
	She speaks Armenian to her daughter,	(28)
	Even though no one uses that language at all,	(29)
Stella	Their children try to speak Hebrew or Arabic?	(30)
Samir	() Arabic, it's Arabic, for everything,	(31)
Stella	In my case, for example,	(32)
	My parents spoke Moroccan with me,	(33)
	And I understand—	(34)
Samir	That's their mother tongue,	(35)
	Eh— no, that problem doesn't exist here, no no,	(36)
Stella	I don't know Moroccan,	(37)
	But I understand when they speak with me,	(38)
Samir	Yes, yes, no, they speak well, they speak Arabic,	(39)
	Just like someone from Egypt,	(40)
	Or from— I don't know—	
	maybe with a different accent,	(41)
	Like in Syria and Lebanon, you know,	(42)
	Arabic— they know Arabic well,	(43)
	Better than Syria— ((laughs))	(44)
	They know Arabic well, very well,	(45)
Stella	OK, I for example don't understand	
	my mother's tongue, Morocc—	(46)
	I don't understand Moroccan,	(47)
	I understand, but I don't know	
	how to speak, you know what I mean?	(48)
	My parents spoke with me—	(49)
Samir	They speak only Arabic,	(50)
	But they know Hebrew,	(51)
Rhoda	That is, they don't, ...	(52)
	It's as if they don't dare speak,	(53)
	Eh— the opposite,	(54)
Stella	What don't they dare speak?	(55)
Rhoda	OK, I— my son too, when—	(56)
	So eh, TV, neighbors,	(57)
	But to come and speak with him	
	instead of Arabic to speak Hebrew,	(58)
	There's no reason at all,	(59)
	He needs to know—	(60)
	And it'll take root in him,	(61)

	That Hebrew is the lang—	(62)
	Arabic is his mother tongue,	(63)
	And Hebrew is a language that can—	(64)
	It may be that it'll be the language of the street,	(65)
	But, not at home,	(66)
	OK, good, and all, but not to feel that that— that it's equal, (),	(67)
	Maybe, after there is peace, maybe there will be—	(68)
	And the Jews, too, will learn (),	(69)
Lisa	No, for me— personally I never even thought about them speaking Hebrew, ...	(70)
	(193B:2:20–5:20)	

A number of interesting points emerge from this awkward stretch of interview. Most prominent is that Palestinian Israelis do not imagine Hebrew, the language of dominant society, to be a home language. In the interview, Lisa and Samir were so shocked by Stella's question "What language do you speak with your children" (line 1), that they at first misunderstood her. In suggesting that a Palestinian Israeli family might use Hebrew in the home, Stella's question is naïve, but not insincere. Stella perceives a similarity between herself, as a Mizrahi Jew, and Lisa and Samir's child: both grew up in Arabic-speaking homes. Stella finally manages to explain this perceived parallel, when she says, "In my case, for example, my parents spoke Moroccan with me ... I don't know Moroccan, but I understand when they speak with me" (lines 32–39).[20] The import of these issues to all involved in this conversation becomes clear when Samir denies that his attitudes about language in his home are "racist" (line 23). The discussion thread ends with Rhoda's suggestion that Hebrew might be an acceptable mother tongue for Israel's Palestinian residents when there is peace between Jews and Arabs in the region (line 68), but her further suggestion that Jews would learn Arabic in a utopian future (line 69) generates irony, given Stella's own story: Stella grew up surrounded by Arabic, but she never learned it.

Text 5.1 also shows a certain defensiveness among Palestinians on their children's use of Hebrew. Rhoda, for example, says, "It's as if [parents] don't dare speak the other language in the home" (lines 52–54), implying that the children are drawn to Hebrew, even if their parents "can't imagine" such a scenario. Indeed, Rhoda's opinion that it is the political conflict between Jews and Palestinians that justifies separation between Arabic and Hebrew worlds (lines 56–69) appears to contradict Samir's earlier assertion that such separation came naturally (lines 8–15).

In calling Hebrew the "language of the street," Rhoda is referring to a painful and salient problem: Israeli public culture attracts Palestinian children. In cities like Haifa, where Palestinian homes are surrounded by thriving Jewish neighborhoods, commercial centers, and cultural hot spots, the Hebrew voice of television is linked with the Hebrew voices of the street in a powerful lure to identification with the dominant. Palestinian mothers, for example, frequently complained of their children's attraction to the innovative children's programming on Israel's Hebrew-language television.

AN ARAB-JEWISH YOUTH SOCCER CLUB

In general there is very little contact between Arabs and Jews—even in the "mixed" neighborhood of Hadar Elyon. The Shutafut community center set out to increase such interaction by providing badly needed services for children.[21] Toward this end, Shutafut renovated a park, provided daycare for babies, taught art classes for older children, and organized neighborhood soccer teams for school-aged boys. I was put in charge of organizing the soccer activities.

Many Palestinian and Jewish youths from the neighborhood expressed interest in the soccer team, and early on we drew over sixty boys. Both communities were well represented. We arranged to use a school playground, and soon our twice-weekly practices were established and popular. The team's coach, Rafik, was a Palestinian man who taught at one of the Arabic-language high schools in Haifa, and who devoted much of his own time to Arab/Jewish activities. He was a talented coach and good with the kids.

Practices were run in Hebrew—out of necessity. Most of the Palestinian children had a working knowledge of Hebrew, while none of the Jewish children knew any Arabic at all. Command of Hebrew among the Palestinian boys depended on age. The oldest boys spoke Hebrew fluently, while the youngest boys had trouble understanding and speaking. In between were the boys who were most active in the club, and who were clearly frustrated. For these children, Hebrew fluency was a desired goal but a difficult achievement.

While Rafik coached the team, he skillfully mixed Hebrew with Arabic. He was perceptive enough to notice when his Hebrew explanations had been understood by all the boys. When he needed to use Arabic too, he usually spoke in that language first, making the Jewish boys wait for translations—subtly reminding them that it was they who lacked knowledge of the other's language.

When Rafik left our team, the cohesive, bilingual quality of the group left with him, and the club quickly became a site for Palestinian but not Jewish participation. One by one the Jewish boys who had joined us in the beginning stopped coming to practices. Eventually only one Jewish boy remained with the team—Yaakov, whose father was Palestinian and mother Jewish.

Interestingly, overall interest in the team dropped along with its bilingual character. Many Palestinian boys went back to the other soccer clubs run by Palestinian community service providers. It appeared to me that much of what had attracted participation on our team had been its bilingualism.

Palestinian children—those who grow up in the largely Jewish and Hebrew environment of Haifa, and those who grow up in the largely Arab environments of villages and towns—all learn Hebrew formally in school from the first grade. They learn Hebrew as a second language and as a literary language. Teachers are often Mizrahi Jews, recreating a hierarchy of dominance relations: Jews over Arabs, and Ashkenazim over Mizrahim.[22] This domination is keenly felt. Several teachers in Arabic schools maintained that the Jewish Hebrew teachers informed (or would inform) on Arab teachers' attitudes and activities to the Israeli security forces (the equivalent of the FBI in the United States). Informers or not, these Hebrew teachers are frequently the children's first, and sometimes their only, personal contact with Jews.

"Using Language as a Tool"

Nabil grew up in Rami, a village many miles from his parents' hometown of Iqrit. The latter town, along the border with Lebanon, was evacuated by order of the Israeli army in 1948 and demolished some years later. All that remains now is the church. Nabil's father is active in the political struggle waged by the displaced families of Iqrit to regain rights to their land—a struggle they have waged so far in vain.[23] Nabil remembers not liking Jews when he was young, despite his father teaching him to distinguish between the Israeli government and individual Jews.

Nabil now lives in Haifa, away from his family. He works part-time with an organization called Yami, "Children Teaching Children," a program that brings Palestinian and Jewish children together to further mutual understanding.[24] As facilitator, Nabil must translate for Palestinian and Jewish children engaged in debates that sometimes become quite heated, even hurtful. Nabil says he doesn't always translate exactly what the children say: he doesn't allow either side to use language "as a tool."

While language was at times a tool during Yami encounters, it was always a problem. I observed the Children Teaching Children program throughout a school year, following one pair of schools (one Palestinian, one Jewish) as their students met and interacted. The program was designed to focus on language in order to bridge the power gap between Arab and Jewish children. Organizers hoped that Palestinian children's command of Hebrew—in comparison to the Jewish children's complete lack of any knowledge of Arabic—would counterbalance contextual inequalities. Actual experience, however, proved otherwise. Conversation was carried out exclusively in Hebrew, and Palestinian children were frustrated by their limitation in that language.

Encounters like those orchestrated by programs like Yami constitute for most Palestinian participants their first need to use conversationally the Hebrew they learned in school. Even in Haifa most Palestinian children have limited direct contact with the Jewish world, since school systems are separate, residence patterns are segregated, and social lives are distinct. Many Palestinians, then, only begin to use Hebrew intensively when they enter the university or the world of work.

Text 5.2.   Group Work in a Foreign Language

A RESEARCH ASSISTANT, NURIT, AND I INTERVIEWED RA'ID AND HIS WIFE, JAMILA, IN THEIR HAIFA HOME. RA'ID AND JAMILA HAD BOTH STUDIED AT THE UNIVERSITY OF HAIFA.

EARLY IN THE INTERVIEW I ASKED ABOUT THEIR EXPERIENCES MOVING FROM AN ARABIC-LANGUAGE HIGH SCHOOL IN NAZARETH, WHERE THEY GREW UP, TO THE HEBREW-LANGUAGE ENVIRONMENT OF THE UNIVERSITY.

Ra'id	Now there's a problem,	(1)
	That the Arab student comes with his	
	high school Hebrew,	(2)
	But my Hebrew that I learned in high school,	(3)

	80 percent of it doesn't help me at the university,	(4)
Nurit	Why?	(5)
Ra'id	Not the Bible that I studied,	(6)
	And not the literature of Haim Nahman Bialik,[25]	(7)
	And I don't know what else ...	(8)
	It doesn't help me, not to speak Hebrew, not at all,	(9)

...

Jamila	I'll give you an example from my	
	personal experience, that I'll never forget,	(10)
	In the first year of social work school,	(11)
	There's a workshop ... that's really critical ...	(12)
	Whoever doesn't pass doesn't continue,	(13)
	And this workshop consists of talking,	
	a really verbal workshop,	(14)
	Role-playing games, how to play roles	
	of applicant and caregiver and patient,	(15)

...

And with all the technicalities of the therapy,	(16)
And I remember how difficult that was	
for me as an Arab (woman) ...	(17)
To play this game, in another language,	(18)
And it was a real competition,	(19)
I remember that the groups were really small,	
twelve to fifteen people,	(20)
And we all just had to compete ...	
everyone had to prove himself,	(21)
And at the end we'd get a grade based on	
how much we took initiative,	(22)
How much we talked, how we talked,	
the types of sentences we used,	(23)
That was really difficult,	(24)
I remember how tough that was for me,	
and (I was relatively good in Hebrew)	(25)

...

Because my parents had Jewish friends	
I had some experience speaking Hebrew,	(26)
And even so it was so hard for me to speak, ...	(27)

(37A:35:35–36:00, 38:37–40:40)

Many Palestinian Israelis have very similar experiences in the working world. Language, of course, is critical in many jobs, and finding work in Israel is difficult enough for Palestinians, who face systematic discrimination in the labor market because many high-paying jobs are restricted to those who have done military service—an impossibility for most Palestinians.

Learning Hebrew is the theme of the Israeli author Sami Michael's 1987 novel *Xatzutzra ba-Vadi*, "Trumpet in the Wadi." The novel, which is set in Haifa in the 1980s, romanticizes Arab-Jewish relations through the symbolism of learning and teaching Hebrew. The story unfolds in Wadi Nisnas, an Arab neighborhood of Haifa (see chapter 2). Huda, a young Palestinian woman, holds a good job as a travel agent at a Jewish-owned agency in downtown Haifa. She falls in love with a Russian Jewish immigrant who has just arrived in Israel and who moves into an apartment in Huda's building without knowing a word of either Hebrew or Arabic. The poignant, and eventually tragic, tale of their love focuses on the irony of the Palestinian Huda teaching Hebrew to the Jewish immigrant. The novel embeds the universal human story of language learning in the particularly Israeli master narrative of Jewish homecoming. Ultimate acceptance of Jews, Israel, and Hebrew comes in the form of the native Arab herself doing the teaching.

Arabs learning Hebrew was also thematized in an earlier and much more famous novel, A. B. Yehoshua's *Ha-M'ahev*, "The Lover." In Yehoshua's novel, which is also set in Haifa, a Jewish girl, Dafna, and a Palestinian boy, Na'im, fall in love. Na'im works for Dafna's father and is smitten with love the first time he lays eyes on her, but Dafna sees Na'im only as a curiosity at first. It is when Na'im recites from memory the poems of Nathan Alterman, a classic poet (like Bialik) of romantic Zionist themes, that Dafna begins to take an interest.

The poetry of Alterman and Bialik, the classic Zionist texts in difficult, esoteric Hebrew, still formed a core component of the Hebrew curriculum in the early 1990s in Arabic-language schools in Israel, as Ra'id alludes to in text 5.2. Palestinian learners of Hebrew thus continued to study these texts even as Israeli Hebrew-language schools had modernized their literature curricula. This disparity signals that Hebrew has been successfully revived, but that Israeliness must still be imposed.

Palestinians feel necessity and pressure to speak Hebrew in the working world. It is in the workplace that one finds Palestinians code-switching between Arabic and Hebrew (see "Arabic-Hebrew Code-Switching," this chapter), and it is in the workplace— even Arab sector workplaces—that use of Hebrew becomes an active and creative part of the Palestinian repertoire.

TEXT 5.3.   ARABIC IN THE WORKPLACE

LATER IN THE INTERVIEW WITH RA'ID AND JAMILA (SEE
TEXT 5.2), THE CONVERSATION HAS MOVED ON TO LANGUAGE
USE AT WORK.

Jamila	Where I work, for example, we're all Arabs and Dru—	(1)
	There aren't any Jews,	(2)
	So all the (memos) they do in Hebrew,	(3)
	And even the agency, we belong to an agency,	(4)
	So they do all the memos to the agency in Hebrew,	(5)
	And staff meetings, even when they write that there's a staff meeting, the protocol,	(6)
	They do everything in Hebrew,	(7)
	When they answer the telephone immediately they answer in Hebrew,	(8)
	"*Boker tov*" [Hebrew: "Good morning"],	(9)
	And "*Mo'atza*" [Hebrew: "agency"],	(10)
	And things like that …	(11)

And that really grates on me, and it's annoying,   (12)
So I rebel, I kind of really try to speak Arabic ...   (13)
Especially when I speak with social workers,   (14)
And ... I— right when I started to work
    at Dalia,[26]   (15)
I really—   (16)
It made me switch back, to try and make
    an effort to speak Heb— in Arabic,[27]   (17)
And I even took on the job of organizing
    the staff meetings,   (18)
And all of a sudden they don't understand,   (19)
And they really argued with me,   (20)
"Why are you writing in Arabic?   (21)
Write in Hebrew, it'll be easier for you",   (22)
Because I really didn't find some words
    in Arabic,   (23)
And I— it's real clear to me,   (24)
Old women who don't even know
    how to read or write,   (25)
You see them start talking with you in Hebrew,   (26)
Even when they pronounce it all wrong,   (27)
But they speak Hebrew,   (28)
I'm going along the street,   (29)
I meet children aged three to four,   (30)
And they're speaking Hebrew with each other,   (31)
It's simply become— ... (37B:17:55–19:44)   (32)

Jamila's narrative relates an unpleasant memory of feeling pressure to use Hebrew even as a social worker who provided services exclusively to Arabic-speaking Israelis. Her Druze coworkers urge her to use Hebrew at work, arguing that it is easier to write and speak about technical matters in Hebrew, which has highly developed technical vocabularies. As Jamila notes in line 23, the underdevelopment of Arabic as it is spoken in Israel is a serious problem (see Amara and Spolsky 1986), but such vocabulary "underdevelopment" is a social, not a linguistic, phenomenon. Many of the technical terms used in Hebrew are borrowed from English—and might also be borrowed into Arabic.

Learning Arabic

For Palestinian Israelis, the negotiation of identity through the nuanced use of Hebrew occurs within the context of a bilingual, or dual, language system in which the primary assertion of identity is the maintenance of Arabic as a mother tongue and the primary language of Arab identity. The linguistic negotiation of Arab identity in Israel is therefore first and foremost accomplished by speaking, learning, and teaching Arabic. Yet even this assertion of Arab identity is significantly influenced by the control and power of dominant Israeli, Hebrew society.

Palestinian identity is richly associated with the Arabic language, as Jamila's feelings about work, expressed in text 5.3, indicate. For Jamila, the (perceived) lack of technical vocabulary development in Arabic constrains the bounds of Palestinian identity. She and others look to the surrounding centers of Arab culture—Cairo, Damascus, Beirut—for models, but find little guidance. Attitudes toward language are deeply imbued with tradition, religion, and heritage in Arab society.

In a broader, Middle Eastern context, Palestinian identity is an emergent and vigorous phenomenon, coincident with a growing cultural leadership of the Palestinian intelligentsia. In Jordan and elsewhere linguists have noted that new prestige dialects involve the adoption of Palestinian forms (Abd-el-Jawad 1986, 1987). Palestinian writers, including Emil Habibi, Mahmoud Darwish, and Samih Al-Qasim, have become leading figures in modern Arabic literature. In Israel, however, this association of Arabic with Palestinian identity cuts two ways: it expresses Arab identity, and it divides Israeli citizens and residents of the Occupied Territories.

SPEAKING (ARABIC) FOR THE PALESTINIANS

When the great Palestinian writer Emil Habibi was awarded the Israel Prize for Literature, I decided to attend a ceremony in his honor. The ceremony marked the first time that Israel's most prestigious literary honor had been given to a Palestinian writer.

Habibi was an elder statesman both in the Arab literary world and the Israeli political scene—a striking combination. His literary masterpiece, *The Secret Life of Saeed, The Ill-Fated Pessoptimist*, skillfully adapted the satirical style of Voltaire's *Candide* to portray the impossible situation faced by Palestinians living in Israel after 1948.[28] His political life included serving as editor of *Al-Ittihad*, "The Union," Israel's Arabic-language daily newspaper, and as a member of Parliament for many years.

Speakers at the ceremony included Sasson Somekh, a Jewish Israeli professor of Arabic literature, who spoke about Habibi's place in the Arabic literary world, Habibi himself, and Faisal Husseini, a leading figure at the time in the Palestinian resistance in the Occupied Territories. The meeting was conducted in Hebrew despite the vast majority of Arabic speakers in the audience.

Habibi was an elderly man at the time. As he spoke I was struck by the difficulty with which he strung Hebrew words together into sentences. He spoke haltingly, almost painfully searching for words and expressions. Most striking about language-use at this ceremony, though, was that for the first time I heard Faisal Husseini speak in Hebrew. His Hebrew was fluent, flawless, and elegant.[29]

My surprise at hearing Husseini speak Hebrew paradoxically reflects the increasing symbolic value of Arabic in the struggle for Palestinian identity. I had heard Husseini speak on Israeli television many times, but in such formal, public, and official contexts, he spoke either in English or in Arabic. The popular Israeli novelist David Grossman provides a good example of the meaning attached to the use of Arabic in Palestinian encounters with Israelis in his book *Sleeping on a Wire: Conversations with Palestinians in Israel*.[30] In one chapter Grossman describes a meeting he had set up among residents of the former Barta'a, a town that the 1948 armistice divided between Jordan (i.e., the West Bank) and Israel. Barta'a remains divided today, and Grossman invited to this meeting representatives of East Barta'a, which is in the Occupied West Bank, and West Barta'a, which is in the State of Israel. Grossman describes a strikingly choreographed pattern of language use. All participants in the conversation knew both Hebrew and Arabic fluently, yet the residents of (Occupied) East Barta'a spoke Arabic to Grossman, while those from (Israeli) West Barta'a spoke to him in Hebrew (Grossman 1992:39–54). What is striking about this interaction is the persistence of the Israeli Arabs in using Hebrew, even in the presence of their Palestinian cohorts (and former neighbors). This marked usage also brings into direct relief the power of the Arabic language to symbolize and constitute a Palestinian identity.

The connection to a modern Palestinian identity is, however, inseparable from the associations of Arabic with Arab culture, tradition, and heritage. Arabic, as the language of the Qur'an, the language of the proud history of scientific, philosophical, and literary writings, and the language that unites peoples from Baghdad (in Iraq) to Marrakech (in Morocco), partakes also of an important spiritual connection to Arab culture. This culture is renowned for a love of language, both in the centrality of oral and poetic forms (Abu-Lughod 1986; Caton 1990) and the celebration of ancient roots, such as the proud association of Bedouin speech with the classical form. Indeed even the wide gulf between spoken and written forms of the language (a phenomenon linguists call *diglossia*), which positions all discourse within a hierarchy, serves to make the formal style of written Arabic more special and exalted.

Within Israel, however, there is a growing tendency for leading Arab writers to write in Hebrew, coincident with a parallel interest on the part of Hebrew Israel to access the writings of Arab Israelis. Representative of the latter trend is the publication of a collection of Palestinian short stories translated into Hebrew as *Xayalim Shel Mayim*, "Soldiers of Water," in 1989. Amazingly, this was one of the very first instances of Palestinian literature being published in Israel in Hebrew translation. Definitive of the former trend is Anton Shammas's notorious novel *Arabeskot*, "Arabesques," which came out in 1986 and took Jewish Israel—or at least its literary elite—by storm. The book's impact stemmed in part from the fact that Shammas—a Palestinian—wrote the book in Hebrew, rather than Arabic. Even more striking, however, was the quality of Shammas's language: *Arabeskot* was written in a rich and eloquent Hebrew—a Hebrew worthy of Bialik.

Yet these trends do not indicate an emergent bilingualism in Israel. There is little bilingualism in this officially bilingual country. Arabic and Hebrew coexist as dual languages, as paired languages, as opposed languages. Although many Palestinians speak Hebrew fluently, none do so in the home. Nowhere do Arab children speak to their parents in Hebrew. Nowhere do Arab children struggle to retain fluency in the ancestral language. And in very few places do Palestinians switch back and forth between Arabic and Hebrew within the same conversation.

ARABIC-HEBREW CODE-SWITCHING 1

Beit Ha-Gefen is a well-funded institution that promotes Arab-Jewish interaction in Haifa and that is relatively well known throughout Israel. Several times a year it sponsors high-profile events, such as Arabic Book Month, the National Dabka Festival,[31] or periodic exhibits of artwork by Palestinian and Jewish artists. Most of the time, however, the facility serves as a community center for the adjacent Arab neighborhood, Wadi Nisnas, its pretensions of bringing Arabs and Jews together in any active sense being limited to some school-based hafgasha programs.[32]

More than anything else Beit Ha-Gefen symbolizes Israeli pluralist ideology—Jewish visions of plurality. In a concrete sense, Beit Ha-Gefen is the establishment's means of contact with the Arab community. As such, it is suspect within the Palestinian community, where it is seen as providing only a hegemonized means of representing an Arab voice in Haifa.[33]

I tried to arrange an interview with the Palestinian director of Beit Ha-Gefen without much success. On several occasions a scheduled interview was postponed; once an appointment simply passed by without his arriving. After the latter experience I mentioned my frustration to a friend who had once worked at Beit Ha-Gefen. With my friend's help I finally managed to meet with the director.

The interview was conducted in Hebrew. In the middle of our conversation, the director took a long phone call, which I overheard. His phone conversation was conducted mostly in Arabic, but it was laced with conspicuous, sentence-length code-switches into Hebrew.

ARABIC-HEBREW CODE-SWITCHING 2

My fieldwork in Haifa included participant observation in the emergency ward of a Haifa hospital. I hoped to study real-life constructions of and negotiations over identity, and the emergency room staff was interested in how language affected the provision of services.

In observing language use in the hospital setting, I was struck by a pattern of code-switching between Arabic and Hebrew among many of the emergency room doctors. Of the four senior doctors who staffed the emergency room, three were native speakers of Arabic.[34] In casual conversation, while on duty but during the pauses between actively treating patients, these Palestinian doctors switched casually back and forth between Arabic and Hebrew.

The code-switching I saw in the hospital emergency ward was the most pervasive Arabic/Hebrew code-switching I witnessed among Palestinians. The fact that Palestinian Israelis do not, in general, switch between Arabic and Hebrew in casual conversation stands out in Israel because many other kinds of code-switching as an unmarked choice (Myers-Scotton 1982) are common. Educated Israelis from all backgrounds, for example, switch into, and out of, English (Cooper 1977; Maschler 1994). Jewish Israelis switch between Hebrew and a heritage language, such as Yiddish, Spanish (Berk-Seligson 1986), or Arabic (Schely-Newman 1991).

In this context the code-switching among Palestinian doctors in a Haifa emergency room demands an explanation, and a second observation about language use in the hospital emergency room provides one. The hospital emergency room was the one place in Israel where I, as a native-speaker of English with limited Hebrew and a thick American accent, was never addressed in English. This was surprising, since the doctors and nurses who worked on the ward were all highly educated and knew English well, and these conditions generally led Israelis to switch into English while speaking with an American. These two observations suggest that the hospital constituted an exceptional domain of language use, a context where Hebrew was defined as the language to be used, even when such use violated broader societal norms.[35]

Israel is officially trilingual, with Hebrew, Arabic, and English all sharing status as official languages. The position of Arabic as an official language alongside Hebrew is reflected in the government television broadcasts in Arabic and in the separate Arabic-language school system (see chapter 4) but in few other aspects of Israeli life. In general, the patterns of when, where, and how Arabic is spoken, heard, written, or seen in Israel reproduce and represent the dominant social hierarchy in Israeli society.

For example, in their 1991 book *The Languages of Jerusalem*, Bernard Spolsky and Robert Cooper provide a fascinating analysis of the languages used (and not used) in the street signs of the old city of Jerusalem (Spolsky and Cooper 1991:74–94). The authors carefully document dramatic changes in the use of Hebrew, Arabic, and English on these signs over the past hundred years, and how these changes of language use coincide with social and political changes. They note, for example, that during the period of Jordanian sovereignty, 1948–1967, signs excluded Hebrew, and the Arabic version was placed at the top of the sign. When Israel gained control, in 1967, however, Hebrew was placed on top. They further note that recent changes in Israeli politics have resulted in the removal of Arabic from signs on many public buildings (e.g. police stations), despite the fact that over 70 percent of the local population are native speakers of Arabic, not Hebrew.

A similar analysis could be made of street signs in other parts of Israel. In Haifa, for example, very old street signs include three languages, Arabic, Hebrew, and English, but one sees these signs primarily in Arab neighborhoods, like Wadi Nisnas.[36] Many new street signs are also trilingual, but these signs are posted only on main thoroughfares. Thus road signs that give real traffic information are provided only in Hebrew and English outside of specifically Arab neighborhoods.

The distribution of languages in public is similar for other domains as well. Money, for example, displays Arabic and English as well as Hebrew, but store signs include Arabic only in neighborhoods that are heavily Arab demographically. Even here one almost never finds a store sign that does not include Hebrew. Hebrew newspapers were found everywhere in Haifa, but Arabic newspapers were sold only in the Arab neighborhoods (see "Buying an Arabic Newspaper" in chapter 2). Radio and television broadcasts treat Hebrew and Arabic on parallel footing in some respects, but in other ways the position of Arabic is distinctly subordinated. Movies from European countries, for example, are shown on television with subtitles, and these are usually provided in both Hebrew and Arabic. Movies shown in theaters, however, rarely include Arabic subtitling. And the prime-time television news program *Mabat la-Hadashot* provides only Hebrew subtitles for the many interviews and stories that unfold in English.[37]

Beyond such forms of institutional language use are subtler, more finely tuned patterns of when and where languages are spoken and heard. As with written Arabic on signs and in newspapers, spoken Arabic is also highly constrained in its geographic distribution. In Haifa one rarely hears Arabic spoken outside of specifically Arab neighborhoods. Hadar, for example, is a thriving commercial hub, bustling with activity, movement, and talk. Even though Hadar adjoins Wadi Nisnas, Haifa's largest Arab neighborhood, one rarely hears Arabic spoken in Hadar.[38] Hebrew is used in any social interaction that includes a Jewish Israeli, no matter how large the majority of Arabs (see "Speaking (Arabic) for the Palestinians," this chapter). At a retreat for Re'ut, the Jewish-Arab youth group (see chapter 4), a talk given by Palestinian journalists from the West Bank about Palestinian identity was given alternately in Hebrew and in translation into Hebrew from Arabic. The question-and-answer session following the journalists' presentation was dominated by questions from the Palestinian youth, yet the structure of marked Hebrew use and/or laborious translation to and from Arabic continued.

"Bir Zeit University"

At the university one day I was waiting for a class to begin. I sat down in a chair at the end of a long hallway, near windows that afforded a scenic view. Suddenly I realized that I heard only Arabic being spoken around me, and I recalled that many Jews in Haifa derisively refer to the University of Haifa as Bir Zeit, the name of a West Bank university, because it "feels" to them like an Arab environment. The percentage of Palestinian students is not much greater than the percentage of Palestinian Arabs in the city as a whole, but Haifa University is a place where Arabic can be—and is—spoken freely.

In my interviews with Arab Israelis in Haifa, I often asked whether there were contexts in Israeli life in which Palestinians felt uncomfortable speaking Arabic. Response to this question was nearly unanimous: in most places of public interaction Palestinians felt self-conscious speaking one of Israel's official languages. One woman I interviewed said that she felt so uncomfortable speaking Arabic in public that she would speak to her Palestinian friend in Hebrew while riding on Tel Aviv buses.

TEXT 5.4.   HARASSMENT IN A DEPARTMENT STORE

Cynthia	Actually in Haifa it's more comfortable	
	than in Tel Aviv,	(1)
	I remember in Tel Aviv,	(2)
	Actually at that time I was very religious,	(3)
	And I walked around with a cross,[39]	(4)
	And I went into a department store on Allenby,[40]	(5)
	Eh— He asked me for my identity card,[41]	(6)
	I said,	(7)
	"Why"?	(8)
	And I saw that he was looking at the cross,	(9)
	You know at the entrance,	(10)

I said to him,	(11)
"Why? because I'm wearing a cross?	(12)
Or because I'm an Arab?"	(13)
So he said,	(14)
"I don't know that you're an Arab,	(15)
But you look foreign",	(16)
I said,	(17)
"Because of the cross?"	(18)
...	
He actually held onto my identity card,	(19)
...	
Afterwards my friend told me he's not allowed	
to do something like that,	(20)
I went back to him,	(21)
"I know it's forbidden for you to keep	
my identity card,"	(22)
But someone was following us around,	(23)
I couldn't continue,	(24)
I left,	(25)
There I really felt people were following us,	(26)
I really felt it, ... (33A:32:23–34:02)	(27)

NEWS OF TERRORISM

I vividly recall riding home on a crowded Haifa bus one afternoon when the radio news announced an act of "terrorism" in northern Israel. A hush filled the bus and lasted for several minutes after the news report had ended. The experience impressed me deeply—even though I did not feel personally threatened by the news.

When Arabic is spoken in Israel, it is inflected as *Israeli Arabic*. One veteran American observer of Arab societies remarked, upon visiting Israel for the first time, how differently Arabic was spoken in Israel from in the centers of Arab culture outside Israel. He cited a lack of demonstrativeness and effusiveness. Israeli Arabs themselves describe their Arabic as heavily influenced by Israeli culture and Hebrew. The popular stereotype of Hebrew influence on Israeli Arabic is the prominence of certain Hebrew lexical items that have been widely incorporated into Arabic. The word *b'seder*, for example, means "OK" in Hebrew, but has come to be used much more generally as a discourse marker in Arabic conversation (Katriel and Griefat 1988). Similarly, Israeli Arabic is peppered with Hebrew words and phrases for technical terms or Israeli institutions (Amara and Spolsky 1986). The impact of Hebrew on the Arabic spoken in Israel goes well beyond lexical items and discourse markers, however, as several of the Palestinians I interviewed told amusing stories about their Arabic being so infused with Hebrew that they had difficulty making themselves understood while traveling in Egypt.

Such stories were told tongue-in-cheek, referring more positively to the identification with an Israeli identity than to any real shame she felt with respect to Egyptians, but the perception persists that prestigious Arabic is spoken outside of Israel. This perception stems in part from the period of isolation from 1948 to 1967, when Palestinians who remained in the territories that became Israel were cut off from communication with the rest of the Arab world. Dramatic changes and developments in the Arab world took Israeli Arabs by storm in 1967, when communication with Egypt and Jordan increased through the newly occupied territories of the West Bank and Gaza. It also derives, however, from Israeli discourse, which devalues Arabic in relation to Hebrew. Arabic literature produced in Israel receives little critical attention in Israeli literary circles, despite its importance in the Arab world.

Israeli discourse also devalues Israeli Arabic in the way that Arabic and Arabic literature are taught in Israeli schools and universities. The Arabic curriculum—which until recently was determined by national ministries controlled by Jewish officials—is rigidly traditional in its approach to language and literature. According to Samir, the Palestinian schoolteacher quoted in text 5.1, the national aptitude tests that all Israeli high-school students take, and that determine a student's chances of studying at a university, are much more difficult for Palestinian students than for Jewish students. Samir argued that these "psychometric" tests put Arab students at a disadvantage because they must take an Arabic literature exam that is heavily oriented toward a classical and scholastic Arabic that has little relevance for students today. Another Palestinian schoolteacher I interviewed noted that Palestinian teachers face many obstacles when they try to introduce modern, topical, and close-to-home materials into the curriculum. The government, by insisting on a classical curriculum, effectively prevents Israeli/Palestinian Arabic from being presented as a high-status model for spoken and literary language.

The control Israel exerts over the teaching, learning and use of Arabic is clearest at the university. Palestinian university students gravitate toward the humanities, and often specifically to Arabic language and literature, because finding employment in technical fields, for which military experience is often prerequisite, is difficult. Such students are often shocked to learn that Arabic literature courses are taught by Jewish professors—in Hebrew. Many Palestinian students arrive at the university straight from small-town high schools far from centers of Jewish population, and for some the university constitutes their first real encounter with Jews, with Hebrew, and with non-Arabic education (see text 5.2). Moreover, these classes often generate awkward encounters, since many of the Jews who study Arabic at the university level do so for official, military, or surveillance (i.e., "security") purposes (see "Arabic and Soldiers," this chapter).

Israeli discourse thus places contradictory constraints on Arabic. On the one hand, the systematic separation of Arab education, television, residence, and so on, maintains a relatively impermeable boundary between the two groups. On the other hand, discouraging use of Arabic in public and preserving a classical Arabic pedagogy enforce a switch to Hebrew. These contradictory tendencies can be seen in the language use of one Israeli group that is intermediate between Arab and Jewish identities, the Druze.

TALK AT THE UNIVERSITY POOL HALL

Hamdan and I were a team at the pool table. Hamdan was a dashing young man—tall and handsome, with a congenial manner. He had always been particularly friendly to me, inviting me to visit his family, for example, in a Druze village near the university. He was also a good pool player, but on this occasion, teamed with me, he had no chance. We lost.

Playing pool at the campus club was socially structured much like the basketball and soccer games I participated in (see chapter 4). Thus pool-playing teams usually recreated the distinction between Arab and Jew, and it was even rare that Arab teams and Jewish teams would play against each other.

Hamdan was different. He hung out with Jews. He dated a Jewish woman. He played pool with Jewish partners. He spoke Hebrew. On this particular night a struggle developed. Some of the other Arab and Druze men objected to Hamdan's speaking Hebrew when he spoke with them. Hamdan responded aggressively, and the conflict seemed ready to explode into violence when it was at last defused.

Learning "Morokayit"

Arabic is an important language for many Israelis. For Palestinian Israelis it is the language of nation, of home, of politics. For Mizrahi Israelis it is the language of heritage, of the past, of stigma. For Jewish Israelis it is the language of conflict. Paradoxically, Jewish Israel unlearns Arabic, only to relearn it, as the processes of language shift discourage Mizrahi children of Arabic-speaking immigrants from learning their parents' language, while the necessities of Israeli security mandate that knowledge of Arabic is Israel's best defense.

A FAMILY CONNECTION

Of the several research assistants I worked with during my years in Israel, I got along best with Stella. She and I hit it off on a personal level in a way that never crystallized in the other pairings. We found that we shared interests and habits. One day, for example, while riding a bus to an interview across town, we discovered that we shared the quirky habit of counting stairs—I counted 144 steps as I ascended from the bus stop to my home; Stella counted a few more along her own route home.

Stella also took a personal interest in my research. She confided to me one day that our interviews with Palestinians interested her because her father, just before his death, had told her of his fond memories of warm relations he had had with his Arab neighbors in Morocco before moving to Israel. Our interviews gave her an opportunity to find out more about this nostalgic past, and to come to terms with the apparent contradictions between her father's fond memories and the official history of discrimination she had learned in school.

One reason that Stella enjoyed our interviews with Palestinian Israelis is that the social separation between Arabs and Jews in Israel is so great that for her—indeed for all of the research assistants I worked with—our first interview with a Palestinian Haifan constituted her first personal encounter with an Israeli Arab. As a Moroccan Jew, whose mother's mother tongue was Arabic, Stella seemed to be working through in a personal way the very problems of Mizrahi identity that I was working through in a professional way: the close ties with Arabness, in contrast to a deep-seated opposition to Arabs. Thus her naïve questions to Samir and Lisa in text 5.1 were genuine. Stella wondered if Palestinian families in Haifa were not undergoing the same powerful reidentification process her family had suffered.

TEXT 5.5.   SPEAKING ARABIC IN BEIT SHE'AN

THE FOLLOWING EXCHANGE OCCURRED IN AN INTERVIEW
WITH SALMAN NATUR, A PALESTINIAN DRUZE AUTHOR,
ABOUT THE INTERVIEWS HE CONDUCTED IN BEIT SHE'AN, A
CENTER OF MOROCCAN JEWISH IDENTITY (SEE TEXT 2.6).

Dan:	By the way, did you speak Arabic with the people?	(1)
Salman:	Arabic? eh—	(2)
Dan:	Do some speak Arabic?	(3)
Salman:	Almost all of them, speak Arabic, but Arabic that I don't understand, ...	(4)
	(66A:43:11–43:24)	

When Mizrahi Jews in Israel speak about the language their parents spoke, they rarely call it "Arabic." In text 5.1, for example, Stella repeatedly referred to the language her parents spoke as *Morokayit*, "Moroccan" (e.g., in lines 33 and 37). Strictly speaking, the Jews of Arab lands did not speak Arabic, but rather their own Jewish dialect of Arabic, often referred to as Judeo-Arabic (see Blau 1981a; Chetrit 1985), but labeling the language Morokayit avoids the stigma that attaches to Arabic. Judeo-Arabic is a "Jewish Language" (see Fishman 1985), sociolinguistically similar to the better known example of Yiddish. Both are languages that were used by Jews for in-group communication within Jewish communities that were surrounded by other dominant languages (see Harshav 1990). Judeo-Arabic is, as the name implies, a dialect of Arabic; similarly, Yiddish is a dialect of German. The third great Jewish language is Ladino, a dialect of Spanish that was spoken in Turkey, Greece, and other places in the post-Inquisition Sephardi diaspora (see Harris 1994). Morokayit partakes of *moreshet*, "heritage," which is Jewish, and not Arab (see Dominguez 1989).

A PALESTINIAN JEW

When I arrived in Israel I was introduced to a family who were not related to me but who, through their kindness and generosity, made me feel as if they were. Sarah and her husband, Moshe, lived with their youngest daughter in a modest Haifa apartment. A distant aunt of Sarah's was very sick, dying of complications from cancer, bedridden, and in and out of hospitals. The old woman's own family was split by bad feeling and feuds, and care and visiting had fallen to Sarah. I began to go with her to visit the aunt.

The old woman was weak and in pain, but a warm and vibrant personality shone through nonetheless. My relationship to her was distant at best, and my command of Hebrew very poor at the time. Nonetheless, the old woman spoke with me as best she could, mixing Hebrew and Arabic with some English she had learned half a century before. She had grown up in Haifa before there was an Israel. She was a Palestinian Jew. Hebrew she had learned from her children; her own first language was Arabic.

Sarah spoke a combination of Hebrew and Arabic with her aunt, switching constantly between the two languages, but she rarely spoke Arabic to anyone else. Only once did I hear her use Arabic with a Palestinian, for example. On our way into the hospital one day she whispered a friendly greeting to an Arab woman also on her way to visit a patient. None of Sarah's children speak or understand Arabic.

Language shift among Jewish Israelis is very pronounced. Few children learn the languages of their parents. None of the children of the Moroccan families I interviewed had learned Arabic in childhood, although several said they had chosen to study it later, in school.

NOT LEARNING IRAQI JEWISH ARABIC

Sharon's parents came from Iraq and spoke (Jewish) Iraqi Arabic at home when she was growing up. As an adult Sharon had decided to move back into the neighborhood where she had been raised. In the intervening twenty years the neighborhood had returned to being an Arab, Muslim neighborhood, and Sharon was proud that her young son was learning Arabic from the neighborhood children. Sharon herself speaks Hebrew with her Palestinian neighbors, even as she expresses hope that her son will learn Arabic. The passive knowledge of (Iraqi) Arabic that she received from her parents does not allow her to converse in Arabic.

TEXT 5.6.   "THEY'RE JEWISH ARABS"

IN AN INTERVIEW WITH DALIA, A YOUNG, ASHKENAZI ISRAELI WOMAN, MY RESEARCH ASSISTANT, NURIT, WHOSE FATHER WAS MIZRAHI (SEE "AN UNTAPED INTERVIEW," CHAPTER 3), HAS ASKED WHETHER DALIA DISTINGUISHES ASHKENAZI FROM MIZRAHI ISRAELIS:

Dalia	() I mean I could also make a mistake,	(1)
	() that it could be an Arab Jew,	(2)
	I mean eh—	(3)
	That's my definition for Mizrahim here in Israel,	(4)
	I think they're Arabs in essence,	(5)
	Jewish Arabs,	(6)
	But eh— that's not a problem,	(7)
	It's like me being an Ashkenazi (),	(8)
Nurit	Interesting that you say Jewish Arab,	
	how did you arrive at this definition?	(9)
Dalia	They're Jewish Arabs,	(10)
	I mean their tradition, their language,	
	their mentality,	(11)
	It's an Arab mentality,	(12)
	They came from the Arab countries,	(13)
Nurit	Yes,	(14)

Dalia	They're Arabs in essence, they speak Arabic at home,	(15)
Nurit	The new generation too?	(16)
Dalia	I don't think the new generation does,	(17)
Nurit	Are you in contact with people eh— Jewish Arabs?	(18)
Dalia	Not in any special contact,	(19)
	My brother-in-law for example, he—	(20)
	His parents came from Syria,	(21)
	So at their house they spoke Arabic, the parents,	(22)
	But I think (that) the young generation is trying to shake loose from that a bit,	(23)
	How it's an embarrassment for them,	(24)
	This thing of their parents speaking Arabic,	(25)
	And don't know Hebrew, and the—	(26)
	And anyway to say to them that they're Arabs or something it's a terrible humiliation,	(27)
Nurit	Is it more of a shame than English?	(28)
Dalia	Yes … for the educated it's reversed,	(29)
	There's the idea of national pride to turn around and say that I'm Iraqi and I'm Moroccan and I'm proud of that and—	(30)
	But that's only among educated people,	(31)
	Maybe it's also a matter of showing that I'm educated despite the fact that I came from there … (31A:12:40–14:39)	(32)

Dalia's comments in text 5.6 on the shame associated with Mizrahi Jews speaking Arabic are particularly interesting, given that Dalia had many Palestinian friends in Haifa, had dated a Palestinian man, and had tried to learn Arabic herself.

TEXT 5.7. STUDYING ARABIC AS A SECOND LANGUAGE

LATER IN THE SAME INTERVIEW WITH DALIA, WE ASK ABOUT HER RELATIONS WITH PALESTINIANS IN HAIFA:

Nurit	And you speak Arabic?	(1)
Dalia	No, I'm sorry to say it, but I don't speak Arabic,	(2)
	I tried, but that was for me— th—	(3)
	It was in a course that I took with Yehudit,[42]	(4)
	It was a course on Arab-Jewish coexistence in education,	(5)
	So we worked in pairs, a Jew and an Arab in schools,	(6)
	And there was one Arab man who didn't have a partner,	(7)
	And they decided to assign him the project to teach the Jewish folks in the class Arabic,	(8)
	Naturally there was a powerful crush of interest,	(9)
	I was the only one,	(10)
	Great people the Jews,	(11)

So that was it,	(12)
He was a guy I couldn't get along with,	(13)
I mean—it wasn't—and I gave up that idea fast,	(14)
It didn't work, but I understand a little ...	(15)

(31A:8:48–9:30)

Liberal Jews in Israel, those interested in what is called in Hebrew *du-kiyum*, "coexistence," frequently express the desire to learn the language of the Other. Many Hebrew-language schools offer Arabic—indeed the government periodically requires its study—but the harsh connection to military utility is never far beneath the surface of learning Arabic in Israel.

ARABIC AND SOLDIERS

Ulpan Akiva was widely regarded—both in the United States and in Israel—as the best place to study spoken Arabic in Israel. Unfortunately, I learned that when it comes to teaching Arabic in Israel, the very best should not be mistaken for good.

I had just arrived in Israel. Since I had studied Arabic for four years in graduate school and had only recently begun to learn Hebrew, I understood Arabic better than Hebrew. But the Arabic I had learned in college was of little use to me. Because of the powerful Arabic diglossia—in Israel, just as in every country where Arabic is spoken—the spoken vernacular differs considerably from the formal written variety. My university training had taught me only the written variety. I could therefore read a newspaper, but I had difficulty understanding even the simplest of conversations.

To be sure, one sometimes hears the formal Modern Standard Arabic (*fusha*) spoken—in political speeches, in network news broadcasts, in old Egyptian movies—but this just exacerbated the situation: when I spoke my formal Arabic with Arab friends in the university dorms, my interlocutors broke up in peals of laughter. Broadcast news sounded very funny coming out of the mouth of a jeans-clad, baby-faced American. After some persistence, of course, my friends did get used to hearing me speak fusha, but they always laughed at one another when they adopted the formal style so that I could understand. This was just too embarrassing. Those whose English was good switched to that language, but, in deference to those who knew less English, we mostly spoke Hebrew.

For this reason I enrolled at Ulpan Akiva, hoping to learn enough colloquial Palestinian Arabic to converse. My course coincided with the Gulf War, which produced some extraordinary conditions. In my class—the advanced class—there were only six students: a retired engineer and a young music teacher who just wanted to learn Arabic; myself, who needed Arabic for my research; and three officials in the Israeli administration of the Occupied Territories, including two young tax collectors.

Periodically we were joined by a soldier. The first time this happened the two tax collectors played a joke on me. They introduced a young man dressed in a green army uniform and carrying an automatic rifle as a "Palestinian"[43] who had signed up with the Israeli army. I was confused for a few moments, caught between their improbable story and several other equally implausible scenarios, until the soldier himself laughed, slapped

me on the back, and said, "You don't have to be afraid. I'm not really a
Palestinian. I'm a Jew, like you!"

The vast majority of those studying Arabic at Ulpan Akiva were women
soldiers. The women were participants in an extensive program to train
Arabic language teachers. After several months of the training at Ulpan
Akiva, these young women would be sent into elementary schools throughout Israel to teach—in full uniform—basic Arabic to young children.

The director of the Arabic program at Ulpan Akiva was a Muslim
Palestinian, and the main teacher for the women soldiers was a Druze soldier,
but those who taught my course were all elderly men who had come to
Israel from Iraq. The style of teaching contrasted starkly with that of the
Hebrew classes at Ulpan Akiva. In the Hebrew ulpan, classes were conducted
in Hebrew, spoken proficiency was encouraged, and communicative
competence was emphasized. In the Arabic ulpan, spoken Arabic was taught
in Hebrew, exercises involved line-by-line translations of written sentences,
and the readings consisted of folktales, legends, and myths that portrayed
Palestinians as anachronistic peasants, if not simpletons.

Some school programs, such as Yami (see chapter 4), that bring Palestinian and
Jewish students together explicitly focus on the learning and teaching of Arabic.
Shutafut, the Hadar neighborhood center (see chapter 4), offered Arabic lessons, but
low levels of commitment and attendance limited progress to the learning of token
words and phrases. On two occasions I suggested to Palestinian friends, who wanted
to improve their English skills, that we exchange practice speaking Arabic for practice
speaking English, but both attempts degenerated into chats in English or Hebrew.
Such projects were doomed to fail for solid sociolinguistic reasons: Jews who choose
to speak Arabic with Palestinians attribute low social status to their interlocutors. A
Jewish Israeli anthropologist, for example, who was fluent in Arabic, told me that
Palestinians she interviewed often preferred to speak Hebrew with her. In general,
Palestinians do not appreciate the choice of Arabic in conversation.

TEXT 5.8.   CURSING IN ARABIC

Cynthia	I just got on the bus,	(1)
	I had a little girl with me,	(2)
	Some old man behind us, he pushed me and said something in Arabic,	(3)
	He used— I don't remember the word, something rude,	(4)
	You know specifically coarse Arabic,	(5)
	And he really pushed me,	(6)
	And I almost fell down,	(7)
	And I wasn't even in his way,	(8)
	I asked,	(9)
	"Why did you push me?"	(10)
	People behind him started shouting at me in Arabic too,	(11)
	Really funny, those Ashkenazim and they're yelling in Arabic,	(12)
	And suddenly they're laying the blame on me,	(13)

And I had the little girl ... so I really got mad,   (14)
"Yes, you all are yelling because you see
    that I'm an Arab, black and Arab,   (15)
So you deserve it",   (16)
And then there was lots of shouting in the bus,   (17)
One woman was really fair and said
    that I was right,   (18)
And the guy attacked her too,   (19)
... (33A:30:25–32:03)

The Israeli ideology of language holds that Hebrew—the revived sacred language—does not have curse words of its own, and that Israelis therefore needed to adopt curse words from Arabic. In point of fact, many Hebrew phrases are used in swearing and rough speech, but the use of Arabic phrases for such purposes is very prominent.

Indeed, David Grossman's story of his meeting with Palestinian citizens from West Barta'a and Palestinian noncitizens from occupied East Barta'a (cited earlier in this chapter) also addresses the low status accorded the use of Arabic in Israel. The Palestinians from "Israeli Barta'a" insisted on speaking Hebrew in part as an assertion of identity vis-à-vis their noncitizen neighbors, but in part too their choice of language was a claim to status (vis-à-vis Grossman himself) within Israeli social and symbolic structures.

Learning English

The Israeli state may be politically "binational" (Jewish and Arab), but it is linguistically trilingual (Hebrew, Arabic, and English), and English plays an important role in Israeli ways of speaking. The importance of English in the land of Hebrew stems from many factors, including the prominence of English-speaking Jewish immigrants in Israel; Israel's dependence on financial, political, and military support from the United States; and the general cultural and political hegemony that America currently enjoys, reflected in a widespread swing toward English as a world language.

English also plays an important role in Israeli language learning. Many Israelis acquire English in the home, as did members of my own Israeli family. My aunt and uncle emigrated from the United States to Israel in the 1950s. Their four daughters were born in Israel and are native speakers of Hebrew. The language of the home, though, is English, and, as a result, all four daughters speak English well.

For the vast majority of Israelis, however, acquisition of English is a slow and painful process that begins in school. English is as important economically and socially for Palestinians as it is for Jews, but the structural circumstances of its acquisition disadvantage Palestinians. As a result, the use of English reproduces and reinforces the political economy of language based fundamentally on the norms of use of Hebrew and Arabic. In Hebrew-language schools English is the first foreign language children study. The study of English is mandatory; it begins in the first year of elementary school, and it continues through the final year of high school. Many Israeli Jews gain a high degree of proficiency in English in this way. In Arabic-language schools, however,

Palestinian students must first learn Hebrew. Hebrew is introduced as a foreign language from the first year of schooling, and English is put off until the third year. Both languages are then taught throughout primary and secondary education, but the burden of studying two foreign languages compounds the disadvantage for Palestinians that stems originally from the two-year delay.[44]

Palestinian Israelis also have less access than do Jewish Israelis to informal means of learning English. Television and cinema, for example, constitute an important source of exposure to English for many Israeli children. English-language shows shown on Israeli television have subtitled translation, but only a few are translated into Arabic as well as Hebrew. American and British pop music provides another point of access to English. One young Palestinian acquaintance, who was very interested in American pop music, liked to ask me to explain the lyrics to his favorite songs.

THE YOUTH GROUP CALLED "RE'UT"

It was Wednesday evening, and the weekly youth group meeting was about to begin. This particular week the Haifa branch of Re'ut, the national Arab-Jewish youth organization, was hosting a group of German high-school students who had hosted a delegation of Re'ut participants in Germany the summer before. The Germans see parallels between Jewish-Arab relations in Israel and German-Turkish relations in Germany. There are no Turkish Germans in the group that has come to Haifa, however.

The meeting coalesces slowly, casually. A dozen or so high-school kids—nearly all Arab boys and Jewish girls—are milling about. The group has appointed leaders, but they are kids too, and no one takes much authority. The boys are talking loudly in Arabic—nervously, but also ostentatiously. Jokes are exchanged in Arabic. Now and then a joke is translated into Hebrew. The boys are uneasy and out of their element. Speaking Arabic gives them a certain power.

The Germans do not speak Hebrew or Arabic, and few Israelis learn German, so the discussion takes place in English. Among the Israelis, the Jews dominate the floor. One Jewish Re'ut member is the child of an American. Several others have learned English very well, apparently in school. The Palestinian participants are quieter than usual.

Knowledge of English becomes crucial when students enter the university. Instruction at the university is in Hebrew (see text 5.2), but in most fields textbooks and journal articles must be read in English. Knowledge of English is therefore a decisive factor in success or failure at the university level. For Palestinian students, while Hebrew may be a major social hurdle, English is their biggest challenge. And in meeting this challenge they face several disadvantages. Jewish students begin their university studies after two or three years of military service, while Palestinians, most of whom do not serve in the military, enter college directly upon finishing high school. Palestinian students recognize the advantages of maturity and experience away from home that come with entering school at a more advanced age.[45] The extra years also help linguistically. Many Israeli Jews take a year off after they finish their military service and travel to places like Thailand or California, where they gain experience using English. Exposure to English is also dependent on the size and Jewishness of the city—English is pervasive in Tel-Aviv, but rare in small villages. Most Palestinian students, however, come to the university from villages, where their experience with English, as with Hebrew, is limited to school.

THREE ISRAELI GAMES OF LANGUAGE CHOICE

(1) A PASSOVER INVITATION AT THE UNIVERSITY DORMITORIES

At the beginning of my fieldwork in Israel I stayed in a dormitory at the University of Haifa. The dorms offered a convenient microcosm of Israeli society because the residents were an unusually diverse group. Since the dormitories were arranged in six-person suites, I was assured of living with Israelis.

Unfortunately, the dormitories turned out to be a terrible place to learn Hebrew. Four hundred Israeli students shared these dormitories with about one hundred American exchange students, most of whom were enrolled in semester-abroad language-study programs. Most Americans treated their studies as a vacation, showing more interest in travel and flirtation than in scholarship or language learning. Few made any serious attempt to use Hebrew with their Israeli roommates, and those who did try were usually defeated in the Israeli game of language status, as the following experience demonstrates.

A male student (Jewish, Israeli) came into my suite one evening with a female student (Jewish, Israeli). The students worked part time for the dormitory administration, and they had come to see us on official business. I was sitting at a table chatting, in Hebrew, with Hagai, an Israeli suite-mate, and Mike, an American. Like me, Mike spoke Hebrew well and insisted on Hebrew in his interactions with Jewish Israelis. The male student spoke to Mike and me in a fluent, but accented English, inquiring whether we had plans for the upcoming Passover Seder.[46] Mike answered him in Hebrew, thanking him for his consideration, noting that we were well accounted for ourselves, but asking what plans the dormitory was making for its American (Jewish) residents. The visitor responded in English, and Mike asked several more questions, each time in Hebrew: "Were they also asking Russian immigrant students if they needed a place to celebrate?" "Why were they so concerned about Americans?" And so on.[47] Each question was asked in Hebrew and answered in English, and the conversation continued in this manner for some time.

The female visitor was very quiet at first. When she did join the conversation, she did so in Hebrew. I interpreted her silence to mean that she felt her English was not good enough to warrant participation in that language.

(2) ORDERING PIZZA AT A HAIFA CAFE

My Israeli cousin and I once had dinner together at a Haifa pizza restaurant that catered to tourists. We sat at a small outdoor table and were engaged in a lively conversation—she spoke English to me, and I spoke Hebrew to her—when the waitress surprised us. Actually, it turned out to be the (Jewish)

Israeli waitress who was surprised, when, displaying proper communicative competence for Israel, she addressed the person-speaking-English (my Israeli cousin) in English, and the person-speaking-Hebrew (me) in Hebrew. Our respective accents soon gave us away, and language-use reverted to Hebrew for ordering.

(3) LANGUAGE AND DATING

Soon after I arrived in Israel, my cousin introduced me to Dorit, an unmarried female friend of hers, thinking we might hit it off. Over the course of my two years in Israel, we did spend a lot of time together, but we never became romantically involved. There was always a certain tension between us. At our last meeting, a few days before I was to return home, she admitted to me that my speaking to her in Hebrew had always annoyed her. Her English was flawless, stemming from a childhood spent in Holland going to an international school.

While Palestinians have less access to English-learning environments than do Jewish Israelis, the use of English may carry even more social meaning for them.

A FORM OF BROKEN HEBREW

Salim is a Palestinian Re'ut member, whose musical interests led him to ask me to translate English pop-song lyrics. I noticed that when Salim spoke Hebrew he often stopped in midsentence, hesitant, searching for a word. Sometimes he would ask me for the word in Hebrew, and sometimes he would just use the English word instead. This pattern persisted despite the fact that his Hebrew was very good. It seemed to me that Salim was quite happy to represent himself as someone who knew only passing Hebrew, and whose English was perhaps better (see "A Ship's Chandler," chapter 1).

Learning *Israeli* (Learning to Negotiate)

When discussing language, Israelis jokingly distinguish between *ivrit*, "Hebrew," and *yisra'elit*, or "Israeli" (language). The joke's humor refers to the diglossia in Israel, according to which written, formal, and biblical Hebrew is the idealized model for one's speech, while actual performance follows the very different rules of colloquial vernacular.

Yet the idea of "Israeli" as a language goes well beyond the grammatical simplifications and phonological mergers usually thought of as the difference between formal Hebrew and vernacular speech. Rather, "Israeli" is the repertoire of linguistic varieties meaningfully deployed in Israeli discourse, the range of social meanings associated with such varieties, and the set of rules for their appropriate use. "Israeli" is the language of interaction, of negotiation, of struggle, of change. "Israeli" is the language Salim speaks when he hesitates to speak Hebrew fluently. It is the language he uses when he inserts English words into Hebrew conversation. By using English while speaking Hebrew, Salim fluently deploys a systematic code of social meaning shared throughout Israel.

A closer look at some patterns of incorporating English into Hebrew discourse will demonstrate this point. Linguists distinguish three primary processes through which multiple languages are incorporated in talk:

- *Code-switching* involves a switch from one language to another within a speaker's utterance.

- *Borrowing* involves adoption of a word from one language into another, retaining some phonological and grammatical material from the source language. For example, the word *genre* is a borrowing from French into English that (often) retains French phonology.

- *Loanwords* are borrowings that have been so thoroughly integrated phonologically and grammatically into the adoptive language that speakers (and grammars) barely recognize the distinction. Examples from English include *café* (from French), *gesundheit* (from German), and *algebra* (from Arabic). Commonly borrowed words often become loanwords, and the distinction between these concepts can be subtle in English. In other languages, like Hebrew, however, the difference can be far more salient.[48]

In Israel all three processes are commonly used to inject English into Hebrew conversation, but the ability to use English loanwords deftly and creatively is a core feature of "Israeli."

A large number of common words in colloquial Hebrew were borrowed from English but are sufficiently integrated into Hebrew phonology and morphology that we may call them loanwords. Table 5.1 shows examples of the integration of the loanwords into Hebrew phonological and morphological systems. English source words are stripped to their consonantal frames and truncated to no more than four consonants, conforming to Hebrew structure, which is based on three- or four-consonant roots. Thus from English "organize," the Hebrew root ?.R.G.N is formed. Israeli usage then incorporates the consonant patterns into Hebrew's system of verbal and nominal derivation, as can be seen in the formation of the infinitive, *l'argen*, the verbal noun, *irgun*, and the derived reflexive verb, *l'hitargen*. Phonological incorporation can be

Table 5.1. Some English Loanwords in Hebrew.

Source	Verbal Infinitive		Derived Forms	
organization	*l'argen*	to organize	*irgun*	organization
			l'hitargen	to get organized
torpedo	*l'tarped*	to torpedo	*tarpedet*	torpedo boat
			turpad	sabotaged
bluff	*l'valef*	to bluff		
telephone	*l'talpen*	to call		
depress	*l'dapres*	to depress		
fabricate	*l'fabrek*	to fake		

seen in the case of "bluff." The infinitive, *l'valef*, shows the effect of the regular Hebrew phonological process, called spirantization, in which /b/ is "softened" to [v] when it is not the first sound in a word or syllable.[49] (Other forms derived from this loanword, including the verbal noun, *biluf*, "bluffing," do not show spirantization.)

Loanwords such as those shown in table 5.1 are common, highly nativized features of colloquial Hebrew—and "Israeli" incorporates hundreds of them. There is a certain "Israeli hip" quality to introducing as wide a range of English words as possible into one's Hebrew speech. Integrating loanwords into Hebrew grammatical patterns shows linguistic virtuosity and creativity—and often humor as well. Thus alongside the formal prestige attached to using English itself, a covert prestige (see Trudgill 1972) attaches to the smooth integration of English with Hebrew, as the following language-related news stories demonstrate:[50]

- David Levi, for many years foreign minister of Israel and a very prominent politician, was the butt of many jokes based on his supposed lack of English skills.[51]

- A survey published in an Israeli magazine in the early 1990s revealed an intriguing fact: Israeli yuppies preferred the English-language television news broadcasts to the longer, much more substantive, and presumably easier to understand Hebrew-language news.

- A radio commercial for a car dealership featured an American man's voice intoning an entire sentence in English in the middle of an advertisement otherwise completely in Hebrew.

- My aunt, who reviewed American and British books for an Israeli publishing company, advising them on which books to translate into Hebrew and publish in Israel, related an interesting story. One book that she rated as a "must-translate," because she thought it would be of great interest to Israelis, was indeed marketed in Israel, but it was never translated into Hebrew: Market research had shown that in some topic areas Israelis prefer to read books in English.

English use is a powerful marker (and therefore resource) in the negotiation of status and identity. Jews and Palestinians alike use English to claim and assert high status, but in this domain, as elsewhere, Jewish and Palestinian patterns are distinct. A study of Hebrew and English borrowings into the Arabic spoken in a Palestinian town in Israel (Amara and Spolsky 1986), for example, indicates a preference for drawing on English where possible. Similarly, use of English has high symbolic importance for Palestinian as for Jewish Israelis, but with a crucial difference in polarity: English is used by Palestinians—in their Arabic, as in their Hebrew—in part to distance themselves from mainstream Israeli identity.

Yet the use of English in Hebrew privileges Jews because their increased access to contexts of English-learning generates increased fluency in that language. The kind of lexical incorporation shown in table 5.1 was far more typical of Jewish Israeli speech than of Palestinian speech.[52] Palestinians, however, use English in other ways to distance themselves from mainstream Israeli identity, as a segment of talk from my interview with Cynthia, cited earlier this chapter (see text 5.8), shows. Text 5.9 presents the relevant section in transliterated Hebrew (shown in boldface italic type):

TEXT 5.9. CURSING IN ARABIC (EXPANDED)

Cynthia ...

People behind him started shouting at me	
in Arabic too,	(11)
Really funny, those Ashkenazim	
and they're yelling in Arabic,	(12)
And suddenly they're laying the blame on me,	(13)
And I had the little girl with me,	(14)
ze noten yoter ledjitimizeshn she— lo litz'ok	(14a)
[which provides more legitimization that—	
not to shout],	
So I really got mad,	(14b)
"Yes, you all are yelling because you see	
that I'm an Arab, black and Arab,	(15)
So you deserve it",	(16)
And then there was lots of shouting in the bus,	(17)

Cynthia's use of the English word "legitimization" takes the form of the relatively unintegrated *ledjitimizeshn*, rather than the common loanword *ledjitimatzia*. Cynthia's usage is therefore more akin to a one-word code-switch into English than an application of a Hebrew ("Israeli") rule of loanword incorporation. Such switches were common in Cynthia's speech during our interview.

While English in Israel functions primarily to reinforce symbolic hierarchies grounded in the respective roles of Hebrew and Arabic, it can also serve resistant purposes, as the following case of status reversal shows.

A REVERSAL AT YAMI

At one Yami staff meeting, the teachers and Yami officials (and myself) were joined by the principal of the Arab school where the meeting was being held. This private school was funded and run by the Catholic Church, and the principal was a nun who had been born in France. Although she had been in Israel for years, the principal did not speak Hebrew. When she spoke with schoolchildren she used Arabic, but with her faculty, as with the assembled Yami staffers, she used English.

A striking reversal in the customary roles of leadership within the group emerged, as it became clear that the English skills of the Palestinian teachers greatly exceeded those of the Jewish teachers. The three Palestinian teachers, who are usually less talkative and less animated than the Jewish teachers, dominated the talk at this meeting.[53]

"Israeli," or the various forms of public, intergroup language, also needs to be learned, and here a paradox arises: intergroup interaction is actually quite rare in Israel, where a high degree of segregation prevails. While the segregation between Arab and Jew in Israel is more-or-less official (Lustick 1980) and widely acknowledged, segregation between Mizrahi and Ashkenazi is unofficial, and poorly recognized. Thus when I arrived in Israel with my project of studying Israeli identity by looking at talk in actual crosscultural encounters, Israelis found the idea puzzling: Arab-Jewish encounters were seen as too rare and artificial to study in that way, and Mizrahi-Ashkenazi encounters too ubiquitous and routine to be of interest. How, then, are the forms and meanings of "Israeli" learned? In the following chapter I will argue that the primary source is the media—broadcast, print, and commercial.

6

Tropes of Identity
in Public Culture

As children acquire language they are ushered into a world of communication that proceeds much as they choose, but not with the tools of their choosing. A language provides words, constructions, and idioms for some—but not all—of the potential ideas a child might want to express. Hebrew, for example, has no equivalent for the way Americans use the word "embarrassed." On the other hand, Hebrew encourages the distinction between two ideas usually conflated by Americans in the word "sorry."[1] Adult speech is, in this sense, a negotiation between the set of possible thoughts and the set of tools for articulating those thoughts.

As children are socialized into society they are introduced to a world of interaction that also proceeds somewhat as they choose, but not entirely with the tools of their choosing. A society consists of images and practices that, while subject to change, have histories and politics that add inertial weight. In the 1880s, for example, when Jews began to resettle Palestine, "Israeli" was a new idea, while today it carries a welter of meanings.[2] Adults in any society negotiate their identities, but they cannot do so just as they please. Face-to-face interaction is a complex negotiation that involves much more than just the human interlocutors. Conversational negotiations of identity also involve an active negotiation between the ideas of identity an individual feels (and wishes to assert) and the images of identity public culture provides. In this chapter I characterize the relationship between conversational interaction and public discourse as a negotiation, a spiral trajectory influenced by the coordinate processes of

169

entextualization and (re)contextualization (see Briggs and Bauman 1992; see also chapter 3).

Media images play a central role in Israeli negotiations of identity, as the following interview segment reveals.

"Nurit Ben"

In the course of my interview with Hagit and Nurit, two Jewish Israeli women who know each other as neighbors, and as parents of classmates at school, the topic of musical tastes came up. Popular music is a rich topic in Israel, and musical tastes are heavily marked for ethnicity. Hagit, who is Ashkenazi, said, "Ashkenazim can't stand Mizrahi music." Nurit, who is Mizrahi, admitted liking Mizrahi music.

Pursuing this topic, Hagit said that Mizrahim disliked "Land of Israel songs," the folksy tunes she grew up on,[3] but Nurit took offense at this, claiming that she too grew up loving Land of Israel songs.

At this point in the interview I posed what I knew would be a provocative question: I asked the two women what they thought of the Eurovision controversy.[4] Hagit responded immediately, saying: "Oh, you mean what happened to Nurit Ben?"

I felt embarrassed for Hagit, and I quickly rephrased my question so as to emphasize the singer's actual name, "Zehava Ben." Nurit gave no indication of having noticed her friend's slip of the tongue.

This segment of interview conversation is remarkable for the incorporation of public discourses on identity into face-to-face negotiations of identity. Throughout this three-hour interview, the two friends, Hagit and Nurit, explored what it meant to be Israeli through a stimulating interrogation of their mutual differences. These two women, one Ashkenazi, one Mizrahi, played with and negotiated identities, through discussion of family, neighborhood, children, religion, military service, and other topics. In chapter 8 I will return to this interview, examining in detail some of the linguistic resources the women deployed in their negotiated claims to dominant and resistant identities. Here I am interested in the converse: how public media discourses influenced the face-to-face interaction.

In the interaction just described, the everyday, conversational identity negotiation between two friends became entangled in prominent public discourse images of identity, as Hagit inadvertently inscribed "Nurit," her friend's name, onto the image of a popular Israeli singer and symbol of Mizrahi identity, "Zehava Ben." Hagit's slip appears "Freudian": the Ashkenazi Hagit is so conscious of her friend's Mizrahi ethnicity that she momentarily identifies her with the Mizrahi singer. Freud's great insight into such conversational phenomena, however, was to recognize that the slip is also a comment (Freud 1960:2–7; Wollheim 1971:77–84). By inscribing Zehava Ben's identity onto Nurit, Hagit is asserting—indirectly—that her friend is like Zehava Ben. Just as a metaphor, such as "Love is war," maps attributes of a source domain, "war," onto a target domain, "love," in order to assert about love that it can be rough, dangerous, unruly, and so on (Lakoff and Johnson 1980), Hagit has mapped characteristics of what she knows about the media figure, Zehava Ben, onto what she feels about her friend, Nurit. A brief examination of the media discourse about Zehava Ben at that time will illuminate the content of Hagit's inadvertent comment about Nurit.[5]

The interview took place just a few months after the 1992 Eurovision preliminary contest. That year the Eurovision competition had drawn special attention in Israel because Zehava Ben decided to enter a song. At the time Ben was not only the most popular singer of Mizrahi music, but also Israel's top-selling pop star overall. Not surprisingly, then, the precontest expectation was that she would win easily. In fact, however, Ben finished in tenth place, dead last, despite singing a popular song and performing it well.

Ben's music, while popular, was heavily stigmatized as *muzika mizrahit*, "Mizrahi music" (see Halper, Seroussi, and Squires-Kidron 1989), which meant that it was neither the right genre nor the right ethnicity. The Eurovision contest offered Israelis an opportunity to present themselves to the European world, and this opportunity generated enormous pressure to present a mainstream image. While the contest appeared to draw a range of songs and acts, in fact rigid constraints were applied to the style of music Israelis would hold up to Europe as a representation of Self. Most songs that appeared in this contest were exemplars of what might be called Ashkenazi music, broadly similar in tone and style to the "Land of Israel songs" Hagit brought up in the interview. Ben's participation in Eurovision, like her introduction of a Mizrahi song into the contest, was a bold attempt at crossover popularity.

It was the acceptability of Mizrahi music as a representation of Israeliness that I had meant to raise with my question to the two women in the interview, but the original issue had been overshadowed by its coverage in the media and by subsequent events. Ben had not taken her defeat gracefully. Instead, she had cried foul. The following day's newspapers had covered her tears and anger in splashy detail, as the artist and her (Mizrahi) fans raucously complained of racism and discrimination. Thus the narrative that emerged from the 1992 Eurovision contest—that "Mizrahi" was not (yet) "Israeli"—was constructed in mutually reinforcing ways:

- Mizrahi music was not Israeli music.

- Mizrahi artists could enter and win the Eurovision contest—but not with a Mizrahi song.

- Bad sportsmanship, intense disappointment, and violent protest are un-Israeli, and these behaviors retroactively justified the contest's dismissal of Ben's claims to mainstream Israeliness.

Thus it seems likely that it was Zehava Ben's post-Eurovision behavior as reported and presented in the Israeli media that Hagit responded to—and inadvertently attributed to her friend, Nurit. By asserting that her friend, Nurit, was like the singer, Zehava, Hagit may have been saying she felt Nurit to be too emotional. I can't know for sure. What is of interest here, though, is the way that media images became—literally—the language with which Israelis talk about identity.

To understand the dynamics of conversation we must engage not only with the broad social context of talk but also with the specific social histories of particular tropes. Talk derives its social meaning from webs of dialogic connection that are both synchronic and diachronic in nature. Talk of music in Israel is linked synchronically to ethnicity, as mention of "Land of Israel songs" leads to mention of its opposite, *muzika mizrahit*. And these associations have social histories, as talk of "Land of Israel songs" evokes cultural memories of Israel's golden age of pioneering in the 1920s and 1930s (see Katriel and Shenhar 1990), when they were written, or of Israel's heroic independence struggle in the 1940s and 1950s, when they were popularized, or of Israel's traumatic Gulf War confinement in the 1990s, when they were replayed endlessly on the radio and television.[6]

Tropes, images, symbolic forms of all kinds are actively dialogic in that the contextual and historical meanings they evoke are constantly changing. The 1992 Eurovision contest added a powerful new meaning to the dialogism of ethnicity and music in Israel, and, in turn, Hagit's incorporation of (her memory of) this public culture media image into her conversational interaction further inflected the discourse. This example also demonstrates a third kind of dialogism: reflexive dialogism. Coverage of the 1992 Eurovision competition was reflexively dialogic because media coverage of the contest literally represented to Israelis their own discourse. Contest winners and losers were determined by popular vote, tallied in real time. Israeli television viewers were thus consuming representations generated from their own representations. This case highlights a relationship that obtains more generally. Individuals negotiate identities with respect to media images they consume, but the media images themselves are representations drawn from the kinds of identities negotiated in face-to-face interactions. The media provides powerful models for identity by representing to Israelis their own performances of identity. The negotiation between individuals and public culture is thus also a spiral, in which meanings are negotiated between public and private forms of discourse. Images, like the sounds and grammatical forms of a dialect, originate in practice, find structure through entextualization in the media (or grammaticalized in language), and return (recontextualized) to conversations.

This chapter discusses the role of public discourse in the conversational negotiation of identity by looking at the ways Israeli identities are represented in the media, and how such representations articulate with social and cultural power. I will look at how media representations of identity constitute tools of power, constraining the subjectivities and actions of individual Israelis. Symbols of identity lend power to public discourse images because identity naturalizes ascriptions, and because they implicitly contain affect. A look at some symbols that are shared by Jewish and Palestinian discourses of identity shows their meanings to be generated in part from their dynamic opposition—the meaning of the symbol in the discourse of Jewish identity derives from the meaning the symbol carries in the discourse of Palestinian identity, and vice versa. An in-depth analysis of the shared symbol of the "victim" as it played out in a media drama highlights the powerful role of emotion in media representations of identity. This chapter concludes with a discussion of the sharing of the symbol "Israeliness" and the ways in which media representations of identity constrain individual agency in the negotiation of identities in everyday interaction.

Shared Symbols in Dynamic Opposition

One implication of the synchronic dialogism of symbolic practices is that identities are negotiated in dynamic opposition to each other. In Israel, Jewish and Arab identities are been formed and re-formed through their mutual encounter. Images of identity are negotiated in the complex field constructed by the Self's imaginings of Self and Other, and bounded by the Other's imaginings of Self and Other.

WHO IS THE NATIVE?

While studying Arabic at an American college I attended a lecture given in formal Arabic by Yemen's ambassador to the United States. I have long since forgotten the topic of his lecture, but his response to a student's question stands out in my memory.

The student, an earnest young man named Yaakov, stood up and, in the halting Arabic of a beginning student, conveyed the poignant story of his (Jewish) family's escape from the Holocaust, refuge in Israel, and ultimate immigration to the United States. He then asked the ambassador to address Yemen's position on Israel.

In response, the ambassador told a story of his own: Upon arrival in Washington as the new ambassador, he had been welcomed by the "Jewish caucus"—the cohort of Jewish senators and representatives. In the midst of this reception, one senator had said to him: "Why do you, the Arab nations of the Middle East, not welcome Israel as a neighbor, the way we, American senators, are welcoming you as an ambassador?" To this the ambassador had responded: "Would you American senators also welcome American Indians who came back to reclaim their land?"

This narrative strategically reverses the expected images of Palestinian and Israeli identities. Instead of representing Palestinians as the aboriginal inhabitants of the disputed land, and the Israelis as colonial occupiers, the Yemeni ambassador rhetorically accepted the Israelis' own construction of themselves as aboriginals with the "right of return." By explicitly comparing Jews to Native Americans, the ambassador positioned the American (Jewish) senators in the place of Palestinians. Prominent symbols in the Israeli/Palestinian negotiation over identity take on a double polarity here. Both Jews and Palestinians claim to be the natives of Palestine/Israel. Jews claim to be natives by virtue of the biblical history of their residence in, and dispersal from, Palestine. Palestinians claim to be natives by virtue of nearly two millennia of continuous residence in Palestine since the Jewish diaspora. The negotiation over the meaning and reference of "the native" therefore resolves into a struggle over legitimacy, authenticity, and belonging.

Israeli discourse encompasses a contentious negotiation over the meaning of a number of such shared symbols, which are claimed by both sides, with divergent meanings. Like the negotiation over the meaning and reference of the idea of the "native," the meaning of images such as "tree" and "farmer" are also negotiated in public discourse.

The Tree

The forest is a rich symbol of Israeli identity, with many dialogic connections. Most directly, forests are linked with the Zionist discourse of reclamation. The Jewish return to Palestine was conceptualized as reclaiming land in the dual sense of reclaiming (through settlement) an ancestral territory, and of reclaiming (through husbandry) a green oasis. Trees were especially important in the second reclamation sense, since they were instrumental in draining swamps, producing food, and providing shade and building materials for Jewish settlements. Perhaps even more important, though, trees functioned symbolically to link this ecological sense of reclamation to a spiritual sense of reclamation. Zionist discourse sought to reclaim Jewish identity through a return to physical, productive work, symbolized by agricultural labor, of which the planting of trees was a mythologized centerpiece.[7]

If the forest is a rich symbol of Israeli identity, the tree serves as an equally rich symbol of Palestinian identity. Palestinian Israelis I visited in Nazareth fondly recalled the trees that graced the courtyards and gardens of the homes they grew up in. For many these trees exist now only in memory, as spacious and green courtyards have given way to additions to the houses needed to accommodate growing families on shrinking plots. The olive tree, in particular, carries great symbolic significance, in part because of the great age these trees attain and in part because of the central role olives and their products have played in Palestinian lives, livelihoods, and economies for hundreds of years (Doumani 1995:132).[8]

The discursive struggle over this symbol is poetically represented in A. B. Yehoshua's famous short story "Facing the Forest."[9] In this story the (Jewish) image of forests-that-built-a-nation is symbolically transformed into the (Palestinian) image of trees-that-displaced-villages. Yehoshua's tale revolves around two men: the young Jewish proprietor of a forest and his employee, an elderly Palestinian caretaker. The caretaker quietly plots to burn the forest down, stowing pots of kerosene throughout the forest and waiting for the moment to set it ablaze. When the caretaker finally acts, he appears to do so with the passive consent of the Jewish proprietor, who has discovered the kerosene but does nothing to prevent the fire. The blaze levels the forest and exposes the stone walls and cactus plants that mark the outlines of what had been the caretaker's village.[10] The village had been razed by the Jews during the 1948 conflict.

The current negotiation, or struggle, over the symbolism of trees draws from these various reservoirs of meaning:

THE RABBI ALAN S. GREEN FOREST

The pine forests that now cover the rocky hills west of Jerusalem are a source of great pride to Israeli and diaspora Jews alike. Each time I took the long, slow bus ride up those slopes into Jerusalem I recalled the days of my youth spent in Sunday School, where we celebrated the Jewish holiday, Tu B'Shvat, by contributing quarters toward the planting of trees in Israel. Each week my mother sent me off with a coin, and when my contributions had reached a certain total I received a certificate commemorating my "purchase" of a tree that would be planted in the forest named for my temple's rabbi.

While in Israel I frequently rode the bus into and out of Jerusalem. Each time, as I rode past these forests, I wondered where the Rabbi Alan S. Green forest was and what it actually looked like. But I often had trouble seeing the forest for all the stones and walls among the trees.

The Farmer

Like the symbol of the tree, the image of the farmer is also a core symbol of identity, historically claimed by Palestinian and Israeli nationalist movements, and currently struggled over in Israeli public discourse:

THE TRACTOR AND THE HORSE

On the eastern slope of the Jezreel Valley a *kibutz*[11] has established a museum that commemorates the pioneering days of early Zionist (Jewish) settlement in Palestine.[12] I have joined a University of Haifa professor and her class as they tour the museum.[13]

Our guide, an elderly, white-haired man, enthusiastically shows us around the spacious museum. His enthusiasm stems, in part, from the popularity such nostalgia enjoys. These museums glorify the role men like him played in founding the Israeli state. Ironically, though, the museum celebrates the kibbutz—and the agricultural and communal lifestyle it stood for—just when that lifestyle fades from Israeli life. Doubly ironic is that the kibbutz built the museum in part as an economic venture because the traditional kibbutz economy the museum celebrates has failed.

Following the museum's chronological layout, our guide begins with stories about draining swamps and coexisting with Arab farmers, as he leads us past displays of the wooden and rusted-iron farm implements Palestinian peasants traditionally used.

The centerpiece of the display is a huge black-and-white picture framed and mounted on the museum's wall, surrounded by eighteenth-century farm implements. The picture shows two fields separated by a low stone wall. In the foreground an Israeli *kibutznik*[14] plows one field with a tractor. In the background a Palestinian *fallah*[15] plows the other field with a horse. Our guide makes an idyllic spirit of cooperation radiate from the photograph, as he nostalgically tells us about his friendship with his Arab neighbors in those days.

The farmer is central to current constructions of Israeli identity because agriculture was central to the historical reclaiming of Jewish nationhood. Agriculture joined forestry in mythologically justifying the Jewish reclamation of Palestine, and the farmers who practiced it became celebrated images of a new Israeli Self. The image of the Jewish farmer also realized the Zionist desire to reclaim manual labor as a Jewish practice, and thus farmers—especially kibbutz farmers—encapsulated all that seemed good and worthy in the pioneer Israeli.

Similarly, the farmer is currently an important signifier of Palestinian identity because the fallah, "peasant," was central to historical re-constructions of Palestinian nationhood. Palestinian nationalism emerged in the 1930s in response to the growing influence of

Jewish settlements and the growing incursion of Zionist agriculture on Palestinian village life. Jewish agricultural practices displaced the Palestinian peasantry. Jewish settlers bought land from absentee Arab landowners, but the Zionist return to productive labor prevented Jewish farmers from hiring Palestinian peasants. Many Palestinian peasants were thus alienated from their land and means of production (Rosenfeld 1978). During the Arab Revolt of 1936–1939, the Palestinian peasantry emerged as a leading nationalist group, and the fallah (represented by the *kufiya*, the traditional peasant head covering) as a powerful national symbol (Swedenburg 1995). The image of the fallah symbolically contested Zionist reclamation by asserting Palestinian claims to the land, to productive labor, and to authenticity.[16]

Images of the Victim: The Bat Yam Murder and Riots

Israeli social groups play with a set of shared symbols in their negotiations of identity, but they do not do so just as they please. Such negotiations are weighted by inequalities in the distribution of the power to represent. The prominent photograph featured by the museum tour guide, like the similar picture that frames *Arab and Jew*, the book by David Shipler discussed in chapter 4, evokes uniquely Jewish Israeli representations of Self and Other. Such representations delegitimize the conflict over Palestine by framing it in images of serene coexistence that erase the cause of conflict. Such images silence Palestinian voices even as they establish the symbols with which Palestinians must negotiate their identity. The power of representation resides with the powerful: Jews, Ashkenazi Israelis, and the Hebrew institutions. Palestinians, and to a lesser extent Mizrahi Jews, are forced to resist. It is within this field of power that Palestinian, Mizrahi, and Ashkenazi discourses struggle over imagery.

The media is a domain in which the power to represent is distributed unequally. Arabic newspapers, radio stations, television programs, films, and other forms of media exist, but the Arab(ic) media are limited, constrained, and subordinated. The Palestinian voice in Israeli media is disproportionately small. While 20 percent or more of Israeli citizens speak Arabic as a mother tongue, the slice of Israeli media that is produced in Arabic is proportionately small and much less significant. In the early 1990s the government television station (Channel 1)[17] set aside a block of time each day for Arabic-language programming, but this block occurred in the late afternoon when audiences were small. Nor was Israeli Arabic television as imaginative or as well funded as the Hebrew television. Arabic-language movies were aired most afternoons, but the old-fashioned Egyptian films that were broadcast rarely captured the interest of young Palestinians (who preferred the American and European films shown later, with Hebrew subtitles). Similarly, an evening news program was broadcast in Arabic, but a 1995 survey showed that over 64 percent of Israeli Palestinian respondents preferred to watch the Hebrew news (Smooha 1999:15). One explanation for this finding lies in the greater depth and quality of the Hebrew news. But another factor is certainly the subjection of the Arabic news to intervention by the government censor (see Halabi 1981). During accounts of "terrorist" actions, for example, the Arabic news program focused far more visual imagery on dead Palestinian terrorists than did the Hebrew news.[18]

Palestinian Israelis may represent themselves in and through Arab media, but they may not represent themselves just as they please. The marginalization of Arabic in the Israeli media was perhaps most egregious during coverage of major sporting events. Soccer and basketball games were often shown in the early evening, preempting the regularly scheduled Arabic programs. Play-by-play announcers broadcast the game in Hebrew, but every fifteen minutes or so an Arab broadcaster was called in to hastily summarize the game in Arabic. The tokenism of this Arabic translation was not lost on Israelis: adult Palestinians understood the Hebrew, and the brief translations added little to children's enjoyment of the game.[19] A similar situation obtained with regard to print media, where three main newspapers were published in Arabic in Israel, but these had limited readership and limited influence.[20] Two weeklies, *al-Sinnara* and *Kul al-'Arab*, were published in Nazareth, the largest Palestinian Israeli city, and the daily, *al-Ittihad*, was published in Haifa as the journal of the Israeli Communist Party.[21] Many Haifa Palestinians read one of the Nazareth weeklies on a regular basis, but only for what they called "family news."[22] Most relied on the Hebrew press for news. The suppression of the Arabic-language press in Israel is clearest when compared to the Russian-language press (see "Buying an Arabic Newspaper" in chapter 2). Haifa newsstands carried several Russian-language newspapers in the early 1990s, and for a while some of the Hebrew papers even included a page of news in Russian each day. This dramatic contrast flies in the face of central aspects of the Israeli ideology of language: Russians, who, according to this ideology, "should" learn Hebrew, read non-Hebrew newspapers, while Palestinians, who "should" maintain Arabic, read the Hebrew press. (See chapter 5 for discussion of ideological implications of language learning and language shift.) Palestinian citizens of Israel are therefore forced to negotiate their representation with and through the mainstream Hebrew media.

I turn now to a case study of the representation of a third important shared symbol, the "victim." The case study looks at a particular set of events that occurred in the spring of 1992 and their coverage in Israel's largest-circulation newspaper. The coverage presented to Israelis a powerful narrative of Israeli identity that is internally complex and functionally important. The media narrative is complex because it interweaves potent images of all three social groups. It is functionally important because, by drawing on taken-for-granted discourses of emotion, this media narrative naturalizes particular representations of identity, thereby setting the terms for their deployment in conversational negotiations of identity.

The Events

The dramatic set of events that formed the basis for the extraordinary media drama can be summarized as follows:

- On Sunday morning, May 24, 1992, a Palestinian man from Gaza stabbed and killed a fifteen-year-old Jewish Israeli girl.

- The girl was attacked while waiting for a school bus in the central square of Bat Yam, a working-class suburb of Tel Aviv.

- The Palestinian attacker was caught by witnesses and handed over to the police.

- Crowds of Jewish Israelis formed mobs and attacked Palestinian workers who happened to be in the area.

- Violent demonstrations continued for three days, involving thousands of Jewish Israelis.

- The demonstrations turned into violent confrontations with the Israeli police.

- On Wednesday night, May 27, 1992, a massive police deployment brought the riots to a halt as water cannon were turned on the crowds.

This story attracted particular attention because it cogently re-presented to Israelis a narrative that is intimately familiar, and viscerally felt to be true. The story of violent action and violent reaction in Bat Yam replayed well-known and deeply articulated narratives of Israeli identity. Stories that represent Israelis as *victims* and Palestinians as *terrorists* re-present core aspects of the Israeli discourse of legitimacy—even as they evoke sadness and feelings of loss. These public discourse representations of well-known narratives reinforce and reproduce the ready-made images into which individuals are socialized. The significance of the initial stabbing and the subsequent rioting extend far beyond the lives of the individuals directly affected, however, as the acts of violence became symbols that, through their presentation and re-presentation in the media, were embedded in an overarching national narrative.

The Coverage

The very intensity of the events' coverage in the media brought this story enormous attention. The Bat Yam incident captivated the attention of Israeli by virtue of its monumental coverage in the media, just as the Los Angeles riots in 1992[23] and the September 11 attack in 2001 captured American attention through television's saturation coverage. The day after the stabbing in Bat Yam, newspapers appeared in the double-width format usually reserved for weekend and holiday editions. Banner headlines and large color photographs on the front pages called attention to the story for several consecutive days. Articles, pictures, and commentaries describing and analyzing events in Bat Yam dominated the news sections of Israel's newspapers for most of that week.

In Israel the press of current events, or what is affectionately called *ha-matzav*, "the situation," is so intense it is almost overwhelming. Travel abroad is one of the few opportunities Israelis have to escape, and long journeys occupy a central place in Israeli rites of passage. Upon completion of their military service, for example, many (Jewish) Israelis take extended trips to Nepal, Thailand, California, and other distant places. Israelis often say that what they appreciate most about such travel is the *sheket*, "quiet," by which they mean the distance achieved from ha-matzav.

In this news-saturated environment, the media are particularly influential. On city buses, for example, drivers turn the volume up on the radio every half-hour, so that passengers can hear the news broadcasts (see "News on the Bus" in chapter 1). At home, many families congregate each evening to watch the news together. At times the prime-time nightly news show *Mabat la-Xadashot* has been the highest rated show on television.[24] Dinner-party conversations are often dominated by talk of current events, and in social gatherings of all kinds, *kiturim*, or griping about the country's affairs, is "an ever-present speech activity" (Katriel 1991:35).

Within the Israeli news culture, print media play an especially important role. The importance of newspapers derives from their nearly universal readership, their national distribution, and their intimate connection with other domains of Israeli intellectual life. Newspaper readership is extremely high in Israel, an unusually literate country in general (Lavie 1992:86), and nearly all Israelis read a newspaper on a daily basis. All of the major daily newspapers in Israel are national in their distribution and coverage, shrinking the geographically and demographically small nation even further (see Anderson 1991).[25] Perhaps most significant, however, Israeli intellectual life is deeply integrated with all its media, and especially with its print media. It is quite common for popular novelists, respected scholars, or government ministers to contribute articles to the "op-ed" pages of the national newspapers.

The "Bat Yam Violence" media drama played out across all Israeli media, but the analysis to follow will focus on its coverage in *Yedioth Ahronoth* (henceforth *Yedioth*), Israel's largest circulation daily newspaper.[26] *Yedioth* occupies a centrist position among Israeli newspapers, in that it is not aligned with either of the major political parties. (As in many European countries—and quite in contrast to the situation in the United States—many Israeli newspapers are aligned with specific political parties.) *Yedioth* is also centrist in a sociolinguistic sense. Israeli newspapers vary significantly in the variety of Hebrew used. *Ha-Aretz* and *Ma'ariv*, the other major national Hebrew papers, use a grammatically and stylistically elevated Hebrew, while *Yedioth* uses a style of Hebrew more in tune with the mainstream (spoken) vernacular. *Yedioth*'s coverage can be interpreted, therefore, as an expression of mainstream Israeli discourse.

While the newspaper coverage of the Bat Yam violence seeks to report an objective sequence of events, it does not do so transparently. For example, although daily shifts of focus in the coverage corresponded to the evolving course of events in Bat Yam, the newspaper made countless choices of emphasis and inflection. Monday's paper focused on the attack and the initial riots. Tuesday's paper covered the victim's funeral. And Wednesday's paper emphasized the violent clashes with police. But within this apparent fidelity to "events" the reportage narrates through choices, such as: Which ideas are represented in pictures, and which are relegated to print? How are various images juxtaposed with each other? What labels are used to identify images and to summarize events?

The newspaper coverage thus unavoidably narrativizes the incidents it reports. Coverage frames the events in particular ways, elaborating some aspects while silencing others. Newspaper narratives inscribe social meaning onto objective events, just as narratives of personal experience told in conversation inscribe interactional meaning onto objective events. In chapter 4 I argued that the narrator of "The Lazy Susan" skillfully embedded simple events in a complex moral frame. The simple events involved trips to a store; the moral frame encompassed attitudes about generosity and friendship, wealth and position, social role and cultural values. Media framing of news stories similarly embeds the "events" in a moral order. *Yedioth*'s narrativization of the Bat Yam violence embeds the objective events in a national frame, by orienting events and participants within a metanarrative of Israeli identity. One important difference, however, between the public discourse narratives printed in newspapers and the narratives of personal experience told in conversation is the institutional power that stands behind the stories told by the former. News stories become powerful allegories that a society tells about itself. These allegories construct models for hero and villain and tempt readers to identify with one or the other.

Yedioth Ahronoth's coverage of the Bat Yam violence opposes two powerful symbols: *victim* and *terrorist*. To be sure, the "facts" of this case lent themselves to such a metanarration, and the closeness of fit facilitates this particular story's becoming an immense media drama. But the newspaper's representation accentuates the opposition and creates an allegory by inscribing social identities, Israeli Jewish and Palestinian Arab, onto the respective symbols, "victim" and "terrorist."

The coverage accentuates the victim/terrorist opposition by polarizing it. One part of this polarization is the idealization of the victim. In this case the actual victim is already close to ideal. As a young girl cut down on her way to school, this victim bears many attributes of ideal victimhood: as a child she is innocent; as a girl she is vulnerable; as a dutiful student she is virtuous. The newspaper coverage augments this ready-made image through repetition. Articles and picture captions throughout the first days of coverage refer to the victim's age—fifteen. Numerous photographs recall the victim's gender. Quotations from bereaved friends and family reiterate that this young girl was on her way to school. The front page of *Yedioth*'s first day of coverage demonstrates all three of these tendencies in a single spread. Figure 6.1 shows the large color photograph of the (healthy, prestabbing) victim that dominated the spread. Her image is framed by the title "The Murdered Girl,"[27] and above the picture a headline cites the bereaved father saying, "In the morning I sent a girl to school, in the afternoon I was called to identify her corpse."

Beyond such repetition, though, the coverage also augments the ideal victim image by making this actual victim intimately known and deeply familiar to a nation of readers who in fact do not know her. On the front-page spread just described, for example, the picture of the victim is framed on the bottom by a caption that gives the victim's name: Helena Rap. This simple caption begins an extended personal introduction to the victim. Throughout the coverage Helena is referred to by name—often by first name. Indeed, the newspaper's coverage encapsulates and summarizes the entire set of events as "Helena" by visually and textually elaborating images of the victim. On the third page of Monday's coverage, for example, an enormous spread of photographs features images of Helena (see fig. 6.2). This spread shows Helena's family mourning the loss of their daughter. The spread is composed of three separate pictures. On the right side of the newspaper page is a large picture of Helena's father holding, in his hand, a snapshot of Helena. On the left side of the page is a picture of Helena's brother comforting their mother. And in the top left corner of the page is a very small picture of Helena's face. This small image of Helena's face appears in the top outside corner of each of the

הנרצחת

Figure 6.1. "The Murdered Girl." (Source: *Yedioth Ahronoth*, May 25, 1992, p. 1. Reprinted by permission of *Yedioth Ahronoth*.)

seven pages of Monday's edition of *Yedioth Ahronoth* that are devoted to coverage of the Bat Yam violence. (See figs. 6.4, 6.6, and 6.15 for the positioning of this image on other pages.) The image of the victim's face (shown in fig. 6.3) is thus made into an icon representing the events. As an icon, the image of the victim's face is framed, above and below, by the words "the murder and the rage."[28] Repetition of the icon helps frame the newspaper's narrative of the events as a story about victimhood, just as its textual message helps frame an affective orientation toward the stabbing and the response.

The dual textual processes of idealizing the victim and iconizing her image enhance the symbolizing value of the victim image. This process of representing Helena as the subject of the newspaper's narrative is powerfully reinforced by some subtle aspects of the semiotic structuring of the pictorial spread shown in figure 6.2. For example, the image of Helena's face that appears in the corner icon bears the same head tilt and facial expression as the larger image of her face that appeared (in the same issue) in the front-page photograph shown in figure 6.1. Indeed, both of these images appear to be derived from the snapshot that Helena's father is holding in his hand in the right-hand image in figure 6.2. This iconic repetition of the image of victimhood projects, in Roman Jakobson's (1960) terms, a paradigmatic opposition onto a syntagmatic progression. The poetics of the imagery calls attention to itself, beginning the transformation of an objective documentation of reality into a narrative with a moral point.

The striking parallelism is further developed by other structural features of the imagery in figure 6.2. The spread is structured along two intersecting diagonals. One

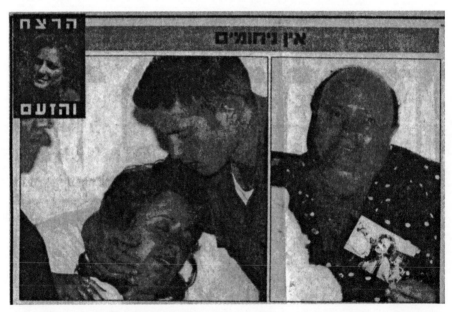

Figure 6.2. "There Is No Consolation." (Source: *Yedioth Ahronoth*, May 25, 1992, p. 3. Reprinted by permission of *Yedioth Ahronoth*.)

הרצח
והזעם

Figure 6.3. "The Murder ... And the Rage." Corner icon. (Source: *Yedioth Ahronoth*, May 25, 1992, p. 3. Reprinted by permission of *Yedioth Ahronoth*.)

diagonal—from the lower left corner of the spread to upper right corner—is defined by the lines formed by the parallel tilts of the heads of Helena (in the corner icon and the snapshot in her father's hand), her mother (resting on a pillow, held by her son), and her father. The second diagonal—from the lower right corner of the spread to the upper left corner—is defined by the angle of the snapshot held in the father's hand and the tilt of the son's head in the center. The reader's gaze is directed along the second of these diagonals, from lower right to upper left.[29] This diagonal directs the reader's gaze to the corner icon, linking the icon to the snapshot. The reader is thus drawn to contemplate the three images of the victim. From the original snapshot (fig. 6.2), to the front-page enlargement (fig. 6.1), to the corner icon (fig. 6.3), there is a progressive loss of context. The snapshot shows the girl from the waist up, surrounded by a house and garden that we assume to be her home. The icon in the header, in contrast, shows only the girl's face. This progressive loss of context helps transform the picture from an objective copy to a morally charged signifier.

The iconism described here represents Helena as the subject of the newspaper's narrative, and her subjectivity is further elaborated (on inner pages of the first day's coverage) by articles that describe intimate details of her life, her family members' reactions, her friends' feelings, and so on. The coverage narrativizes her life as it reports on her death:

DESCRIPTION OF HELENA RAP

> It was 7:10 am when Helena Rap, fifteen and a half years of age, left her home on S.Y. Agnon Street in Bat Yam for the bus stop on Ben Gurion Street, on the municipal boardwalk. She was supposed to get on bus #10, on her way to the WIZO-France School,[30] where she was a student in the photography track. (*Yedioth Ahronoth*, May 25, 1992, p. 2)

Such detailed narrativization of Helena's last moments, repeated in several articles early on in the coverage, constructs her as the subject of the coverage and of reader interest. Readers are persuaded to identify with Helena by virtue of the fullness with which they come to know her.

In dramatic contrast to the fullness of voice attributed to "Helena" in death, the Palestinian man who killed her is characterized by an absence of voice. In the week of coverage, encompassing more than twenty full articles and at least that many pictures, the agent of the original violence receives only two or three mentions. This man was centrally involved in many of the "events"—he stabbed Helena; he was caught by a passerby; he was beaten by the crowd; he was interrogated by police; he was jailed by prosecutors; and so on—yet he plays almost no role in how these events are reported.

Yedioth Ahronoth's construction of the Arab terrorist works through silence. Even when he is mentioned, the Palestinian man is narrativized as lacking a voice. When reporting on the suspect's first appearance in court, for example, *Yedioth* represents him as silent and mute, refusing to make eye contact (*Yedioth Ahronoth*, May 27, 1992, pp. 2–3).[31] When speech is attributed to the suspect, the words are framed as nonsensical and irrational (see "Representations of Jewish Emotion," this chapter). The attacker's name is rarely used, even though his full name is provided early on in the coverage. In contrast, the victim is repeatedly referred to by name—even by her first name. And while the victim's life is richly narrativized, the attacker's motivations for his outrageous action are not discussed. Visual representations also deface the terrorist's subjectivity. Figure 6.4 shows the picture that appeared in *Yedioth*'s first day of coverage, where he is shown literally faceless, hidden by a black ski mask on his way to jail. In the early 1990s the Israeli discourse on terrorism was so powerful that "terrorist" could be narrated even without explicit discussion. This implicit discourse derives from the deep resonances attendant to images of terrorism—and victimhood—in Israeli discourse. These resonances have historical roots.

Historical Resonances of "Victim" and "Terrorist"

The images of victim and terrorist in the coverage of the Bat Yam violence derive their meaning and power in part from historical resonances—dialogic references to popular memories. Thus to explicate the social drama occasioned by the nationalistic violence and its discursive elaboration in newspaper coverage, I turn to a discussion of the resonances that these images evoke, and that give them social meaning.

The inscription of victimhood onto the Israeli Self recalls prominent historical discourses of Jewish victimhood. The Israeli construction of Self revolves around—while crucially contesting—the notion of the Jew as victim. The originary core for these constructions lies in the biblical and historical narratives of Jewish diaspora. Jews chronicle a long history of displacement, including the Exodus from Egypt of (approximately) 1280 BC, the Babylonian Exile of 587 BC, the Roman Exile of 70 AD, and the great diaspora in 135 AD (Scheindlin 1998). The latter event, occasioned by the fall of the Bar Kokhba Revolt, led to the dispersal of the Jewish people throughout the world that came to be known as the Diaspora.[32] These mythologized displacements

Figure 6.4. Image of the Suspect in the Stabbing. (Source: *Yedioth Ahronoth*, May 25, 1992, p. 5. Reprinted by permission of *Yedioth Ahronoth*.)

form an important part of Jewish memory and are commemorated in religious observances. The festival of Passover and the fast of Tisha B'Av, for example, recall the Exodus from Egypt, and the Babylonian and Roman Exiles, respectively.

A secular history of Jewish victimhood takes place in Europe. Jewish history in Europe is a fantastical roller coaster of peaks and troughs—golden eras of prosperity and belonging followed by dark periods of persecution. Jews flourished in Spain, for example, for hundreds of years until they were massacred and expelled in the Spanish Inquisition of 1492 (Sachar 1994). Jews prospered in France in the eighteenth and nineteenth centuries, until 1894 when the infamous trial of Alfred Dreyfus led to a cycle of vicious anti-Semitic attacks (Telushkin 1991:262). Ironically, France had been the first European country to grant Jews full citizenship and equal rights. Jews did well in Germany, too, where they were among the leaders of German high culture, until the middle of the twentieth century, when they were decimated in the Holocaust. The Holocaust is merely the most recent and the most powerful of these memories of victimhood.[33]

Modern Israeli discourse continues to marshal the power of the victim symbol, largely through the image of the Holocaust. The state of Israel arguably owes its establishment to the horror felt by the Western world in the wake of the Nazi Holocaust during World War II (see Morahg 1997:143), and the Holocaust remains a prominent signifier in Israeli discourse today. Holocaust memorials, for example, are commonplace elements of urban Israeli landscapes. I passed a striking memorial sculpture many times each day while living in the student dormitories of the University of Haifa. The Holocaust Museum, Yad Va-Shem, is a required stop for visiting dignitaries from abroad, as well as a major tourist attraction.[34] Holocaust Day is marked each year by a dramatic two-minute moment of silence, in which a siren sounds, and all traffic, all activity comes to a complete stop. Schools instruct children from an early age in the meaning of this event, and in the proper emotional response to it.[35] During the early 1990s a Holocaust-related issue drew newspaper coverage almost weekly. One such media debate involved a controversy over whether or not the Israeli Symphony Orchestra could play music by Richard Wagner, the reputedly anti-Semitic German composer whose music had been championed by the Nazis.

Israel also marshals the victim image in more active ways. Israel has historically represented itself as a small, poor, and weak country in the midst of large, rich, and powerful Arab neighbors. Israel's War of Independence in 1948, for example, is represented in mainstream Israeli historiography as a miraculous victory of an Israeli "David" over an Arab "Goliath." More sober evaluations, however, judge the two sides to have been fairly even in military strength and preparedness at the time hostilities broke out (Flapan 1987:187–199). Even after the Six Day War in 1967, when military fortunes dramatically reversed and Israeli technical superiority was clearly established, Israeli discourse continued to represent Israel as small, vulnerable, and victimized. Israelis frequently refer to themselves as one Jewish country in the midst of twenty-two Arab countries, as a small country in the midst of large countries, as a poor country in the midst of (oil) rich countries, as an island of democracy in a sea of autocracies.[36] Israel claims victimization also when the world singles it out for special scrutiny, as in 1976 when the United Nations passed a resolution equating Zionism, the Jewish nationalist movement, with racism. During the 1991 Gulf War, Israel represented itself as a victim when Iraq attacked Israel with Scud missiles, even though Israel was not an official combatant. Israelis noted that their stature in the world improved so long as Israel suffered the attacks without striking back: Jewish Israel once again played the victim.[37]

The image of "victim," though, is one of the many symbols shared by Jews and Palestinians in their common struggle over Israeli discursive terrain. Like the "tree," which means "erasure" to Palestinians by virtue of its meaning "reclamation" to Jews, "victim" is a symbol whose meaning stems from its dynamic opposition in the symbolic repertoire of two nationalist discourses. Thus Israeli constructions of Self as "victim" are intimately related to constructions of Other as "terrorist."[38] As the Israeli journalist Danny Rubinstein has put it, "in order to be a victim ... you have to create a picture of the enemy as a huge monster" (quoted in Shipler 1986:183). By the 1980s, as Shipler (1986:123) notes, Israeli public discourse had a very powerful image of the terrorist:

In official communiqués, in Israeli newspapers and broadcasts, even in conversation, the word ["terrorist"] had become synonymous with the PLO[39] and, in many quarters, with Arabs generally. ... Israel radio and television, and [newspapers] almost always referred to the PLO as nothing other than a "terrorist organization" with "terrorist bases" in Lebanon containing "terrorist buildings," "terrorist trucks," and launching "terrorist boats." Palestinian refugee camps in Lebanon were merely "terrorist bases" or "terrorist headquarters" ... somehow the term became almost a catechism in Israeli discussion, a chant that masked the human faces behind the enemy lines.

Currently the dominant Israeli construction of the Palestinian Other may be as "terrorist," but this was not the first Zionist image of Palestinians. Theodor Herzl's initial writings on the imagined Jewish State do not mention Palestinian Arabs at all. In *Judenstaat*, "The Jewish State," written in 1896, before he had actually been to the Middle East himself, Herzl describes an imaginary society of Jews in Palestine. Herzl imagines this utopian society down to the minutest details, such as the design of middle-class homes (Herzl 1988:108–109) and the text of extradition treaties (Herzl 1988:148–149), but he does not mention a resident population. In this book Herzl is intensely concerned with the physical parameters of the land: how the land would be mapped, subdivided, settled, and made productive. Early Zionist constructions of the Palestinian Other merged the local population with the natural topography. In this way Herzl helped construct the powerful image of "a land without people" (i.e., Palestine) for "a people without land" (i.e., Jews).

In developing this image of the Other, European Jews were treating the Middle Eastern people they encountered much in the way other Europeans had encountered other natives. European Jews, like European colonial ventures elsewhere, mis-understood and misrepresented land-use patterns that were different from their own. While some of the early Zionist settlements reclaimed land not traditionally used by the Palestinian residents, such as the Hula swamps in the Galilee and many of the coastal wetlands, other settlements bought or usurped lands that were used for grazing. The uncultivated vegetation of these communally held and communally used lands looked, to the European mind's eye, empty.[40] Jewish pioneers also either misrecognized or overlooked Palestinian systems of land-ownership, as their purchases of land from absentee landowners displaced Palestinian peasants (Shafir 1989). The image Israelis constructed of the Palestinian thus shares many features with the image American colonists created of the American Indian: Palestinians, in Zionist mythology, are *noble savages*. Palestinians were constructed as noble because they lived in and knew of the (Jewish) homeland (Benvenisti 2000; Idinopulos 1998), because they worked the land and herded the flocks in ways that recalled (Jewish) biblical practices (see "The Tractor and the Horse," this chapter), and because they retained their Semitic mother tongue, so similar to the Hebrew that Zionists were struggling to revive (see chapter 7). Palestinians were constructed as savage because they appeared poor and backward, and because they opposed Jewish settlement—sometimes violently.

Indeed, the encounter of European Jewry with real Palestinians markedly changed Zionist imagery. After visiting Palestine in 1902, for example, Herzl wrote the book *Altneuland*, "Old New Country," a fantasy of what a future "Israel" might be like. In this work Arabs are mentioned, but they appear as grateful beneficiaries of, and enthusiastic participants in, the Jewish return. This image of the Palestinian beneficiary of Zionist colonization remains strong in Israeli identity discourses today, but in the wake of increasing—and increasingly violent—conflict between Jewish settlers and Palestinian residents, a companion image emerged, namely the Palestinian as a "fearsome, violent figure of immense strength and duplicity" (Shipler 1986:182). It was this image that was consolidated into the symbol of the "terrorist."

Standing in opposition to the Israeli discourse of peaceful coexistence (see "The Tractor and the Horse," this chapter) is a long history of violence between Jewish settlers and Palestinian residents. Violent conflict began in earnest in the 1920s. Riots and counterriots broke out in several cities—in Hebron in 1922; in Jaffa in 1929; and so on—and led to numerous deaths on both sides. Palestinian resistance became organized in the 1930s, during the Arab Revolt (Swedenburg 1995), and reached full-scale warfare in 1947. The establishment of the State of Israel in 1948 was a watershed event that wrought many dramatic changes. In the wake of the Jewish defeat of the Palestinian resistance, organized violence to the Jewish State was taken over by Arab states. A stunning number of wars ensued, including the 1956 Sinai Campaign, the 1967 Six Day War/June War, the so-called War of Attrition between 1967 and 1973, the 1973 Yom Kippur/October War, and the 1982 Lebanon War. All of these wars involved Israel, Egypt, Jordan, Syria, and Lebanon, with the Palestinians themselves more-or-less sidelined (until the 1982 Lebanon War). Indeed Palestinian quiescence was jointly managed by Israel internally (Lustick 1980) and by the Arab "frontline" states outside Israel (Hudson 1977). This quiescence was challenged only after the 1967 "Six Day War." This war destroyed the military and political prestige of the Arab countries, when Israel demolished the Egyptian and Syrian air forces and conquered the Sinai Peninsula, the West Bank, the Gaza Strip, and the Golan Heights. As a result, Palestinians took their resistance into their own hands (Khalidi 1997).

Palestinians grabbed control of their own destiny when Yasir Arafat gained control of the PLO and embarked on a dramatic campaign to bring the Palestinian issue to world attention. Arafat's leadership was first established in guerilla military actions inside Israel, including daring raids across the Jordanian border into Israeli territory. In the 1970s a series of spectacular airline hijackings helped bring international recognition to the Palestinian nationalist struggle. A series of equally spectacular attacks inside Israel, including a 1978 attack on a bus that killed thirty-three Israelis (Shipler 1986:85) and a 1980 attack on Kibbutz Misgav Am that killed several children (Shipler 1986:112–115), indelibly inscribed the image of "terrorist" onto the identity of "Palestinian" in Israeli discourse.

Despite the very real human toll, terrorism—like victimhood—is most powerful as a signifier in discourse. As many commentators have noted, terrorism's efficacy stems from inciting terror, not inflicting physical damage. As Shipler (1986:84) writes,

Arab terrorists rarely manage to kill more than about twenty people in Israel each year, compared with two to three times that number of ordinary murder victims, more than 200 who commit suicide, and an average of about 425 who have been dying annually in traffic accidents in recent years. Between 1982 and 1985, a total of 654 Israeli soldiers died in Lebanon to prevent Palestinian guerillas from continuing attacks that had cost a total of 29 lives in northern Israel in the four years from June 1, 1978, to June 5, 1982.[41]

The symbol "terrorist" wields far more power than the activities of terrorists, but this discursive power can be deployed to various effects.

Representations of Jewish Violence

Despite the suggestive power of the narrative of Jewish victim and Palestinian terrorist, the events in Bat Yam, and their coverage in Yedioth Ahronoth, resisted this simple opposition. May 1992 was a time of persistent violence between Israelis and Palestinians, including a series of knife attacks by Palestinians on Israeli citizens in the months leading up to the Bat Yam stabbing. All of these events had drawn front-page newspaper coverage, but only the Bat Yam stabbing attracted the extraordinary attention described earlier. The special coverage accorded the Bat Yam incident is due to the violent response by Jewish residents of Bat Yam.

Three kinds of violence are represented in the media coverage of the Bat Yam stabbing and riots:

- The violence of the stabbing
- The violence of the mob
- The violence of the police

Of these three kinds of violence, the coverage focuses most heavily on the violence of the mob. Strikingly, the stabbing itself is virtually unnarrativized. Neither photographs nor articles explicitly represent or analytically discuss the stabbing. In Monday's edition, on the second page of coverage, an item under the heading "Sequence of Events" details how the crime took place (see fig. 6.5), but it depicts the crime diagrammatically, with an almost medical precision and detachment.[42] Toward the end of Monday's coverage, on the seventh page of the newspaper, a small picture shows the victim's corpse (see the righthand photograph in fig. 6.6). But even here the body is completely covered by a blanket, and one must read the caption in order to interpret the image. Indeed, as mentioned earlier, the Palestinian terrorist himself is almost entirely absent from the coverage. Similarly, police violence is only minimally narrativized.

In sharp contrast, however, Jewish violence—the violence of the mob—became a graphic focus of the narrative attention. For example, on *Yedioth Ahronoth*'s front page on Monday, the first day of coverage, the large color photograph of Helena

Figure 6.5. Diagrammatic Representation of the Stabbing. (Source: *Yedioth Ahronoth*, May 25, 1992, p. 2. Reprinted by permission of *Yedioth Ahronoth*.)

(discussed earlier as fig. 6.1) appeared as part of a full-page spread, in which it was juxtaposed to an even larger color photograph of a mob smashing a car (see fig. 6.7). These two pictures are labeled, respectively, "The Murdered Girl" and "The Riots."[43] This juxtaposition of images links the death to the riots. Significantly, the newspaper allotted twice as much space to the Jewish violence as to the ideal victim. The focus on Jewish violence becomes even clearer a bit further into the first day's coverage. Figure 6.6, for example, shows a photograph of the bloodied and bandaged face of a policeman injured by a rioter, and figure 6.8 shows a second large photograph of Jewish rioting.[44] The second day of coverage is dominated by the victim's funeral, and there are no pictures of the ongoing violence (though violence does play a role in many of the day's articles), but mob violence returns to the headlines on the third day of coverage. Figure 6.9 shows the two color photographs that appeared on the front page of Wednesday's *Yedioth Ahronoth*. One photograph shows a fire raging in a dumpster against a shadowy backdrop of men in chaotic motion, and the second photograph shows policemen wrestling with rioters. By Thursday the front-page headline reads: "Riots Peak in Bat Yam," and on an inner page a large black-and-white photograph (fig. 6.10) shows Bat Yam residents being subdued by mounted police.

Thus, while the story narrated by the coverage appears to involve Palestinian violence and Israeli victimhood, the media actually becomes preoccupied with the meaning of Jewish violence. This focus can be seen in subtle shifts in the framing of the news items and their representations. Images of Jewish violence early in the coverage are relatively mild, while subsequent images become increasingly harsh. Figures 6.11 and 6.12, for example, show two images of Jewish violence. Figure 6.11, which appeared on the front page of Monday's newspaper (and which re-presents the left side of fig. 6.7), portrays a violent act (toppling a car) as a relatively calm and serene event. The image is violent, to be sure, but in a relaxed, almost peaceful way. The sunny day and colorful clothing contribute to this effect. The crowd appears at its leisure. Some bystanders are clapping; others are smiling. Most are watching; only a few are acting. One man is even taking a picture. In the foreground of the picture (bottom right), a distinguished-looking man is helping push the car over. His wristwatch, clean white shirt, and carefully groomed hair contest the violent context. Even the car itself seems only slightly the worse for wear (since the damage is out of sight).

Figure 6.6.   Images of Injured Policeman (left) and Stabbing Victim (right). (Source: *Yedioth Ahronoth*, May 25, 1992, p. 7. Reprinted by permission of *Yedioth Ahronoth*.)

Figure 6.7. Front-Page Spread. (Source: *Yedioth Ahronoth*, May 25, 1992, p. 1. Reprinted by permission of *Yedioth Ahronoth*.)

Figure 6.12 (which re-presents the picture from fig. 6.8 along with the title that framed it), portrays what appears to be the same scene as that shown in figure 6.11, but figure 6.12 represents this scene very differently. In this picture, too, men are destroying a car, but here they seem exerted. The scene is rough. We see grimaces on the men's faces and damage to the car. The wristwatch in this photo has been stretched out of shape.

While the first image showed mob violence justified by terrorist violence, subsequent images contest this representation. The justification of the violence in the first section of the newspaper stems in part from the linkage articulated between the stabbing and the reaction. Monday's front-page spread (fig. 6.7) juxtaposes a picture of Helena, the victim, with a picture of the serene mob, suggesting the following predication:

Stabbing → violent reaction

This predication is reinforced throughout the seven pages of Monday's coverage by the corner icon (fig. 6.3; the icon also appears in figs. 6.2, 6.4, 6.6, and 6.15), which frames the image of the victim's face with the words: "the murder and the rage." The icon thus reiterates the causal link between the originary and reactive violences, justifying the latter by reference to the former. The icon suggests that the violent actions are caused by rage and justified by murder, or:

Figure 6.8. Image of Rioting on Cover of Inner Features Section. (Source: *Yedioth Ahronoth*, May 25, 1992, "24 Hours," p. 1. Reprinted by permission of *Yedioth Ahronoth*.)

Murder → rage → riot

On the cover of the inner features section (fig. 6.12), however, we see a much harsher image of the violence that is framed differently. The image of Jewish men toppling a car in figure 6.12 is framed by the words "the frustration and the rage," whereby the rage is justified by a different, and arguably lesser cause. Here the predication is:

Frustration → rage → riot

The altered framing introduces a subtle but weighty shift in emphasis. Figure 6.12 no longer narrates violence justified by the murder. Rather, figure 6.12 narrates a "frustration" that leads to violence. But from the text (and from Israeli contextual knowledge of Bat Yam) this frustration refers not only to Palestinian violence against Jews but also to Ashkenazi domination of Mizrahim. Thursday's major headline indicated that the orientation of the protests had become antiestablishment, rather than anti-Palestinian, saying: "Cries of Death to Arabs Switched to Death to the Police" (*Yedioth Ahronoth*, May 28, 1992, p. 3). With the violence now directed against Jews

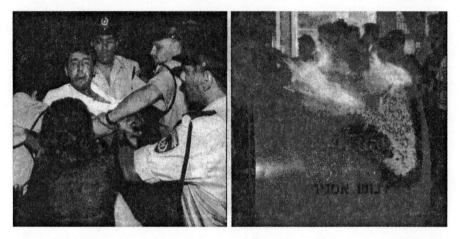

Figure 6.9.   Images of Rioting. (Source: *Yedioth Ahronoth*, May 27, 1992, p. 1. Reprinted by permission of *Yedioth Ahronoth.*)

(i.e., the Israeli police), its visual representation in *Yedioth* is characterized by extreme roughness (see figs. 6.9, 6.10). These images of violence, however, are no longer on the front page of the newspaper.

Historical Resonances of Jewish Violence

The media's focus on Jewish violence undermines the moral clarity of the simple dichotomous opposition between Jewish "victim" and Palestinian "terrorist." Indeed, the image of Jewish violence, especially the out-of-control violence that characterized the Bat Yam rioting, highlights a paradox in the mainstream construction of Israeli identity. While Israelis represent themselves as victims of Palestinian violence, they pride themselves on not being victims. The coverage rhetorically resolves this paradox through a dual process of gendering victimhood and racializing violence. The Hebrew press inscribed victimization onto the female Israeli Self, and violence onto the ethnic Israeli Other. It achieves this resolution by evoking Jewish ethnicity, an image that has its own powerful historical resonances.

The image of the Jew as victim is a deeply ambivalent symbol in Israeli discourse because it recalls an anachronistic, pre-Israeli Jewish identity that is diametrically opposed to the Zionist reconstruction of Jewish identity in the form of the "New Jew" (Almog 2000; Zerubavel 1995). The construction of the New Jew was an attempt to reverse popular memories of (European) Jewish history, which Zionist historiography characterized as one of victimization. The New Jew was conceived as the very antithesis of the victim. Zionist social theory blamed Jewish victimization on the material conditions of Jewish lifestyles in Europe, and especially eastern Europe, where the majority of European Jews lived prior to the Holocaust. Historically denied the right

Figure 6.10. Images of Rioting. (Source: *Yedioth Ahronoth*, May 28, 1992, p. 3. Reprinted by permission of *Yedioth Ahronoth*.)

to own land, Jews had evolved into free professions as merchants, bankers, lawyers, and doctors. Zionism sought to redress the tragic history of discrimination and dispossession by normalizing Jewish life, by re-creating a Jewish tie to land, to labor, and to the body.[45] The tie to the land materialized in the return to Palestine. The tie to the labor and the body materialized in the Zionist celebration of the farmer, the worker, and the soldier.

The construction of the Israeli Self involved a complex reconceptualization of Jewishness—from religious to ethnic, and from cultural to national. Israeli discourse thus ironically distinguishes between "Jews" and "Israelis," attributing weakness, victimhood, and defeat to "Jewish," while asserting strength, agency, and victory as "Israeli." This discourse of Israeli identity resonates in Israeli military strategy: attacks on Israeli citizens tend to generate strong, aggressive, military responses, even when negotiation and conciliation might save (Israeli) lives. The strength of this discourse was revealed in a hostage incident from 1992. Palestinian fighters took Israeli hostages and barricaded themselves in a small house. A standoff ensued, and Palestinian leaders negotiated with Israeli military and political officials in an effort to end the incident without further bloodshed or loss of face on either side. The Israeli military, however, did not wait for negotiations to succeed, launching a raid on the house in which the Palestinian fighters and the Israeli hostages were hidden. In the raid the Palestinian attackers were killed, but one of the hostages was killed as well. The following day the press reported that negotiations had been close to an agreement that might have saved the life of the Israeli hostage. The power of the "New Jew" rhetoric is manifested in the paucity of criticism of the military for its only partially successful, and very tragic, raid. The Israeli abhorrence of victimhood was so strong that it trumped the desire to

המהומות

Figure 6.11. "The Riots" (detail of fig. 6.7). (Source: *Yedioth Ahronoth*, May 25, 1992, p. 1. Reprinted by permission of *Yedioth Ahronoth.*)

Figure 6.12. "The Frustration and the Rage" (perspective of fig. 6.8). (Source: *Yedioth Ahronoth*, May 25, 1992, "24 Hours," p. 1. Reprinted by permission of *Yedioth Ahronoth*.)

save lives. Accordingly, when during the Gulf War Israel agreed to play the victim, suffering the Scud missile attacks without attacking Iraq, the media and the public expressed great tension over the role.

This struggle between victim and fighter emerges in the coverage of the Bat Yam stabbing and riots. An article that appeared in the Friday edition of *Yedioth Ahronoth* that summarized and interpreted the Bat Yam events was entitled "Anaxnu lo Frayerim," "We Are Not Suckers" (Barnea 1992). The Hebrew word *frayer*, "sucker," is a slang term with a complex cultural meaning (Bloch 1990). *Frayer* refers to the heavily stigmatized condition of being victimized—by fast drivers, by clever salesmen, by government bureaucracy, or by terrorists. In this context—the author's title comes from a comment made by a resident of Bat Yam—the usage refers to the feelings of Bat Yam residents that they have been taken advantage of, and that the riots were their rejection of the "sucker" identity.

This Israeli concept of Self therefore forms part of a triadic set of oppositions—the (old) Jewish victim, the (new) Israeli soldier/farmer,[46] and the Palestinian terrorist—defined in terms of relations to violence. The Jewish victim represents a nonviolence that leads to suffering violence. The Palestinian terrorist represents the uncontrolled application of amoral violence. And the Israeli soldier represents the controlled application of morally justified violence.

The representation of police actions in the Bat Yam media drama is instructive. The Israeli police play a prominent role in the events being described, but they play a minimal role in the description. Police apprehend the man who stabbed Helena; police are injured in the rioting; police question the suspect; police confront the mobs of rioters; police imprison residents of Bat Yam; mounted police turn water cannon and clubs on unarmed citizens; and so on. The coverage of the police activities, though, is minimal, and its character is striking.[47] Where the coverage does describe the actions of the police they are shown to exhibit coolness and to apply violence in measured ways. Control is the central metaphor. The apprehension of the suspect, for example, is described somewhat breathlessly as a heroic chase by passersby and a bloody attempt at a lynching by the mob. The police, however, are described as acting coolly: they hold off the mob; they shield the suspect; and they take him into custody. Similarly, descriptions of violent protests in and around Bat Yam, in which crowds of angry residents searched for Arab workers to attack, are described quite racily as regards the actions of the mobs, but the police are noted as defending those attacked and calming the tempers of those enraged. The description of one particular incident is representative: It is reported that an off-duty military officer, who happened to be passing by at the time, rescued an Arab worker from attack. This representation of Israeli official authority as exerting controlled violence comes in the context of considerable debate in Israeli society over the treatment of Palestinians in military and civilian custody. As Shipler (1986:88–90) notes, Israeli security forces sometimes react passionately to Palestinian terrorists, and when this happens many Israeli media institutions comply in covering up such images.

The triad—Jewish victim, Israeli soldier, Palestinian terrorist—is simultaneously mapped onto the domain of ethnicity in Israel, as Mizrahi identity becomes a synonymous signifier for (old) Jewish identity. Virginia Domínguez (1989) describes the important distinction in Israeli discourse between "heritage" and "culture," and the mapping of this distinction onto social identities. In an insightful study of the distribution of two Hebrew terms, *morasha*, "heritage," and *tarbut*, "culture," in the Israeli popular media, Domínguez shows that the former is used to describe Mizrahi cultural practices, while the latter is used to describe Ashkenazi cultural practices (Dominguez 1989:123). Mizrahi heritage is represented as anachronistic, while Ashkenazi culture is represented as modern, advanced, and rational.

The uncontrolled nature of (Jewish) violence inscribes Mizrahi identity onto the media representations of Bat Yam. The Bat Yam coverage was, in fact, filled with indirect references to Mizrahi identity. The media's focus on the "Death to Arabs" slogans shouted by the demonstrators evokes the Israeli discursive tradition of associating irredentist hatred of Arabs with Mizrahim (Shohat 1989; see also "Living-Room Talk and Shower Talk" in chapter 2 and "A Family Connection" in chapter 5). Further, discussion of the riots focuses on the poverty, unemployment, and low quality of living in Bat Yam, and these are qualities that recall Israeli discourses linking Mizrahim with "slum" neighborhoods and other social problems (see text 2.4).

The coverage of the Bat Yam stabbing and riots reinforced these historical resonances by semiotically linking Jewish violence and Arab identity. For example, the coverage repeatedly inscribed Palestinian identity onto the angry and violent responses of Jewish residents of Bat Yam. References abound to burning tires, stone throwing, and commando knives, which at the time were powerful symbols of the Palestinian Intifada. The editorial cartoon in figure 6.13, for example, shows an Israeli policeman overwhelmed by smoke billowing from a burning tire, which is labeled "Bat Yam." Helena's father is reported to arrive at the police station holding a stone in one hand and a commando knife in the other (see figure 6.14). These representations construct a Mizrahi Jewish identity as violent through a link to the Jewish-Arab identity (see text 5.6).[48]

Rioting itself recalls a well-known history of Mizrahi urban protest movements in the 1960s and 1970s (Hasson 1993; Sachar 1989:538–542; see also "Wadi Salib" section in chapter 2), and the media's representation of violence in Bat Yam resonates with prominent stereotypes of a Mizrahi Other. An ugly history of media representations of Mizrahi immigrants in the early 1950s remains a powerful popular memory in current Israel. Early representations of Mizrahi immigrants to Israel belie a virulent racism. Ella Shohat (1989:116), for example, cites a passage from a 1949 editorial that appeared in Israel's liberal newspaper, *Ha-Aretz*, in which the columnist refers to the Mizrahi immigrants as a "primitive race of people"

> whose level of knowledge is one of virtually absolute ignorance, and, worse, who have little talent for understanding anything intellectual. ... These Jews ... are totally subordinated to the play of savage and primitive instincts.[49]

This stereotype was propagated in many popular cultural forms. Shohat (1989:122) notes, for example, that Mizrahi men prominently played roles of violent and criminal characters in Israeli cinema. Thus the representations of mob violence in Bat Yam narrated a Mizrahi identity, just as protestations of discrimination narrated a Mizrahi identity in the aftermath of Zehava Ben's defeat in the 1992 Eurovision contest (see

Figure 6.13.   Cartoon Depicting Bat Yam as the Palestinian Intifada. (Source: *Yedioth Ahronoth*, May 29, 1992, p. 23. Reprinted by permission of *Yedioth Ahronoth*.)

"Nurit Ben," this chapter). In both cases it was not just violence that created this narrative of Israeli antiidentity, but the conjunction of violence with emotionality. In both cases it was the inappropriate control of emotion that characterizes the non-Israeli, but Jewish, Self. Thus the Old Jew/New Jew opposition is reconstructed in terms of violence and control of emotion. Mizrahim are stereotypically constructed as quintessentially emotional: on the one hand violent and criminal and on the other warm, familial, and affectionate (Shohat 1989). In this way, discourse on affect and its expression becomes a resource through which the ethnic difference is constructed and enforced. I therefore turn now to the representation of emotion in the Bat Yam media drama.

Narratives of Emotion

The simple We/They, Self/Other, Israeli/Palestinian dichotomies were subverted by the media's focus on emotion as well as by representations of Jewish violence. Indeed, the association of violence with Mizrahim works through the discourse of emotion. Yedioth Ahronoth drenched their coverage of the stabbing and rioting in Bat Yam in striking representations of emotion. This focus dramatizes the notion of victim, and naturalizes it by associating it with bodily (re)actions.

בעקבות הרצח והמהומות

Figure 6.14. Helena's Father with Rock and Commando Knife. (Source: *Yedioth Ahronoth*, May 27, 1992, p. 3. Reprinted by permission of *Yedioth Ahronoth*.)

Emotionality becomes a focus through elaborated representations of crying, sadness, and anger. Figures 6.1–6.3 show the three major images of the victim that appeared in the first few pages of the first day's coverage in Yedioth Ahronoth. As discussed earlier, the three images all derive from the snapshot in Ze'ev Rap's hand, embedded in figure 6.2. The progressive loss of context, from the embedded snapshot to the front-page enlargement to the icon miniature, coincides with a change in the emotional valence of the facial expression. In the snapshot, surrounded by family, home, and warm sunshine, Helena appears to be smiling. In the enlarged front-page photo, Helena appears wistful, with an expression that can be read in this context as sadness. In the corner icon, which shows only Helena's face, she appears to be crying.

Inner pages of the first day's coverage further elaborate the representation of emotion through additional images of sadness and crying. In figure 6.2, for example, which appeared on the third page of Monday's coverage, two photographs show crying by the victim's family. In the lefthand photograph, the victim's brother attempts to console the mother, who is crying. In the righthand photograph, the father's eyes are moist and lips spread in grief as he holds the snapshot of his deceased daughter. The entire visual spread is framed by the title "En Nixumim," "There Is No Consolation."

The focus on crying continues throughout the early stages of this media drama. On the fifth page of Monday's coverage, for example, a large black-and-white photograph (fig. 6.15) shows two young girls crying. This image is framed by text above the picture that reads "They Lament the Friend Who Is No Longer Here" and by a caption below the picture that reads "Two of Helena's Friends, Arm-in-Arm, After Her Death Was Made Known."[50] The next day's coverage of Helena's funeral included a

Figure 6.15.   "They Lament The Friend Who Is No Longer Here." (Source: *Yedioth Ahronoth*, May 25, 1992, p. 6. Reprinted by permission of *Yedioth Ahronoth*.)

photograph of girls crying (fig. 6.16) under a header that reads "Tears on Helena's Grave,"[51] and a picture of Helena's parents weeping at her grave (fig. 6.17).

The text, too, highlights and elaborates the focus on sorrow, tears, and lamentation. An article entitled "They Sit in the Classroom and Cry" describes the reactions of Helena's classmates at school (*Yedioth Ahronoth*, May 25, 1992, p. 7). Another report on Helena's funeral ends with the following description:

> One of the girls, who stood next to her father, sobbed so hard that no sound escaped from her mouth. Her eyes reduced to two narrow cracks, and her mouth was wide open. Another friend, Dafna, her eyes swollen from tears was led far from the crowd. She sat down on a stone and mourned in silence there. (*Yedioth Ahronoth*, May 26, 1992, p. 2)

And an interview with the bereaved father begins:

> Ze'ev Rap, Helena's father, speaks in a broken voice. He sits on her bed, and the tears flow from his face without end. His sons, the soldiers Avi and Dedi, sit at his side, and their faces are red from weeping. The mother, Rivka, sits in the living room, her face pale, and she refuses to be reconciled. (*Yedioth Ahronoth*, May 25, 1992, p. 2)

The Hebrew media thus constructed the Israeli Self as a victim through an abundance of sadness. In contrast, it is the absence of emotion that most powerfully constructs the

דמעות על קברה של הלנה

Figure 6.16. "Tears on the Grave of Helena." (Source: *Yedioth Ahronoth*, May 26, 1992, p. 1. Reprinted by permission of *Yedioth Ahronoth*.)

Figure 6.17. Helena Rap's Parents Mourn Their Daughter at Her Funeral. (Source: *Yedioth Ahronoth*, May 26, 1992, p. 3. Reprinted by permission of *Yedioth Ahronoth*.)

Palestinian Other as a terrorist. The faceless representation of the Palestinian attacker in figure 6.4, where he is pictured with his face covered by a mask, powerfully denies him an affective voice by obscuring the primary visual keys to human emotional expression. The coverage represents the attacker as having acted without cause for his extreme actions and without remorse over their deadly consequences. The attacker's name is reported, but it is seldom used in the narrative. Few details are reported about the attacker as an individual. We learn nothing about his background, for example, or about his motivations for the attack. His actions are represented as lacking any rational cause or emotional justification. The visual image that shows him masked and faceless (fig. 6.4) is juxtaposed to (and thereby associated with) an article whose headline presents his words as irrational: "I decided: If I don't find work I'll slaughter Jews" (*Yedioth Ahronoth*, May 25, 1992, p. 5). Palestinian terrorists are thus constructed as violent in an uncontrolled, irrational, and—literally—inexplicable way.

Indeed, even the stabbing itself is drained of its emotion in this representation, as the victim's body—as a victim—is deemphasized (see fig. 6.6, far right), and the "Sequence of Events" feature, which details how the incident unfolded, depicts the crime diagrammatically, with great detachment (see fig. 6.5).

The Coverage Concludes

By Thursday night the rioting had subsided, and as the dramatic week came to an end, so too did the coverage in Yedioth. In Friday's edition the main reference to the Bat Yam stabbing and riots is a long article that summarizes, analyzes, and repackages the whole drama. Accompanying this article is one last visual image of Bat Yam on the cover of the newspaper's "Week-in-Review" section.[52] In this picture, reproduced as figure 6.18, the riot appears remarkably quiet, and almost serene. The scene is early morning, and hundreds of people are milling about at a major intersection (*Yedioth Ahronoth*, May 29, 1992, "Friday Supplement," p. 1). From the distance and height of the photo, the scene could be a celebration. The accompanying articles focus once again on the riots as expressions of anti-Arab feeling.

The media representations of the Bat Yam drama have thus traced a spiral trajectory. At the beginning of the week the coverage narrated Jewish violence against Palestinians justified by Jewish sorrow and Jewish rage. As the week progressed, the media representations focused more heavily on Jewish mob violence against Jewish authority, and the narrative did not seek to justify the violence. By the end of the week coverage returned to representations of the drama as violence against Palestinians, but without the justificatory rhetoric.

The media drama's metanarrative deals with the proper deployment and control of emotion. The coverage spectacularly juxtaposed Jewish affects (sadness and anger) with Jewish affective behaviors (crying and rioting), constructing sadness-that-leads-to-tears and anger-that-leads-to-violence as natural responses to the stabbing of a young girl. The media representations simultaneously create and reflect Israeli imaginings of ethnic difference as they construct affective response to nationalistic violence, and channel this emotion into the naturalized domains of social identity. Newspaper accounts

Figure 6.18.   The Final Images of Rioting in Bat Yam. (Source: *Yedioth Ahronoth*, May 29, 1992, "Friday Supplement," p. 1. Reprinted by permission of *Yedioth Ahronoth*.)

of the two events, the stabbing and the rioting, differentially inscribed sentiments of sadness, anger, and frustration onto representations of the Jewish Self and the Palestinian Other in bodily responses such as crying and violence. Tears that express the sadness of bereavement and violence that expresses the anger in response to attack are ascribed to the Jewish Self. The Palestinian Other, in contrast, is represented as lacking proper emotion and cause for violence.

But extreme emotionality and violence are problematic images for the dominant Israeli discourse of Self, and representations of the Bat Yam rioting therefore undermined the simple dichotomy of Jewish-Arab difference. Sadness and rage construct Jews in opposition to Palestinians, but extreme sadness and extreme rage construct Mizrahi Jews in opposition to an Ashkenazi Self. The media coverage of the Bat Yam rioting sutured any possible rupture to dominant Israeli discourses of identity by discursively locating Jewish violence in the domain of Mizrahi Jewish identity. Jewish violence that is extreme, out of control, or unjustified is ascribed to the Arab-Jewish Self, the Mizrahi Other, in opposition to the Ashkenazi Self. In so doing, the Bat Yam narrative continues a long tradition in Israel of Ashkenazi domination of Palestinians being exercised by way of domination over Mizrahim (Shohat 1989:136).

Media Images and Identity

The newspaper coverage of the Bat Yam stabbing and rioting is important because of three interconnected patterns:

- The story of the stabbing is narrated through the polarized images of "victim" and "terrorist" that recall deeply familiar popular memories.

- The story of the rioting is narrated through coded images of social identity.

- The story's metanarrative is naturalized through its reference to emotions and the consequent bodily responses.

The construction of affective response to violence in Israel, and its mapping onto social identities, essentializes ethnic difference. Emotion is a powerful resource in such constructions because emotion seems so inherently natural and so impossibly cultural. Public discourse forums, like newspapers, gain their power in large part through their narrativization of the proper regimes of feeling and expressions of emotion.

Violence, Emotion, and Ethnicity in Israel

Structures of feeling have great power to mold representations, as Raymond Williams (1977:128–135) has noted. Ironically, this lasting power derives from emotion's inchoate and evanescent nature. The power of feeling is misrecognized precisely because feeling seems weak, tenuous, and inherently variable. And yet, as Williams argues, social formations exert tremendous power by assuring the uniformity of feeling. Paradoxically, structures of feeling draw their social power also from their posited location in the individual body. Emotions, as Catherine Lutz (1988) has pointed out, are assumed to be natural because we perceive them to be located in the body and because we associate them with bodily dispositions, such as crying and violence. The emotions themselves are thus taken for granted. Felt to precede thought, emotions are widely assumed to be independent of social control or cultural definition. Because emotions often go unarticulated, they are often thought to be inarticulable. Thus the affective work done by representations goes largely unnoticed, and, when noticed, largely unchallenged. These views of the nature of emotion and its role in society, however, are heavily ideologized, as Lutz and others have argued. Such scholars see emotions as culturally variable, as historically specific, and as socially constructed (Abu-Lughod and Lutz 1990). Emotion is thus produced in and through discourse, but discursively produced emotions are constructed as if they were natural. The naturalization of emotions differentially inscribed onto cultural Selves and cultural Others gives media dramas enormous cultural power.

The role of emotion is central to the meaning of the Bat Yam social/media drama, and the transformations in images of emotionality and violence in the Bat Yam newspaper narrative reflect an ongoing struggle among Ashkenazi, Mizrahi, and Palestinian claims to identity in Israel. Control over emotion is a highly valued Israeli ideal manifested in core institutions, such as the kibbutz and the army. A defining feature of the kibbutz lifestyle in Israel is the deconstruction of the nuclear family as the seat of personal emotion (Katriel 1991) and the reorganization of affect around age-grade cohorts.[53] The kibbutz movement created cohesive cohorts through the control of familial emotion on the one hand and the incitement of cohort-based emotion on the other.

If the kibbutz effects the control of love, the military asserts control over Jewish violence. The Israeli military is a prominent and highly respected institution in Israeli life, and it is a powerful force in disciplining both violence and emotion. The mandatory military training, while teaching all Israelis to apply controlled violence, also enforces a strict discipline on emotion, constructed in part through a dual separation of adulthood from childhood, and individuals from the family.

The value placed on emotional discipline finds symbolic representation in the Sabra, a classic symbol of the Israeli Self. The fruit of the prickly-pear cactus stands for the new, Israeli, Jew by symbolizing an ideal of personal comportment: the sabra (fruit), like the Sabra (Israeli), is said to have a soft and sweet interior that is protected by a prickly and impenetrable exterior. So, too, the Zionist ideal of the new Israeli was defined, in part, in emotional terms, idealized in the image of the scholar/soldier: a soft and vulnerable interior life protected by an impenetrable armor.

Tropes of Inclusion and Exclusion

The case study of the Bat Yam media drama demonstrated some patterns of representation that characterize Israeli public discourse more generally. Public discourse reflects individual choices, but it also imposes powerful constraints and influences on individual behaviors. Intermediate between the discourse of everyday conversation and the discourse of authoritative voices, public discourse spirals between these poles of variation. In Israel public discourse mediates the complex three-way struggle over the terms of Israeli identity. The media takes images from everyday practices and from official ideologies and re-presents them. Mediated images are redeployed in conversations, where they serve the pragmatic purposes of self-presentation and strategic negotiation, just as the media image of the Mizrahi singer, Zehava Ben, was redeployed in the interview conversation between Hagit and Nurit described at the outset of this chapter. Such images, though, are redeployed newly vested with the power of institutional authority.

Images of identity in Israeli public discourse form tropes of exclusion from, and inclusion in, Israeliness. Media representations of Palestinians exclude "Arab" from the domain of "Israeli," while media representations of Mizrahim seamlessly include "Mizrahi" in the domain of "Israeli." As a result, Palestinians are hyperpresent in Israeli media, while Mizrahim are erased from public discourse.

Arab identity is hyperpresent in Israeli media because any newspaper story that has involved Palestinian citizens of Israel in some way has come to be a story about Arabness. In the early 1990s Israeli newspapers addressed mostly Jewish concerns, as the vast majority of news, features, and images related to Jewish personalities, Hebrew literature, and majority culture. This preponderance of "Jewish" material in the Hebrew media was disproportionate even when taking into account that Jews comprised 80 percent of Israel's population. Despite being rare, however, articles about Palestinians were regular features of the Hebrew press. Most Friday editions of *Yedioth Ahronoth*, for example, included a feature article about a Palestinian actor, writer, politician, or other public figure (see "The Israeli Kid" in chapter 3). It is the regular presence of such articles, rather than their proportional absence, that constituted a "discourse of exclusion," because these features about Israeli Palestinians were about Arabness—not Israeliness.

This hyperpresence of Arabness in the Hebrew Israeli press was constructed, in part, through practices of naming. Palestinian Israeli individuals, when they appeared in the press, were identified and labeled as Israeli Arabs. In the early 1990s the Israeli media systematically distinguished between "Palestinian" and "Israeli-Arab." The Hebrew word *falastinai*, "Palestinian," unambiguously referred to noncitizen residents of the Occupied Territories, while the Hebrew phrase *araviye yisra'el*, literally "Arabs of Israel," (or, more colloquially, "Israeli Arabs"), referred to Palestinian citizens of Israel.[54] This linguistic and conceptual distinction played an interesting role in the Bat Yam coverage. The coverage consistently specified all references to Palestinians as either "Israeli-Arab" or "Palestinian." Stories, for example, about the lynch mobs that searched for Palestinian workers to beat up used the term *falastinai*, "Palestinian." In contrast, two articles that report on a Palestinian Israeli who was beaten up by a mob referred to him as an "Israeli Arab."[55]

Indeed, one of the first details provided in all news reports of violence in Israel was a classification of the violence into one of two categories: *al reka le'umani*, "nationalistic," or *al reka plili*, "criminal."[56] This categorization of nationalistic and criminal rephrases the underlying semantic distinction between "terrorism" and "crime," as it recodes a social distinction between "Palestinians" (terrorists) and "Arabs" (criminals). Reports also tended to specify the place of residence of the suspected agent of the violence, providing another clue to the all-important distinction between "Palestinians" and "Israel's Arabs."

Arab Israeli victims of "Palestinian" violence garner heavy coverage in the Israeli Hebrew media. Arab Israelis are sometimes hurt in "terrorist" attacks. In the Bat Yam riots, for example, the media paid a great deal of attention to the Palestinian Israeli who was beaten by the angry mob. Both citizen and noncitizen Palestinians were beaten in the course of the rioting in Bat Yam, but the media represented the two cases very differently. Such "positive" representations of the Arab in the Israeli media also function to delimit Palestinian identity by polarizing it. The rare cases in which Palestinian Israelis carry out "terrorist" attacks become the focus of intense media scrutiny, police investigation, and disciplinary actions.[57] Arabs in the Israeli press are thus narrativized either as "loyal" or as "terrorists."[58]

Such naming practices discursively construct Palestinian Israelis as hyphenated Israelis. Hyphenated identities are qualified identities that require specification and delimitation and that are therefore marginalized. Hyphenated individuals must assert Israeliness, rather than presuppose it. Arabs in Israel are thus "open persons" (Gardner 1984:150): like children, women, and men-carrying-pianos, Palestinians are people whose inherent nonnormativity makes them always out-of-role. Being Arab in Israel makes one constantly subject to comment, qualification, and hyphenation.

In dramatic contrast to the hyperpresence of Arabness in the Hebrew media, Jewish difference is rendered invisible. Jewish identity difference is so silenced it is almost taboo. Mizrahi identity is rarely represented explicitly in newspapers, and stories about Mizrahi Israelis are represented first as being about unhyphenated Israelis. Stories about Mizrahim are about Israeliness—not about Mizrahiness. The ethnicity of a Jewish writer, singer, or public official, for example, is rarely the focus of attention—even when, as in the case of popular music, the identity is crucial to the story (see "Nurit Ben," this chapter).[59]

One source of the taboo is the dominance of the idea of assimilation in Israeli social scientific (and political) discourses. The social scientific discourse of assimilation dominated Israel in the early decades of its existence. Many prominent books were written on the assimilation of Mizrahi immigrants into Sabra Israeli culture and society (e.g., Eisenstadt 1967, 1985). The power of this taboo can be seen in the Bat Yam coverage. The summarizing article in the final day of coverage is entitled "We Are Not Suckers." The place (Bat Yam), the events (violent protest), and the phrase ("suckers") all index Mizrahi identity in Israel, but the author, Nachum Barnea, makes no explicit reference to Jewish ethnicity at all. Even though Bat Yam is a town rent by ethnic tensions, Jewish Israelis are homogenized as unhyphenated Israelis.

But the taboo on explicit mention of Mizrahi identity does not entail that Mizrahi identity is absent from media discourse. Indeed, Jewish ethnicity regularly explodes into public discourse, but it does so indirectly—in disguised form, in veiled and coded ways. Discourse on cultural heritage (Dominguez 1989) and social disadvantage are imbued with implicit reference to Mizrahi identity. Articles on "development towns," urban slums, social inequality, educational failure, and numerous other topics are potent signifiers understood to encode Mizrahi identity. "Poverty" is a code word for Mizrahi identity in Israel, just as "crime" has been a code word for African-American identity in the United States (Mendelberg 1997).[60]

Such stories appear regularly in the press, often coinciding with the publication of a new book, or the release of a new research finding. The publication of a survey of educational achievements nationally in 1991 provides an excellent example. The survey showed significant and persistent differences between Ashkenazim and Mizrahim in educational achievement, and the findings attracted a great deal of media attention. Newspapers were filled with articles, analyses, and editorials for days. Television news coverage focused on the problems faced by the school system in Kiryat Shmona, a "development town" in northern Israel, airing interviews with teachers, principals, and city officials. Despite the nationwide hand-wringing, the media discussion downplayed several important factors unrelated to ethnicity, such as reduced classroom hours and problems in religious schools, while focusing on ethnic differences. Even in this case, however, the references to ethnicity were largely indirect.

In the early 1990s Mizrahi identity also emerged onto the national media scene in the political domain, primarily in the person of David Levi. At the time Levi was one of the most important figures in Israeli politics, serving for many years as foreign minister of Israel. Levi was also the highest ranking, and most successful, Mizrahi politician, and he became a prominent representative of Mizrahi Israeli identity. His family had come to Israel from Morocco, where he was born, and his Israeli residence in Beit She'an made the small town a center of the Mizrahi political heartland, as well as a salient symbol of Mizrahi identity.[61] Levi speaks Hebrew, at times, with a prominent Mizrahi accent (see chapter 7), which he shifts into and out of depending upon the (media) context. Levi's political fortunes reflect the fundamental tension in Israeli politics between electoral and ideological power. The conservative Likud government came to power in 1977 on the strength of the Mizrahi vote, but its leadership has always been primarily Ashkenazi.[62] By the 1990s the Likud was still held in power by the Mizrahi plurality in Israel, but the years had brought few changes in social and economic conditions for Mizrahim. And the Likud power structure had changed little to reflect in its composition the ethnic makeup of its constituency. Levi was therefore considered crucial to the electoral success of the Likud party. Nonetheless, he was portrayed as an incompetent official[63] and was repeatedly humiliated by then prime minister Yitzhak Shamir. Levi kept his ministerial position because of his popularity among Mizrahi voters, for whom he remained a potent symbol of progress. In the elections of 1992 an open split emerged between Shamir and Levi, as Shamir slighted Levi at every opportunity, including denying him a role in the high-profile Madrid Peace Conference, for example. Levi, in turn, cried ethnic discrimination, and it is this cry that hit the media full blast. This split eventually cost the Likud the election.[64]

Public Discourse and Negotiations of Identity

The media have a powerful—but not determining—influence on our patterns of thought and speech. Images gleaned from the media enter our conversations inadvertently— just as Hagit conflates her friend with a prominent Mizrahi singer by combining their names in conversation. The telling mistake—a "Freudian" slip—reveals the extent to which Hagit identifies her friend as a Mizrahi woman, in this case subsuming the friend under a series of images that take on rather negative value. It would be tempting to say that the media had determined (to some extent) Hagit's feelings toward her friend, but that would not be a satisfactory characterization of the process. Rather—as the interview interaction between Hagit and Nurit in fact proceeded to demonstrate— media images become resources in an ongoing, spiral negotiation. The negotiation is spiral because the incorporation of media images into everyday conversations feeds back into the ways that such images are presented in the media. Media images of

Mizrahim in Israel, for example, have changed dramatically since the 1950s—and they will continue to change. The relation between the structure of public (media) discourse and the emergent meanings of face-to-face conversations is also spiral because the situated meaning of an image deployed in public discourse depends upon the myriad inflections that language provides its speakers. Socially meaningful variation in language constitutes a counterbalance to the power of institutional discourses, as speakers turn public symbols to their own agencies.

7

Phonology and the Negotiation of Arab Identity

Language is important to the study of social life because it mediates between structure and agency. Whereas the previous chapters looked at the power of language to produce, enforce, and re-produce structure, this chapter and the one to follow look at the agency of speech to resist. In so doing I move from the domain of institutional discourse to the domain of face-to-face talk interactions, and I switch levels of analysis from the macro-linguistic to the microlinguistic.

In drawing this distinction between the "power of a discourse" to enforce social norms and an individual's "power in discourse" to reformulate social relations, I am drawing on the work of Norman Fairclough (1989:43–68). Discourses, as Foucault (1972) has pointed out, are inherently powerful, and they lend some of this power to any utterances made through them. Ideas about rioting, for example, and their embedded narratives about identity, gain authority by virtue of being published as "articles" in a newspaper. Similarly, ideas about identity draw authority by fitting into broader discourses, master narratives of nation.

I am also drawing on the ideas of "play" developed in chapter 3, according to which the play in discourse, the variability of form, and the negotiability of meaning in discourse (in the sense of actual utterances situated in ongoing social interaction) opens up a space for individual agency and resistant voices. Thus in Hagit's conversation with Nurit, discussed at the outset of the previous chapter (see "Nurit Ben" in chapter 6), the Israeli media presented Hagit with powerful images of Mizrahi identity in the form of its representations of the singer, Zehava Ben, but it was up to her how she deployed them in her conversation with Nurit. Similarly, the discourse of language learning in Israel determines that Palestinian Israelis must use Hebrew to negotiate their identities, but many Palestinians choose nonstandard forms of Hebrew in doing so. Chapters 7 and 8 examine two domains of play in the linguistic structure of Israeli Hebrew—phonology and intonation—and the social meaning generated by such play.

This chapter examines social variation in the use of two phonological variables that are crucial elements in the linguistic construction of Arabness and that therefore constitute a core trope in Israeli constructions of Self and Other. The phonological variables involve variable realizations of the two Hebrew pharyngeal phonemes /ʕ/ (called "ayin") and /ħ/ (called "het").[1] Each variable ranges between pharyngeal and nonpharyngeal pronunciations. Data show that Jewish Israelis avoid pharyngealized forms, while Palestinian Israelis embrace them. In what follows, I will explicate the strategic use to which variation in pharyngealization is put in social interaction, beginning with a discussion of the social and linguistic history of the pharyngeal phonemes.

I focus on the pharyngeal variables because they form an important part of the negotiation of identity in Israel. While these variables comprise only a fragment of socially meaningful variation in Israeli Hebrew, the pharyngeal phonemes /ʕ/ and /ħ/, and their corresponding variables, (ayin) and (het), are prominent, cognitively salient, and affectively powerful markers of language style. The power of these variables stems from the conjunction of three factors:

- Pharyngeal forms of the variables are prestigious features of the formal variety of Hebrew prescribed by the Hebrew Language Academy.

- Pharyngealized Hebrew bears an iconic resemblance to Arabic.

- Pharyngeal pronunciation of Hebrew is a characteristic of the dialect spoken by Mizrahi Jews.

The use of pharyngeal variables to demarcate language style is thus a socially meaningful action with political implications: the pharyngeal variables link all three Israeli social groups—Palestinian Arabs, Mizrahi Jews, and Ashkenazi Jews—in a common contestation over Israeli identity, and the choice of language style constitutes a strong claim to a specific social identity.

On Phonological Variation

Formal theories of language posit invariant underlying structures as cognitive entities, subject to variation only by virtue of their (necessary) realization in performance. The phonology, or sound system of a language, for example, is said to be made up of a fixed number of phonemes, which are abstract underlying sound-archetypes. Writing systems are often designed to represent each phoneme of a language with a unique symbol. English, for example, uses the same graphical symbol "p" to represent all instances of the phoneme /p/, despite the fact that the phoneme is realized in acoustically distinct ways. The phoneme /p/ is realized differently, for example, in each of the three words *pit*, *spit*, and *tip*, as follows.

(1) a. The /p/ in *pit* is aspirated.
     b. The /p/ in *spit* is unaspirated.
     c. The /p/ in *top* is unreleased.

Linguists refer to the different realizations of an underlying phoneme as allophones of the phoneme. The three allophones of /p/ are represented as [pʰ], [p], and [p˺], respectively. The circumstances under which each variant occurs are strictly rule governed. The linguistic conditions that determine which allophone of /p/ English speakers use are as follows.

(2) [pʰ]   word-initial
     [p]   word-medial
     [p˺]   word-final[2]

Selection of a particular form is governed by rule for any given instance. Allophonic alternation therefore does not involve speaker choice. In sociolinguistic variation, on the other hand, speakers are constantly engaged in making strategic linguistic choices, as an overview of the sociolinguistic variable (r) in American English will demonstrate. Studying the speech of New York City residents, William Labov (1982a) found variation in the pronunciation of words conventionally spelled with "r." The word "car," for example, may be pronounced with or without a consonantal constriction (i.e., articulation of the consonant /r/) at its end.[3] We can define for the variable what Weiner and Labov (1983) called an "envelope of variation," or the set of environments in which either variant may occur. All Americans always employ consonantal constriction for the initial sound in "radio," for example. There is therefore no variation when /r/ occurs at the beginning of a word. There is variation, however, in how Americans (especially those from the Northeast) pronounce words like "car," in which /r/ occurs at the end, and in words like "park," in which /r/ follows a vowel and precedes another consonant.

Within this envelope of variation it is impossible to predict when a particular variant of (r) will occur. All speakers (for whom (r) is variable) will sometimes pronounce a word like "park" with constriction, and sometimes without. In this sense the variation of (r) differs fundamentally from the alternation of /p/. A speaker may choose which variant of (r) to use in any given speech situation, and it is this choice that generates the social meaning attendant on linguistic variation.

In his landmark study of sociolinguistic variation in New York City, Labov (1982a) found that while the variant used in an individual token could not be predicted, speakers do adhere to a relatively stable frequency of use. Social and contextual factors have regular and systematic effects on speakers' use of (r) and other sociolinguistic variables, leading to remarkably robust patterns of variation at the level of the speech community. For example, the socioeconomic class of the speaker and the relative formality of the context of speech influence (r): the higher an individual's socioeconomic class the more often that individual uses the constricted variant of (r) across situations of use. Similarly, all individuals—regardless of their socioeconomic positioning—use the constricted variant more often in formal social settings of talk, such as a job interview, than they do in informal contexts, such as a chat with a close friend.

These observations are summarized graphically in figure 7.1, which is based on data from a large number of sociolinguistic interviews conducted in New York City (Labov 1982a). Labov designed the interviews so as to elicit speech in a range of different styles. Along the horizontal axis of the graph in figure 7.1 the styles are arranged in order of increasing formality. Labeled A through D, the styles correspond to casual speech, careful speech, reading style, and the recitation of word lists, respectively. Speech that counts as "casual" is the extremely fluent speech often generated in response to questions that elicit emotionally powerful recollections of personal experience. At the other end of the continuum, for style D, interviewees were asked to read lists of words aloud.[4] All of the words containing the variable (r) within a given style of speech are coded for the variant used, and an index is calculated, ranging from 0 to 100. Figure 7.1 shows (r) indices across speech styles for a sample of speakers grouped by socioeconomic class.[5]

Labov found that within each style speakers' performance is correlated with their social class, such that the higher the class group the higher the (r) index (i.e., the more frequent the consonantal, or "rhotic," pronunciation of /r/). As figure 7.1 shows, in absolute terms the class groups differ in their behavior: members of higher socio-economic groupings use more rhotic pronunciations in each style than do members of

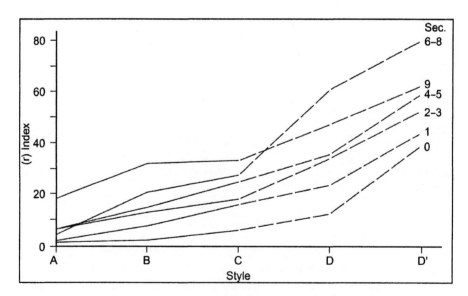

Figure 7.1.   Social Variation in (r) in American English. (Source: Labov 1972a:114. Reprinted by permission of the University of Pennsylvania Press.)

lower socioeconomic groups in the same style.[6] In relative terms, however, all groups participate in the same sociolinguistic pattern, since each group shifts their (r) usage toward the more formal end as the formality of the style increases.

Two further points about the variable (r) in American English are worth noting. First, variation in the pronunciation of /r/ in the United States is a salient marker of identity.[7] Speakers from the American Northeast are immediately identifiable by virtue of their r-less dialect. Experiments that test individuals' subjective reaction to various dialects regularly indicate that Americans judge r-lessness to indicate low socio-economic class status and education levels (alongside friendliness and trustworthiness!).

Second, the social evaluation of (r) is neither new nor constant from an historical perspective. Labov (1972a:144–145) notes that the social evaluation of variation in /r/ pronunciation has come full circle since World War II. Prior to World War II, the r-lessness of Received Pronunciation in Britain (i.e., the high-status style of British English, often called "RP") formed the model for the high prestige accorded r-less articulation in the United States. In the wake of American hegemony after World War II, however, the British-sounding r-less dialect went out of favor, and the r-ful dialects of the American heartland (the so-called broadcast standard of the American Midwest) came into favor. During this period formal speech in prestigious contexts, such as political debate in the American Congress, was characterized by r-ful articulation. In the late 1960s sociolinguistic fashion reversed again. Ethnic pride movements led to the rebirth of regionalism and a reclaiming of r-less dialects in the Northeast (and South), though the association with British nobility was replaced by an imagined link with an emergent American ethnic regionalism.

Sociolinguistic Variation in Israel: An Example from Public Discourse

Hebrew, like English, has a number of sociolinguistic variables subject to strong social evaluation, including the variable pronunciation of an /r/ phoneme. Hebrew /r/ is realized either as an apical flap/trill, [ɾ/r], or as a uvular trill, [ʁ]. The two variants help define the two main social dialects in Israeli Hebrew: Mizrahi Hebrew (MH) and Ashkenazi Hebrew (AH). Typically, speakers of MH use apical (r), while speakers of AH use uvular (r). As is the case in much of Israeli Hebrew sociolinguistic variation, the ver-nacular norm, or what the high-prestige speakers use, contrasts with the prescriptive norm, or what the Hebrew Language Academy adopted as correct usage. Thus, the apical, Mizrahi (r) bears official prestige, even though its use is stigmatized as a vernacular form.

A recent study of the (r) variable in Hebrew found a striking difference between formal and informal contexts of use. Malcah Yaeger-Dror (1988, 1991) analyzed the pattern of variation in the use of (r) by a range of popular Israeli singers, comparing their use of (r) in the relatively casual style of a radio interview (which Yaeger-Dror refers to as "interview speech") to the much more formal style of sung lyrics on commercial recordings (which Yaeger-Dror calls "song register"). Building on the importance of popular music styles and tastes for signaling Jewish ethnic identification in Israel (see Halper, Seroussi, and Squires-Kidron 1989; Shiloah and Cohen 1983), and the role of Mizrahi singers, like Zehava Ben (see "Nurit Ben," in chapter 6), as focal points of Mizrahi ethnic identification, Yaeger-Dror selected twenty singers and classified them along a continuum of social identification from MM (Mizrahi singers of Mizrahi music) at one pole, to AA (Ashkenazi singers of Ashkenazi music) at the other pole. Figures 7.2–7.4 summarize Yaeger-Dror's findings on (r) variation among the singers.[8] Figure 7.2 maps an index of (r) performance in song register for each of the singers Yaeger-Dror studied. This (r) index is constructed so that high values of the index (near 100) correspond to frequent use of apical (r), the MH norm, while low values of the index (near 0) correspond to frequent use of uvular (r), the AH norm. As figure 7.2 shows, apical (Mizrahi) variants dominate the song register. All but one of the singers used the Mizrahi/official prestige form more than 70 percent of the time.[9] This result is not surprising. The MH pronunciation of (r) coincides with the prescriptive norm for Israeli Hebrew. Since commercially recorded songs that are played on Israeli radio stations are subject to stringent correctness guidelines and even censorship (Yaeger-Dror 1988), one would expect a high degree of prescriptively normative speech.

We note a stark contrast, however, when we look at the (r) variable in the more casual speech produced when the singers were interviewed on the radio. Figure 7.3 shows that instances of apical (r) are quite rare in conversational speech, even in the conversational speech of those singers designated MM—Mizrahi singers of Mizrahi music—who are prominent public symbols of Mizrahi identity. Indeed, only four singers, those Yaeger-Dror identifies as NG, GC, HM, and AM,[10] used apical (r) in their interview speech to any significant degree. This subset is comprised of Mizrahi

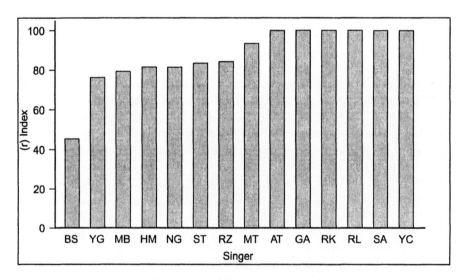

Figure 7.2. Israeli (r) Variable in Song Register. (Source: Malcah Yaeger-Dror, personal communication.)

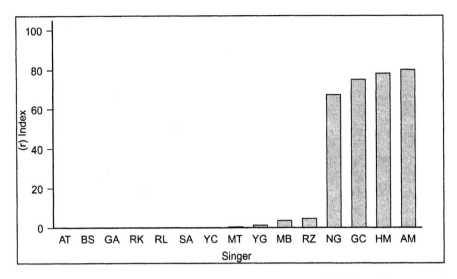

Figure 7.3.   Israeli (r) Variable in Interview Register. (Source: Malcah Yaeger-Dror, personal communication.)

singers who identify themselves, and are identified, with the Mizrahi community. Figure 7.4 re-presents Yaeger-Dror's data, highlighting the stark contrasts among speakers.[11] For each singer the (r) index from interview register is mapped onto the (r) index from song register, creating an "r-space." The figure dramatically illustrates that although both Ashkenazi and Mizrahi singers use high frequencies of apical (r) in song, the use of apical (r) in interview speech is restricted to individuals who identify as Mizrahi. Ashkenazi use of apical (r) in recorded songs is an example of adoption of a variety of Hebrew appropriate to the formality of radio broadcast and commercially recorded music, while Mizrahi use of the same variant symbolizes, and provisionally negotiates, a social identity.[12]

Sociolinguistic Variation in Action: Conversational Negotiations of Identity

Yaeger-Dror's work on (r) demonstrates how Jewish Israelis negotiate identity through language use, but in order to address how Palestinian Israelis fit into the picture I turn to an examination of the Hebrew pharyngeal variables. I begin with three examples of such negotiation that demonstrate the strategic manipulation of the pharyngeal variables and the range of social uses and social identities these variables serve.

A KIBBUTZ MUSEUM GUIDE

I am visiting a Kibbutz museum that commemorates the golden age of Jewish pioneering in Palestine in the early part of the twentieth century.[13]

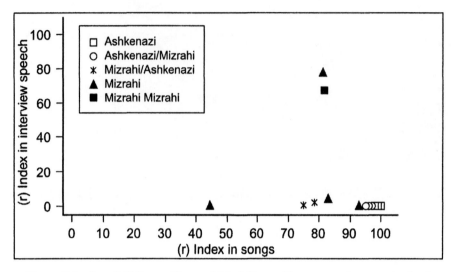

Figure 7.4.   Israeli (r) Space. (Source: Malcah Yaeger-Dror, personal communication.)

The tour guide is an elderly white-haired man who lived through the period he is describing. He seems grizzled by decades of agricultural labor, but he is basking in the current popularity of museums like this one that nostalgically glorify his own role in the establishment of the Israeli state. His enthusiasm spills over into his speech, which is grand and elegant.

The guide devotes much time to the museum's display of eighteenth-century farm implements—those traditionally used by the local Arab population. As he shows us the weathered wooden and iron tools, he takes each one in his hands, reverently explains its use, and lovingly calls it by its name. Plows and saws and scrapers and hitches. I am learning many new words in Hebrew—as are the Israelis who comprise the rest of the tour group. Our group happens to include two Palestinian Israelis, but they do not recognize the old tools either. The Jewish guide seems pleased to be able to teach them something about their own heritage, just as he teaches Jewish Israeli visitors about theirs.

I am fascinated by our guide's pronunciation: he uses a fancy and formal Hebrew with categorical pharyngeal pronunciation. And he mixes in Arabic. As he spins the stories of his interactions, in decades past, with Arab farmers/neighbors/friends, he injects Arabic punch lines, he quotes companions in Arabic, and he always provides the Arabic word for an implement. He engages the two or three Palestinian members of the class in this ongoing conversation, sometimes to ask their confirmation of an implement's use or currency—rarely to solicit words in Arabic, however, a language whose mastery seems a central part of his identity.

As we stand below a huge photograph showing a Jewish farmer riding a tractor next to a Palestinian farmer riding a horse, the guide tells us nostalgically about the spirit of cooperation that existed in those days. He folds this picture into his narrative of identity, similarity, and coexistence, thereby constructing his own identity as a Jewish laborer, a speaker of Arabic, and one who inflects his Hebrew with the Arab sounds it was originally "meant" to have.

A TAXI RIDE IN JERUSALEM

It is late Friday afternoon, and I am waiting at a bus stop in Jerusalem.

Friday afternoons are special times in Israel. A feeling of general bustle takes over, as people leave work early, buy food, newspapers, and other weekend supplies on their way home, and then hurry to clean the house, prepare the dinner, and finish the multitude of chores that need doing before sundown heralds the onset of Shabbat, the Jewish Sabbath.

Shabbat in Israel is a wonderfully quiet, liminal, reflective time. Just before it begins, though, people are tense, as they hustle to finish errands and return home before the last bus leaves—leaving them with no way home.[14]

On this Friday afternoon I was traveling to Jerusalem to visit my cousin. Waiting at the Jerusalem bus stop, I read and reread the elaborate instructions she had given me for getting to her new apartment. I checked and rechecked the posted route information. Still my bus didn't show up. Other travelers came and went, as their buses arrived, took on passengers, and departed, but two other young men and I stood and waited ... ten minutes ... half an hour ... almost an hour. Finally, one of the men suggested we share a taxi, and off we went.

The other two men were Israeli: a young man in army uniform (probably a soldier going home for the weekend) and a man who was closer to my age. At the bus stop they had been chatting about the weekend, about the bus not coming, about the approach of Shabbat, finally about taking a cab. Their conversation was carried out in fluent, colloquial Hebrew—nothing out of the ordinary. When the cab arrived, the young soldier got into the front seat, next to the driver. The driver, an older, gray-haired man, was friendly and chatty. He spoke with a strong Mizrahi accent that was heavily pharyngealized. He asked each of us where we were going and what we did in life. He joked with us, playfully bargaining up the fare. In the back seat we played along for a while.

In the front seat the young soldier suddenly became talkative—and his accent suddenly became strongly pharyngealized. The conversation shifted to the front seat, and I lost the thread as the taxi approached my destination.

AN ELOQUENT GREENGROCER

Dan Shilon is the host of a late-night television talk show that was very popular in the early 1990s. The *Dan Shilon Show* was a heady hour of talk about the major political and social issues of the day, on which many of the leading figures of Israeli public life appeared. In selecting his guests Shilon mixed conservatives with liberals and men with women, and he usually mixed Ashkenazi and Mizrahi guests with Palestinian Israelis as well. Shilon liked to mix it up. He often stimulated lively debate among his guests— and sometimes he provoked it. Shilon brought up controversial topics, juxtaposing as starkly as possible the opinions of guests representing diametrically opposed positions. His show was popular in part because it tapped into the Israeli love for aggressive argumentation.

One night Shilon invited a young Palestinian man with a particularly intriguing story: He owned a vegetable store in a posh, solidly Jewish northern suburb of Tel Aviv. The greengrocer fielded the expectable questions about how he gets along with his Jewish customers, with his Jewish neighbors, with people who don't like him because he is Arab, and so on. But the focus quickly shifted from his business circumstances to the charismatic strength of his character, as his wit and eloquence charmed the other guests. Toward the end of the show, Shilon asked the greengrocer to recite a poem he had written, and the young Palestinian man brought down the house with a bitingly funny lampoon of Israeli society—composed in a style that was impeccably Israeli.

Most impressive was this Palestinian man's command of Hebrew, and his striking accent. His flawlessly fluent Hebrew was heavily pharyngealized.

These three sociolinguistic practices exemplify the range of meanings that individuals can evoke by deploying pharyngealized Hebrew, enacting the multivocal struggle over identity through phonological variation. The three speakers just described, the Ashkenazi "pioneer," the Mizrahi soldier, and the Palestinian greengrocer, all used the same style of Hebrew, which can be approximated by their use of the pharyngeal variables. Yet in doing so the three speakers tapped into different pools of meaning, and they constructed different social identities. In each case socially meaningful linguistic variation was deployed strategically.

For the museum guide, the pharyngeal forms *semiticized* his Hebrew. By using etymologically "correct" forms that are also shared by Arabic, the guide showed learnedness and sophistication at the same time that he symbolically placed Israel in its Middle Eastern context, laying claim to legitimacy for the Zionist presence in Palestine. For the Mizrahi soldier, the pharyngeal forms constituted an in-group language, through which he expressed and claimed solidarity with the Mizrahi taxi driver, whom he recognized as a member of his own identity group. For the Palestinian businessman, the pharyngeal forms *arabized* his Hebrew. By using elegant and prestigious Hebrew that simultaneously sounds like Arabic, the greengrocer claimed membership in Israeli society while simultaneously asserting a Palestinian identity.

In the three-way struggle over Israeli social identity, many Palestinian Arabs, like the Tel Aviv greengrocer, coopted markers of Jewish ethnicity in staking claim to an Arab Israeli identity. This move has interesting social and linguistic consequences. Socially, it reflects a rearrangement of ethnic, national, and class dimensions of social difference. Linguistically, it drives a rearrangement of the linguistic features Israeli Jews use to mark their own identity, namely a shift from phonology to intonation that is the subject of chapter 8. In what follows I show important patterns of current usage in a more systematic fashion through an analysis of data from sociolinguistic interviews. The findings are then embedded within the broader context of Hebrew variation, and within the historical and social development of the meaning of pharyngeal usage.

The Linguistics of the Hebrew Pharyngeal Variables

The pharyngeal variables in Hebrew, (het) and (ayin), correspond to the realization in speech of two Hebrew phonemes, the voiceless pharyngeal fricative /ħ/ and the voiced pharyngeal approximant /ʕ/, respectively. Pharyngeal sounds are produced by constricting the pharynx, the upper portion of the throat. Such sounds are rare among the world's languages, but they are characteristic of Semitic languages. Both Arabic and Hebrew, the two Semitic languages in vernacular use today, retain the historically pharyngeal Semitic phonemes.[15] Pharyngeal sounds are salient in speech, and they give Arabic—and the Hebrew dialects that preserve them—a distinctive sound. Most dialects of Arabic have retained pharyngeal realizations of the underlying phonemes—even while other distinctive Semitic sounds (the emphatic sounds, for example) have disappeared from many vernacular dialects of Arabic.

In vernacular Israeli Hebrew the underlying pharyngeal phonemes are realized in variable ways: as phonetic pharyngeals in the speech of many Palestinian and Mizrahi Israelis, or as phonetically nonpharyngeal sounds in the speech of most Ashkenazi speakers. For Ashkenazi speakers the voiceless pharyngeal phoneme (het) is realized as a voiceless velar fricative, [x], and the voiced pharyngeal phoneme (ayin) is realized as a glottal stop, [ʔ]. In the speech of all Israelis, however, these phonemes condition a number of important morphophonemic alternations.[16]

Figures 7.5 and 7.6 show schematic linguistic histories of the Hebrew pharyngeals. Figure 7.5 looks at the history of the voiced pharyngeal, called "ayin." Hebrew inherited from Proto-Semitic a phonetic and phonemic distinction between the voiced pharyngeal (/ʕ/) and the glottal stop (/ʔ/). Arabic tends to maintain both the phonetic and phonological distinctions, as the minimal pair /qaraʕa/, "he hit/beat," and /qaraʔa/, "he read," demonstrates.[17] The situation in Hebrew, however, is more complicated. The two major dialects of Modern Israeli Hebrew, AH and MH, differ in their treatment of the reflexes of the Semitic pharyngeal phonemes. Both dialects of Hebrew maintain an underlying phonemic distinction that gives rise to morphophonemic alternations (see hereafter). Only the more conservative MH dialect, however, maintains the voiced pharyngeal phonetically, as do Arabic dialects. The AH dialect, in contrast, does not include a voiced pharyngeal in its phonetic inventory, and underlying voiced pharyngeals are realized as glottal stops. These facts are reflected in figure 7.5 by the separate trajectories in the two dialects of the minimal pair of roots, /k.r.ʕ/, "to cut, tear," and /k.r.ʔ/, "to read."[18] In the MH dialect, all forms derived from the root /k.r.ʕ/ (in which the third root consonant surfaces) contain a phonetic pharyngeal. In the AH dialect, all such forms are pronounced as a phonetic glottal stop. Figure 7.5 demonstrates this with the specific example of the third-person, feminine, singular, past tense forms "she tore" and "she read." These forms are distinct in MH ([karʕa] and [karʔa], respectively) but homonymous in AH (both pronounced [karʔa]).[19]

Figure 7.6 shows a parallel history for the voiceless pharyngeal phonemes. Hebrew, like Arabic, inherited from Proto-Semitic a phonetic and phonemic distinction between voiceless pharyngeal (/ħ/) and velar (/x/) fricatives. Dialects of Arabic tend to maintain both the phonetic and phonological distinctions, while a more complicated pattern

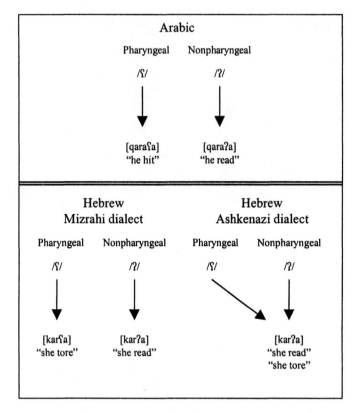

Figure 7.5.   Schematic History of Semitic Voiced Pharyngeal Phoneme.

obtains in Modern Hebrew. As with the voiceless pharyngeal, Hebrew maintains a phonological distinction (that conditions morphophonemic alternations) but has lost a surface phonetic distinction between the two phonemes. The two dialects of Modern Hebrew, however, differ as to how these underlying segments are pronounced. As with the voiceless pharyngeal, the more conservative MH dialect maintains a surface pharyngeal articulation that the AH dialect does not have. These facts are reflected in figure 7.6 by the different trajectories the two dialects trace for the words for "salt" and "brother." The final sounds in the Arabic words are distinct: [milħ], "salt," ends in a pharyngeal, while [ax], "brother," ends in a velar. Figure 7.6 shows that the Hebrew cognates of these words end in the same sound in each dialect—but this sound is pharyngeal in MH ([melaħ] and [aħ]) and velar in AH ([melax] and [ax]).[20]

This analysis of Israeli Hebrew phonology relies on an important abstraction. If we treat the two dialects of Hebrew, MH and AH, as underlyingly similar, we must posit for the AH dialect an abstract phonemic distinction that never surfaces phonetically. That is, we must argue that the AH dialect includes an abstract phoneme whose phonetic qualities are identical to another phoneme. Support for such an argument comes from rules of morphophonemic alternation. Even though speakers of AH do not have phonetic pharyngeals, they obey a number of phonological rules whose statement is simplified if we assume that the Ashkenazi dialect maintains an abstract, underlying distinction between the phonemes /ʕ/ and /ʔ/.[21] Linguists posit the existence of an abstract distinction because the two phonemes condition different phonological effects on surrounding sounds in a range of morphological alternations. The forms in table 7.1 illustrate one such alternation: a-insertion in present tense verb forms. Here the a-insertion is triggered by the occurrence of the underlying pharyngeal phoneme, /ʕ/, in the Hebrew word for "he tears." These morphological alternations are common to both dialects: for speakers of the MH dialect the alternation has a phonetic explanation, while for speakers of the AH dialect one must posit the abstract underlying phonemic difference in order to explain the surface morphophonological effect.

The Sociolinguistics of Pharyngeal Usage

Palestinian Arabs, Mizrahi Jews, and Ashkenazi Jews differ widely in their use of the pharyngeal variables: Palestinians use pharyngeal variants in their speech most, and

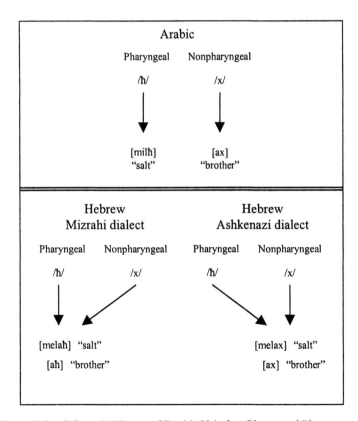

Figure 7.6. Schematic History of Semitic Voiceless Pharyngeal Phoneme.

Table 7.1. A-Insertion Triggered by Underlying Voiced Pharyngeal (AH Dialect).

Grammatical Form	Read		Tear	
Underlying root	k.r.ʔ	to read	k.r.ʕ	to tear
Masculine singular past	kara	he read	kara	he tore
Feminine singular past	karʔa	she read	karʕa	she tore
Masculine singular present	kore	he reads	korea	she tears

Ashkenazi Jews use them least. Indeed, in casual conversation the latter group uses almost no pharyngeal variants at all (which is what made the speech of the [Ashkenazi] tour guide at the kibbutz museum so striking).

Social variability in the use of the pharyngeal variables in colloquial Israeli Hebrew is summarized in figures 7.7–7.11. Data for these graphs are taken from the socio-linguistic interviews with Palestinian, Mizrahi, and Ashkenazi residents of Haifa described in chapter 4. For clarity of exposition, the graphs represent a speaker's pharyngealization as an index, such that high values of this index correspond to highly pharyngealized speech. Thus an index of 100 corresponds to categorically pharyngeal pronunciation, while an index of 0 corresponds to categorically nonpharyngeal speech.[22]

Figure 7.7 shows aggregated data for the two pharyngeal variables, (ayin) and (het), plotting average indices for Ashkenazi, Mizrahi, and Palestinian Israeli interviewees. The two pharyngeal variables pattern similarly, although index values for (het) are somewhat higher. For each variable the average pharyngealization index for Palestinian Israelis is greater than that for Mizrahi Israelis, and the average pharyngealization index for Mizrahi Israelis is greater than that for Ashkenazi Israelis. It is worth noting that since the Ashkenazi speakers in my sample do not pharyngealize (ayin) at all, the

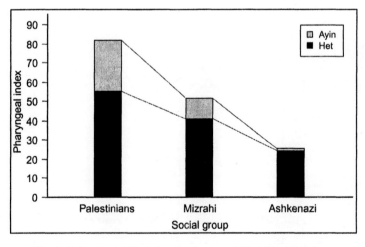

Figure 7.7. Social Variation in Pharyngeal Variables in Hebrew.

pharyngeal realization of this variable by Mizrahi and Palestinian speakers stands out as a salient marker of identity.

The distributional pattern becomes clearer when we look at the performance of individual speakers. Figures 7.8–7.11 compare individual speakers in terms of the frequency with which they pronounced tokens of the variables (ayin) and (het) with phonetically pharyngeal sounds. These graphs form a composite picture of a speaker's pharyngeal usage, a "pharyngeal space," by mapping an individual's (het) index (along the vertical axis) onto the same individual's (ayin) index (along the horizontal axis).

Three important patterns emerge from the comparison of Palestinian and Jewish speakers in figure 7.8.

1. Most Jewish speakers (represented on the graph by triangles) use no pharyngeal variants at all and therefore cluster at the lower left of the pharyngeal space.

2. Three Jewish speakers use some pharyngeals in their speech and thus appear in the middle section of the pharyngeal space.

3. Palestinian speakers (represented on the graph by squares) vary widely in their use of pharyngeal forms and show up throughout the diagram, but three Palestinian speakers cluster at the upper right of the pharyngeal space, reflecting nearly categorical pharyngeal use.

Figures 7.9 and 7.10 provide greater detail on the first two patterns. Figure 7.9 focuses on the pharyngeal usage of Jewish speakers and distinguishes between Ashkenazi Israelis (empty triangles) and Mizrahi Israelis (filled triangles). Figure 7.9 shows that among Jews in Israel only Mizrahim pharyngealize their speech to any significant extent. Of these, three speakers stand out as using relatively high levels of pharyngealization in their interview speech. These speakers have (ayin) indices between 30 and 40, and one uses pharyngeal variants for the (het) variable nearly categorically.

On the other hand, figure 7.9 also shows that many Mizrahi speakers are

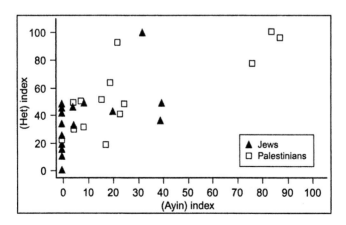

Figure 7.8.   Hebrew Pharyngeals: Jewish and Palestinian Israelis.

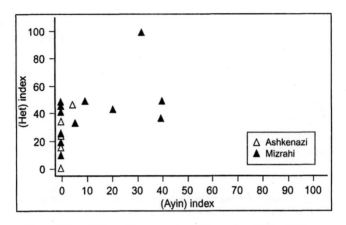

Figure 7.9.   Hebrew Pharyngeals: Ashkenazi and Mizrahi Jews.

indistinguishable from Ashkenazi speakers in terms of their pharyngeal use. Figure 7.10 provides an explanation for these two divergent findings: pharyngealization is associated, among Jews, with older Mizrahim. Figure 7.10 re-presents the pharyngealization data from figure 7.9 to show the pattern of pharyngeal speech by age among Jewish speakers. In figure 7.10 younger Jewish speakers (less than forty years of age) are represented by empty triangles, while older speakers (over the age of forty) are represented by filled triangles. Figure 7.10 shows that Mizrahi speakers who used pharyngeal forms in their interview speech are all above the age of forty and that younger Mizrahim show no significant use of pharyngeal variants, thus patterning with Ashkenazim of all ages. Thus the young Mizrahi soldier, with whom I shared a taxi (see "A Taxi Ride in Jerusalem," this chapter), deployed the young-Mizrahi/Ashkenazi-speaker pattern while waiting for the bus, and shifted to the older-Mizrahi pattern in speaking with the taxi driver.

Figure 7.11 shows pharyngeal usage among Palestinian speakers and explores the third of the three patterns just described. A striking gender pattern emerges from figure 7.11, in which Palestinian men are represented by filled squares, and women by empty squares. Palestinian women, whose graphing symbols show up at the lower left of the pharyngeal space, use very little pharyngealization in interview speech, while Palestinian men, whose graphing symbols show up above and to the right of those for the women, use noticeable amounts of pharyngealization. Most important, the three speakers whose graphing symbols appear in the extreme upper right of the pharyngeal space are all men. Their speech shows nearly categorical pharyngealization of both (ayin) and (het) variables. The contrast between the speech styles reflected in data points on opposite corners of figure 7.11 is quite striking. Speakers appearing at the lower left of figure 7.11 are mistaken for Jewish, while speakers who appear at the upper right of the figure are recognized as speaking in a very distinctive way (the greengrocer from the example given at the outset of this chapter would appear here). The extreme pharyngeal pronunciation of these latter speakers far exceeds the pharyngealization of any of the Jewish speakers in my sample (though the museum guide's speech approached this level). The difference between these trends does not correspond to differences in speakers' age or class affiliation. Rather, this difference represents—and is exploited in order to construct—an expression of Palestinian Israeli identity.

Sociolinguistic Resonances

These simple patterns of language use generate complex social meanings that constitute the play-in-language through which a three-way struggle over Israeli identity is negotiated. To understand the meanings of the language-use patterns, we must look both to the historical context of the revival of Hebrew in Israel and to the (socio)linguistic context of Hebrew diglossia.

The Hebrew Revival

The revival of the Hebrew language is the cornerstone, and arguably the most enduring, accomplishment of Zionism, the Jewish nationalist movement. Zionist nationalism grew out of the European nationalisms of the 1800s. The Zionist call for an identity rooted in territory and a lifestyle based on manual labor and working the land (see chapter 2), was paralleled by a desire to be—like other European nations—a *Volk* with a unique language.

The revival of Hebrew in modern Israel is, as Jack Fellman (1973a:7) has argued, "one of the outstanding sociolinguistic phenomena of modern times." Eliezer Ben-Yehuda, a Russian-born autodidact, is usually credited with the success of this revival. Ben-Yehuda compiled a magnificent dictionary of Hebrew, worked tirelessly to promote the use of Hebrew in daily life, and eventually succeeded in getting Hebrew adopted

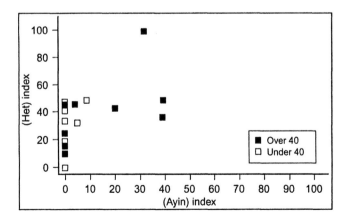

Figure 7.10.   Hebrew Pharyngeals: Jewish Speakers by Age.

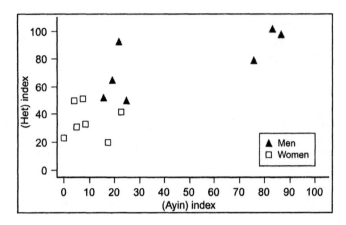

Figure 7.11.   Hebrew Pharyngeals: Palestinian Speakers by Gender.

as the language of instruction in Jewish schools of mandatory Palestine. In 1904 a Language Committee was established to oversee the standardization of the revived language. By 1953 this committee had grown and transformed into the Hebrew Language Academy (Rabin 1970:328), which remains an influential institution in Israel to this day.

While Hebrew needed to be revived as a spoken vernacular in the nineteenth century, it had never died out as a language used in other ways (Fellman 1973a; Spolsky and Cooper 1991). Indeed, as many scholars of the revival have pointed out, it is precisely the active, two-thousand-year history of the use of Hebrew by Jewish communities that enabled its revival as a spoken vernacular (Alter 1988; Harshav 1990). Hebrew was used as a liturgical and scholarly language by Jewish communities throughout the world. Hebrew was long an important language for poetic expression. In some communities Hebrew may even have been used as a lingua franca, enabling communication between Jews from different parts of the world. The primary source of Hebrew knowledge remained religious observance, generating some deep disparities within Jewish communities in sociolinguistic competence. Men and women, for example, differed greatly in the amount of access they had to Hebrew (Seidman 1997). There were also important class differences. Prior to the emergence of Israel and the revival of Hebrew as a spoken language, thorough knowledge of Hebrew was associated with wealth and prestige. Families that could afford to encouraged sons to devote their lives to religious studies. Thus relatively conservative and orthodox communities had greater command of Hebrew, and within such communities men had much greater knowledge of Hebrew than did women, and wealthier families had greater knowledge than poorer families (Spolsky and Cooper 1991).

Not all Zionist settlers advocated the use of Hebrew in Israel. Indeed, a spectacular debate broke out in the early days of the Zionist return to Palestine over what language should be used in the new nation. Many Zionists, for example, argued for German because it was the world's leading literary and scientific language at the time. Others argued for Yiddish on the practical grounds that most of the pre-state settlers already spoke that language, while all settlers would have to learn Hebrew. Theological arguments supported those who called for Yiddish to be the language of the Jewish Return. Since Hebrew was the sacred language of religious texts, some orthodox Jews believed that its everyday use for mundane purposes would be a profanity (Sachar 1989:82). To this day many ultrareligious Jews conduct their private lives in Yiddish, using Hebrew only for prayer—and for their necessary contacts with the broader Israeli society (Isaacs 1998).[23] In 1913 this language struggle spilled over from academic and political debates into actual physical confrontations, as riots broke out over the use of Hebrew for instruction at Israel's technical university (Sachar 1989:84).

At the time of the revival much discussion focused on the question of which version of Hebrew to adopt. A great deal of research went into establishing "correct" forms for that variety. The debate juxtaposed different modern traditions of liturgical pronunciation, literary traditions from various periods and genres, and reconstructions of spoken practice at various times in Jewish history (Alter 1988). Differences had emerged over the generations, for example, in the liturgical traditions for pronouncing Hebrew. A major split had developed between Sephardi (Mizrahi) and Ashkenazi traditions, as these two broad communities had relatively little contact after the first millennium of the Common Era.[24] Indeed, scholars believe that by the second century AD (the time of the Diaspora from Palestine) significant differences had already emerged between the liturgical language (Biblical Hebrew) and the language of the street (Aramaic). Biblical Hebrew was used as a formal variety, while Aramaic was used as a vernacular form (Spolsky and Cooper 1991). The vernacular Aramaic influenced subsequent literary forms of Hebrew, and centuries of literary production led to increasing grammatical and lexical separation from Biblical Hebrew (Rabin 1970). The Hebrew Language Academy adopted Sephardi pronunciation as the official model for the revived spoken language in modern Israel, alongside many of the grammatical and lexical innovations of postbiblical literary Hebrew (Blanc 1968; Rabin 1970).

The Hebrew Diglossia

One consequence of the revival process—going from written language to spoken language—is the development in modern Israeli Hebrew of what linguists call "diglossia." Diglossia describes speech communities that systematically use two varieties of the same language in functional complementarity (Ferguson 1959). A "high" variety (conventionally represented as H) is used in writing and in formal speech contexts. A "low" variety (conventionally represented as L) is used in casual conversation. Typically, all members of the speech community control both varieties, although in practice the command of the H-variety depends upon formal education.

While the Hebrew Language Academy enforces adherence to prescriptive norms for the H-variety in formal and written discourse, a vibrant youth culture, centered around the universal (for Jews) military service, has led to many (ongoing) changes. As a result, a gap has emerged between the formal language of newspapers (for example) and the vernacular language of the street.[25] The vernacular is increasingly characterized by the inclusion of loanwords, borrowings, and even code-switches (see chapter 5), as well as by violation of many of the prescriptive rules of formal grammar. For example, the L-variety of Hebrew is undergoing many processes of simplification and analogic leveling, which have the effect of widening the gap between H and L varieties.

Table 7.2 shows one example of this process, the simplification of the complex Semitic grammar of noun-noun compounding. In formal Hebrew, *smixut*, "noun-noun compounding," involves a complex set of rules for agreement and morphological alternation. Spoken Hebrew, however, simplifies such expressions, either by substituting analytic phrases for the compound[26] or by reinterpreting common noun-noun compounds as single lexical items. Table 7.2 shows a common instance of the latter process. The common compound *bet-sefer*,[27] "school," is composed of the words *bayit*, "house," and *sefer*, "book." The syntax of noun-noun compounding in Hebrew involves attributive meaning, such that the compound *bet-sefer* means "house of book" or, by convention, "school." As the first two rows of table 7.2 show, Hebrew marks definiteness with the particle *ha-* prefixed to the definite noun. Prescriptively in compounds, definiteness is marked only on the second element of the compound, as in *bet ha-sefer*, "the school." Colloquial usage in informal contexts, however, includes the common form *ha-betsefer*, "the school," where the compound has been reanalyzed as a single lexical item.

Table 7.2. Marking Definiteness in Noun-Noun Compounds (Formal Hebrew).

Word	Indefinite		Definite	
House	*bayit*	a house	*ha-bayit*	the house
Book	*sefer*	a book	*ha-sefer*	the book
School	*bet-sefer*	a school	*bet-ha-sefer*	the school

Such simplification processes are quite productive in vernacular Israeli Hebrew, rapidly increasing the distance between the formal and written variety of Hebrew on the one hand and the spoken vernacular on the other. As a consequence, however, the deployment in conversational speech of constructions characteristic of the formal variety becomes a powerful resource in the linguistic construction of identity.

The Social Context of Pharyngeal Use in Israel

The special value of the Hebrew pharyngeals as resources in the linguistic negotiation of identity stems from their social history. The history of language revival, the relations among Jewish diaspora groups, and the social conditions pursuant to the establishment of Israel combined to create a situation in which the same forms share three mutually contradictory social meanings:

- High prestige as the officially sanctioned norm for educated speech in a diglossic community

- Stigma as the stereotyped forms used by the lower of the socioeconomic class groups in Jewish Israeli society

- Symbolic association with "Arab" and "Oriental" dimensions of identity in Israel

The revival of Hebrew involved a host of very conscious language-use practices. At the time of the revival, use of Hebrew in everyday conversation constituted a relatively marked and formal style. This was especially true because in the diaspora Hebrew had been an H-variety, functionally restricted to religious observance, scholarly writing, poetry, and other serious literary genres (Rabin 1970). The revivers of Hebrew were heavily invested in maintaining the purity of the language, and the Hebrew Language Academy worked hard to produce Hebrew or Semitic pedigrees for the thousands of new words that modern discourse required. Because of the enormous influence exerted by the Hebrew Language Academy, the form of Hebrew selected for revival became an H-variety. Historically, the academy has been very successful in its insistence that high-prestige speech contexts, such as school classrooms, television news broadcasts, and political speeches, be domains for the use of the formal variety of Hebrew.

Because the traditional Sephardi pronunciations were adopted as the *tiknit*, "correct," forms for Israeli Hebrew, Mizrahi pronunciations, including pharyngealized variants of (het) and (ayin), as well as the apical variant of (r), carry high social prestige. Vernacular norms, however, evolved differently. The European Jewish immigrants, who comprised the vast majority of newcomers in the period prior to statehood, did not adopt the Mizrahi phonological forms into their everyday speech, and the pharyngeals emerged as hallmark features of the prestige dialect not adopted into the vernacular.[28]

The waves of immigration during the 1950s brought to Israel, for the first time, large numbers of Mizrahi Jews, who were habitual users of the Sephardi (liturgical) traditions for pronouncing Hebrew. These speakers maintained the tradition of pharyngeal (het) and (ayin) in their own communities, and they brought this tradition with them to Israel.[29] The immigrants from Middle Eastern countries entered Israel as a Jewish underclass, subject to large-scale discrimination, residential marginalization, educational, occupational, and political underachievement, and, above all, cultural subordination. Mizrahi Jews were systematically settled on the margins of Jewish Israeli society, in frontier development towns on the borders with the Arab neighbors, and in hastily constructed slum neighborhoods at the edges of the Jewish cities (see chapter 2). Mizrahim took over manual labor jobs in industry and agriculture and were considered primitive and inferior by the Ashkenazi elite.

Thus the form of Hebrew used by Mizrahi immigrants was stigmatized, even as the very same forms held official prestige. Use of the pharyngeal forms was sufficient to evoke negative stereotypes of Mizrahi Jews propagated in movies, books, and popular discourse (Shohat 1989:117). Linguistic usage patterns quickly changed, and younger

Mizrahi Jews abandoned the newly stereotyped linguistic forms of their parents (Bentolila 1983; Blanc 1968; Davis 1984; Yaeger-Dror 1988).

Against this backdrop, the Palestinian cooptation of pharyngeal variants (see fig. 7.11) takes on enormous social meaning. It constitutes simultaneous assertions of Israeli prestige and Arab identity. It is an assertion of Arab identity for two reasons. First, the pharyngeal variants make Hebrew sound more like Arabic. As figures 7.5 and 7.6 show, many Hebrew words have transparent cognates in Arabic, and Arabic cognates that contain pharyngeal sounds are pronounced pharyngeally in Arabic. Many words pronounced in the Mizrahi dialect do sound more like Arabic than when they are pronounced by Ashkenazi speakers.

Arab use of Hebrew pharyngeals also asserts Arab identity by virtue of its cooptation of the association between the pharyngeal variables and Mizrahi Jews. Within the Jewish community, pharyngeal forms are stigmatized precisely because they link these Jews with the Arab lands they left behind. Palestinian Israelis, who adopt pharyngeal pronunciation in their Hebrew, are thus revitalizing stigmatized symbols in order to turn the stigma on its head. They are using the stigma—Arabness—against itself.

But Arab appropriation of Hebrew pharyngeals in Israel is more than just a claim on Arab identity. The association of pharyngealized Hebrew with *ivrit tiknit*, "correct Hebrew," makes of this language style a claim on belonging and status within Israeli society. Indeed, the phenomenon is clearly a Hebrew phenomenon—not interference from, or imposition of, Arabic. This important point is demonstrated by the fact—discussed earlier—that the Hebrew variable (het) has merged two sounds that are distinct in Arabic (see figs. 7.5 and 7.6). The two dialects of Hebrew differ in the form that (het) takes, but in each dialect a single sound corresponds to the two Arabic sounds. The Palestinian speakers highlighted in figures 7.8 and 7.11, for example, do not use pharyngeal articulations only for Hebrew words whose Arabic cognates have pharyngeal sounds. Rather, these speakers are extremely fluent speakers of a rich and colloquial Hebrew. By choosing nearly categorical pharyngeal variants, they are making linguistic choices wholly within the framework of Hebrew.

Conclusion

This look at socially meaningful phonological variation in Israeli Hebrew demonstrates one aspect of the linguistic negotiation of Israeli identity. Palestinian Arabs have coopted the forms and meanings associated with the pharyngeal variables in Hebrew. In so doing, they have highlighted certain of the forms' meanings (their official status) and altered the polarity of others (their association with Arabness), such that a negative stigma is reinflected as a positive emblem.

These language practices constitute an abstract negotiation. Sometimes abstract negotiations take concrete form, as when a young Mizrahi soldier alters his phonology to talk to an older Mizrahi taxi driver (see "A Taxi Ride in Jerusalem," this chapter)— or when a Palestinian chandler makes his Hebrew sound American in an interview with an American researcher (see "A Ship's Chandler" in chapter 1). In these cases the abstract negotiation is made concrete by inscribing it onto a face-to-face interaction between individuals. But ultimately an individual negotiates identity with discourse, not with other individuals, and, in this abstract negotiation, habitually used language styles stake out the various positions. By adopting a categorically pharyngeal speech style, the Palestinian speakers highlighted in figures 7.8 and 7.11 are negotiating their identity with respect to others who are present in the discursive context, if not actually physical partners in the instance of talk itself. This is what makes "dialect" so powerful a symbol.

But symbolic representations of identity (such as dialects) are formed and used in dynamic opposition to other groups copresent within a community of discourse. The social meaning of the emergent pharyngealized Palestinian dialect of Hebrew, for example, refers not only to the Ashkenazi dialect, which it opposes (pharyngeal/ nonpharyngeal) but also to the Mizrahi dialect, which it supersedes (pharyngeal/ formerly pharyngeal). Widespread adoption of pharyngealized Hebrew by Palestinian Israelis affects the language-use practices of Mizrahi and Ashkenazi Israelis as well. In the next chapter I look at socially meaningful variation in Hebrew intonation as a space of "play" for the negotiation of Mizrahi Jewish identities in the discursive realm where the pharyngeal phonemes have been effectively coopted.

8

Intonation and the Negotiation of Sabra Identity

In Chapter 7 I showed that Palestinian Israelis adopted a pharyngealized style of Hebrew and argued that this pattern of language-use constituted a negotiation of identity in Israel. Palestinian Israelis claimed an Arab Israeli identity by emphasizing Arabness and linking it to the high prestige of *'ivrit tiknit*, "Standard Hebrew," the prescriptive norm for Israeli Hebrew. Such language choices decenter dominant tropes of Israeli identity by contesting the equivalence of "Jewish" and "Israeli."

This pattern of language use coopts the symbolic value of the pharyngeal variables traditionally associated with Mizrahi Jewish identity. Adoption of these symbols by Palestinian Israelis provides impetus for their abandonment by Mizrahim. Once used by Palestinians to enunciate Arabness, their value in enunciating Jewish heritage diminished. Yet the importance of the Mizrahi/Ashkenazi social difference did not decline, and the motivation to mark this difference linguistically remains high. In this chapter I argue that the negotiation of Jewish Israeli identity has shifted to a different domain of language structure, namely intonation.

AN "ISRAELI" INTONATION

My interest in the social meaning of Israeli intonation began one night in the late 1980s while watching the *MacNeil/Lehrer Newshour*.[1] Discussion focused on the Intifada, the 1988–1992 Palestinian popular uprising in the

236

Israeli Occupied Territories. Two men had been invited to debate the issue. One man was identified as an official of the Israeli government, and the other as a representative of the "Palestinians."

The discussion became acrimonious, as it juxtaposed two diametrically opposed positions. At one point, however, the Palestinian speaker found it necessary to assert that he was also an Israeli citizen, contesting the identity the interviewer had imposed upon him.[2] In doing so he used—in his English—an intonation contour that is typically Israeli.

This negotiation of identity has its source in the overlap of identity categories in Israeli discourse. In the colloquial Hebrew of the time, the words for "Arab" and "Palestinian" unambiguously referred to two different identity categories: "Arab" in this context referred to citizens of Israel, while "Palestinian" referred to noncitizen residents of the Occupied Territories.[3] This distinction is not maintained in English, and it was lost both on the American audience, and, temporarily, on the journalist. In part, the distinction was lost precisely because blurring this boundary had been useful for both panelists—the Israeli Jewish man and the Israeli Palestinian man.

In provisionally (re)claiming his Israeli identity, the Palestinian man used a drawn-out, rising-and-falling melody that sounds quite distinctive in English, but which is quite common in colloquial Israeli Hebrew. This chapter describes this intonational contour in terms of its occurrence in Hebrew conversation, its function in conversational negotiations of identity, and its contribution to the social meaning of language. Use of the intonation is marked for Israeliness, but generalized (and frequent) use is associated with Mizrahi Jewish identity. Palestinian Israelis, especially those who use the pharyngealized style of Hebrew discussed in chapter 7, use a distinctive variant of this tune. This intonation pattern, like the phonological variables discussed in the previous chapter, lies at the crux of a three-way struggle over the meaning of linguistic symbols, as follows.

- A stylized variant of a common linguistic form comes to stand for the nation (or at least its dominant group).

- Mizrahim, whose pharyngealized dialect was stigmatized and subsequently coopted by Palestinians as a marker of Arabness, adopted an intonational style characterized by the generalized use of the tune.

- Palestinians adapt the tune to mark their speech as Israeli—but distinctively so.

The Nature of Intonation

Dwight Bolinger, a pioneer in the study of intonation, joked, "Intonation is a half-tamed savage. To understand the tamed or linguistically harnessed half of him one has to make friends with the wild half" (Bolinger 1978:475). Bolinger's metaphor, comparing intonation to a beast that is partially tamed but still partially wild is apt in many respects. Intonation is a highly salient dimension of human languages, but linguists understand relatively little about its structure. I will therefore discuss how intonation works in language in general before addressing the specifics of the Hebrew intonational variable introduced here.

Intonation is formally simple but functionally complex. In a formal sense intonation is simple because the single parameter of pitch fully defines intonational form. In contrast, a great number of physical features (placement of the tongue, lip, velum, etc.) combine to create phonemic distinctions. Further, the parameter of pitch has only a single dimension of variability—higher or lower. In contrast, features that are involved in phonemic distinctions usually have multiple alternates: there are numerous sites of articulation, several manners, and so on. Yet intonation is functionally complex, since it is implicated in the expression of many different kinds of meaning, from gender identity to grammatical distinctions. In contrast, the many multiply variable parameters of segmental phonology function primarily to distinguish lexical meaning. The "tame" part of intonation is harnessed to grammar, where, for example, it distinguishes statements from questions in many languages. A "wilder" side of intonation expresses emotion. Intonation is half-tame and half-wild also because it occupies the borderlands of language and the liminal zones of linguistic theory. Intonation straddles the boundary between the phonetic and the phonological, the physical and the mental, the continuous and the categorial. For all of these reasons intonation is also of great interest.

Intonation is the patterned rising and falling of pitch in speech. Pitch itself is a perceptual phenomenon best correlated with the physical quantity called the fundamental frequency (abbreviated F_0), or the frequency with which the vocal chords vibrate during speech. The fundamental frequency is determined by the length and tenseness of the vocal chords. The shorter the vocal chords, or the tenser the vocal chords, the higher the F_0, and the higher the perceived pitch of the speech. Women's voices tend to be higher than men's voices, for example, because their smaller bodies have correspondingly shorter vocal chords.[4] Similarly, people may raise the pitch of their speech when they are angry, in part because the emotion increases the tension in their throat.[5]

Linguists refer to intonation as a suprasegmental feature of language because it coincides with, or is superimposed upon, the segmental, or phonemic structure. If I were to utter the simple phrase "Annie's driving my Mazda,"[6] my lips, tongue, and other vocal articulators would position themselves in various ways for each segment, but my pronunciation of the /d/ in "driving" would have no effect on my articulation of the /m/ in "my." However, if I were angry when uttering the same phrase, I might utter the entire sentence with raised pitch. Intonational phenomena also occur over much longer stretches of discourse, as, for example, when a speaker indicates a shift in topic by raising or lowering the pitch (see Hirschberg and Pierrehumbert 1986).

Intonation is just one of many suprasegmental features of language that together are called speech prosody. Prosody also includes speech rate, loudness, and voice quality. In expressing anger, for example, many speakers also vary their speech rate, either uttering the phrase very quickly, or very slowly.[7] Alternatively, speakers might use marked loudness to signal anger, yelling "ANNIE'S DRIVING MY MAZDA!" or marked voice quality, as when a growled rendition would serve the same function.

These examples point up one complexity in the study of intonation: the lack of a one-to-one, or "biunique," relationship between form and function. Raised pitch does not uniquely express anger, nor is anger uniquely expressed by raised pitch. Speech uttered with high pitch is not always heard as expressing anger. Conversely, anger can also be expressed by rapid speech, by loud speech, by growled speech. The absence of a biunique relation does not imply that intonation and emotion are unrelated, but it does indicate the complexity of the relationship. In Bolinger's words, intonation is only half-tamed.

Intonation is a salient feature of language use, but it has been particularly resistant to linguistic analysis. An introduction to one textbook on intonation, for example, says that

> linguists ... have been convinced for a long time that prosody is a legitimate issue ... but they have also been aware that it is a fairly elusive subject matter. By their very nature as utterance-long components, prosodic features are more difficult to observe, transcribe and analyse than are their segmental counterparts, and attested formal differences along any prosodic dimension cannot be given a functional interpretation as easily as is the case with a segmental contrast. ... Given the formal and functional complexities of prosodic features, one cannot investigate all of them at the same time. ('t Hart, Collier, and Cohen 1990:1–2)

Despite these difficulties, the linguistic description of intonation has made great progress. Early work (e.g., O'Connor and Arnold 1973) sought correspondences between pitch contours and sentence types. Most languages, for example, associate questions with rising intonation and assertions with falling intonation, as does English (Bolinger 1978). Figure 8.1 show intonation contours for the following typical English declarative and interrogative sentences.

(1)   a. Annie's driving my Mazda. (declarative)
      b. Annie's driving my Mazda? (interrogative)

Figure 8.1a is a pitch-track of the phrase "Annie's driving my Mazda" uttered as an assertion (1a), and figure 8.1b is a pitch-track of the corresponding question "Annie's driving my Mazda?" (1b).[8] On each graph the horizontal axis maps time as the utterance unfolds (measured in seconds), and the vertical axis maps the fundamental frequency (measured in hertz). The points of the graph plot the fundamental frequency of the speaker's voice at a particular moment in time, and vertical dashed lines indicate the boundaries between individual words. Of note in comparing the two contours is that the pitch falls at the end of a declarative (fig. 8.1a), while it rises at the end of an interrogative (fig. 8.1b).

Dwight Bolinger (1972) criticized this correlational approach, pointing to intonational phenomena that failed to correlate with sentence type. Bolinger noted, for example, that in English, as in many languages, speakers can emphasize almost

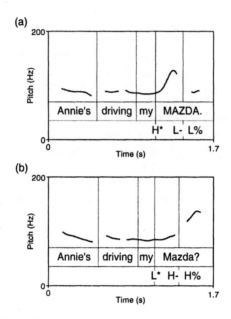

Figure 8.1. Pitch Tracks Showing Intonation on Declarative and Interrogative Utterances in English.

any word in a phrase by raising or lowering the pitch on that word. Linguists call such emphasis "focus," and they call such pitch prominences "pitch-accents." The four versions of the sample phrase "Annie's driving my Mazda" shown in (2) and pitch-tracked in figures 8.2a–d have subtle, but important, differences in meaning.

(2)   a. ANNIE's driving my Mazda.
       b. Annie's DRIVING my Mazda.
       c. Annie's driving MY Mazda.
       d. Annie's driving my MAZDA.

Phrase (2a) implies that it is *Annie* (and not someone else) who is driving my Mazda, while phrase (2c) implies that it is *my* (and not some other) Mazda that Annie is driving. And so forth. Focus can be thought of as a speaker's tendency to bring to the foreground information that is new (to a discourse) and to relegate to the background information assumed to be already shared. There are many ways speakers can focus on particular elements of a phrase, but intonation is a particularly common strategy.[9] Figure 8.2 illustrates the influence of focus on pitch. In each of the four example utterances, a pitch peak occurs over the focused word. In all four pitch-tracks (figs. 8.2a–d) the general shape of the pitch prominence over the focused word is the same—a rise to a maximum, followed by a fall to the original level.

English has a number of different kinds of pitch-accent, as the sample sentences

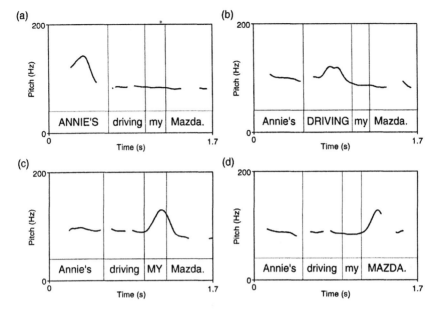

Figure 8.2.   Pitch Tracks Showing Intonation and Focus in English.

pitch-tracked in figure 8.1 indicate. In both utterances (1a) and (1b), English speakers perceive focus on the final word, *Mazda*, but figure 8.1 shows that the pitch contours over the two words are different. Janet Pierrehumbert (1980; Pierrehumbert and Beckman 1988) proposed five distinct pitch-accents for English, differing in pitch movement and timing relative to word-stress. The different pitch contours on *Mazda* in figures 8.1a and 8.1b, for example, can be explained by positing a "high" pitch-accent, H, in the declarative utterance (fig. 8.1a), and a "low" pitch-accent, L, in the interrogative utterance (fig. 8.1b). Both of these pitch-accents also have the alignment feature that the major pitch movement (up to H and down to L) is timed to coincide with the stressed syllable of the focused word—in this case the first syllable of *Mazda*. By convention, the pitch movement aligned with lexical stress is designated with an asterisk, resulting in the notations H* and L*.[10]

To fully account for the pitch movements over utterances such as those represented in (1) and (2) and pitch-tracked in figures 8.1 and 8.2, Pierrehumbert and Beckman (1988) posited three types of pitch phenomenon:

- Pitch-accents, which align with the syllable of a word bearing primary stress

- Phrasal tones, which follow the final pitch-accent in an intonational phrase

- Boundary tones, which align with the first and last syllables of an intonational phrase

With this descriptive apparatus, pitch contours can be transcribed as a sequence of tones that are either "high" or "low." An "intonational phrase" consists of one (or more) pitch-accent(s) followed by a phrasal tone and a (final) boundary tone. The notational conventions that "-" and "%" designate phrasal tones and boundary tones, respectively, allow the full specification of the contours over the declarative and interrogative utterances from (1) as shown in figure 8.3.

Meaning in Intonation

While theoretical and technological advances have facilitated progress in the description of intonational form, a great deal remains to be learned about what intonation means— the "wild side" of intonation. Generative approaches to intonation (e.g., Pierrehumbert and Beckman 1988) have brought rigor and creativity to formal description of intonation, but they have largely ignored the domain of meaning. Scholars who have studied intonational meaning differ widely in their approaches. Gussenhoven (1983), for example, argues that intonational forms bear only very general and abstract meanings. On this view, the specific interpretations that some tunes generate depend for their meaning upon context and inference. Liberman and Sag (1974) argue essentially the opposite, namely that at least some intonational tunes have specific meanings that are independent of context and almost idiomatic in function. Their study

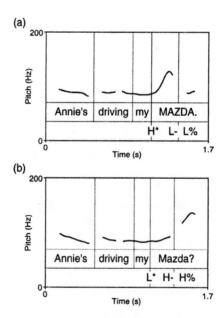

Figure 8.3.   Pitch Tracks of Declarative and Interrogative Utterances with Tonal Specifications.

of the "contradiction contour" in American English, for example, found that the tonal sequence L*H ... L* H- L% (i.e., any sequence beginning with an L*H pitch-accent, ending with an L* pitch-accent, and followed by an H- L% phrase-accent and boundary tone) regularly expressed "contradiction," or the speaker's attitude that the phrase the speaker utters is true, and that it is true despite the interlocutor's assumption to the contrary.[11]

The Sociolinguistics of Intonation

Unfortunately, the breakthroughs in formal analyses of intonation have not been matched by sociolinguistic research on intonation. Relatively few scholars have looked at the social meaning of pitch variation, or the ways in which intonation functions indexically. As Alan Cruttenden (1986:134) has complained, when it comes to regional or social dialectal variation in intonation "our knowledge of basic descriptive facts is either minimal or disputed."

A pioneering study of social variation in intonation looked at the distribution of the "high rising terminal" (henceforth HRT) in Australian English (Guy, Horvath, Vonwiller, Daisley, and Rogers 1986). Guy and his colleagues found that the HRT, a rising phrase-final contour usually associated with questions, was being used on declarative utterances in mainstream dialects of Australian English. This study broke new ground by treating an intonational phenomenon as a quantifiable linguistic variable, and by linking variation in intonation to the marking of social identity in speech.

The Israeli Rise-Fall Tune

I return now to the distinctively Israeli intonational contour that I heard on the *MacNeil/Lehrer Show* and that occurred frequently in the conversational Hebrew of Israelis. This tune is a particularly useful indicator of the ways in which social variation in Hebrew is used by Israelis to construct, enact, and negotiate their social identities in crosscultural interaction. Investigation of the social structure of its use sheds light on the struggle over Israeli identity.

The intonational contour in question is a rise-fall melody that occurs at the ends of phrases. I transcribe this contour as H* L- H:%, henceforth HLH.[12] This formalism captures the three defining characteristics of the tune:

(3)   a. A high pitch-accent aligned with a stressed syllable (H*)
       b. A fall to a relatively low pitch close to the end of the phrase (L-)
       c. A sustained high pitch over a lengthened phrase-final syllable (H:%)

Figure 8.4 shows a pitch-track of a typical instance of this contour. The phrase analyzed in figure 8.4 is given as:

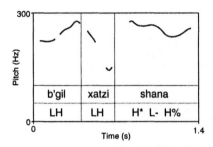

Figure 8.4.   Pitch Track of Typical Utterance Containing Israeli HLH Phrase-Final Contour.

(4)   ve—b'gil xatzi SHANA,[13]
       When I was six months old,

Figure 8.4 illustrates many of the characteristics of the tune just described. The general shape of the pitch contour shows the high-low-high melodic shape over *shana*, "year," the final word of the phrase. Pitch levels over this word vary. The pitch begins high, reaching a maximum of 270 hertz near the beginning of the word. The pitch then falls to a (local) minimum of 235 hertz, only to rise again to a drawn-out level tone of 260 hertz at the very end of the phrase. The pitch peak is timed to coincide with the second syllable in the word *shana*, the syllable bearing primary lexical stress.[14] The final syllable is lengthened, lasting twice as long as any other syllable in the phrase. Finally, relative to the overall pitch-range of this particular speaker, the phrase shown in figure 8.4 begins at a midlevel tone but ends at a level much higher than most of this speaker's phrase-final lows.

The HLH contour is often used to introduce new topics. The phrase in (4), *b'gil xatzi shana*, "when I was six months old," was uttered as a way of introducing an extended narrative:

(5)   ve—b'gil xatzi SHANA,
       When I was six months old,

       horai eh—nas'u le—moroko ...
       my parents went to Morocco ...

The phrase in (5) is the initial line of a narrative told at the outset of a sociolinguistic interview. In answer to an interview question, the speaker began a dramatic story about her family's immigration to Israel in the 1950s. She used the HLH contour to launch the narrative.

Hebrew has many other ways to introduce topics, and this tune has many other discourse functions in addition to topicalizing. For example, the HLH contour often occurs when a speaker is contrasting two entities, as in this example, taken from a narrative told during a sociolinguistic interview, in which the narrator recalls a party she threw for her son's Bar Mitzvah:[15]

(6)   asinu aruxa, v'zehu,
       We did a meal and that was it,

       ze haya ba tarix ha'ivri,
       That was on the Hebrew date,

       ki bar mitzva xogegim (batarix) ha'ivri,
       Because you celebrate a Bar Mitzvah according to the Hebrew date,

       axshav ha tarix ha LO'AZI, ...
       Now the Western date, ... (77B:505)

The narrator used the HLH tune (on *lo'azi,* "Western") to contrast two dates. Israelis use two different calendar systems. For most secular purposes Israelis use the Western, Gregorian calendar used in the United States, but Israelis also use the traditional Jewish (lunar) calendar to mark birthdays, religious and national holidays, and certain other important dates. This calendrical overlap leads to the pleasant situation in which children may celebrate their birthdays twice: once on the anniversary of the Western date of birth, and again on the anniversary of the Jewish date of birth. Such is the case with the narrator's son's Bar Mitzvah. After briefly mentioning a modest marking of the occasion on the Hebrew birth date, the narrator moves on to tell much more elaborately about the large party she threw to mark the Western date of her son's thirteenth birthday. Here the speaker articulates the word *lo'azi,* "Western," with the HLH tune, sharpening the contrast between the two dates.

When speakers use the HLH contour to contrast two entities in this way, they often inject affect into their utterance, expressing approval of one of the two contrasted entities. The following passage, for example, is taken from a gripping story told by a woman who found out after the fact that her daughter had been hospitalized and had undergone an emergency appendectomy. The daughter, a married woman with children of her own, did not tell anybody about her illness. Despite her daughter's silence, the narrator says, she had had an intuition. She frantically searched for her daughter, and, having located her in a hospital, rushed to be at her side when she awoke from anesthesia. The narrator employs the HLH contour when she introduces her own actions into the narrative:

(7)   tov, lo amra shum davar,
       OK, so she didn't tell anybody,

       ha-misken ha-ze,
       the poor guy, [i.e., her husband]

       histovev ita mi-sheva ba-boker,
       stayed with her from seven in the morning,

       ad she-hi nixn'sa l'xadar nituax b'xamesh va-xetzi,
       till she entered the operating room at five thirty,

ben kol ha-rof'im she-rak efshar, she badku ota,
what with all the doctors that examined her,

hu haya kol kax umlal,
he was so miserable,

ANI, ba-yom SHENI, ...
as for me, on Monday, ... (77C:100)

The mother tells this narrative of personal experience as part of an effort to construct an image of herself as a "good mother." She begins this story by setting the stage: the daughter gets sick; she doesn't tell anyone; her husband worries. When introducing herself, however, the narrator uses the HLH rise-fall contour. Here the narrator uses the topic-introducing intonation to contrast the disapproved actions of the daughter to her own actions, which she approves of.

Intonation in Discourse:
The Rise-Fall Contour in Narrative

To investigate the social meaning of the Israeli HLH contour in actual discourse, I look at two interviews in which the politics of identity was especially salient. Analysis of these interviews as sites for the negotiation of Self and Other and attention to the details of speech for the multiple layers of dialogic meaning it contains highlight the role of the HLH contour in negotiating identity.

Interview 1

The first interview involved two middle-aged Jewish women, whom I call Nurit and Hagit.[16] The women were good friends as a result of their sons being in the same school class. The interview was held at Nurit's home, in a lower-working-class neighborhood of Haifa. In conducting this interview I was joined by an Israeli research assistant, a native speaker of Hebrew. The two interviewees have recognizable accents: Nurit has a strong Mizrahi accent and Hagit an equally strong Ashkenazi accent. The accent difference, however, does not involve the pharyngeal variables discussed in the previous chapter. In terms of phonology the speech of the two women is quite similar. Rather, the accent difference resides in the domain of prosody.

Israelis have clear intuitions on the relationship between intonation and Jewish Israeli identity: Mizrahim are said to "sing" more than Ashkenazim, an observation often correlated with statements about more expressiveness in other domains, including gesture. The perceptual effect of "singing" is achieved through a wide range of specific intonational and prosodic phenomena: wide pitch range, relatively short prosodic phrases, frequent H* pitch-accents, and stylized intonational contours. Nurit's speech is characterized by many of these features. She uses a wider pitch range than does Hagit, as well as a higher pitch register, and more stylized intonation. The HLH rise-fall tune described earlier, for example, is one of the stylized contours. This contour occurs more than twice as frequently in Nurit's speech as it does in Hagit's speech.

The role this intonational contour plays in dialect differentiation, however, is more complicated than mere frequency, as a comparison of two narratives from the interview shows. The two narratives to be examined here are transcribed as texts 8.1 and 8.2. These narratives are presented in both transcribed (transliterated) Hebrew and a relatively free English translation. Numbered lines correspond to prosodic units that are defined in terms of phonetic pause structure. Text 8.1 reproduces the narrative Nurit told at the outset of the interview of her family's emigration from Morocco to Israel in the 1940s. Text 8.2 reproduces a narrative Hagit told much later in the interview about growing up on a kibbutz. Hagit's story was not a direct response to an interview question; rather, it emerged spontaneously from the ongoing flow of conversation. (In the transcription of the two narratives, I have marked occurrences of the HLH contour with boldface and small caps.)

The narratives reproduced in texts 8.1 and 8.2 both relate strongly ambivalent experiences of childhood. Nurit's narrative, for example, tells of her parents' harrowing journey from Morocco to Israel in the 1940s, just before the State of Israel was formed. This is a familiar story in Israel, a nation of immigrants (see chapter 2), but Nurit tells it in a way that contests dominant representations of the Mizrahi immigration. Nurit represents her father, for example, as a Zionist pioneer. By noting that he brought his family to Israel in 1946, before the formation of the state in 1948, Nurit contests official Israeli ideology, which privileges Ashkenazi immigrants as heroic founders (see Elon 1981) and marks Mizrahi immigrants as reluctant pioneers.[17] Nurit also represents her parents as Jews who maintained close ties to their Moroccan origin even after making the move to Israel. Her story shows them moving back and forth between Israel and Morocco, constructing fluidity of identity that contradicts official Israeli discourses that posit an abrupt rupture between Israeli and Arab Jewish identities. The rupture is based upon the related notions that the Jews were persecuted in Arab countries, that they were uniformly ecstatic to come to Israel, and that once in Israel they avenged their former persecution by developing an irredentist hatred of Arabs. In stark contrast, Nurit's narrative shows Israelis (her parents) moving back to Morocco after having come to Israel, Jews (her grandmother) electing to stay in Morocco rather than emigrate to Israel, and a pleasant and safe life in Morocco contrasted to a difficult and risky life in Israel.

Hagit's narrative, shown in text 8.2, also relates a deeply ambivalent family experience, and this story, too, contests dominant images of Israeli identity. Hagit's story tells of growing up on a kibbutz and of her feelings of alienation from the other children and the community's intense social atmosphere. Hagit's portrayal of being ridiculed by her age-mates for wanting to be close to her parents contests the idealism of the kibbutz movement, which celebrated peer culture and separation from parents. Hagit, too, counters powerful Israeli tropes of identity that privilege the kibbutznik as the model for the new (Israeli) Jew (see chapter 3).

Text 8.1. Nurit Narrative, Hebrew Transcription

ve— b'gil xatzi SHANA,	(1)
horai eh— nas'u le— moroko,	(2)
v'az Haya li gam ax nosaf, ben shnatayim,	(3)
v'han'siya hazot ba'a b'ikvot eh— eh— laxatz shel ha— ima shelo,	(4)
she— amra shehi muxr'xa lir'ot oto,	(5)
ki avi ala LA'ARETZ,	(6)
v'azav et MOROKO,	(7)
b'shnat arba'im v'shesh, mashehu kaze,	(8)
ala 'im aliyat hano'ar,	(9)
ve— b'arba'im v'SHEVA, tafsu otam, b'kafrisin, b'maxanot,	(10)
ve— sham hu shaha shana b'erex,	(11)
sham hu hikir gam et ima sheli,	(12)
(…)	
she gam alta, aval yaxad im horeha,	(13)
ve— b'shnat arba'im v'SHMONE,	(14)
k'she haya kvar heter la'alot la'aretz hem nixn'su la'aretz,	(14a)
ve— hitxatnu,	(15)
ima sheli, eh— hitxatna balaxatz shuv hahorim,	(16)
shelo titgayes latzava, od lo yod'im ma ze, v'ex ze,	(17)
hixlitu shehem m'xatnim ota,	(18)
ve zehu, az noladnu ani v'axi,	(19)
ve— hamilxamot shehayu kan,	(20)
ha— ima shel AVI,	(21)
sham'a k'ilu shehu— neherag b'axat hamilxamot,	(22)
ve— hi shalxa et ha'ax shela,	(23)
et eh— ax shel AVI,	(24)
eh— la'alot la'aretz, k'de l'xapes oto,	(25)
v'az b'emet eh— hu ba v'xipes, v'sha'al, v'matza oto,	(26)
v'ham'anyen hu she hu matza oto bidiyuk eh—	
kama yamim lifne haxatuna,	(27)
v'hu— eh— hispik afilu l'hishtatef baxatuna,	(28)
v'shalax la'ima shelo TMUNA,	(29)
she hine hu matza oto, ve—	(30)
v'az ha'ima hitxila b'laxatz shel eh—	
bo'u, l'kan, ze tov, v'po, v'sham,	(31)
b'kitzur hahorim sheli azvu kan et hakol v'nas'u l'xutz la'aretz,	(32)
sham hem shahu b'erex eh— shnatayim v'xetzi shalosh,	(33)
benatayim nolad li od ax,	(34)
b— b'moroko,	(35)
ve— b'shnat eh— xamishim v'SHESH,	(36)
hahorim sheli xazru la'aretz,	(37)

TEXT 8.1. NURIT NARRATIVE, ENGLISH TRANSLATION

When I was six months old,	(1)
my parents went to Morocco,	(2)
and I had a brother then too, two years old,	(3)
and the trip came about eh— because of pressure from his mother,	(4)
who said she needed to see him,	(5)
because my father came to Israel,	(6)
and left Morocco,	(7)
in 1946, something like that,	(8)
he came with The Youth Aliya,	(9)
and in 1947, they caught them, in Cyprus, in camps,	(10)
and he spent about a year there,	(11)
and he met my mother there,	(12)
(...)	
she immigrated (to Israel) too, but together with her parents,	(13)
and in 1948,	(14)
when people were finally allowed in, they came to Israel,	(14a)
and they got married,	(15)
my mother, eh— married under parental pressure,	(16)
not to get drafted for the army,	
don't know what that is, or what it's like,	(17)
they decided to marry her off,	(18)
and that was it, then my brother and I were born,	(19)
and the wars here,	(20)
my father's mother,	(21)
heard that he— had been killed in one of the wars,	(22)
and she sent her son,	(23)
eh— my father's brother,	(24)
eh— to come to Israel, to look for him,	(25)
and then he eh— really did come, and looked,	
and asked, and found him,	(26)
and what's interesting is that he found him	
just days before the wedding,	(27)
and he was even able to take part in the wedding,	(28)
and he sent his mother a picture,	(29)
that see, he found him, and—	(30)
but then the mother panicked, come here, it's good, and there—	(31)
in short, my parents left everything here, and went abroad,	(32)
they lived there about eh— two to three years,	(33)
in the meantime another brother was born,	(34)
in— in Morocco,	(35)
and in eh— 1956,	(36)
my parents returned to Israel.	(37)

TEXT 8.2.   HAGIT NARRATIVE, HEBREW TRANSCRIPTION

ani zoxeret oti b'tor yalda,	(1)
ani lo yoda'at m'efo haya li ha'ometz,	(2)
ani kol layla,	(3)
v'yaxal l'hiyot geshem haxi— geshem zel'afot,	(4)
hayiti boraxat l'xeder hahorim,	(5)
v'ima sheli haita m'tapelet, bagan, kol hashanim,	(6)
v'ex ze,	(7)
she hi m'tapelet,	(8)
v'habat shela m'iza lavo lishon b'xeder horim,	(9)
az hayu maxbi'im oti b'argaz,	(10)
ki lamita haya argaz kaze', mi barzel, (...)	(11)
ad lifnot boker,	(12)
lifnot boker, baxashai,	(13)
atufa b'smixa hayu maxzirim oti,	(14)
shema yuvada l'mishehu,	(15)
(...)	
yashanti im hahorim,	(16)
yoter m'uxar, shehayinu b'vet sefer,	(17)
hayiti yoshevet,	(18)
omedet al hamirpeset, kol layla v'boxa,	(19)
kvar lo baxiti ima,	(20)
baxiti abale,	(21)
v'ani— hayiti omedet v'boxa, um'xake she yavo lakaxat oti,	(22)
(...)	
at yoda'at ma, haya li pa'am xerem xevrati,	(23)
im hakita,	(24)
ani m'od ahavti et xug habait shel hahorim,	(25)
ki haya li ken m'od xam,	(26)
bet horai, ze haya mashehu, kodem kol ze haya	
tamid markaz xevrati,	(27)
kol erev male xaverim,	(28)
(...)	
m'od ahavti,	(29)
v'az, bat'kufa shelanu,	(30)
lahov et xeder hahorim, ze haya ason,	(31)
at— at pashut at lo normalit,	(32)
im at ohevet lihiyot im hahorim shelax,	
ze mashehu— dafuk etzlex basexel,	(33)
v'ani zoxeret she eze erev hayiti im hahorim sheli,	(34)
v'kol hakita, ba m'axure hadelet, v'dafku, v'tzaxaku, ...	(35)
(...) yesh li xavera, shehi mitgoreret axshav b'artzot habrit,	(36)
hi bidiyuk haita axshav b'bikur,	(37)
hi haita semel shel anti-horim,	(38)
HAYOM, ani omeret labat, ex at margisha im ze,	(39)
ex HAYOM, shehi BA'A, ani omeret la,	(40)
ani margisha she at m'od rotza xazara,	(41)
ratzit l'galgel axora, l'hitkarev LAHORIM,	(42)
ki at pashut daxit otam,	(43)

TEXT 8.2.   HAGIT NARRATIVE, ENGLISH TRANSLATION

I remember myself as a young girl,	(1)
I don't know where I got the courage,	(2)
every night,	(3)
and it could have been the biggest rain— pouring rain,	(4)
I would run away to my parents' room,	(5)
and my mother was caretaker, in the kindergarden, all those years,	(6)
and how could this be,	(7)
that she's the caretaker,	(8)
and her own daughter dares to come sleep in the parents' room,	(9)
so they would hide me in a box,	(10)
because those beds had boxes, out of metal,	(11)
till dawn,	(12)
at dawn, in secret,	(13)
wrapped up in a blanket, they would return me,	(14)
lest someone should find out,	(15)
(…)	
[that] I slept with my parents,	(16)
later on, when we were in school,	(17)
I would sit—	(18)
stand on the porch, every night and cry,	(19)
I didn't cry for Mommy anymore,	(20)
I cried for Daddy,	(21)
and I— I would stand and cry, and wait for him to come take me,	(22)
(…)	
you know what? I was once excommunicated,	(23)
from my class,	(24)
I really loved my parents' circle of friends,	(25)
because I had a very "warm nest",	(26)
my parents' house, that was really something,	
it was always a social center,	(27)
every night full of friends,	(28)
(…)	
I really loved it,	(29)
but then, in those days,	(30)
loving the parents' room, that was a disaster,	(31)
you're— you're just not normal,	(32)
if you love to be with your parents,	
something's screwed up in your mind,	(33)
and I remember that one evening I was over at my parents',	(34)
and my whole class came to the door, and knocked, and laughed,	(35)
(…) I have a friend, who lives in the U.S. now,	(36)
she was just here on a visit,	(37)
she was a symbol for [being] "anti-parents",	(38)
today, I said to [her], how do you feel about that,	(39)
so now, when she comes, I said to her,	(40)
I feel that you really want to go back,	(41)
you wanted to go back, to get closer to the parents,	(42)
because you just rejected them.	(43)

The two narrators use their stories to negotiate their own identities with respect to the dominant Israeli discourse of identity. The stories are thus told in order to counter general stereotypes of their respective identities, as the two women struggle over the meaning of Israeli identity. But retelling these familiar stories also functions pragmatically in the interview, since the stories are also told to counter specific stereotypes held by their interlocutor—despite their mutual friendship. Thus in analyzing the narrative speech we must read a speaker's utterance in terms not only of the broader contestation over Israeli national identity but of the interpersonal interaction of the interview as well.

The two women tell these narratives to each other, as it were. During the interview both women actively contested the other's narrative construction of identity. Hagit interrupted Nurit's growing-up narrative to inject an experience from her army service. Hagit's inserted story told of Mizrahi immigrants' avoidance of military duty and thereby reasserted dominant images of Mizrahi identity that Nurit was contesting.[18] Similarly, and perhaps equally pointedly, Nurit interrupts Hagit's narrative about growing up on a kibbutz to contest her negative portrayal of kibbutz life. Her own relatives, she asserts, have had much more positive experiences of the kibbutz. This interview interaction was thus very much a negotiation of identity, in which narratives of personal experience were deployed as emotionally charged expressions of Self.

But the narrators negotiated their discursive identities through the play of language form, as well as the play of narrative content. Nurit, for example, uses a marked intonational style to assert her Mizrahi identity, as an analysis of the prosody of the two narratives will show. In particular, the use of the HLH contour distinguishes the two prosodic styles.

Nurit uses the HLH rise-fall contour more than twice as frequently (nine times in 36 lines) as Hagit (four times in 43 lines), but a closer look at the distribution of the rise-fall tunes in the two narratives reveals an even more striking difference. Figure 8.5 shows two different patterns of use of the HLH tune in the two narratives. This

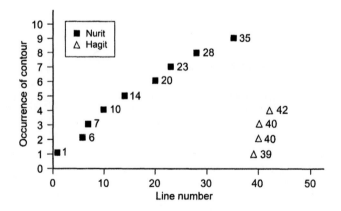

Figure 8.5.   Distribution of HLH Contour in texts 8.1 and 8.2.

figure graphically compares the distribution of HLH contours in the two narratives, mapping for each narrative the occurrence of an HLH contour onto its sequential position in the narrative. The nine occurrences of the HLH tune in Nurit's narrative (text 8.1) are represented in figure 8.5 by filled squares, and the four instances of the HLH tune in Hagit's narrative (text 8.2) are represented by empty triangles. The number to the right of the graphing symbols in figure 8.5 indicates the number of the line (from texts 8.1 and 8.2) in which the HLH tune occurred. In Nurit's narrative the nine HLH tunes are spread regularly and evenly throughout the narrative, while in Hagit's narrative the four HLH tunes are clustered in the final few lines of her story.

A clear pattern emerges when this distribution is linked to the content of the two narratives. In text 8.2, Hagit argues that the kibbutz ideal of separation from family failed. The early part of her narrative is told in a detached, analytical, and self-effacing manner. In the following segment, Hagit tells how her classmates had ridiculed her:

(8)   But then, in those days,
       Loving the parents' room, that was a disaster,
       You're— you're just not normal,
       If you love to be with your parents, something's screwed up in your mind,
       And I remember that one evening I was over at my parents',
       And my whole class was behind the door, and they knocked, and they laughed, ...
       (text 8.2, lines 30–35)

But a pronounced shift in attitude occurs abruptly in line 36, when she provides poignant evidence that kibbutz ideals damaged family relationships: even the girl who was most central to the peer group culture came to regret her alienation from her parents:

(9)   (...) I have a friend, who lives in the United States now,
       She was just here on a visit,
       She was a symbol of "anti-parents",
       Today, I said to [her], how do you feel about that,
       So now, when she comes, I said to her,
       I feel that you really want to go back,
       You wanted to go back, to get closer to the parents,
       Because you just rejected them, ...
       (text 8.2, lines 36–43)

This is the affective crux of Hagit's narrative. She marks this crux with several dramatic linguistic devices: an accelerated speech rate, a tense-shift from the simple past to the historical present, a switch from indirect to direct speech, and the deployment of the HLH contour four times in six lines. Hagit thus begins using the rise-fall tune at precisely the point in her narrative where she becomes maximally involved as narrator. In so doing Hagit merges affectively powerful intonation with affectively loaded content.

Nurit employs the rise-fall tune in a very different way. Figure 8.6 is a flow chart that maps the sequence of topics and segments Nurit's narrative into its component themes. The overarching narrative of her family's brief return to Morocco is told through

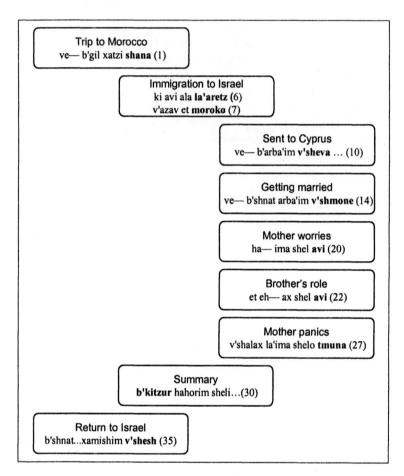

Figure 8.6. Narrative Flow and the HLH Contour in text 8.1.

a sequence of embedded stories: her parents' original move to Israel; their eventful wedding; and Nurit's grandmother's concerns over their safety. The beginning of each of these narrative subplots is marked by the HLH contour. Nurit thus uses the HLH contour systematically as a marker of discourse units in narrative.

The two narratives differ in other ways as well. While Hagit tells a narrative of personal experience, Nurit's narrative is a narrative of vicarious experience. Hagit relates events that she actually witnessed and presumably remembers. The emotions she attributes to herself as a young child are presumably the emotions she recalls herself feeling. Nurit, in contrast, tells of a period before her own personal memory, and her narrative thus is comprised of reported speech about the personal experiences of others. Nurit never becomes particularly involved in the telling, despite the powerful feelings her story evokes.

It is thus striking that Hagit's use of the rise-fall tune is concentrated in specific discourse contexts where the marking of speech with affect is important. In contrast,

Nurit does not mark specific foci of affectivity with the HLH tune.[19] Both speakers use the rise-fall contour, and in the speech of both women the intonation functions to express and evoke affect, but in the narrative speech of Nurit, the Mizrahi Israeli woman, the rise-fall contour has been generalized as a regular marker of topic change and discourse structure. This difference indicates that an iconically meaningful intonation (i.e., one that expresses affectivity) has become an indexically meaningful marker of Mizrahi identity.

Interview 2

The rise-fall tune is also an important linguistic resource in the marking of Palestinian identities in Israeli Hebrew. As was shown in chapter 7 for the pharyngeal variables, Palestinians in Israel vary a great deal in the degree to which they adopt Jewish Israeli linguistic norms. A meaningful adaptation of the Israeli rise-fall tune commonly occurs in the speech of Palestinians as part of a linguistic construction of a Palestinian Israeli identity.

Figure 8.7 shows a Palestinian variant of the HLH contour. This contour is broadly similar to the contour described in figure 8.4. The relevant difference between this contour (which I call the Palestinian HLH, or PHLH) and the general Israeli rise-fall tune is that the pitch movement in the PHLH occurs in the middle of the speaker's pitch range, rather than at the top of that range (see fig. 8.4).

The PHLH fulfills the same range of functions that the general Israeli HLH does. The PHLH also introduces new discourse topics, contrasts opposed entities, and expresses affectivity. The token described in figure 8.7, for example, *ani ba-misrad*, "(as for me), in the office," introduced a narrative about the speaker's experience as a Palestinian lawyer working with Jewish clients and colleagues, as the broader discourse context shows:

(10) ani ba-MISRAD,
       in my office,

      yesh li hamon klientim yehudim, shel ha-misrad, she ani oved itam, ...
      I have lots of Jewish clients, (clients) of the office, that I work with, ...

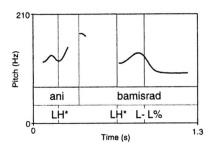

Figure 8.7.   Pitch-Track of Typical Utterance Containing Palestinian Israeli PHLH Phrase-Final Contour.

TEXT 8.3. HANI NARRATIVE (HEBREW TRANSCRIPTION);
RESPONSE TO THE INTERVIEWER QUESTION:
"HOW DID THE AWARENESS OF YOUR PALESTINIAN IDENTITY DEVELOP?"

ani, k'shehayiti KATAN,	(1)
v'katan ze ad kita vav naneax l'mashal,	(2)
ani lo hirgashti shum davar—	(3)
etzli bazehut hafalastinit l'xalutin,	(4)
ani afilu hixHashti et ze,	(5)
lo hayiti magdir et atzmi k'falastinai—	(6)
b'shum panim v'ofen ad kita vav,	(7)
en shum siman lazehut hazot,	(8)
mi shehaya sho'el oti, hayiti yisra'eli l'xol davar v'inyan,	(9)
v'hayiti m'od sameax sherov ha—	(10)
l'mashal she Einstein haya yehudi, …	(11)
v'she Freud yehudi,	(12)
she harbe mad'anim hem yehudim,	(13)
sheani Hai b'm'dina,	(14)
shekol kax xaxama,	(15)
she yesh la koax tzvai mamash xazak, …	(16)
v'ze b'emet kaxa, …	(17)
n'kuda rishona she hafxa…lanitzotz harishon, ze…yom ha'adama, …	(18)
ani zoxer az,	(19)
kaxa hayiti mamash ad oto yom,	(20)
ani zoxer she b'oto yom, ani katavti shir,	(21)
ze lo haya pa'am rishona she katavti shir,	
aval b'oto yom ani katavti shir, …	(22)
lo, ani zoxer et ze, b'emet, …	(23)
ani xoshev shehat'kufa she ba'a axare ze, xativat haBENAYIM,	(24)
lo shinta harbe, aval haya kvar nitzotz,	(25)
ani zoxer mamash n'kudot eh z'man, kaxa,	(26)
axare ze ba'a b'shiv'im v'tesha, hitnagshut b'Sheq'a,	(27)
bashlishi lashishi,	(28)
ani xoshev sheze haya, …	(29)
v'az asu atzuma b'vet hasefer,	(30)
im ani zoxer miYALDUTI,	(31)
et hakomunistim osim d'varim TOVIM,	(32)
ulai ze haya exad hadvarim, …	(33)
axare ze hayiti xaver bamiflaga hazo,	(34)
aval ze exad hadvarim shehayu TOVIM,	(35)
v'az eh— haya— ze nitzotz axer,	(36)
b'ota SHANA,	(37)
hayiti tzarix LIHIYOT, …	(38)
v'az hayiti tzarix l'hishtatef kaxa b'eru'im,	(39)
v'az hitxalti likrot, …	(40)
kol yalduti hayiti bolea sfarim b'kamuyot,	(41)
v'az hitvadati lsug xadash shel sfarim tov yoter,	(42)
ani zoxer kama s'farim shemamash KRIATAM,	(43)
hishpi'a al tafniot hat'fisa sheli,	(44)
mamash ani zoxer et ha sefer v'et kriato,	(45)

TEXT 8.3. HANI NARRATIVE (ENGLISH TRANSLATION);
RESPONSE TO THE INTERVIEWER QUESTION:
"HOW DID THE AWARENESS OF YOUR PALESTINIAN IDENTITY DEVELOP?"

As for me, when I was little,	(1)
and little means up to the sixth grade let's say,	(2)
I didn't feel anything,	(3)
of Palestinian identity in myself, not at all,	(4)
I even denied it,	(5)
I wouldn't have defined myself as a Palestinian,	(6)
no way, till the sixth grade,	(7)
there wasn't any sign of such an identity,	(8)
anyone who'd have asked I'd have told them I'm totally Israeli,	(9)
and I was very happy that most of the—	(10)
for example that Einstein was Jewish, ...	(11)
and that Freud is a Jew,	(12)
that many scientists are Jews,	(13)
and that I live in a state,	(14)
that's so clever,	(15)
and that has such a strong army, ...	(16)
and it's really like that, ...	(17)
the point that became the first spark, is definitely Land Day, ...	(18)
I remember then,	(19)
really up to that very day I was like that,	(20)
I remember that on that day I wrote a poem,	(21)
it wasn't the first time I'd written a poem,	
but I remember writing one on that day, ...	(22)
no, I really do remember that, ...	(23)
I think that the period that came after that, junior high school,	(24)
didn't change much, but there was a spark already,	(25)
I remember actual points in time like that,	(26)
after that came in '79 the clash in (Sheq'a),	(27)
on the third of the sixth,	(28)
I think it was, ...	(29)
and then they had a demonstration at school,	(30)
if I remember from my childhood,	(31)
the Communists doing good things,	(32)
maybe this was one of them, ...	(33)
(even though) I was a member of the party after that,	(34)
but maybe this was one of the things that were good,	(35)
and then eh— there was— another spark,	(36)
the same year,	(37)
I was supposed to be, ...	(38)
and then I had to participate in all sorts of events,	(39)
and then I began to read, ...	(40)
my whole childhood I used to eat up books,	(41)
and then I got acquainted with a different kind of book,	(42)
I remember a few books that reading them,	(43)
influenced the patterns of my understanding,	(44)
I really remember the book and its reading,	(45)
one, was the newspaper *al-Ittihad*,	(46)

TEXT 8.4. FARHA NARRATIVE (HEBREW TRANSCRIPTION);
RESPONSE TO THE INTERVIEW QUESTION:
"WHAT HAPPENED TO YOUR FAMILY IN 1948?"

ma m'saprim,	(1)
eh— b'natzeret lo hayu— anashim lo azvu et habatim shelahem,	(2)
k'dai lishmoa et hasipur shel ima shelo,	(3)
ze mamash sipur m'anyen,	(4)
ima selo— anashim sham,	(5)
avru l'livanon, v'xazru,	(6)
xazru b'nes, mamash, eh—	(7)
eh— b'natzeret lo kara shum davar, eh—	(8)
anashim nish'aru babayit,	(9)
lo b'etzem lo, ma ani m'daberet,	(10)
lo, mishpaxa shel aba sheli,	(11)
hem azvu, hem azvu b'arba'im v'SHMONE,	(12)
v'yatz'u l'livanon,	(13)
aval higi'u l'Rama, l'kfar Rama,	(14)
haya blok baderex,	(15)
v'lo yaxlu L'HAMSHIX,	(16)
v'hem xazru,	(17)
ken, ze ma she ani yoda'at,	(18)
lo higi'u l'livanon,	(19)
xazru,	(20)
aval aba sheli L'MASHAL,	(21)
hu lamad, bauniversita ha'amrikait b'berut, lifne arba'im v'shmone,	(22)
hu gamar b'arba'im v'xamesh, arba'im v'shesh,	(23)
v'xazar lifne kol ha— dvarim ha'ele,	(24)
v'ima shel— nish'aru ba—	(25)
mishpaxa shel ima sheli L'MASHAL,	(26)
nimtzet b'livanon,	(27)
hem azvu b'xamishim v'tesha,	(28)
k'de limtzo avoda sham,	(29)
v'hi gam lo xazru,	(30)
az hi l'vad po b—	(31)
kol ha'axim shela,	(32)
mfuzarim b'xol ha'olam ha'aravi,	(33)
Abu-dabi, v'kuwet, v'sa'udia, v'livanon,	(34)
kol mine m'komot, ...	(35)

TEXT 8.4. FARHA NARRATIVE (ENGLISH TRANSLATION);
RESPONSE TO THE INTERVIEW QUESTION:
"WHAT HAPPENED TO YOUR FAMILY IN 1948?"

What do they say,	(1)
eh— in Narareth there weren't— The people didn't leave their homes,	(2)
you should hear his mother's story,	(3)
it's really an interesting story,	(4)
yea, his mother, the people there,	(5)
they went to Lebanon, and came back,	(6)
they came back by a miracle, really, eh—	(7)
in Nazareth nothing happened,	(8)
people stayed at home, and—	(9)
no, actually not, what am I saying?	(10)
my father's family,	(11)
they left, they left in '48,	(12)
and they headed for Lebanon,	(13)
but they got to Rama, to Rama Village,	(14)
and there was a block there,	(15)
and they couldn't continue,	(16)
and they came back,	(17)
yea, that's what I know,	(18)
no— they didn't get to Lebanon,	(19)
they came back,	(20)
but my dad for example,	(21)
he studied at the American University, in Beirut before 1948,	(22)
he finished in '45, '46,	(23)
and he came back before all— those things,	(24)
and my mother, they stayed in—	(25)
my mother's family for example,	(26)
is in Lebanon,	(27)
they left in '59,	(28)
to find work there,	(29)
and they didn't return,	(30)
so she's alone here,	(31)
and all her brothers,	(32)
are scattered throughout the Arab World,	(33)
Abu-Dhabi, and Kuwait, and Saudi Arabia, and Lebanon,	(34)
in all sorts of places,	(35)

This variant of the HLH tune thus functions as a topicalizer, just like the phrase analyzed earlier in figure 8.4.

To examine Palestinian use of the Israeli rise-fall tune I turn to an interview conducted with Hani and his wife, Farha. Hani grew up in a small Palestinian town in northern Israel and had moved to Haifa in pursuit of higher education and employment. During his student days he had been very active in Palestinian politics, and at the time of our interview he worked as a lawyer for a medium-sized, Jewish-owned law firm.

Hani and his wife used diametrically opposed styles of Hebrew. We can get a feeling for these divergent styles by looking at their respective use of the pharyngeal variables discussed in chapter 7. While Hani was among the most pronounced users of pharyngealized Hebrew, his wife, Farha, used almost entirely nonpharyngeal forms (see fig. 7.11). Their deployments of socially meaningful intonation, and specifically the HLH tune focused on here, parallel their respective uses of the pharyngeal variables, as demonstrated by a close analysis of the two narratives transcribed here as texts 8.3 and 8.4.

In the narratives presented here as text 8.3, Hani uses two variants of the HLH contour: a mainstream form similar to that described in figure 8.4, and the PHLH variant similar to that shown in figure 8.7. (In the transcripts here, occurrences of the HLH tune are marked, as earlier, by boldface and small caps; in addition, the PHLH variants are italicized.) The overall distribution of the rise-fall tune in texts 8.3 and 8.4 parallels the distribution of pharyngeal forms discussed in chapter 7. Figure 8.8 illustrates that Farha, who had a low pharyngeal index, uses the intonation relatively frequently, and that it is evenly distributed throughout her speech.[20] Hani, on the other hand, uses the form infrequently, and the occurrences of the tune are clustered at particular junctures of his narrative. Specifically, Hani's use of the PHLH tune is concentrated in the part of his narrative where he describes the origins of his self-identification as a Palestinian. At such points—when Hani uses the tune frequently—he alternates between the mainstream form and the Palestinian variant.

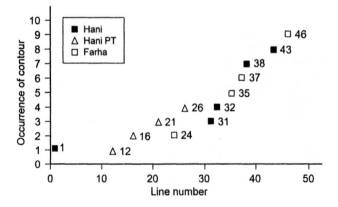

Figure 8.8.   Distribution of HLH and PHLH Contours in texts 8.3 and 8.4.

Embedding the narrative speech in its interpretive context, we see that Hani's description of his own youthful pride in being Israeli, symbolically expressed through attachment to Einstein, Freud, and Jewish intellectual achievements (see lines 9–17 in text 8.3) dialogically evokes (while resisting) official discourses of Israeli nationhood.[21] He provisionally accepts, for example, Israeli discourses that erase Palestinian presence, symbolized as an empty and barren Palestine, "a land without people for a people without land," which the returning Jews redeemed with hard work and ingenuity (see chapter 2). Hani also parodies the voice of Israeli educational policy, according to which Arab school curricula feature Jewish history and literature, including the classics of Jewish nationalism, while omitting Palestinian history and restricting Arabic literature to non-Palestinian authors and premodern genres (see text 5.2). Finally, Hani parodies the voice of American Jews, who come to Israel in great numbers, looking for their roots, and for whom Israel unproblematically represents the very things Hani parodies.[22]

The clear parody contributes to the rhetorical power of the message, as Hani skillfully constructs the shift in footing through a pronounced change in prosody. This section of Hani's narrative is composed of short phrases. Each phrase is uttered to a distinct cadence. And this rhythm becomes increasingly prominent, climaxing on the lines

(11)   She-ani ḥai b'-m'dina,
       and that I live in a state,

       she-kol kax xaxama,
       that's so clever,
       (text 8.3, lines 14–15)

wherein the Hebrew word *m'dina*, "state," rhymes with *xaxama*, "clever."

Toward the end of the narrative, Hani again uses intonation to insert dialogically connected voices into his speech. The HLH contour occurs most frequently in the portion of Hani's narrative in which Palestinian identity is an important part of his consciousness, and this section contains both variants. Hani's use of these contours phonetically constructs the blurred Israeli-Palestinian identity he semantically evokes throughout this narrative segment. Hani's use of the HLH tune, much like Farha's use of the tune, claims membership and position in Israeli society. His modification of the tune asserts the Palestinian basis for his Israeli identity, much the way his pronounced use of pharyngeal articulations lays claim to an Arab and Israeli identity.

Thus the HLH intonation is embedded in a web of intertextual and dialogic meanings that evoke Israeliness in part through the contour's evocation of affect. While all Israelis use the rise-fall tune to express speaker involvement and affective engagement, subaltern Israelis use the tune distinctively. Mizrahi Israelis deploy the tune as a systematic discourse-marker in narrative speech, and Palestinian speakers use a distinctive variant of the tune. The rise-fall contour contests *sabra* ideals of constrained emotionality (see chapter 6), thereby decentering received notions of mainstream Jewish Israeli identity. The use patterns described therefore constitute linguistic expressions of oppositional identities, while providing evidence for the emergence of social dialect differences.

9

Conclusion:
Negotiations, Dialogues,
Power, and Language

Israel/Palestine stands for the intersection of West/East and North/South in international politics. This contested site constitutes a bridge at times—though more frequently a divide—between Western modernity, democracy, and colonizing power and Eastern tradition, patriarchy, and colonial subalternity. Where once the tensions between the United States and the Soviet Union were manifest, now other global tensions, such as that between the hegemony of international capitalism and the resistance of fundamentalist revitalisms, play themselves out on the same soil. Events in this small piece of land influence global relations of power. The everyday practices of domination and resistance in Israel/Palestine therefore take on a significance that extends far beyond their quotidian scope. A study of local politics therefore has implications for global politics.

I have focused on the strategic manipulation of linguistic variation in face-to-face interactions because the use of language forms a lens through which to view underlying social processes. In contrast to the wide scope of their implications, these everyday practices of domination and resistance are understood through the fine detail of their enactment and achievement. Understanding the relationship between the dynamics of politics and the politics of talk in Israel sheds light on general processes of social dynamics applicable to other places and other regions. More specifically, though, understanding the dynamics of Israeli social life illuminates the dynamics of a crucial nexus of international relations.

The theme of this book is the interactional negotiation of identity, and I have explored this theme by looking at situated occasions of language use. Analysis of the language used in interaction has revealed interplay between structure and agency, lived experience and public discourse, conflict and conformity, identity and difference. That Israel/Palestine is a site of conflict is well known, but the complexity of this conflict is not often adequately portrayed. International observers of Israel usually focus on the Palestinian-Jewish dimension of the conflict as the engine driving the regional Arab-Israeli conflict. This focus obscures, however, the important identity politics within the Jewish Israeli community. On the other hand, Israeli social scientists tend to focus on internal Jewish dynamics, thereby obscuring the role played by Arabs, Palestinians, and Arabness. This book has contested such erasures by arguing that conflict within Israel is best seen as a three-way struggle among Palestinian, Mizrahi, and Ashkenazi Israelis over ideas and symbols that crosscut and interlink the three groups in complex ways. "Arabness," for example, is an image that joins Palestinian and Mizrahi identities, while "Jewishness" constructs a link between Mizrahi and Ashkenazi identities.

These twin erasures (of Jewish Israeli "ethnicity" outside of Israel, and of Palestinian presence within Israel) maintain their currency in scholarship on Israel in part because Israeli identity is constructed oppositionally. Being "Jewish" in Israel is accomplished by being not-"Arab." Jewish Israeli identity is constructed out of a common set of symbols and a shared field of discourse as an opposition to Arab identity.

But the oppositionality is situational. Identities are neither stable nor permanent. Rather, they are subject to negotiation and manipulation. Individuals manipulate negotiable identities toward pragmatic and strategic ends, but they do not do so freely. Rather, they negotiate these identities from within specific relations of power. The relations of power are themselves not accidental; they derive from specific historical processes.

Negotiations of identity are situated in actual talk interactions, as well as in a broader context of the individual's interpellation into subjectivities suggested by public discourse. Individual speech acts evoke powerful social and historical resonances because of their dialogic links to public discourse. The emergent identities that result are provisional—because situated in the pragmatic contexts of speech, in discourse. The notion of discourse, as used here, is inherently dual. On the one hand, discourse is the material domain of language use, the phenomenon of signifying practices actually deployed in social interaction. On the other hand, discourse is also the abstract domain of Bakhtinian dialogue, the space of meaning that recalls earlier utterances and evokes other scenes. Discourse is, to adapt Joel Sherzer's (1987) phrase, the nexus between language and identity.

Identities that are negotiated are simultaneously subject to hybridization. An underlying hybridity inflects the surface wholeness of Israeli identities, deconstructing the bond between power and identity. Hybrid identities form powerfully resistant symbols and are often deployed as powerful resistances.

This study looked at linguistic negotiations of identity in Haifa, Israel. Haifa is one place in Israel where Palestinians, Mizrahim, and Ashkenazim interact, but this research also questioned the nature of such interaction. Contact among groups is highly structured, as a bus ride up Mount Carmel in Haifa reveals. Neighborhoods touch on neighborhoods. Historical changes in residence and culture are inscribed onto landscapes, hewn into rock, written onto signposts. A physical slope re-presents an economic slope as it represents social structure. The landscape is imbued with meaning as traversal recalls the voices and narratives of people who live there. Everyday journeys, like a bus ride, offer the illusion of interaction but provide only representations of the Other.

The climb up Haifa described in chapter 2 illustrated a negotiation over discourse and history. The power of nostalgia mingled with the pain of current struggles to form and re-form mythologies of place. Signs of struggle emerged from physical conjunctions of poverty and wealth, and from the structured distribution of identities along this line of difference. The struggle was observed in the inscription of identities onto urban places through the (re)naming of city streets and the (re)making of neighborhoods. And it was seen in individuals' practices of inscribing—resistant practices of naming, narrating, remaining, and remembering.

Recognition of the process of negotiation allows one to avoid the dual temptations of dichotomy and determination. Viewing identity as a negotiation resolves the complex struggles into a play of dichotomous oppositions and shared significations, of provisional identities and (momentarily) fixed identities.

Two parallel frameworks—one theoretical, the other methodological—were established to study identity processes in Israel. The theoretical framework developed a way of conceptualizing Israeli identity that would encompass Arab and Jew within a common process—even as they are opposed. The methodological framework established a way of studying identity negotiation—even when such negotiation is quite abstract. Language, it was argued, is extremely important as a resource for constructing identities and as a location for their negotiation. Fine-grained analyses of the details of language-use informs our understanding of broader processes of inter-action because crosscultural encounter in Israel plays out in discourse. Identity emerges in the discursive nexus linking public culture with material practices.

To investigate the negotiation of identity at the various levels at which language works, and the multiple meanings it generates, a correspondingly multiple methodology is applied. This methodology triangulates toward an elusive object by approaching from various directions. Thus a technical approach to language complements an abstract approach to discourse. A detailed description of intonational phenomena in narrative speech, for example, is linked to the images of identity presented in the written discourse of national newspapers. In this case, emotion forms the link between these disparate realms of discursive performance and analytical practice. Public discourse in Israel constructs ideal Israeliness in part in terms of the proper deployment of emotion. With respect to this ideal of the dominant identity, subaltern identities are constructed as deficient. In the case of the Bat Yam riots discussed in chapter 6, for example, news-paper discourse maintained the image of the ideal Israeli by inscribing culturally devalued forms of emotional comportment onto Palestinian and Mizrahi Others. Positioned by emotion, Mizrahi identity parodies power in Israel when it is claimed with a speech style characterized by intonation that suggests emotion (see chapter 8).

The power of the resistance is proportional to the power of the oppression: emotion is a powerful tool of hegemony, and therefore it is also a powerful weapon of the weak (Scott 1985).

The two parallel frameworks—theory and method—are joined through the idea of narrativity. Narrative structures experience in language while it simultaneously structures language as experience. Narratives of personal experience, for example, are an important means Israelis have for expressing in conversation ideas and attitudes that are difficult to say directly. Other kinds of narrative similarly encode social meaning in semiotic signs. Newspapers narrate news stories—while reporting them—and this gap between narrative and report is filled with ideological meaning. Narrative also structures language in ways that constitute experience. Narrative is the site of a dialect's most systematic manifestation. Narrative is also the site of a speaking tradition's most elaborate poetic entextualizations. By structuring language (in these and other ways) narrative becomes a focus of interaction and negotiation. Meanings emergent from situated tellings of emotionally charged narrative sediment out as experiences—that are themselves retold in a spiral of narrativity.

Language constructs the focal opposition in Israeli society between integration and segregation. Israelis assumed that distinctive Mizrahi Hebrew had disappeared, and that Palestinian Hebrew was distinctive by virtue of its being "broken"—characterized by imperfect learning, ungrammatical forms, and pronunciation influenced by interference from Arabic. These ideas about language parallel ideas about identity. Israelis' own image of intergroup relations posits complete Mizrahi-Ashkenazi integration alongside complete Arab-Jewish segregation. Both sets of notions departed from the Israeli practices I observed. Palestinian-Jewish interaction was far more common than (Jewish) Israelis reported, and Mizrahi-Ashkenazi interaction was far less common than (Jewish) Israelis assumed. This gap between attitudes and practices formed a space of ideology—the dominant Israeli ideology of identity.

Patterns of language learning maintain and reproduce this integration/segregation opposition. The linguistic negotiation of identity through deployments of socially meaningful variation in Hebrew takes shape against a backdrop of language choice in a multilingual society. An initial move in any negotiation of Israeli identity is the choice of language, primarily Hebrew, Arabic, or English. The learning and unlearning of languages is thus a key factor in the disciplining of identities. The teaching and learning of Arabic and English reproduce the social hierarchy constituted by the use of Hebrew. Arabic remains the home language of the Palestinian community in Israel— there are relatively few contexts of code-switching, for example—but it is actively maintained in a state of underdevelopment compared with Hebrew. The testing of Arabic language skills in Israeli (Arabic-language) high schools is more difficult than parallel testing for Hebrew language skills. Arabic, as it is used in Israel, lacks technical vocabulary in many fields, enforcing a pattern of borrowing from Hebrew (and from English). Arabic taught at universities is often taught in Hebrew. And the Jewish Israeli population's own orientation to Arabic shows the same patterns of preservation/ limitation. Mizrahi Jews are discouraged from maintaining Arabic as a home language, at the same time that learning Arabic later in life (in the military, for example) is highly valued.

The knowledge and deployment of English also reproduces dominant relations of power and authority. At the university, for example, knowledge of English serves pragmatic as well as social functions, and Palestinian students face a disadvantage because they must learn English as a second second-language. When Jewish children begin learning English, Palestinian children begin learning Hebrew.

Encounters with the Other are moments of language learning. Language learning characterizes such encounters because individuals are exposed to new ways of using language to create social meaning—not because they actually acquire the Other's language (see "Yami," in chapter 4). The overwhelming presence of public discourse—media—in modern Israeli life means that individuals' first encounters with the Other (identity) precedes their first contact with Other (people). Discourse immerses the individual in images of Self and Other, and such institutional forms of identity construction have a powerful impact on an individual's negotiation of identity. Individuals must negotiate with institutional sources of discourse over the force and meaning of identity images. Such negotiations carry implications for the relation between individual action and institutional power, as individuals locate their face-to-face interactions within the discursive context of institutional discourses on identity. Individual subjectivities are, in part, the result of structure, but structure is also, in part, the result of individual subjectivities.

If negotiated identities begin with images gleaned from public discourse, they evolve in conversation. The images of identity that come ready-made in the discourse that surrounds individuals are channeling or constraining but not determining influences. In face-to-face conversations people take up, reject, or adapt these discursive constructions. Discourse determines the tools of talk, but it cannot interpellate subjectivity "just as it pleases." Linguistic analyses show that the negotiation of identity in face-to-face interaction reuses preexisting forms in creatively refashioning symbolic power. A close look at the use of long-meaningful forms of phonological variation in Hebrew, for example, showed that, while the Ashkenazi form of Hebrew has taken hold as the Jewish Israeli norm, and Mizrahim, especially younger Mizrahim, have abandoned the stereotyped forms of their parents' generation, some Palestinian Arabs are forging a new lect of Hebrew that highlights precisely those formerly stereotyped forms. This spiraling of form and meaning draws power from the diglossia of Israeli Hebrew. The Hebrew forms that carry the stigma of (old) Mizrahi usage are the same forms as those that carry the prestige of *ivrit tiknit*, "standard (correct) Hebrew."

Hebrew dialects also refer to Arabic for their social meaning. The phonological variables discussed in chapter 7, for example, are salient markers of Arabness because the pharyngealized forms of those variables make Hebrew sound like Arabic. Thus Palestinian appropriation of a stigmatized-but-prestigious form of Hebrew makes two powerful identity moves. On the one hand, it claims Israeli identity by adapting Israeli discourses of power, prestige, and belonging. On the other hand, it indexes discourses of Arabness, both by emphasizing linguistic forms in Hebrew that are iconic of Arabic itself and by adopting linguistic forms conventionally associated with the "Arab" component of Mizrahi identity. In this way the Palestinian dialect of Hebrew expresses a resistant identity—stressing Arabness in opposition to the hegemonic symbols of Jewish Israel.

If the study of phonology reveals a resistant use of Hebrew by Palestinian Israelis, the study of socially meaningful intonation highlights a resistant use of Hebrew by Mizrahi Israelis. The emergence of intonational styles, which index an emotionality considered un-Israeli, deploys affect to deconstruct dominant images of the Israeli Self. The rise-fall intonation studied in chapter 8 indexes both positively and negatively valued aspects of dominant Israeli constructions of Self. It is on the one hand aggressive and oppositional, similar to the *dugri* speech prescribed for the Israeli Self (Katriel 1986) and on the other hand emotional in a manner proscribed by dominant Israeli discourse. The intonational sign is for Mizrahi Israelis, then, precisely what the phonological sign was for Palestinian Israelis, namely a multivocal symbol claiming both inclusion in, and difference from, the hegemonic forms of Israeli identity. The phonological and the intonational phenomena thus both constitute dialogic spirals of meaning.

On Variation and Meaning in Language

The results of this research on linguistic negotiations of identity in Israel hold general relevance for a number of linguistic, sociolinguistic, and anthropological issues. Israel offers a unique opportunity to study the emergence of social dialects in real time. Debate over the origins of African-American Vernacular English, for example, has raged for decades in part due to the absence of crucial evidence—how African Americans actually spoke in the eras before their language was reliably recorded (see Labov 1982b). In contrast, the revival of Hebrew as a spoken language has taken place almost entirely within the era of instrumental recording, and contact between (speakers of) Arabic and Hebrew is an even more recent phenomenon. The cohort of Palestinian speakers of Hebrew studied here is probably the first generation of Arabic-speakers immersed in a Hebrew environment and generating a Palestinian Israeli Hebrew.

The focus on the use of Hebrew by Palestinian Israelis also contributes to the neglected topic of socially meaningful variation in bilingual contexts of language learning. Although Labov argued long ago that immigrant populations play a crucial role in the introduction of innovative forms to the sociolinguistic system (Weinreich, Labov, and Herzog 1968), most quantitative studies of language variation nonetheless focus on language as it is used by native speakers. The linguistic behavior of the second-language speakers is posited as the source of change, but the language-use of the innovators is rarely examined directly. This tendency derives from linguists' reliance on notions of vernacular language, but it is perpetuated by the paucity of opportunities to study the emergence of dialects in real time.

The study of intonation as an element of social dialects (see chapter 8) broadens sociolinguistic notions of dialect. Intonation and other aspects of prosody have long been acknowledged as distinctive components of (social) dialects, but to date few studies have systematically described dialect differences in terms of intonation. Moreover, most extant work of this type has focused on just a few languages—primarily English. This study therefore contributes to a description of intonation in a Semitic language, Hebrew, as well as to a description of the sociolinguistics of an intonational dialect.

By systematically comparing and contrasting trends in intonation and phonology, and by specifically linking these two spheres in terms of their social correlates, attention is also given to the ways in which different levels of linguistic and sociolinguistic structure may be involved in the dialogic spiral of linguistic symbols and their social meanings. I have suggested that changes in the sociolinguistics of Israeli Hebrew phonology stimulated changes in the sociolinguistics of Israeli Hebrew intonation. Abandonment by Mizrahi Israelis of stigmatized phonological forms coincided with the uptake of socially meaningful variation in intonation by the same group. Such an analysis suggests a general explanation of how subaltern groups avoid stigmatized forms without forfeiting the ability to mark socially significant relationships in speech. Such a theory would apply Labovian conceptions of chain shifting, the linked cycling of sound changes within the phonological subsystem (Labov, Yaeger, and Steiner 1972) to socially meaningful relationships among linguistic subsystems.

The focus on intonation also positions the field of language and affect as central to the conjunction of (socio)linguistic and anthropological interest. Anthropologists are becoming increasingly concerned with affect as a site of the production and disciplining of identities and subjectivities. And language plays a particularly central role in the production of affect, yet few studies relate the production and manipulation of affect in actual talk interactions to the details of linguistic codes. Intonation is a key element in this relation—but one that has remained largely unexplored.

On Identity and Its Conceptualization

Viewing the negotiation of identity in Israel as a three-way struggle unites—in struggle—disparate parts of Israeli cultural discourse. Received dimensions of social difference, such as race, ethnicity, and nationality, are useful as starting points in the analysis of identity discourses. Such notions are symbolic resources that are used, manipulated, and changed in actual negotiations of identity. They are way stations along the spiral of historical alternations between structure and agency. The interweaving of contradictory identity struggles highlights the dialogic nature of identity symbols— and of discourse more generally. The range of social meanings associated with pharyngeal forms of phonological variables in Hebrew, for example, shows that the discourse of status and power in Israeli society is interwoven with—at the same time that it is opposed to—the discourse of Arabness and subalternity in Israel.

Identity processes in Israel also address the interaction between race, ethnicity, and nation more generally. As Ella Shohat has noted, there are "structural analogies between the oppression of Blacks in the New World and the situation of Sephardim in Israel. If the Palestinians can be seen as the aboriginal 'Indians' of the dominant discourse, the Sephardim constitute its 'Blacks'" (Shohat 1989:117). Israel thus recapitulates the American opposition of melting and nonmelting groups. Palestinians and Mizrahim in Israel, like Native Americans and African Americans in the United States, are non-melting groups that are legally included in the state's citizenry but discursively excluded from the nation's imagined community. Ashkenazi Jews, on the other hand, like "white" Americans, are melting Israeli groups—hyphenated only in a historical sense. This simple opposition is complicated, however, by an Israeli ideology of identity that deploys notions of "nation" and "ethnicity" to obscure and justify racialized divisions in Israeli society.

Discourses of identity and difference in Israel unfold against a backdrop of conflict that starkly highlights emergent symbols such as Mizrahi and Palestinian dialects of Hebrew. The multivocality of discourse argues for a conception of identity itself—because it is discursively produced—that is multivocal and hybrid. The hybridity of identity in Israel, where identities are extraordinarily polarized and politicized, suggests that notions of hybridity may have a more general role to play in anthropological studies of identity.

On the Relationship Between Language and Culture

Paradoxically, at the very moment that sociolinguists and cultural anthropologists seem to be converging on a view of language as the site of, and the means for, deploying and contesting power, divergent trends are emerging. Sociolinguistics has increasingly bound itself to language—instead of talk—as the object of study (even while approaching language via speech), and cultural anthropology has bound itself to increasingly abstract levels of language as its object of study. The juxtaposition of these paradoxically opposed trends within an anthropological linguistics (or a linguistic anthropology) places the field at an important crossroads.

Discourse offers a resolution theoretically and methodologically. Discourse provides a productive way to conceptualize the relationship between language and culture at the same time that it provides a methodology for investigating this relationship. Methodologically, a discourse approach (Sherzer 1987) focuses ethnographic description on the form and function of language as it is used. Integrating quantitative sociolinguistic analyses of linguistic form with qualitative interpretations of speaking practices facilitates a thorough understanding of Israeli discourse by attending both to details of form and abstractions of context. Integrating a variety of approaches to language and society also suggests a holistic conception of the language/culture nexus that is consistent with the original formulations of the ethnography of communication (Hymes 1967).

The focus on discourse is also a theoretical position. Discourse demands a systematically dual conception of social process and language use. The study of discourse encompasses—without eliding—broad regimes of discursive power (Foucault 1979, 1980) and situated occasions of speech embedded in ongoing social practices.

Attention to the duality of discourse enables the study of language-use to address issues of social process. Discourse is simultaneously structured and structuring (Bourdieu 1977), and power is both exercised and resisted in and through discourse. The interplay between Foucaultian regimes of discourse and Sherzerian instances of discourse generates the dynamism in both that I have represented metaphorically as a spiral—and as a negotiation.

On Negotiation and Hybridity

Negotiation is a metaphor that bridges gaps between various perspectives on identity as it captures the dialectic of structure and agency. Based on notions of play, as developed by Gregory Bateson, Erving Goffman, and Joel Sherzer, the metaphor of negotiation highlights the inherent variability encompassed by structured systems of symbols and posits this variability as the source of change, resistance, and creativity. William Labov's brilliant contribution to the social analysis of language is the ability of quantitative linguistics to locate and specify the "play" in linguistic systems. The metaphor of negotiation maps variation in form to variation in function, focusing inter-pretive attention on the emergent, hybrid, and provisional aspects of identity. Negotia-tion thus refers not only to talk interactions (in which literal negotiations are possible) but also to abstract negotiations, such as those that occur between individuals and the dispersed sources of interpellative power—be they school textbooks, persons of authority, images from public discourse, or structures of language.

The metaphor of negotiation also contests received views of identity that emphasize binary dichotomies, such as male/female, powerful/weak, rich/poor, and so on. Such dichotomization suggests essentialization, since Self and Other are seen as diametrically opposed and unitary entities (Boyarin 1992). Dichotomizing discourses themselves, however, tend not to stop at the binary stage but to recursively split into embedded subdichotomies (Gal 1994). The Jewish/Arab distinction in Israel, for example, is often represented as a quintessentially binary opposition, but each term recursively splits into a multitude of further oppositions. The Ashkenazi/Mizrahi opposition resolves into a more complex structure, as the Mizrahi category is subdivided into Moroccan, Yemeni, Iraqi, and other categories. A similar process subdivides the subaltern member of the Jewish/Palestinian dichotomy (see chapter 3). This construction of an internal Other (see Boyarin 1992) is a potentially infinite regress of subdivided identities. The process introduces such complexity to the idea of Self and Other that the utility of the opposition breaks down. Moreover, the discursive representation of identity as a Self/Other distinction functions to obscure the dimensions of interrelation and overlap among identities. Thus the integrity of Jewish and Palestinian identity domains is compromised by images of the Mizrahi Israeli as an Arab-Jew (see Lavie 1992) and of the Druze Israeli as a Jewish-Arab (see Dominguez 1989). Metaphorizing the identity process as negotiation thus suggests metaphorizing identities themselves as "hybrid."

Viewing language use semiotically, we can posit two paradigmatic sets—one of identities, and the other of linguistic forms. The syntagmatic chain of semiosis is generated by a sequence of choices from among the paradigmatic sets. Each specific choice at the level of language form suggests a set of corresponding signifiers at the level of identity—and vice versa. Social meaning is complex and thoroughly hybrid because cooccurrence relations among the paradigmatic sets (such that initial choices restrict the range of subsequent options) are relatively weak. The semiotic model suggests two locations for this hybridity. Hybridity resides on the one hand in the syntagmatic juxtaposition of paradigmatic choices and on the other hand in the addition of a new, internally hybrid signifier to a paradigmatic set. The negotiation model of identity, conceptualized as a dialogic spiral, suggests that the two processes work in complementary fashion.

Hybridity models of identity make relatively conservative claims about resistance. These models suggest, as Smadar Lavie has phrased it, an imploding of hegemony from within (Lavie 1992). In what ways are the resistant discourses—of Mizrahi and Palestinian Israelis—truly resistant, oppositional, or powerful? And which discourses do they resist? The discourse of Arabness, which both Mizrahi and Palestinian Israelis approach in their resistant usages, locates Israel as a hybrid nation within the Middle East. Indeed, it is difficult to see how any use of Hebrew could exceed the overall hegemony of Israeli discourse—how it could be anything other than an aspect of the consent given by the subordinate to rule of the dominant.

On Narrative, Representation, and Voice

In this book I have argued that linguistic analysis can identify and analyze the abstract processes of hegemony. Viewed as an assertion of discursive, rather than coercive power, and as a flexible negotiation of dominating, resistant, and incorporative tendencies (Williams 1977), hegemony can be seen in the relationship between situated deployments of specific forms of Israeli Hebrew speech and structured enactments of institutional authority in Israeli society. The dynamism of hegemony as a process emerges from linguistic practice—quantitative aspects of language-use as it changes over time.

These chapters are tied together through their focus on Israel—a place of struggle and conflict; a place of neighbors, schools, and children; a place of Jewish homeland and Palestinian subalternity. Abstract social process and minute linguistic detail run the risk of losing sight of the lived experiences of Israelis themselves. Having taken apart the seamless flow of life to look at its component parts, I hope also to have stitched the interlocking pieces back together.

This motivation to deconstruct without losing sight of lived experience lies at the heart of recent critiques of representation in anthropological discourse. The power to construct the Other, and to do so in ways that may significantly influence the Other's lives, resides with the Western anthropologist in drastically unequal proportions. Anthropologists have searched for new strategies by which to represent their work. Discourse-based approaches to anthropological research and writing seem promising. In this book I have given to personal narrative a central role, both analytically and representationally. Narrative speech is the quintessential vehicle for expression of Self and of ideas about Self and Other. It is also the locus of affectivity and involvement in speech, so important to linguistic analyses of vernacular. Use of narrative speech in this text—related directly, even if via translation—enables the subject's voice to be represented. Narratives are presented here with (as much as possible) the slips and starts and fumbles of everyday speech, and they are presented within the context of ongoing interaction, replete with interruptions and hesitations. Moreover, an attempt was made to place these narrative pieces in juxtaposition to my own analytic voice, thereby evoking rather than determining interpretation of others' voices.

In narrative, however, the situated and pragmatic nature of speech is also foregrounded, and thereby the multivocality of social life in general and the multivocality of ethnographic practice in particular. Basing these analyses of language form and function on linguistic data taken from small-group sociolinguistic interviews led directly to an incorporation of the ethnographer as an integral part of the fieldwork experience and the interpretive process. For not only was the ethnographer a participant in the talk interactions, but his language, English, became a factor in the negotiation. This work positions ethnography within everyday life, not in opposition to it. The ethnographic encounter is, for me, every bit as hybrid a negotiation as the ebb and flow of Israeli life I'm trying to understand.

On Israel, Palestine, and Peace in the Middle East

As I write this book's final words, I reflect back upon its initial words, written so long ago, which reflect upon the rapidity of change and its perceptibility. In recent years a Jordanian king has visited Israel and signed a peace treaty. Morocco, Tunisia, and other Arab nations have initiated diplomatic ties with Israel. At the same time, however, deadly violence has continued, and diplomats have been withdrawn. States draw boundaries in sand, but people make their boundaries with talk. As the borders between an autonomous Palestine and the State of Israel wax and wane, the negotiation of identities within Israel grows in significance. New identities are created out of political necessity, and they use the resources that are available—the warp and weft of language. Subtle differences that are available when a crucial distinction needs to be drawn make weak weapons strong.

Notes

Chapter 1

1. The momentous events I am referring to here are, respectively, the Persian Gulf War, which began in January 1991, the Madrid Peace Conference, held in October 1992, and the Israeli parliamentary elections of June 1992, which led to sweeping changes in Israeli policies (see Arian and Shamir 1995; Elazar and Sandler 1995).

2. I use the terms "Palestinian" and "Arab" interchangeably to refer to Palestinian Arabs, whether citizens of Israel or not. The semiotics—and politics—of this usage will be discussed hereafter.

3. The many individuals who helped me in my research—either as research assistants or as interviewees—are referred to by pseudonym. Only public figures are referred to using their actual names.

4. The conventions used in transcribing conversational discourse are given in the preface.

5. Interview material is referenced by tape number and position.

6. For Rhoda, "after there is peace" referred fairly specifically to the establishment of a Palestinian state in the Occupied Territories.

7. Nearly ten years later, in 2000, this cycle repeated itself in equally tragic ways. The summer of 2000 saw dramatic developments in the peace process, including negotiations brokered by the American president Bill Clinton that were dubbed "Camp David II." The two sides seemed tantalizingly close to a major breakthrough, but the eventual failure of the negotiations led to an enormous escalation of violence. Sadly, at the time of writing, this violence remains prominent in Israel/Palestine.

8. Following the pathbreaking work of Benedict Anderson (1991), Tom Nairn (1977), Hugh Seton-Watson (1977), and others, social scientists in a range of disciplines have begun to look

at the historical emergence of nationalisms. Several excellent historical studies look at Israeli and Palestinian nationalisms, including Kimmerling and Migdal (1993), Swedenburg (1995), and Zerubavel (1995).

9. This diagram represents a greatly simplified situation, since African-American uses of "bad" encompass both positive and negative valences, while many Whites have adopted this usage from African-American Vernacular English.

10. The Hebrew term *Mizrahi* (plural: *Mizrahim*) refers to Jews of Middle Eastern heritage, in contrast to *Ashkenazi* (plural: *Ashkenazim*), which refers to Jews of European heritage. "Mizrahi," as an identity category in Israel, overlaps with *Sfaradi* (plural: *Sfaradim*), much the way "Palestinian" overlaps with "Arab." And just as with terms for Palestinian identity, so too the alternative terms for Mizrahi identity also carry important connotations. In this text I use "Mizrahi" exclusively, but see hereafter on the politics of such usage.

11. Interestingly, American Jews also figure prominently in the right-wing ultranationalist and ultraorthodox groups that currently play a major role in the settlement of the Occupied Territories. In the spring of 1995, for example, a recent immigrant from the United States, Baruch Goldstein, entered a mosque in the occupied Palestinian city of Hebron and opened fire with a machine gun, killing thirty-five Palestinians as they prayed.

12. This incident occurred in 1992 at a Nashim b'Shaxor, "Women in Black," demonstration outside the Israeli town of Tzomet Ra'anana.

13. In Arabic and Hebrew the /r/ phoneme is trilled or flapped, and phonemically monophthong vowels have no off-glides.

14. The pseudonym "Louis" was chosen to reflect the characteristics of the interviewee's actual name. Both Louis and his wife used English first names, as did many of the Christian Palestinians I met in Israel. Edward Said (1999:3) notes in his memoir *Out of Place* that his English given name was an important component of his identity growing up Christian and wealthy in Cairo, Egypt.

15. In fact, several Palestinians I interviewed used the phrase "I am a citizen of the world" in answer to questions about their identity.

16. The Grimm brothers, Jakob and Wilhelm, best known for their anthology *Grimm's Fairy Tales*, were Herderian research assistants—and great linguists as well. Jakob Grimm made an important contribution to historical linguistics by discovering Grimm's Law, the set of systematic sound correspondences that link all Germanic languages.

17. The language is usually referred to as Serbo-Croatian. The popular local perception of difference draws strength from the fact that the two religiously differentiated communities have followed different traditions for representing the language in writing. While the Catholic Croats use Latin orthography, the Orthodox Serbs use the Cyrillic alphabet. A similar pattern obtains in the case of Hindi and Urdu, spoken by Hindus and Muslims, respectively, in India and Pakistan.

18. The term mi'ut is also used—infrequently—to refer to the differences between Muslim, Christian, and Druze Arabs.

19. It turned out to be a good (research) decision to remain in Israel during the Persian Gulf War, and it did become an important "way in" to Israeli society. Gulf War narratives became a focus of the sociolinguistic interviews I conducted, and these interviews were greatly facilitated by my having shared with interviewees the experience of having been in Israel during the war.

20. An American friend born to Palestinian parents privately expressed analogous feelings with respect to living in the Occupied Territories during the Intifada, the Palestinian popular uprising against the Israeli occupation that dominated the Occupied Territories from 1988 through the outbreak of the Gulf War.

21. Television news focused attention, for example, on crowds of ultraorthodox Jews, many of them American immigrants to Israel, clogging the airport in their haste to leave. Similarly,

the mayor of Tel Aviv provoked intense debate by calling Tel Aviv residents who left the city for safer regions (in Jerusalem, or the Negev desert, for example) "deserters." Conversely, news reports also focused attention on the record numbers of Russians who were immigrating to Israel just at that time, a fact that was discursively constructed as an act of Jewish (perhaps even Zionist) solidarity. In contrast, a small group of Russian immigrants who fled Israel for Berlin, Germany, attracted critical coverage.

22. In Hebrew such emigrants from Israel are referred to as *yordim* (singular: *yored*). The literal meaning of the word is "those who descend," and the metaphor stands in parodic opposition to the older usage, *olim* (singular: *ole*), which literally means "those who ascend," for immigrants to Israel.

23. This list includes, among others, the former mayor of New York City Ed Koch, the noted writer Elie Wiesel, and the famous musician Zubin Mehta.

24. This call was recorded from Israeli Army Radio, *Gale Tzahal*, on January 23, 1991, at 8:00 p.m.

25. The linguistic resources that allow Sharon to weave such an identity are the subject of chapters 7 and 8 of this book.

Chapter 2

1. At least two additional airports have been built in Israel/Palestine since 1990, one in the southern Israeli resort city of Eilat, and one in the Palestinian Autonomous region of Gaza.

2. Jaffa is the Palestinian city adjacent to the Israeli city of Tel Aviv. In the late nineteenth century, when Jews first began to settle in Palestine, Jaffa was an important center of culture and commerce, while Tel Aviv barely existed. In the century since then, Tel Aviv has become Israel's largest city, while the fortunes of Palestinian Jaffa have declined.

3. See Slyomovics (1998:66–68) and Benvenisti (2000:11–54) for excellent discussions of the renaming of places in Israel.

4. In general I have transliterated Arabic words and phrases so as to represent actual pronunciations, rather than underlying forms. The Arabic term *an-nakba*, for example, is underlyingly /al-nakba/, but a morphophonological process assimilates the consonant of the definite article, /al/, to following coronal consonants, leading to geminates. Exceptions to this practice include names and phrases that have conventional romanizations, such as the names of Arabic-language newspapers.

5. I once experienced this thorough investigation myself—by mistake. I first traveled to Israel as a thirteen-year-old boy. My family was spending a year in Vienna, Austria, where my father had a sabbatical, and we flew to Israel for my school's Christmas vacation. Our travel arrangements were somewhat complicated. My mother took my sister and me with her, and my father, who had some business to attend to, came separately. As my mother encountered the security check, the Israeli airline official asked what we (Americans) were doing in Vienna, and why my father was not travelling with us. My mother explained that he worked in "Laxenburg" (a small town just south of Vienna), but the agent heard it as "Luxembourg" (a country quite far from Vienna). This initiated a series of pointed questions. Once the misunderstanding was cleared up we were able to proceed. When my mother realized why we had been interrogated, she felt secure because the Israeli system had been so thorough. Before that, however, she (and her children) had experienced the anxiety of being interrogated. My family's discomfort stemmed from a mistake, but the discomfort Palestinian Israelis feel every time they pass through their airport stems from the indelible mark of their identity.

6. A *moshav* is a semicommunal settlement in Israel, in which families may own their own

homes and fields, while sharing with their neighbors communal ownership of community buildings, marketing cooperatives, and some fields.

7. In fact, it can be argued that many Zionist ideas about Palestine came from the European Christian rediscovery of the Holy Land in the eighteenth and nineteenth centuries. The paintings of David Roberts and the cartography of Edward Robinson are two influential examples of European Christian representation of Palestine that shows up in early Zionist imaginings of a Jewish homeland. Ben-Arieh (1979) and Idinopulos (1998) provide interesting discussions of this point.

8. The moshav was close enough to Tel Aviv that many such farms had been incorporated into exurbia.

9. The Hebrew word *blok* (plural: *blokim*) is a borrowing from English, "block," and has roughly the same range of meanings, from "apartment block" (as here), to "city block," to "cement block."

10. Isfiyya and Daliat Ha-Carmel are Druze villages where Arabic is the home language. In Arabic the latter town's name is Daliat al-Karmel. I have transliterated the Hebrew name for this town in keeping with the way the names appear on Israeli maps, and consistent with the politics of language use in Druze communities in Israel (see text 2.6).

11. I have adopted the conventional romanizations for these place names, as they appear in English on many Haifa street signs. Phonetically, Ahuza would be represented *axuza*.

12. Wadi Nisnas is an Arab neighborhood, and its name is sometimes pronounced—even when speaking Hebrew—as it would be in Arabic. The name means "Nisnas Valley," *wadi* being the Arabic word for a small valley. Hebrew and Arabic are closely related languages, and the cognate Hebrew word, *vadi*, has the same meaning. Israelis therefore sometimes refer to this neighborhood as Vadi Nisnas, but I use the Arabicized name in this text.

13. As was common in Israel among restaurants that catered in part to the tourist crowd, the restaurant's name appeared in three languages, Arabic, Hebrew, and English. The three versions were direct translations of each other.

14. The Israeli Communist Party lost support and influence coincident with the fall of communism in the Soviet Union.

15. This incident actually took place in the 'Abbas neighborhood of Haifa, which is both physically close to the Wadi Nisnas neighborhood described earlier and demographically similar to it.

16. Dr. Max Nordau was a friend of Theodor Herzl, the founder of Zionism (Sachar 1989:39).

17. The name Hadar comes from Hebrew words meaning "elegance."

18. *Hagana*, "defense," is the name used to refer to the umbrella organization of Jewish paramilitary forces during the British Mandate. After Israeli independence in 1948 the Hagana formed the core of the Israeli Defense Force (IDF).

19. *Mellah* is a term used to refer to the old Jewish quarters of Middle Eastern cities.

20. The Hebrew term *Mizrahim* is sometimes translated as "Orientals," as here. The Hebrew word literally means "easterners," derived from *mizrah*, the ordinary word for "east." See chapter 3 for more on the politics of this language use.

21. *Mapai* is a Hebrew acronym that forms the name of the Israeli political party in power at the time of the Wadi Salib riots. The acronym stands for *mifleget po'ale yisra'el*, "Party of the Workers of Israel." Histadrut is the name of the national Israeli labor union.

22. Christians comprise only about 10 percent of the total Palestinian population in Israel, but these proportions are reversed in cities like Haifa.

23. Jewish Israelis, both male and female, are required to do mandatory military service at age eighteen. Non-Jewish Israelis are, in general, exempt (in fact, prohibited) from military service, but there are two notable exceptions: Druze men are required to serve, and Bedouin

men may serve voluntarily (and many do). The policy referred to in the text sought to change the status of Christian (Arab) men to that of Bedouin men. Arab women are not conscripted.

24. Nabil grew up in Rami, a small Palestinian town in northern Israel.

25. Nabil is describing the location of the old Palestinian town, Iqrit, in terms of two Jewish towns, Ilon and Shomera. He has correctly assumed that Nurit, the young Jewish Israeli research assistant, is not familiar with the names of Arab Israeli towns.

26. Nabil is referring to David Grossman's book, *Noxaxim Nifkadim*, literally "Present Absentees," which was published in 1992, shortly after our interview. Chapter 13 of this book tells the story of Nabil's family and village. (The English translation appeared under the title *Sleeping on a Wire*.)

27. *Bagatz* is a Hebrew acronym that stands for *bet din gavoa l'tzedek*, "High Court for Justice." Its function is similar to that of the federal appeals courts in the United States.

28. David Ben-Gurion, Israel's first prime minister, led the country from 1948 to 1953 and again from 1955 to 1963.

29. This point is discussed in greater detail in chapter 6.

30. An interesting example of this discourse comes from a recent tour guide to Israel. Frommer's 2000 edition of its Israel guide includes the following description of Haifa: "In a society unlike any other in the Middle East, Jews and Arabs live and work side by side; 25% of Haifa's population is either Muslim or Christian. In 1898, Theodore Herzl, the father of modern Zionism, wrote his prophecy of the Jewish homeland that would one day be reborn: 'Next to our temples, you find Christian, Mohammedan, Buddhist, and Brahmin houses of divine worship ... my comrades and I make no distinction between people. We ask for no one's religion or race but let him be a Man, that is enough.' With its Baha'i Center, churches, synagogues, and mosques, as well as its politically progressive, hard working Jewish and Arabic population, Haifa, more than any other city in Israel, has come to fit that vision" (Ullian 2000:299).

31. Statistics on the percentage of Arabs in Haifa are very sensitive to how the boundaries of the urban area are defined. According to the *Statistical Abstract of Israel*, Arabs comprised 18 percent of Israel's total population in 1998, 21 percent of the population of Haifa District (a census district that includes many of the towns surrounding Haifa), and 8 percent of the population of the city of Haifa itself.

32. Ironically, at the other end of David Raziel Street, at the end farthest from Halisa, the very same kind of building, the old stone houses built in a Middle Eastern style, are maintained as fashionable and desirable homes of middle-class Jews.

33. This anecdote comes from a talk Somekh gave at a ceremony honoring the great Palestinian writer Emil Habibi. The ceremony was held in Haifa in 1992. Habibi has since passed away.

34. This anecdote comes from a talk Shammas gave at the University of Texas in Austin in 1993. See the discussion of pharyngeal variables in chapter 7 for a fuller discussion of the pronunciation of Hebrew and Arabic words for "salt."

35. *Krayot* is the plural form of the Hebrew word *kirya*, "village." East of Haifa are a number of relatively new communities that begin with the word *kirya*, as in Kiryat Motzkin, "Motzkin Village." Collectively these communities are known as the *Krayot*.

36. "Palmach" is the common romanization of *palmax*, a Hebrew acronym for *plugot maxatz*, "strike units," one of the elite units in the Hagana (Jewish paramilitary force) in mandatory Palestine.

37. *T'un tipuax* (plural: *t'une tipuax*) is the official Hebrew phrase for "disadvantaged child." The phrase means literally "in need of care."

38. Tira is a small town just south of Haifa. Formerly a separate Arab community, it was incorporated as a suburb as Haifa's growth encroached upon the surrounding villages (see fig. 2.2a).

39. Ako is the Hebrew name for Acre, a medium-sized town on the Mediterranean coast of Israel about midway between Haifa and Israel's border with Lebanon. Acre is famous among tourists for its Roman ruins.

40. Isha l'Isha is the name of a large women's organization in Israel. The Hebrew means "Woman to Woman."

41. "The Carmel" refers to the wealthier, more fashionable, primarily middle-class, and heavily Ashkenazi neighborhoods that lie higher up the slopes of Mount Carmel.

42. Bus routes do not actually link Neve Yosef with Carmel Center. I have taken poetic license, conflating two actual routes into a single trip in order to include a full range of neighborhoods within a single trajectory.

43. Street signs on major thoroughfares and large intersections are trilingual in Hebrew, Arabic, and English, but most other signs exclude Arabic. See chapter 5, or Spolsky and Cooper (1991), for further discussion of the language of street signs in Israel.

44. *Eged* is the name of the Israeli national transportation cooperative best known for running the public bus system. Atzma'ut Street is a main thoroughfare in downtown Haifa. *Atzma'ut* is Hebrew for "independence."

45. Kiryat Eliezer is a working-class Jewish neighborhood in downtown Haifa. Many interviewees mentioned this particular high school as a model of coexistence. By the early 1990s, however, its curriculum and structure had long since changed.

46. In the aftermath of World War II, Germany made reparations payments to victims of the Holocaust and their families. Such payments had a significant effect both on Israel's fiscal solvency in the 1950s and on the rise to middle-class status of individuals who received them.

47. Bet ha-Kranot (literally, "Foundation House") refers to a prominent square in central Hadar. Haifans referred to the whole area by the name of the most prominent building on the square. Bet ha-Kranot was much closer to Ya'el's parents' home than was Café Pe'er, which was higher up at Carmel Center.

48. Bet She'an is a development town in northeastern Israel that was populated in the 1950s by Mizrahi immigrants from Morocco. The town is a popular tourist site due to a well-preserved Roman amphitheater.

49. Bet She'an gained national notoriety as the home and political base of David Levi, the best known and most successful Mizrahi politician at the time. Levi served as the Israeli foreign minister several times in the 1980s and 1990s, in the cabinets of the Israeli prime ministers Yitzhak Shamir, Yitzhak Rabin, Benjamin Netanyahu, and Ehud Barak.

50. Gush Emunim, "Block of the Faithful," is the Jewish nationalist religious political organization that has actively supported Jewish settlement activity in the Occupied Territories.

51. *Ahlan* is colloquial Arabic for "hello," and *shalom* is the same in Hebrew. Salman is suggesting, I think, that Bet She'an residents began to greet him in Arabic and Hebrew to show their acceptance of him as a Palestinian, but *ahlan* is also a common borrowing into Hebrew, often used as a slang greeting in casual conversation among Jewish Israelis.

52. *Moledet*, "homeland," is the name of an ultra right-wing Israeli political party.

53. Farid Al-Atrash and Umm Kulthum are famous Egyptian pop singers.

Chapter 3

1. I am indebted to Joel Sherzer for this application of the various meanings of the word "play."

2. Socially meaningful variability in language extends well beyond vocabulary. Indeed, language structure is filled with points of variability that are exploited to express social meaning. Active and passive constructions are a common example of syntactic variability, for example.

3. The coffee pot example is taken from an actual conversation I had as a newly hired assistant professor. The "boss" was the newly appointed, female chair of the department, and her indirection was probably part of a complex role negotiation, including her assertion of authority vis-à-vis the secretary, and her modeling (for my benefit) of respectful relations between faculty and staff.

4. I treat work attributed to Bakhtin and that attributed to Vološinov as stemming from the same individual, whom I refer to as "Bakhtin."

5. The British poet Naphtali Herz Imber wrote the Hebrew poem "Ha-Tikvah," "The Hope," in 1886. It was subsequently put to music by Samuel Cohen. (Source: www.stateofisrael.com/anthem.)

6. A parallel can be drawn to American identity discourses, which metaphorize identity either as "race" or "ethnicity." In the United States, "race" refers to difference between White and Black Americans, while "ethnicity" refers to difference among Whites. The dual American discourses of identity break down in the case of social groups that do not fit comfortably in either classification. Hispanic Americans occupy this intermediate position at present, but Jews and Italians have played the role historically.

7. The category of *l'om*, "nationality," also encompasses a third type, "Druze."

8. Constructing Palestinian identity as contained by Arab nationhood recapitulates in cultural terms what Israeli diplomats have long expressed in political terms: "Jordan is Palestine."

9. Data are cited for 1961, the year of Israel's first postindependence census.

10. At the same time that the Jewish population in Israel doubled, the Palestinian population (in what became Israel) decreased precipitously. Estimates put the pre–1948 war Palestinian population at just over one million (calculated from Sachar 1989:334). Official Israeli statistics for 1949, one year after the state was established, estimate that only 160,000 Palestinians remained in the State of Israel (Government of Israel 2000:2–7). This demographic upheaval is even more dramatic when viewed in terms of relative proportions. In 1947 Palestinians comprised just over 50 percent of the population in mandatory Palestine, but by 1949 they comprised only 14 percent of Israelis. Israeli Palestinians were thus transformed within the span of just a few years from a majority to a tiny minority.

11. One historical cause of class differentials in Israel is the reparation payments that the German government provided to Holocaust survivors and to relatives of Holocaust victims. These payments were controversial, as (then) prime minister David Ben-Gurion passionately opposed accepting them. They subsequently became a point of bitterness because of the wealth differentials they created. See text 2.5.

12. As Virginia Dominguez (1989:70) has pointed out, Israeli public discourse first dealt seriously with the racial nature of identity distinctions in Israeli culture during crises over the position of Ethiopian Jewish immigrants to Israel. The public debate over Ethiopian identity, however, stopped short of an analysis of race that includes either the Jewish/Arab distinction or the Mizrahi/Ashkenazi distinction.

13. The analysis suggested by figure 3.1 is intended to be representative, rather than exhaustive. Two important dimensions of Israeli identity left out of the diagram are the religious/secular and male/female oppositions. Problems for this analysis—i.e., orthogonalities to the two dimensions of "Easterness" and "Israeliness"—include the Israeli identities "Anglo-Saxon," which is close to "Ashkenazi," but far from "Real Israeli," and "Ethiopian," which is a non-Eastern Jewish identity that is high on alterity.

14. This restaurant chain created a very complex set of significations. The slogan *kef temani*, "Yemenite fun," can also mean "Yemenite marijuana," since *kef*, "fun," was also a common slang term for "pot." Similarly, the overt visual imagery on the walls of the restaurants of matronly women dressed in colorfully embroidered dresses and traditional beads worked in

dialogue with a covert set of visual images in (some of) the menus showing young, partially undressed women.

15. Whereas elsewhere in the book I spell "Mizrahi" with an "h," in this chapter I am spelling it at times with an "x." The Hebrew word *mizrax* ends in one of the pharyngeal phonemes to be discussed in chapter 7, and its pronunciation is therefore variable. "Mizrahi" is an etymological spelling that happens to also reflect the pronunciation of some Mizrahi speakers of Hebrew. "Mizraxi" more directly represents current mainstream Israeli pronunciation.

16. As a sociolinguist committed to the empirical study of spoken language, tape-recording interviews was crucial to my research. As a matter of strategy when arranging an interview in advance I sometimes avoided telling potential interviewees that I wanted to tape-record, reasoning that once introductions were made, pleasantries exchanged, and my equipment set up, interviewees would not object to being recorded. This strategy worked well in general, and in more than seventy interviews I met with only this one refusal. I had anticipated difficulties in obtaining permission to tape-record Israelis, especially Palestinian Israelis, on sensitive topics. Throughout the first months of my research, therefore, I was pleasantly surprised to realize that my fears were greatly overdrawn. It was not until my final interview, more than a year later, that a Palestinian speaker asked me to turn off the recorder while he told a story of being harassed by police.

17. In the past decade, and largely as a result of the (first) Palestinian Intifada, Israel encouraged a large influx of foreign workers from Thailand, Romania, and elsewhere. This phenomenon has changed the Israeli socioeconomic hierarchy in ways that are significant, but beyond the scope of this book.

18. Many Bedouin men also serve in the Israeli military, but they do so on a voluntary basis. Military service is mandatory for Druze men.

19. Druze soldiers played pivotal roles in several media dramas related to the "Al-Aqsa Intifada," the Palestinian resistance that emerged in September 2000. One of three Israeli soldiers kidnapped by Hizballah fighters on the Lebanese border was a Druze man, and a Druze soldier was killed defending a Jewish holy site in the West Bank. The latter case was particularly salient because an Israeli military tradition appeared to have been violated when soldiers retreated without making an effort to rescue the trapped (Druze) soldier.

Chapter 4

1. *Kipa* is the Hebrew word for the skullcap, or yarmulke, worn by observant Jewish men.

2. The notion that the resident Arab population benefits from the Jewish presence in Palestine has a long history, stemming from Herzl's *Altneuland* (1960 [1902]). See chapter 6 for further discussion of this point.

3. From a pragmatic point of view, the picture also functions to present a palatable (and attractive) image to the Jewish American public that comprises the book's primary readership. Indeed, Shipler may not have intended the readings of his cover that I am proposing, since authors sometimes have little control over the images that adorn their books' covers.

4. Palestinian Israelis, it should be noted, had a less expansive understanding of the frequency and nature of such contacts.

5. Gabi's Hebrew phrase is *ha-kav ha-adom*, literally "the red line."

6. Amidar refers to a government housing program that helped low-income families purchase apartments.

7. The narrator, Gabi, is referring here to his adoptive family, not his biological parents.

8. Most, but not all of the Russian Jews were recent immigrants to Israel who had arrived in the previous year.

9. *Pe'er* means "luxury" in Hebrew.

10. City regulations for such condemned buildings prevented residents from selling an apartment or renting to other occupants.

11. Indeed, the only time I saw large numbers of people flowing along David Raziel Street, traversing the boundary between these two neighborhoods, was on the evening of the Jewish holiday Yom Kippur, when many residents of Tel Amal attended services at the Halisa synagogues.

12. Schools also cleaved the Jewish Israeli community along religious/secular lines. Ironically (for a "Jewish" state), religion played a relatively insignificant role in early Israeli social politics, but this role has grown in recent decades and is now a nexus of social conflict. Mizrahi identity, for example, has been powerfully expressed through religious politics, especially through Shas, the Mizrahi ultraorthodox political party (Lefkowitz 1997).

13. Dormitory space was allotted preferentially to students from poorer families and from distant hometowns. Haifa University is the closest Israeli university to the Galilee, where many Palestinians live. Both factors increased diversity.

14. American students were housed in suites with Jewish Israelis, not Palestinians.

15. Patients at this hospital were quite diverse in terms of Israeli identity group, but less diverse in terms of socioeconomic position. Middle- and upper-class patients tended to go to the newer and more luxurious hospitals higher up the hill, despite the national health insurance system, *kupat xolim*, which (in principle) provided most services free of charge.

16. Palestinians are relatively well represented in many prestigious professional fields, like medicine, in part because Palestinians are barred from serving in the military. Since many jobs in science and technology require military experience, the so-called free professions of teacher, doctor, and lawyer become magnets for Palestinian employment. The parallel to the occupational history of Jews in Europe and the United States is striking. The historically high representation of Jews in the free professions in Europe, for example, was due in part to legal restrictions placed on their ability to own land.

17. Car theft and drug smuggling rings involve Palestinian and Israeli contacts across the border between Israel and the Palestinian Authority. These were said to be among the very few activities to continue uninterrupted during times of intense conflict, such as the Gulf War or the Palestinian Intifada. Such rings are said to involve considerable cooperation between Jewish and Palestinian Israelis as well.

18. *Neve Shalom/Wahat al-Salam* is often conceptualized as an Arab-Jewish kibbutz. The name, in both Hebrew and Arabic, means "Oasis of Peace."

19. The Re'ut youth group is also known by its Arabic name, *sidaqa*. Both words mean "friendship."

20. Yami is a vocalization of the acronym (Y.M.Y.) created from the organization's Hebrew name, Y'ladim M'lamdim Y'ladim, "Children Teaching Children."

21. The expressions *du-le'umi* and *xad-le'umi*, "binational" and "uninational," respectively, for school programs are revealing in the degree to which the idea of *nation* has penetrated even elementary school curricula. The Hebrew word *le'umi* is an adjective formed from the noun *l'om*, "nation."

22. I am adapting Clifford Geertz's famous dictum "Anthropologists don't study villages … they study in villages" (Geertz 1973:22).

23. This strategy for interviewing a representative sample of people within a neighborhood was less successful in the Neve Yosef neighborhood than it was in Hadar Elyon. Despite

considerable effort, my contacts in Neve Yosef never extended beyond the close-knit group of activist families involved in the community center programs.

24. Since most interviews were conducted by a pair of interviewers (myself and one research assistant), almost all of the interviews involved at least three people.

25. As native speakers of Hebrew, these research assistants minimized the extent to which the linguistic data gathered were influenced by my presence, as a nonnative speaker of Hebrew. Since all of the research assistants were women, most interviews were mixed in terms of gender as well. Gendering the assistant position was unintended; most applicants were women, and the one man I hired never showed up for work.

26. I also hired a Palestinian research assistant, but my plan to conduct some of the interviews with Palestinians in Arabic and to do some of the interviews with Jews with a Palestinian interviewer turned out to be impractical. Arabic-language interviews were impractical because my own Arabic never got good enough. Having studied written Arabic in the United States for several years, I seriously underestimated the difficulty of picking up spoken Arabic in Israel (see chapter 5). Hebrew-language interviews with a Palestinian interviewer also turned out to be impractical because the Palestinian woman I hired did not feel comfortable interviewing Israeli Jews in Hebrew on the provocative topics my protocol featured.

27. Figure 4.2 is a simplification of the full interview protocol; only some of the modules are represented.

28. Speech among Israelis was also much more fluent, since it was less influenced by accommodation to my foreign accent, slow speech rate, and occasional lack of comprehension.

29. Not all Palestinian informants identified me as Jewish. See texts 3.1 and 3.2.

30. This question refers to the tumultuous time of the establishment of the Israeli state, the fighting between Jews and Palestinians, and the first war between Israel and its Arab neighbors. Many Palestinian families were displaced by these events, but such stories are rarely acknowledged by mainstream Israeli discourse or known by Jewish Israelis.

31. Palestinian/Jewish relations in Israel were sufficiently tense in the early 1990s that questions that put Palestinian interviewees at ease often made Jewish research assistants uncomfortable. This strategy thus made the job of research assistant difficult, and I employed four assistants over the course of my research in part because some lost enthusiasm after their first few interviews.

32. Indeed, one of William Labov's most important contributions to modern thought was his deconstruction of the widespread conflation of "systematicity" with "formality" in language-use. In a trenchant article, "The Logic of Nonstandard English," Labov (1969) demonstrated that nonstandard, low-prestige varieties of English—when acquired as a native language—are every bit as systematic as the standard, prestige variety of English. Labov argues that the common misconceptions about working-class speech stem, in part, from ideological prejudice, but in part also from a misperception of the way that social context influences speech.

33. This narrative was recorded by Pamela Saunders and is reprinted with her permission. Guests at the party were aware of the recording, but the tape recorder itself was out of view.

34. In fact, all three verbs are past-tense forms. The verb in the first of the narrative clauses, *says*, is a historical present tense (see Schiffrin 1981). The discussion of narrative structure draws heavily on Labov 1972c.

35. This narrative also contains what Labov has called a *coda*, or narrative section that returns the talk to the here-and-now of conversation. In this narrative, the narrator effects this transition through the rhetorical laughter that has been transcribed as *hhhhh*.

36. Interpretation of this narrative does not seem to hinge on whether the audience believes that the narrator actually gave the lazy susan to Goodwill in the "jazzy" box. The narrator's laughter in the coda makes her last line interpretable as a rhetorical flourish that need not be

taken literally. Moreover, donations to bona fide charities, like Goodwill, are evaluated quite differently from wedding gifts: repackaging a cheap donation to look expensive is neither laudable nor suspect, in contrast to repackaging a cheap gift, which is harshly evaluated.

37. *An-Nakba* is Arabic for "the disaster." Palestinians (and Arabs more generally) often use this term to refer to (as well as describe) the loss of Palestine in the 1948 conflict.

38. This interview took place in the months after the end of the "Gulf War" (January to March 1991). Though not an official combatant in the war, Israel was attacked by Iraqi "Scud" missiles on numerous occasions. Due to the fear that Iraqi missile warheads might contain chemical weapons, Israeli authorities had ordered Israeli citizens to protect themselves in their homes (rather than in bomb shelters), in interior rooms sealed against air transfer.

39. As the narrator in text 4.4 notes, Palestinians had deeply ambivalent feelings about the role of the Iraqi military and its leader, Saddam Hussein, in the Gulf War. Palestinian citizens of Israel, and especially those who resided in cities, like Haifa, that suffered missile attacks, probably found such questions quite awkward to answer, given the identities of the interviewers.

40. The initial question itself was not recorded because it was posed just at the moment that my tape ran out. Lisa's response beginning text 4.4 opens the second tape of the interview recording.

41. This phrase was not included in the transcript presented as text 4.5 because it occurred just before my question "And you, did you stay here in Haifa during the war?" which introduces the transcribed excerpt.

42. Samir makes this point subtly, contrasting the potential danger in the village (of an unannounced missile) to the actual fear in the city (of the loud sound of the alarm siren). Samir notes that they did sometimes hear an alarm in the village, but that it was the alarm in the nearby Jewish town of Carmiel (line 34). Samir is thus also describing a situation in which the Jewish State discriminated against its Arab citizens, protecting them less well against attack than its Jewish inhabitants. Such claims were made also about the distribution of gas masks before the outbreak of the war.

Chapter 5

1. Richard Rodriguez's representation of acquiring the language of the majority while losing the language of the home recalls the legends of Eliezer Ben-Yehuda, the man credited with reviving Hebrew as a spoken language. Ben-Yehuda, it is often said, was so obsessed with raising his son to be a native speaker of Hebrew that he refused to speak any other language in his home—despite the fact that his wife knew no Hebrew at all (Fellman 1973a:34). Both stories suggest the symbolism of an ultimate rupture of identity through the rupture of the "mother tongue," or the linguistic connection between (grand)mother and child. See later in this chapter for further discussion of Ben-Yehuda and the revival of Hebrew.

2. See text 5.1 for a discussion of the politics of Palestinians acquiring Hebrew as a native language. The same interview material was discussed in chapter 1, as text 1.2.

3. Many young Mizrahim study Arabic formally in school, or as part of their military service, but the acquisition of Arabic in these contexts takes on very different social characteristics and cultural meanings.

4. Ironically, the original source of these language-teaching methods was the American military (Spolsky and Shohamy 1999:97). It is in Israel, though, that the innovative methods were first applied on a large scale.

5. The Hebrew word *ulpan* (plural: *ulpanim*) literally means "studio," but it is widely used to refer to institutions that teach Hebrew language.

6. Arabic too is a language that is powerfully romanticized by its speakers, but these romanticizations take strikingly different forms. While Arabic is romanticized for its form (its sacred status as the language of the Qur'an, its calligraphic traditions that embody Arab aesthetic theory and practice, its magnificent literary traditions, its monumental vocabulary, and its special place in the hearts and souls of Arab people [e.g. Patai 1973:41–72]), Israeli Hebrew is romanticized for its acquisition.

7. As Seidman (1997) and others have pointed out, the story of Ben-Yehuda's selfless devotion obscures a gendered story of oppression. Ben-Yehuda's wife probably knew little Hebrew because in east European Jewish society girls rarely received formal education. Almost all boys, on the other hand, would have learned a great deal of Hebrew through their religious instruction.

8. The contrast indicates some of the differences between American and Israeli ideologies of language. Americans, for example, feel that their English is a meager and poor version of British English, which is held up as proper, sophisticated, and elegant.

9. Many Israelis tell stories of living abroad and deciding to return home. The chance to live in the United States is highly valued in Israel. America is seen as a place where people can earn money (free from the burden of an enormously high tax rate in Israel) and live in peace (far from wars, military service, terrorism, combative politics, and the incessant press of news). Since Israel and the United States allow dual citizenship, Americans who immigrate to Israel may keep their own American citizenship, and they can pass their citizenship on to their children as well. Many Israelis born to American parents opt for such dual citizenship because it makes travel easier, and because it facilitates spending extended periods of time living, working, or studying in the United States. Indeed, so many Israelis have moved (more or less permanently) to the United States that Los Angeles and New York have become the largest "Israeli" cities in the world—outside of Tel Aviv. An entire sociological literature has grown up around the phenomenon of the *yordim*, or Jews who emigrate from Israel (see Sobel 1986).

10. The borrowed word *breksim* has had the Hebrew plural suffix *-im* added to an already plural English word, "brakes." Such redundant plural marking on borrowed words is not uncommon, as in the English usage "curriculas."

11. The official word for an audiocassette tape, for example, is *kaletet*, which is derived from a Semitic root that means "to absorb, receive, or comprehend." Similar constructions exist for most modern products, although common usage favors the borrowed terms from international languages, primarily English.

12. See "Nation, Not Race! 1" in chapter 1.

13. The student-aged immigrants were particularly motivated to learn Hebrew. Many had been in advanced training programs when they left the Soviet Union. Several classmates, for example, had left in the middle of medical school. As new immigrants they were entitled to special benefits, including lucrative education grants, but these were conditioned upon their gaining acceptance to university programs within their first two years in Israel. Gaining admission depended upon performance on standardized tests, which were administered in Hebrew.

14. While most Israelis (including those on the political right and left) recognize that democratic principles and practices do not extend to noncitizen Palestinians living in the Israeli-occupied territories (i.e., the West Bank and Gaza Strip), they do not see this situation as diminishing the democratic nature of the State of Israel.

15. Indeed the importance the ulpan placed on teaching Israeli values and Jewish identity—alongside Hebrew language—was demonstrated most clearly when a visitor came to our class to speak about the Holocaust. The visiting speaker was an Israeli man who had emigrated from Russia many years before. He told the students about an organization that documented Holocaust victims, in order to solicit information from these newcomers about Russian victims. What was remarkable about his presentation, though, was that he spoke in Russian. At no other time, and

for no other purpose, did the ulpan staff break the language-pedagogic frame of teaching "Hebrew-in-Hebrew."

16. The contradictory attitudes of the ulpan teachers stem from the disparate goals of the ulpan curriculum. Russian students were in fact quite eager to learn the language, and they saw the ideological material as an obstacle in their way.

17. By the late 1990s, language-use in Israel had in fact undergone revolutionary changes. The 2001 campaign for prime minister, for example, included bilingual television commercials—both in Hebrew with Russian subtitles and in Russian with Hebrew subtitles. The two candidates, Ehud Barak and Ariel Sharon, referred to language in their ads and their stump speeches—if only to apologize, as did the Labor candidate Ehud Barak, for being unable to speak Russian. Indeed, Ariel Sharon drew significant electoral support from Russian immigrant voters in part because he was able to represent himself in Russian. This striking change in discourse reflects both the new electoral importance of the Russian immigrant vote and a sea change in Israeli attitudes toward language.

18. This phrase is intended to describe a general pattern, rather than a statistical fact. There may in fact be some individuals who consider themselves Palestinian native-speakers of Hebrew, but such cases would have been quite extraordinary in the early 1990s. Even the children of marriages between Arab and Jewish Israelis rarely considered themselves (or were considered by other Israelis) to be Palestinian native-speakers of Hebrew. Such individuals experienced powerful pressures to identify fully with one group or the other, rather than to straddle the two communities. Thus Yaakov, the son of a Jewish mother and a Palestinian father, spoke no Arabic. Conversely, the young children of Haula and Shim'on, a Palestinian woman and a Jewish man, spoke only Arabic.

19. This text is a longer excerpt from the interview with Samir, Lisa, and Rhoda that was discussed in chapter 1 as text 1.1.

20. Stella uses the Hebrew word *Morokayit*, literally "Moroccan (language)," which is a common Israeli way of referring to the Jewish dialect of Arabic spoken by Moroccan Jews. Israelis did not tend to use such a designation for the distinctive dialect of Moroccan Arabic used by non-Jewish Moroccans, which would have been called simply *aravit*, "Arabic."

21. Shutafut, "Partnership," is the name of a community center in Hadar Elyon that worked to encourage Arab-Jewish coexistence. (See chapter 4.)

22. Ella Shohat makes a parallel point in her book on Israeli cinema, noting that Israeli films long tended to portray Arab characters with Mizrahi actors and Mizrahi characters with Ashkenazi actors (Shohat 1989:136).

23. For a fuller description of the destruction of Iqrit, and of Nabil's family's struggle to regain the community's rights, see text 2.3.

24. See chapter 4 for further discussion of the Yami encounters I observed. Nabil and I were associated with the same program, but we worked with different participating schools.

25. See the discussion of Bialik and the role of his poetry in Israeli education earlier in this chapter.

26. Daliat Ha-Carmel (Dalia, for short) is the largest of several Druze villages near Haifa (see text 2.6). Dalia is a town of native speakers of Arabic, so Jamila's point is that even in an Arabic town her coworkers used Hebrew.

27. The Hebrew words for "Hebrew" and "Arabic" are extremely similar, involving the same three-consonant root. In line 17 Jamila has merely transposed the first two consonants of the word for "Arabic," thus creating something that sounded like "Hebrew." This is a common conversational slip-of-the-tongue.

28. Habibi's masterpiece appeared originally in 1974 under the Arabic title *al-waqa'i' al-gharibah fi ikhtifa' Sa'id Abi al-Nahs al-Mutasha'il*. An English translation appeared in 1985.

29. Sadly, Emil Habibi and Faisal Al-Husseini have both passed away.

30. I have used the title of the English translation of Grossman's book, *Sleeping on a Wire*, for the sake of simplicity. The book's original, Hebrew title, *Noxaxim Nifkadim*, "Present Absentees," bears complex meanings. Grossman's title refers to an Israeli legal term for the status of Palestinian Arabs who left their place of residence during the 1948 conflicts but who remained within the borders of what became the State of Israel. These internal refugees have the official status of "present absentees." (See text 2.3.) The translators of Grossman's book captured some of the feeling evoked by Grossman's Hebrew title, but missed much of its irony.

31. The Dabka is a popular Palestinian folk dance, widely thought of as the Palestinian national dance.

32. For more on hafgasha encounter programs, see chapter 4.

33. The difficulties faced by other Arab-Jewish organizations, like Shutafut, in obtaining funding and cooperation from the Haifa municipality was often justified in terms of the official support given to Beit Ha-Gefen.

34. The most senior of the Palestinian emergency-room doctors was a Druze man, and the other three were Christian Arab men. The prominence of Palestinian doctors in this emergency ward is not surprising. On the one hand, medicine is a career path that is open to Palestinian Israelis, who are excluded from many technical and scientific fields by military service requirements. On the other hand, emergency room duty was a relatively low-status role for a doctor in Israel, where emergency medicine was not a recognized field of specialization.

35. Other languages were used when pragmatic considerations dictated. Russian patients were treated by Russian-speaking doctors, a French-speaking elderly woman was examined by a French-speaking doctor, and Arabic-speakers were cared for by Palestinian doctors. It is precisely this tendency to switch language to facilitate communication that makes the Arabic-Hebrew code-switching and the nonuse of English stand out so prominently.

36. The presence of Arabic on street signs in older Arab neighborhoods may not be a direct function of local readership. The trilingual signs probably predate the Israeli state, and they may have been common in the older Jewish neighborhoods as well. Jewish neighborhoods, however, tend to receive better municipal services than do Palestinian neighborhoods, and the old street signs there may have been replaced by newer ones—which show a different pattern of language use.

37. I discuss the use of language in broadcasting more extensively in chapter 6.

38. I often heard Arabic spoken at one taxi stand near the center of Hadar, but this turned out to be the exception that proved the rule. That particular stand was the point of origin for cab trips to the Druze villages of Dalia and Isfiyya, and the drivers were themselves Druze. At a second taxi stand, just a few blocks away, I heard only Hebrew.

39. Cynthia is a Christian Palestinian woman. She is referring to a cross she wore as a pendant on her necklace.

40. Allenby Street is a main thoroughfare and fashionable shopping district in Tel Aviv, Israel's largest city.

41. Cynthia is saying that she was stopped at the entrance to the department store by a security guard, who demanded to see her *t'udat zehut*, "identity card." Security guards are routinely stationed at the entrance to public buildings in Israel. Guards check the bags of all people who enter. (The practice is a response to the bombings Israel has experienced over the years.) Living in Israel, one quickly gets used to the routine of opening purses, backpacks, and any other closed package for inspection upon entering a public building. Anything but the most cursory inspection of bags, however, was unusual in the early 1990s. In particular, the request to see Cynthia's identity card was highly unusual—and particularly humiliating for Cynthia. A salient feature of Israeli identity cards—which every adult Israeli citizen carries but which are rarely used—is that it specifies a person's *l'om*, "nationality" (see chapter 3). Cynthia was thus outraged that the guard wanted to establish that she was an Arab.

42. Yehudit is a pseudonym for the woman who introduced me to Dalia as a potential interviewee.

43. The Hebrew word my classmate used was *falastinai*, "Palestinian," which in this context unambiguously referred to a noncitizen Palestinian resident of the Occupied Territories. A Palestinian citizen of Israel, in contrast, would have been called *aravi yisra'eli*, literally "Israeli Arab."

44. Several additional factors prevent Palestinian students from gaining the fluency in English that Jewish students achieve, including disparities in the quality of teaching facilities, curricular materials, instructors, and pedagogical styles.

45. Interestingly, Jewish Israelis tend to have the reverse perception. Jews perceive Palestinian students to have an advantage, since they reach the job market two or three years earlier. In fact, many Jews expressed resentment over this difference. Such resentment, however, overlooks the massive advantages military experience gives Jews in the job market. Jews rarely acknowledged the restricted nature of the job market Palestinians face.

46. This conversation took place just a few days before the beginning of Passover, a major Jewish holiday. Passover is the biggest family festival on the Israeli (Jewish) calendar, somewhat akin to Thanksgiving in the United States. The concern that Americans, who were far from their families, would need a place to celebrate the big first-evening meal, called a Seder, was therefore quite considerate.

47. Mike's questions were pointed, and eventually they provoked a lengthy conversation about Israeli attitudes toward Russian immigrants.

48. Distinguishing between a code-switch and a borrowing can be subtle, since phrases as well as words may be borrowed from one language into another. Linguists usually identify code-switches with incorporations of more than word-length fragments of a second language.

49. I have greatly simplified the statement of the Hebrew spirantization rule. For greater detail on this phonological process and its history, see Faber (1986).

50. The covert nature of this prestige derives from its juxtaposition to the overt prestige of speaking Hebrew well in Israel. The ideological role of Hebrew remains so strong that Israeli Jews are embarrassed when confronted with their own (situated) preferences for English.

51. One of the gentler of these "David Levi jokes" poses the question "Why was David Levi found on the roof at a party?" and provides the answer "Because he heard that the drinks were on the house." The idiomatic expression "on the house" is given in English, as a code-switch. The humor of the joke depends entirely on the assumption that Levi didn't understand the English, since the play on words does not work in Hebrew, as it does in English.

52. Jewish members of the Re'ut youth group, for example, sprinkled their speech with English loanwords and borrowings.

53. It may be that the peculiarity of an English-speaking principal accustomed the Palestinian teachers to speaking English, but an alternative explanation also presents itself. The general education level of Palestinians who go into teaching is much higher than that for Jews who go into teaching, in large part because of the occupational barriers to employment of Palestinian graduates in other fields.

Chapter 6

1. The Hebrew *navox* is formally equivalent to English "embarrassed," but it is rarely used in casual speech. Conversely, speakers of American English generally use "sorry" to mean both "apologize" and "regret," which Hebrew speakers distinguish as *hitnatzel* and *hitzta'er*, respectively.

2. Even in the nineteenth century the concept of "Israeli" bore received meanings, since it was fashioned as the "New Jew," which was a reaction against very specific historical, political, and cultural forces.

3. "Land of Israel songs" (in Hebrew, *shire eretz yisra'el*) are popular, folksy songs that are familiar to all Israelis of Hagit's and Nurit's generation. They are played on the radio, taught in schools, and celebrated in festivals. Today they are heard as sentimental and patriotic in tone.

4. Eurovision is an annual television event that is immensely popular in Israel. Each year Israeli pop stars enter songs in a national competition that determines a single act to represent the country in a subsequent competition that encompasses all of Europe. The Israeli act has won the European competition several times in the past, and Israelis take pride in such accomplishments.

5. For a fuller discussion of this incident and its coverage in the Israeli press see Lefkowitz 1997.

6. During the 1992 Gulf War radios filled the hours-long Scud missile confinements with "Land of Israel songs," which were intended—and received—as soothing and comforting.

7. See chapter 2 for further discussion of the role of agriculture and physical labor in Zionist discourses of redemption.

8. As part of an attempt to discourage Palestinian guerrilla and terrorist attacks on Israeli citizens, the Israeli military has long followed a policy of punishing the village of a suspected attacker by uprooting the community's olive trees. This tactic is ironic (from the perspective of Israeli public culture), given the high symbolic value Israelis place on trees. The tactic is also devastating to Palestinians, for whom the trees are often an important part of their livelihood. The Israeli practice thus exerts symbolic violence in equal measure with economic violence, as the planting of Israeli trees on Palestinian villages coincides with the removal of Palestinian trees. The dual strategy parallels Israeli practices of remaking urban space by reclaiming (some) Arab homes as fashionable sites for Jewish residence, while removing (other) Palestinian homes (see chapter 2).

9. The story's Hebrew title, *mul ha-ya'arot*, translates literally as "in front of the forests." Ted Swedenburg's (1995:73–74) insightful analysis first drew my attention to this story.

10. In Yehoshua's story, the prickly pear marks the traditional boundaries of Palestinian villages (see fig. 2.7 and associated discussion in chapter 2). For Israelis, the fruit of the prickly pear, the *sabra* (Hebrew: *tzabar*), is the quintessential symbol of Israeli identity.

11. A *kibutz* (plural: *kibutzim*) is an Israeli collective farm. These farms, based on socialist ideals of manual labor and communal living, were instrumental in the early Jewish presence in Palestine, and they retain today a leading role in Israeli cultural, political, and social life (see Bettelheim 1967; Elon 1981; Hazleton 1977; Spiro 1963). Note that this word is usually rendered "kibbutz" in English, where the doubled consonant reflects an etymological gemination in the Hebrew word that no longer corresponds to actual pronunciation.

12. The time period referred to is the 1920s and 1930s. For more detail on this kibbutz museum and on the Israeli nostalgic commemoration of the *xalutz*, see Katriel 1997.

13. This discussion is indebted to Tamar Katriel's (1997) work on the rhetoric of kibbutz museums in Israel. These specific observations were made during participation in her ongoing research. The segment entitled "A Kibbutz Museum Guide" in chapter 7 describes the same visit.

14. The word *kibutznik* is Hebrew for "a member of a kibbutz," but the word is laden with affective and symbolic meaning. The *-nik* ending is a highly productive suffix in Israeli Hebrew slang. Added to nouns it works like *-ian* in English, creating a noun that means "a person associated with" the noun. The *-nik* suffix, however, also bears a humorous productivity, akin to English *-aholic*, as in *chocaholic* and others. Added to *kibutz*, the ending symbolizes a highly esteemed, if nostalgic, Israeli identity.

15. *Fallah* is the Arabic word for "farmer, peasant," but it too has taken on affective and symbolic meaning. In Palestinian discourse the fallah is a powerful symbol of Palestinian identity (Swedenburg 1995). Interestingly, the Arabic word has also been borrowed into Hebrew slang, where it means "Palestinian villager" but bears negative affect.

16. The image of the fallah also represented a monumental change in the relations between social class groups in the Palestinian community, relations that would change even more drastically after 1948, when almost the entire urban and upper-class Palestinian population ended up outside of the Israeli-held territory.

17. In the early 1990s there were only two broadcast television stations in Israel: Channel 1, which was government run, and the newer Channel 2, which was semiprivatized. With the introduction of cable television since then, the number of television channels and programs has greatly multiplied, but at the time, families needed to purchase an expensive additional antenna just in order to receive the alternative channel, Channel 2.

18. The ideological nature of the reporting on Palestinian violence on Israeli Arabic-language television news is clearest when compared to the English-language news. In the latter forum incidents of terrorism received very brief and superficial coverage, as problematic scenes in general were downplayed in favor of colorful features that were less threatening. The English-language news was oriented toward people the Israeli government wanted to attract to Israel: English-speaking tourists and "Anglo-Saxon" Jews (i.e., those from the United States, Canada, Great Britain, South Africa, and Australia/New Zealand), some of whom might be considering immigration to Israel. As noted in chapter 5, the English-language news broadcasts had gained a surprising popularity. It was widely reported that Israeli yuppies preferred the English-language news, and one explanation was the prestige that attached to competence in English. But in preferring the shorter, fluffier news show, Israeli yuppies were also distancing themselves from the emotionally overwhelming conflict between Israel and its Arab neighbors.

19. As noted in chapter 5, Palestinian Israelis felt the lack of adequate children's television programming in Arabic. Mothers complained that Jordanian television—received in Israel—did not have high-quality children's shows, and as a result, small children made great demands on their mothers to translate the innovative, Western-style shows broadcast mornings in Hebrew on Israeli television. (See chapter 5 for discussion of the role such television plays in Israeli patterns of language learning.)

20. Excluded from this analysis is the vibrant Arabic-language press in East Jerusalem. The East Jerusalem press did not address the Israeli Palestinian community, nor did Israeli Palestinians draw on the East Jerusalem press for their news in the early 1990s. It was difficult to find Jerusalem Arabic-language newspapers in Israel outside of East Jerusalem.

21. The names of the Arabic-language newspapers translate as follows: *al-Sinnara* literally means "the fishhook" but is also an anagram of *an-Nasira*, Arabic for "Nazareth," the town where the paper is published; *Kul al-Arab* means "All the Arabs"; and *al-Ittihad* means "The Union."

22. This pattern partially explains the difficulty buying Arabic-language newspapers in the Arabic-speaking Druze villages (see chapter 2), since Druze had few ties either to the Communist Party or to the Nazareth kinship networks.

23. The Los Angeles riots occurred just a few months before the violence in Bat Yam described here, and Israelis were conscious of the parallels. The symbolic link drawn between these geographically separated events underscores the power of what Arjun Appadurai (1996) has called modern "mediascapes."

24. The show's name, *Mabat la-Xadashot*, translates roughly as "View of the News." In the early 1990s current events talk shows were also very popular.

25. Tel Aviv, Jerusalem, and Haifa are also served by influential local newspapers, but these are weeklies, rather than dailies.

26. The newspaper's name, *Yedioth Ahronoth*, can be translated as "Final Tidings." I have adopted a rather formal (etymological) English transliteration for the name because this is the romanization that the newspaper itself uses. A transliteration more consistent with my practice in this book would represent the newspaper's name as *yediot axronot*, which corresponds more directly to the way it is actually pronounced in vernacular Hebrew.

27. Grammatical differences between Hebrew and English make it impossible to translate the picture's Hebrew title directly. The Hebrew word, *ha-nirtzaxat*, is a passive participle derived from the verb "to murder" that is obligatorily marked for feminine gender—thus "The Murdered Girl."

28. The Hebrew words are *ha-retzax*, "the murder," above the picture, and *v'ha-za'am*, "and the rage," below the picture.

29. The right-to-left Hebrew reading direction augments the tendency for this spread to be read in this way.

30. Many Israeli public schools are supported by outside philanthropical organizations—and are then named after these organizations. Such is the case with Helena's school, which was founded by WIZO, the Women's International Zionist Organization.

31. It is interesting to note that A. B. Yehoshua also represents the Palestinian man as mute in the famous story "Facing the Forest," discussed earlier in this chapter. In Yehoshua's novella, the caretaker's muteness stems from violence inflicted upon him during the 1948 war by Jewish soldiers, who cut out his tongue.

32. Legend has it that a single Jewish community remained in Palestine, living for two thousand uninterrupted years in a small Galilee town called Peki'in (Sachar 1989:18). The town is now an Arab and Druze village—the small Jewish community having left, ironically, in 1948 for other locales within Israel.

33. Though historians of Jews do not speak of a golden age in eastern Europe, the enormous Jewish populations there resulted from periods of relative acceptance. The disastrous history of violent pogroms in eastern Europe in the latter part of the nineteenth century, however, was instrumental in early Zionist emigrations to Palestine.

34. Visits to the Yad Vashem memorial are mandatory as well for ulpan students. See "A Tense Ulpan Class," chapter 5.

35. The insights into school-based training of children to cry during Holocaust Day commemorative activities comes from Julie Spiegel, via personal communication. See Spiegel 2000.

36. Note the conflation of "Arab" and "Muslim," since this rhetoric includes such Muslim, but not Arab, countries as Turkey and Iran. Israel is indeed geographically and demographically small compared to its Middle Eastern neighbors. Roughly the size of Massachusetts, Israel is comparable in size (21,000 km²) and population (5.5 million in 1995) to Lebanon (10,000 km² and 3.7 million), its Arab neighbor to the north, but much smaller than Egypt (1,001,449 km² and 61.9 million), its neighbor to the southwest (Source: 1998 Grolier Multimedia Encyclopedia). Relations of size would look different, though, if phrased in terms of economic production.

37. It is worth noting that a similar phenomenon obtains during the most recent violent conflicts between Israelis and Palestinians, the "Al-Aqsa Intifada." World opinion surges in Israel's favor whenever there is an attack against Israelis, but shifts dramatically when Israel retaliates.

38. In broader perspective the situation is much more complex. As Shipler (1986) eloquently points out, Jews and Palestinians each constructed images of the Other in remarkably similar ways. This chapter looks at half of this picture: the Israeli, Hebrew press. A more inclusive study would look also at the ways that Palestinian constructions of Self and Other interacted with corresponding Israeli constructions.

39. PLO is the acronym for the Palestinian Liberation Organization.

40. The representation of Palestinians occupying empty land retains its ideological force in Israel to this day. The discourse of Jewish settlement in the Occupied Territories, for example, relies on images of an underutilized expanse of underpopulated land. The Jewish settlements on certain hilltops do indeed appear few and far between to Israeli eyes, which are used to seeing Palestine as empty and Israel as vital.

41. The statistics Shipler presents in this excerpt are old, but the pattern has continued, and one could make a similar point with data from 1986 through 2000.

42. Such step-by-step diagrams of a crime's sequence were typical for Yedioth Ahronoth in the early 1990s, appearing for all major accidents or crimes that garnered front-page coverage.

43. In Hebrew the titles are: *ha-nirtzaxat,* "the murdered girl," and *ha-m'humot,* "the riots." The Hebrew writing system's right-to-left directionality reinforces the linkage between these two pictures. The reader's eye tends to read from right to left across the page, from the "victim" to the "riots," suggesting a predication.

44. This second image of Jewish rioting formed the cover of *Yedioth*'s inner "Features" section on Monday. In the early 1990s the weekday *Yedioth Ahronoth* included two sections, a main news section and an inner features section. The features section was called "24 Hours."

45. In constructing its image of the New Jew, Zionism conceptualized a masculine Self. This gendered opposition corresponds in interesting ways to the heritage/culture opposition discussed by Dominguez (1989), as well as to the Hebrew/Yiddish opposition discussed by Seidman (1997).

46. The Israeli image of the farmer and the soldier belong together in many ways. Many of the pioneering agricultural settlements were also military outposts. The kibbutz today stands not only for agricultural production and communal lifestyle but also for an elite class in Israel that contributes disproportionately to Israel's leadership, including its military leadership. Finally, one popular institution within the army itself is an agricultural brigade, called *naxal,* in which conscripts can fulfill their military duty in farming communities along the country's borders (see text 4.1; Gabi, the narrator, had served in a naxal unit).

47. I am using "police" as a cover term for several distinct bodies, including the Israeli army, the Border Guard (Mishmar ha-Gvul), and the local (Bat Yam) police itself. These distinctions are important in Israel, but in this analysis I treat them as similar institutions.

48. The metanarrative of Israeli identity discursively inscribes irredentist hatred of Arabs onto Mizrahi Jewish identity, but, ironically, the public voice of the Bat Yam violence was clearly Ashkenazi. Bat Yam itself was demographically no more Mizrahi than it was Ashkenazi. At the time of the riots the town was about 50 percent Ashkenazi and 50 percent Mizrahi. Typical of Israeli development towns and "slum" urban neighborhoods (see "Neve Yosef" in chapter 2), however, Bat Yam remained semiotically Mizrahi even when its population is largely Ashkenazi. The protagonists of the stabbing story, the Rap family, are themselves Ashkenazi. (The coverage included several references to the Holocaust, in which much of Ze'ev Rap's family perished. His mother, for example, is referred to as a concentration camp survivor.) Moreover, the coverage specifically links the inciters yelling "Death to the Arabs" with activists of several of the right-wing political parties in Israel, including Kach and Moledet, which were then led by Ashkenazi politicians. Nonetheless, it is the nonmainstream identity that is associated with the nonmainstream behaviors represented. Similarly, the current Israeli settler movement is rhetorically associated with Mizrahim, even though it is ideologically led by groups that are Ashkenazi in leadership.

49. The article cited by Shohat was written by Arye Gelblum and appeared in the April 22, 1949, edition of the newspaper *Ha'Aretz,* which is the most liberal of the mainstream Hebrew newspapers.

50. The Hebrew captions are: *m'vakot et ha-xavera she-enena* and *shtayim me-xaveroteha shel Helena, zu bi-zro'ot zu, l'axer she-noda al mota.*

51. The Hebrew caption is: *d'ma'ot al kivra shel Helena.*

52. Hebrew newspapers in Israel publish Friday editions that are larger and include many special features, similar to the Sunday editions in American newspapers.

53. Family residence patterns on kibbutzim became a contentious issue during the 1992 Gulf War, just prior to the Bat Yam incidents described here. The unprecedented safety precautions taken for this war, namely the recommendation that each household take cover in their own home, rather than in communal bomb shelters (because the risks of poison gas were considered greater than the risks of conventional weapons), led kibbutz families to keep their children with them, breaking down the system of age-graded residence.

54. A quirk of Semitic language structure makes this exclusion grammatical. The most general media term for Palestinian citizens of Israel, *araviye yisra'el*, is a construct, *smixut* form, with the literal meaning "Arabs of Israel," or "Israel's Arabs." The connotation of possession is both grammatically present and perceptually salient, but the nonpossessive alternative, the entirely adjectival form *aravim yisra'eliyim*, is rarely used.

55. These usages open up the commonly exploited possibility of using "Arab" more generally to blur the distinction between citizen and noncitizen Palestinians, as the mob's cries of "Death to Arabs," for example, effected.

56. The phrases translate more literally as "in a nationalistic context" and "in a criminal context," respectively.

57. In fact, politically motivated violence by "Israeli Arabs" has been surprisingly rare (see Lustick 1980). A slightly more common occurrence is that noncitizen Palestinians carrying out an attack will be assisted by Israeli citizens. Nonetheless, the rarity of such events and the restraint shown by citizen Palestinians throughout the Intifada in the late 1980s and early 1990s help explain the very spectacular and tragic reaction of the Israeli police to demonstrations in the Galilee toward the beginning of the Al-Aqsa Intifada in the fall of 2000.

58. Ian Lustick (1980) discusses Israel's powerful opposition between the discursive construction of the dangerous and violent Arab and the material reality of an incredibly quiescent populace. There is an interesting parallel to the polarity of the images of the Mizrahi ethnic difference within the Jewish Israeli population, where Mizrahim are stereotypically represented as having inordinate amounts of both love and hate.

59. The exception that proves the rule involved a *Yedioth Ahronoth* article on Samir Naqash, a Jewish Israeli writer who was born in Iraq, and who continues to write in Arabic. The article presented Naqash in terms of his identity: staunchly laying claim to a Mizrahi identity, which was represented as opposed to an Israeli identity. In this case the media treated the Jewish writer as Arab.

60. The semiotic association between social disadvantage and Mizrahi identity stems, in part, from the fact that Mizrahim comprise a disempowered class in terms of income levels, occupation types, educational achievement, and representation in political power and cultural leadership (Swirski 1989). Similar economic disparities distinguish Palestinian and Ashkenazi sectors, but Palestinian and Mizrahi social ills are rarely seen to belong to the same system, and are rarely considered in an integrated fashion.

61. An Ashkenazi acquaintance once confused Beit Shemesh with Beit She'an in conversation. These are two places, with similar names, that have become synonymous with Mizrahi identity. Both are "development towns" that have had their Mizrahiness elevated both to stereotype (of the Other) and emblem (of the Self). Beit Shemesh gained this status when the (Ashkenazi) writer Amos Oz wrote an uncomplimentary essay on the town, drawing the ire of its residents. Beit She'an's symbolic status derives from the prominence of David Levi and his family. The Druze writer Salman Natur (see text 2.6) chose Beit She'an for his study of Mizrahi attitudes toward Palestinians because he wanted to see where David Levi came from.

62. The Likud came to power in the aftermath of the 1973 ("Yom Kippur" / "October") War, as popular confidence in the Labor government plummeted.

63. Interestingly, language frequently entered into this construction. Levi was constantly lambasted for his lack of fluency in English, but he never got credit for his fluency in French. The importance of English, the language of the United States, and the irrelevance of French, the language of Moroccan and other North African Jews, recreates in Israel the Ashkenazi/ Mizrahi hierarchy, even while it reflects the shift in international patterns of language use quite beyond the Israeli scope.

64. More recently much of Levi's popularity and influence among Mizrahi rank-and-file voters has been taken over by the ultraorthodox religious party, Shas. In a fascinating shift of cultural meanings and political tendencies, the religious leadership of Shas has come to index Mizrahi identity the way the secular leader Levi had done previously (see Lefkowitz 1997).

Chapter 7

1. Following convention in Hebrew studies, I use the names of two Hebrew letters, "ayin" and "het," to refer to the pharyngeal phonemes and their corresponding variables. Following general linguistic practice, phonemes are shown between angle brackets, /p/, phones between square brackets, [pʰ], and variables between rounded parentheses, (r). The International Phonetic Alphabet (IPA) symbols, ʕ and ħ, stand for a voiced pharyngeal approximant and a voiceless pharyngeal fricative, respectively.

2. I have simplified the statement of this phonetic conditioning for the sake of clarity. Parallel patterns of allophonic variation hold for the phonemes /t/ and /k/ in English.

3. The presence/absence of consonantal constriction in "car" is often represented as the difference between "car" and "kah."

4. Figure 7.1 includes a distinction between two different word-list recitation styles, which Labov labeled "D" and "D'." For style D' interviewees were asked to read lists that directly juxtaposed words that tested dialect distinctions. For example, interviewees might be asked to read the words "guard" and "God," one after the other. These words are homonyms in an "r-less" dialect but distinct in "r-ful" dialects. Word lists for style D test the same kinds of distinctions, but the interviewee is less likely to be aware of what is being tested, since the words "guard" and "God" would be separated by other words that do not involve the (r) variable.

5. Labov's notation divides the socioeconomic spectrum into ten groups he identifies as socioeconomic class. The division is based primarily on family income. These "class" groups are labeled with numbers, ranging from "0" for the lowest socioeconomic class group to "9" for the highest socioeconomic group (Labov 1982a).

6. The crossover that occurs in the more formal styles (D and D') for the two highest socioeconomic groupings (those identified as "6–8" and "9") is characteristic of sociolinguistic variables in the process of change. The details of this "crossover pattern" are beyond the scope of this book, but see Labov 1972a or Labov 1982a for extensive discussions of the phenomenon.

7. "Marker" is a technical term in quantitative sociolinguistics. Labov (1972a:178–180) distinguishes among three types of linguistic variable, according to the degree of social salience. "Indicators" are the least salient. These variables regularly correlate with various dimensions of social identity, but Americans do not generally remark on their presence. "Stereotypes," in contrast, are linguistic features that are so salient as to make speakers consciously avoid them in any but the most casual of speech contexts. What Labov calls "markers," including (r), lie in the middle of this continuum. Speakers can articulate their awareness of these linguistic features,

and listeners routinely make judgments about speakers based on these features, but they are not avoided in everyday speech.

8. I thank Malcah Yaeger-Dror for providing the specific data used in constructing these figures. Her full study is reported in Yaeger-Dror 1988 and Yaeger-Dror 1991.

9. The apparent exception to this pattern, Boaz Sharabi (whom Yaeger-Dror identifies as BS), the only singer who did not use apical (r) at least 70 percent of the time in song register, is an Ashkenazi singer of Ashkenazi music. Even for Sharabi, though, the level of apical (r) use in song register is much higher than the level of apical (r) use in interview register.

10. The singers' full names are Nissim Garame, Geula Cohen, Haim Moshe, and Avihu Medina, respectively.

11. Some data points are missing on this graph because Yaeger-Dror was unable to get sufficient data from both interview and song-lyric speech styles for all twenty singers.

12. Yaeger-Dror's provocative findings suggest that research on (r) in natural contexts or interview data from the general population in Israel would add much to our understanding of the linguistic negotiation of identity in Jewish Israel.

13. This discussion draws on Tamar Katriel's (1997) work on the discourse of museum building in Israel. The specific observations described in the text were made when I joined her university class for a guided tour of the museum. "The Tractor and the Plow," in chapter 6, is based upon the same incident.

14. In the early 1990s public bus service stopped early on Friday afternoon in most Israeli cities. In Haifa and many other places bus service resumed on Saturdays. Jerusalem, however, was much stricter in its observance of the religious ban on work activities during Shabbat, and no public buses ran in the Jewish part of the city during Shabbat.

15. Arabic and Hebrew are very closely related languages that share numerous transparent cognates. It is therefore ironic that the two languages are written with such different orthographies that they appear quite different visually. This irony is not uncommon around the world, as many geographical regions share closely related languages that are separated by vastly different writing systems. Other examples include Hindi/Urdu in South Asia and Serbian/Croatian on the Balkan Peninsula.

16. The phonological alternations that demonstrate phonemic status for underlying pharyngeals are discussed later in this chapter. These alternations are currently being simplified and analogically leveled, but they remain common in vernacular speech.

17. For simplicity of presentation, the Arabic examples I cite are drawn from Modern Standard Arabic.

18. By convention in Hebrew studies, underlying roots of Hebrew words are represented as strings of three (sometimes two or four) consonantal radicals, "R1.R2.R3." This representation is well suited to Semitic languages, in which vowels play an important role in derivational and inflectional morphology but little role in distinguishing lexical roots.

19. These words are cognates of the Arabic words /qaraʕa/ and /qaraʔa/ discussed earlier. Note that Arabic /q/ corresponds to /k/ in Israeli Hebrew. Hebrew maintains an orthographic distinction between Semitic /q/ (the voiceless uvular stop) and Semitic /k/ (the voiceless velar stop), but the uvular stop is not part of the phonemic inventory of any modern dialect of Hebrew.

20. In the case of the voiceless pharyngeal, the orthographic distinction has been lost in Hebrew as well. The Arabic letters xaa and ħaa represent the Arabic velar and pharyngeal voiceless fricatives, respectively. Hebrew cognates of both reflexes, however, are spelled with Hebrew het (though the two dialects of Hebrew pronounce this letter differently).

21. A parallel argument can be made for the voiceless pharyngeal.

22. To calculate the index scores, thirty tokens of each variable were coded on a three-point scale, and the average was normalized to a number between 0 and 100. Tokens were sampled from the midpoint of the interview recording.

23. Ironically, the emergence of Israel and the revival of Hebrew led to the decline and near-extinction of the great "Jewish languages" of the world. Yiddish, Ladino, and Judeo-Arabic have all declined significantly as the speakers of these languages have moved to Israel where for the most part the social conditions for the classic Jewish trilingualism do not exist. Doubly ironic, then, is the recreation of these conditions by some ultraorthodox Jewish communities in Israel. For these groups, for whom Yiddish remains the home language, Israeli (i.e., vernacular) Hebrew has become the language of communication with the broader society—a role traditionally filled by non-Jewish languages, such as Russian, Polish, or Arabic.

24. A third major pattern of liturgical pronunciation, the Yemenite tradition, existed at the time of the revival of Hebrew, but this form had relatively little influence on the emergent Israeli speech norms (see Blanc 1968).

25. The Hebrew diglossia in Israel thus parallels the Arabic diglossia in Arab countries—but this similarity is rarely noted.

26. As an example of the alternation between noun-noun compound and analytic phrase, the formal noun-noun compound *ovde ha-bank*, "the bank-workers," might appear in a newspaper, while conversationalists would be more likely to utter *ha-ovdim shel ha-bank*, literally "the workers of the bank." The two constructions have the same meaning.

27. Noun-noun compounding involves several morphophonological processes. In this example, the phonetic shape of *bayit*, "house," changes to [bet] when it is the first element of a compound. Such alternations conditioned by compounding are tied to prosodic constraints.

28. Overall, conversational Israeli Hebrew does reflect Sephardi norms of pronunciation. Many standard features of the Ashkenazi liturgical pronunciation, such as t-spirantization and a-backing, are not found in conversational Israeli Hebrew. The pharyngeal variables are thus important exceptions to the general rule.

29. It is tempting to rely on functional arguments to explain Mizrahi retention of pharyngeal articulation (both in the traditional liturgical pronunciations and in the MH dialect as it emerged in Israel) and Ashkenazi abandonment of the pharyngeal forms. The vast majority of Mizrahi Jews either spoke Arabic themselves or lived in an environment where Arabic was used. Therefore, the presence of pharyngeal sounds in Arabic probably facilitated the retention of pharyngeals in the Hebrew of Mizrahim, while the absence of pharyngeal sounds in any European language probably inhibited their retention in Ashkenazi Hebrew. Such arguments, however, may not provide the whole story, as they ignore social and cultural factors. For one thing, many of the Mizrahi immigrants to Israel in the 1950s were not native-speakers of Arabic. Many of those who came from the Maghreb—Morocco, Tunisia, and Algeria—grew up speaking French, rather than Arabic. Moreover, the ease-of-articulation argument cannot explain the rejection of apical (Sephardi) /r/ by Ashkenazi Hebrew. A much better explanation of the latter phenomenon stems from cultural meanings tied to language styles. Ashkenazi Hebrew adopted uvular /r/, similar to the standard French /r/ phoneme, despite the presence of apical /r/ in German, Russian, and most of the other European languages the European Jews of the nineteenth and twentieth century would have spoken or been influenced by. However, the uvular pronunciation of /r/ had been spreading in Europe as a prestige feature for several centuries (and is now the dominant form in many parts of Germany and northern Europe).

Chapter 8

1. *The MacNeil/Lehrer Newshour* was an American public broadcasting nightly news show that gave in-depth coverage to select issues, often through expert panel discussions. The show continues as *The Newshour with Jim Lehrer*.

2. The interviewer subsequently apologized for the confusion he had inadvertently created.

3. Palestinian Arabs refer to themselves as "Palestinians" regardless of their citizenship status in Israel.

4. Interestingly, research has shown that physiological differences between the male and female vocal apparatus do not account fully for the differences in men's and women's pitch ranges. As Cruttenden puts it, "there may...be a tendency for females to exaggerate their femininity and/or males to exaggerate their masculinity" (Cruttenden 1997:131).

5. Robert Ladd has noted that research into the intonational correlates of emotion has yielded a general finding that "active emotions like anger or surprise are generally signaled by higher overall pitch" (Ladd 1996:12, citing Uldall 1964 and Williams and Stevens 1972). Nonetheless, lowered pitch can also be used to signal extreme anger, as a famous segment from a popular film demonstrates: Clint Eastwood's 1971 film *Dirty Harry* is remembered for its signature scene, in which Eastwood intones a deeply pitched threat, "Make my day."

6. Example sentences in the study of intonation often sound a bit odd because they are designed to facilitate instrumental pitch-tracking. Since instruments cannot track the pitch over unvoiced stretches of speech, sample sentences use voiced sounds only.

7. One of the intriguing paradoxes of the study of prosody is that opposite forms often have the same function. Markedly high pitch can reference the same value (anger) as markedly low pitch. Similarly, speakers can express anger either by increasing or decreasing their speech rate.

8. The sample sentences analyzed in figures 8.1–8.4 were voiced by the author. All speech samples were analyzed with an IBM-compatible desktop computer running the Praat pitch-tracking software, version 4.0, developed by Paul Boersma and David Weenink.

9. Many syntactic phenomena, including passive and fronting constructions, function to manipulate focus.

10. Pierrehumbert (1980) originally identified six pitch-accents for American English, but this inventory was later reduced (Pierrehumbert and Beckman 1988) to the following five: H*, L*, H*L, LH*, and L*H. The latter three are "bitonal" pitch-accents, in which significant pitch-effects occur before or after the main lexical stress in the focused word.

11. Liberman and Sag (1974) provide the colorful example "But elephantiasis isn't incurable!"

12. This description follows McLemore (1991) in adapting the system developed in Pierrehumbert and Beckman (1988).

13. The words on which the HLH contour falls are highlighted with boldface and small caps. In most cases only the Hebrew transcription will be so marked because of differences in word order between Hebrew and English.

14. Hebrew is a stress-accent language, generally similar to English in intonational structure. Pragmatic effects like emphasis and focus are relatively freely expressed by means of pitch-accent. Hebrew differs from English, however, in having a regular pattern of predictable word stress. Hebrew stress falls on the final syllable in the word, except for a well-defined set of lexical and morphologically conditioned exceptions. Phonological words are pronounced with a low-high tonal structure, and, since most words have ultimate stress, there is a strong correlation between word stress and pitch rises.

15. A Bar Mitzvah is a festive celebration of a boy's thirteenth birthday that Jewish tradition conceptualizes as a coming of age. Israeli Bar Mitzvah parties were very important occasions. In modern times many girls too mark this occasion, with a Bat Mitzvah.

16. This interview is also referred to in "Nurit Ben," in chapter 6. Examples (4)–(7) in this chapter are drawn from this interview as well.

17. *Reluctant Pioneers* is the title of Alex Weingrod's influential ethnography of Mizrahi immigrants in Israel (Weingrod 1966).

18. Hagit's story clearly touched on a point of discomfort for Nurit. Later in the interview Nurit expressed regret that her parents' traditionalism had prevented her from serving in the military. Indeed when she says (in text 8.1, lines 16–17), "My mother got married under pressure from her parents so as to avoid getting drafted for the army; they didn't know what it was, or what it would be like, and so they decided to marry her off," she might have been speaking of her own experience as well.

19. In other narratives told during the same interview Nurit uses the rise-fall tune to mark affectively loaded segments of narrative, just as Hagit does in the narrative transcribed in text 8.2. Hagit, however, does not appear to use the rise-fall intonation as a systematic discourse marker.

20. Note that Farha's speech adheres to the familiar gender pattern, whereby women adopt mainstream forms more than men do (see Labov 1990).

21. Hani's discussion of an emergent Palestinian identity was prompted by an interview question.

22. Hani knows that I am Jewish, and he plays off this knowledge in constructing his parody.

References

Abd-el-Jawad, Hassan. 1986. The Emergence of an Urban Dialect in the Jordanian Urban Centers. *International Journal of the Sociology of Language* 61:53–63.

———. 1987. Cross-Dialectal Variation in Arabic: Competing Prestigious Forms. *Language in Society* 16:359–368.

Abrahams, Roger. 1963. *Deep Down in the Jungle... Negro Narrative Folklore from the Streets of Philadelphia*. New York: Aldine.

Abu El-Haj, Nadia. 1997. Translating Truths: Nationalism, Archaeological Practice, and the Remaking of Past and Present in Contemporary Jerusalem. *American Ethnologist* 25:166–188.

Abu-Lughod, Lila. 1986. *Veiled Sentiments: Honor and Poetry in a Bedouin Society*. Berkeley: University of California Press.

———, and Catherine Lutz. 1990. Introduction: Emotion, Discourse, and the Politics of Everyday Life. In *Language and the Politics of Emotion*, ed. Catherine Lutz and Lila Abu-Lughod, pp.1–23. Cambridge: Cambridge University Press.

Abu-Nimer, Mohammed. 1999. *Dialogue, Conflict Resolution and Change: Arab-Jewish Encounters in Israel*. Albany: SUNY Press.

Alloni-Fainberg, Yafa. 1974. Official Hebrew Terms for Parts of the Car: A Study of Knowledge, Usage and Attitudes. *International Journal of the Sociology of Language* 1:67–94.

Almog, Oz. 2000. *The Sabra: The Creation of the New Jew*. Berkeley: University of California Press.

Alter, Robert. 1988. *The Invention of Hebrew Prose: Modern Fiction and the Language of Realism*. Seattle: University of Washington Press.

———. 1994. *Hebrew and Modernity*. Bloomington: Indiana University Press.

Amara, Muhammad Hasan, and Bernard Spolsky. 1986. The Diffusion of Integration of Hebrew and English Lexical Items in the Spoken Arabic of an Israeli Village. *Anthropological Linguistics* 28:43–54.

Anderson, Benedict. 1991 [1983]. *Imagined Communities: Reflections on the Origin and Spread of Nationalism*. London: Verso.

Anzaldúa, Gloria. 1987. *Borderlands/La Frontera: The New Mestiza*. San Francisco: Spinsters/Aunt Lute.

Appadurai, Arjun. 1996. *Modernity at Large: Cultural Dimensions of Globalization*. Minneapolis: University of Minnesota Press.

Arian, Asher, and Michal Shamir, eds. 1995. *The Elections in Israel, 1992*. Albany: SUNY Press.

Bakhtin, M.M. 1981. In *The Dialogic Imagination: Four Essays by M.M. Bakhtin*. Edited by Michael Holquist. Translated by Caryl Emerson and Michael Holquist. Austin: University of Texas Press.

———. 1984. *Rabelais and His World*. Translated by Hélène Iswolsky. Bloomington: Indiana University Press.

Barnea, Naxum. 1992. *Anaxnu lo frayerim* (We're Not Suckers). *Yedioth Ahronoth, Ha-Musaf L'Shabbat*, June 27, 1992, pp. 2–3.

Barth, Fredrik. 1972 [1964]. Ethnic Processes on the Pathan-Baluch Boundary. In *Directions in Sociolinguistics: The Ethnography of Communication*, ed. John J. Gumperz and Dell Hymes, pp. 454–464. Oxford: Basil Blackwell.

Barthes, Roland. 1972. World of Wrestling. In *Mythologies*, pp. 15–25. Translated by Annette Lavers. New York: Hill and Wang.

———. 1977 [1972]. The Grain of the Voice. In *Image—Music—Text*, pp. 179–189. Translated by Annette Lavers. New York: Hill and Wang.

Basso, Keith. 1979. *Portraits of "The Whiteman": Linguistic Play and Cultural Symbols Among the Western Apache*. Cambridge: Cambridge University Press.

Bateson, Gregory. 1972. *Steps to an Ecology of Mind*. New York: Ballantine Books.

Bauman, Richard, and Charles Briggs. 1990. Poetics and Performance as Critical Perspectives on Language and Social Life. *Annual Review of Anthropology* 19:59–88.

Beinin, Joel. 1998. *The Dispersion of Egyptian Jewry: Culture, Politics, and the Formation of a Modern Diaspora*. Berkeley: University of California Press.

Ben-Arieh, Yehoshua. 1979. *The Rediscovery of the Holy Land in the Nineteenth Century*. Jerusalem: Magnes Press.

Bentolila, Yaakov. 1983. The Sociophonology of Hebrew as Spoken in a Rural Settlement of Moroccan Jews in the Negev. Ph.D. diss., Hebrew University. (In Hebrew.)

Benvenisti, Meron. 2000. *Sacred Landscape: The Buried History of the Holy Land Since 1948*. Berkeley: University of California Press.

Berk-Seligson, Susan. 1986. Linguistic Constraints on Intrasentential Code-Switching: A Study of Spanish/Hebrew Bilingualism. *Language in Society* 15:313–348.

Berlin, Isaiah. 1976. *Vico and Herder: Two Studies in the History of Ideas*. London: Hogarth.

Bettelheim, Bruno. 1967. *Children of the Dream*. New York: Macmillan.

Blanc, Haim. 1968. The Israeli Koine as an Emergent National Standard. In *Language Problems of Developing Nations*, ed. Joshua Fishman, pp. 237–251. New York: Wiley.

Blau, Joshua. 1981a [1965]. *The Emergence and Linguistic Background of Judaeo-Arabic: A Study of the Origins of Middle Arabic*. Jerusalem: Ben-Zvi Institute for the Study of Jewish Communities in the East.

———. 1981b. *The Renaissance of Modern Hebrew and Modern Standard Arabic: Parallels and Differences in the Revival of Two Semitic Languages*. Berkeley: University of California Press.

Bloch, Linda-Renee. 1990. Communicating as an American in Israel: The Immigrant's Perception. Ph.D. diss., University of Texas at Austin.

Bolinger, Dwight. 1972. Accent is Predictable (If You're a Mind-Reader). *Language* 48:633–644.

———. 1978. Intonation Across Languages. In *Universals of Human Languages II (Phonology)*, ed. Joseph Greenberg, pp. 471–524. Palo Alto: Stanford University Press.

Bolozky, Shmuel. 1985. The Domain of Casual Processes in Modern Hebrew. *Linguistic Analysis* 15:19–27.

Bourdieu, Pierre. 1977. *Outline of a Theory of Practice*. Translated by Richard Nice. Cambridge: Cambridge University Press.

———. 1984 [1979]. *Distinction: A Social Critique of the Judgement of Taste*. Translated by Richard Nice. Cambridge, MA: Harvard University Press.

Boyarin, Jonathan. 1992. *Storm from Paradise: The Politics of Jewish Memory*. Minneapolis: University of Minnesota Press.

Briggs, Charles, and Richard Bauman. 1992. Genre, Intertextuality, and Social Power. *Journal of Linguistic Anthropology* 2:131–172.

Brodkin, Karen. 1998. *How Jews Became White Folks and What That Says About Race in America*. New Brunswick, NJ: Rutgers University Press.

Brubaker, Rogers. 1996. *Nationalism Reframed: Nationhood and the National Question in the New Europe*. Cambridge: Cambridge University Press.

Caton, Steven. 1990. *"Peaks of Yemen I Summon": Poetry as Cultural Practice in a North Yemeni Tribe*. Berkeley: University of California Press.

Chetrit, Joseph. 1985. Judeo-Arabic and Judeo-Spanish in Morocco and Their Sociolinguistic Interaction. In *Readings in the Sociology of Jewish Languages*, ed. J. Fishman, pp. 261–279. Leiden: Brill.

Clifford, James. 1997. *Routes: Travel and Translation in the Late Twentieth Century*. Cambridge, MA: Harvard University Press.

———, and George Marcus, eds. 1986. *Writing Culture: The Poetics and the Politics of Ethnography*. Berkeley: University of California Press.

Cohen, Abner, ed. 1974. *Urban Ethnicity*. London: Tavistock.

Cooper, Robert. 1977. English in Israel: A Sociolinguistic Study. *Anthropological Linguistics* 19:26–53.

Cruttenden, Alan. 1986. *Intonation*. Cambridge: Cambridge University Press.

———. 1997. *Intonation*, 2nd ed. Cambridge: Cambridge University Press.

Davis, Lawrence. 1984. The Pharyngeals in Hebrew: Linguistic Change in Apparent Time. *Folia Linguistica Historica* 5(1):25–32.

Dijk, Teun Adrianus van. 1984. *Prejudice in Discourse: An Analysis of Ethnic Prejudice in Cognition and Conversation*. Amsterdam: John Benjamins.

Domínguez, Virginia. 1989. *People as Subject, People as Object: Selfhood and Peoplehood in Contemporary Israel*. Madison: University of Wisconsin Press.

Doumani, Beshara. 1995. *Rediscovering Palestine: Merchants and Peasants in Jabal Nablus, 1700–1900*. Berkeley: University of California Press.

Eagleton, Terry. 1991. *Ideology: An Introduction*. London: Verso.

Eckert, Penelope. 1989. *Jocks and Burnouts: Social Categories and Identity in the High School*. New York: Teachers College Press.

Eisenstadt, S.N. 1967. *Israeli Society*. London: Weidenfeld and Nicolson.

———. 1985. *The Transformation of Israeli Society: An Essay in Interpretation*. London: Weidenfeld and Nicolson.

Elazar, Daniel J., and Shmuel Sandler, eds. 1995. *Israel at the Polls, 1992*. Lanham, MD: Rowman and Littlefield.

Elon, Amos. 1981 [1971]. *The Israelis: Founders and Sons.* Middlesex, UK: Penguin Books.

Ervin-Tripp, Susan. 1972. On Sociolinguistic Rules: Alternation and Co-occurrence. In *Directions in Sociolinguistics: The Ethnography of Communication,* ed. John Gumperz and Dell Hymes, pp. 216–250. Oxford: Basil Blackwell.

Faber, Alice. 1986. On the Origin and Development of Hebrew Spirantization. *Mediterranean Language Review* 2:117–138.

Fairclough, Norman. 1989. *Language and Power.* London: Longman.

Fanon, Frantz. 1967. *Black Skin, White Masks.* New York: Grove Press.

Fellman, Jack. 1973a. *The Revival of a Classical Tongue: Eliezer Ben Yehuda and the Modern Hebrew Language.* The Hague: Mouton.

———. 1973b. Language and National Identity: The Case of the Middle East. *Anthropological Linguistics* 15:244–249.

———. 1974. The Academy of the Hebrew Language: Its History, Structure, and Function. *International Journal of the Sociology of Language* 1:95–103.

Ferguson, Charles A. 1959. Diglossia. *Word* 15:325–340.

———. 1977. Baby Talk as a Simplified Register. In *Talking to Children: Language Input and Acquisition,* ed. Catherine E. Snow and Charles A. Ferguson, pp. 209–233. Cambridge: Cambridge University Press.

Fishman, Joshua. 1971. The Relationship Between Micro- and Macro-Sociolinguistics in the Study of Who Speaks What Language to Whom and When. In *Bilingualism in the Barrio,* ed. Joshua Fishman, Robert Cooper, and Roxana Ma, pp. 583–604. Bloomington: University of Indiana Press.

———. 1985. The Sociology of Jewish Languages from a General Sociolinguistic Point of View. In *Readings in the Sociology of Jewish Languages,* ed. Joshua Fishman, pp. 3–21. Leiden: Brill.

———. 1991. *Reversing Language Shift: Theoretical and Empirical Foundations of Assistance to Threatened Languages.* Clevedon: Multilingual Matters.

Flapan, Simha. 1987. *The Birth of Israel: Myths and Realities.* New York: Pantheon Books.

Foucault, Michel. 1972. The Discourse on Language. In *The Archaeology of Knowledge and The Discourse on Language,* pp. 215–237. New York: Pantheon Books.

———. 1979. *Discipline and Punish: The Birth of the Prison.* Translated by Alan Sheridan. New York: Vintage Books.

———. 1980. *The History of Sexuality. Vol. 1: An Introduction.* Translated by Robert Hurley. New York: Vintage Books.

Freud, Sigmund. 1960 [1901]. *The Psychopathology of Everyday Life.* New York: Norton.

Friedman, Ina. 2001. Paradise Reconsidered. *Jerusalem Report,* June 18, pp. 16–18.

Gal, Susan. 1979. *Language Shift: Social Determinants of Linguistic Change in Bilingual Austria.* New York: Academic Press.

———. 1994. Media and the Construction of Alternative Models of Minority Language and Identity: Discussion. Paper presented at the American Anthropological Association's ninety-third annual meeting, Atlanta, GA.

Gardner, Carol Brooks. 1984. Passing By: Street Remarks, Address Rights, and the Urban Female. In *Language in Use: Readings in Sociolinguistics,* ed. John Baugh and Joel Sherzer, pp. 148–164. Englewood Cliffs, NJ: Prentice Hall.

Geertz, Clifford. 1973. *The Interpretation of Culture.* New York: Basic Books.

Gellner, Ernest. 1983. *Nations and Nationalism.* Oxford: Blackwell.

Gilad, Lisa. 1989. *Ginger and Salt: Yemeni Jewish Women in an Israeli Town.* Boulder, CO: Westview Press.

Goffman, Erving. 1959. *The Presentation of Self in Everyday Life.* New York: Doubleday Anchor.

———. 1974. *Frame Analysis: An Essay on the Organization of Experience.* Boston: Northeastern University Press.

———. 1983. *Forms of Talk.* Philadelphia: University of Pennsylvania Press.

Goldscheider, Calvin. 2002. *Israel's Changing Society: Population, Ethnicity, and Development,* 2nd ed. Cambridge, MA: Westview Press.

Goodwin, Charles, and Alessandro Duranti. 1992. Rethinking Context: An Introduction. In *Rethinking Context: Language as an Interactive Phenomenon,* ed. Alessandro Duranti and Charles Goodwin, pp. 1–42. Cambridge: Cambridge University Press.

Government of Israel. 2000. *Statistical Abstract of Israel. Vol. 51.* Jerusalem: Central Bureau of Statistics.

Griefat, Yousuf, and Tamar Katriel. 1989. "Life Demands Musayara": Communication and Culture Among Arabs in Israel. *International and Intercultural Communication Annual* 13:121–138.

Grossman, David. 1992. *Noxaxim Nifkadim* (Present Absentees). Tel Aviv: Hasifriya Haxadasha. (In Hebrew.)

Gumperz, John. 1968. The Speech Community. *International Encyclopedia of the Social Sciences* 9:381–386.

———. 1982a. *Discourse Strategies.* Cambridge: Cambridge University Press.

———, ed. 1982b. *Language and Social Identity.* Cambridge: Cambridge University Press.

———. 1982c. Ethnic Style in Political Rhetoric. In *Discourse Strategies,* pp. 187–203. Cambridge: Cambridge University Press.

Gussenhoven, Carlos. 1983. *A Semantic Analysis of the Nuclear Tones of English.* Bloomington: Indiana University Press.

Guy, Gregory, Barbara Horvath, Julia Vonwiller, Elaine Daisley, and Inge Rogers. 1986. An Intonational Change in Progress in Australian English. *Language in Society* 15:23–52.

Halabi, Rafik. 1981. *The West Bank Story: An Israeli Arab's View of Both Sides of a Tangled Conflict.* San Diego: Harcourt Brace Jovanovich.

Halliday, Michael A. K. 1978. *Language as Social Semiotic.* London: University Park Press.

Halper, Jeff, Edwin Seroussi, and Pamela Squires-Kidron. 1989. *Musica Mizrakhit*: Ethnicity and Class Culture in Israel. *Popular Music* 8:131–141.

Handler, Richard. 1988. *Nationalism and the Politics of Culture in Quebec.* Madison: University of Wisconsin Press.

———. 1994. Is Identity a Useful Cross-Cultural Concept? In *Commemorations: The Politics of National Identity,* ed. J. R. Gillis, pp. 27–40. Princeton: Princeton University Press.

Harris, Tracy K. 1994. *Death of a Language: The History of Judeo-Spanish.* Newark: University of Delaware Press.

Harshav, Benjamin. 1990. *The Meaning of Yiddish.* Stanford: Stanford University Press.

———. 1993. *Language in Time and Revolution.* Berkeley: University of California Press.

't Hart, Johan, René Collier, and Antonie Cohen. 1990. *A Perceptual Study of Intonation: An Experimental-Phonetic Approach to Speech Melody.* Cambridge: Cambridge University Press.

Hasson, Shlomo. 1993. *Urban Social Movements in Jerusalem: The Protest of the Second Generation.* Albany: SUNY Press.

Hazleton, Lesley. 1977. *Israeli Women: The Reality Behind the Myths.* New York: Simon and Schuster.

Hertzberg, Arthur, ed. 1959. *The Zionist Idea: A Historical Analysis and Reader.* Westport, CT: Greenwood Press.

Herzl, Theodor. 1960 [1902]. *Altneuland.* Haifa, Israel: Haifa Publishing.

———. 1988 [1896]. *The Jewish State.* Translated by Sylvie d'Avigdor. New York: Dover.

Hirschberg, Julia, and Janet Pierrehumbert. 1986. The Intonational Structuring of Discourse. In *Proceedings of the Twenty-Fourth Annual Meeting of the Association for Computational Linguistics (ACL86)*. Columbia University, New York, June 1986. (Pp. 136–144.)

Hobsbawm, Eric. 1992. *Nations and Nationalism Since 1780: Programme, Myth, Reality*, 2nd ed. Cambridge: Cambridge University Press.

Hudson, Michael. 1977. *Arab Politics: The Search for Legitimacy*. New Haven: Yale University Press.

Hymes, Dell. 1967. Models of the Interaction of Language and Social Setting. *Journal of Social Issues* 23:8–28.

———. 1974. *Foundations in Sociolinguistics: An Ethnographic Approach*. Philadelphia: University of Pennsylvania Press.

———. 1984. Linguistic Problems in Defining the Concept of "Tribe." In *Language in Use: Readings in Sociolinguistics*, ed. John Baugh and Joel Sherzer, pp. 7–27. Englewood Cliffs, NJ: Prentice Hall.

Idinopulos, Thomas A. 1998. *Weathered by Miracles: A History of Palestine from Bonaparte and Muhammad Ali to Ben-Gurion and the Mufti*. Chicago: Ivan R. Dee.

Isaacs, Miriam. 1998. Yiddish in the Orthodox Communities of Jerusalem. In *Politics of Yiddish: Studies in Language, Literature and Society*, ed. D.-B. Kerler, pp. 85–96. Walnut Creek, CA: Altamira Press.

Jakobson, Roman. 1960. Closing Statement: Lingustics and Poetics. In *Style in Language*, ed. T. A. Sebeok, pp. 350–357. Cambridge, MA: MIT Press.

Kadish, Rachel. 1998. *From a Sealed Room*. New York: Berkley Books.

Katriel, Tamar. 1986. *Talking Straight: Dugri Speech in Israeli Sabra Culture*. Cambridge: Cambridge University Press.

———. 1991. *Communal Webs: Communication and Culture in Contemporary Israel*. Albany: SUNY Press.

———. 1997. *Performing the Past: A Study of Israeli Settlement Museums*. Mahwah, NJ: Erlbaum.

———, and Yousuf Griefat. 1988. Cultural Borrowings: A Sociolinguistic Approach. In *Arab and Jewish Relations in Israel: A Quest in Human Understanding*, ed. John Hoffman, pp. 301–331. Bristol, IN: Wyndham Hall Press.

———, and Aliza Shenhar. 1990. Tower and Stockade: Dialogic Narration in Israeli Settler Ethics. *Quarterly Journal of Speech* 76:359–380.

Khalidi, Rashid. 1997. *Palestinian Identity: The Construction of Modern National Consciousness*. New York: Columbia University Press.

Kimmerling, Baruch, and Joel Migdal. 1993. *Palestinians: The Making of a People*. New York: Free Press.

Kristeva, Julia. 1980. *Desire in Language: A Semiotic Approach to Literature and Art*. New York: Columbia University Press.

Kroch, Anthony. 1978. Toward a Theory of Social Dialect Variation. *Language and Society* 7:17–36.

Kulick, Don. 1992. *Language Shift and Cultural Reproduction: Socialization, Self, and Syncretism in a Papua New Guinean Village*. Cambridge: Cambridge University Press.

Labov, William. 1963. The Social Motivation for a Sound Change. *Word* 19:273–309.

———. 1969. The Logic of Nonstandard English. *Georgetown Monographs on Language and Linguistics* 22:1–31.

———. 1972a. *Sociolinguistic Patterns*. Philadelphia: University of Pennsylvania Press.

———. 1972b. *Language in the Inner City: Studies in the Black English Vernacular*. Philadelphia: University of Pennsylvania Press.

————. 1972c. The Transformation of Experience in Narrative Syntax. In *Language in the Inner City*, pp. 354–369. Philadelphia: University of Pennsylvania Press.

————. 1978. The Design of a Sociolinguistic Research Project. In *Papers in Indian Socio-linguistics, CIIL Conferences and seminars series 2*, ed. D. P. Pattanavak. Mysore: Central Institute of Indian Languages.

————. 1982a [1966]. *The Social Stratification of English in New York City*. Washington, DC: Center for Applied Linguistics.

————. 1982b. Objectivity and Commitment in Linguistic Science: The Case of the Black English Trial in Ann Arbor. *Language in Society* 11:165–201.

————. 1984. Field Methods of the Project on Linguistic Change and Variation. In *Language in Use: Readings in Sociolinguistics*, ed. John Baugh and Joel Sherzer, pp. 28–53. Englewood Cliffs, NJ: Prentice Hall.

————. 1990. The Intersection of Sex and Social Class in the Course of Linguistic Change. *Language Variation and Change* 2:205–251.

————, and Joshua Waletzky. 1967. Narrative Analysis: Oral Versions of Personal Experience. In *Essays on the Verbal and Visual Arts*, ed. June Helm, pp. 12–44. Seattle: University of Washington Press.

————, Malcah Yaeger, and Richard Steiner. 1972. *A Quantitative Study of Sound Change in Progress*. Report on National Science Foundation Contract GS-3287. Philadelphia: U.S. Regional Survey.

Ladd, Robert. 1996. *Intonational Phonology*. Cambridge: Cambridge University Press.

Lakoff, George, and Mark Johnson. 1980. *Metaphors We Live By*. Chicago: University of Chicago Press.

Lavie, Smadar. 1992. Blow-Ups in the Borderzones: Third World Israeli Authors' Gropings for Home. *New Formations* 18:84–106.

Lefkowitz, Daniel. 1997. Affect, Identity, and Voting Behavior in Israel: A Discourse Perspective. Paper presented at the American Anthropology Association's annual meeting, November 19, 1997.

Lewis, Herbert. 1989. *After the Eagles Landed: The Yemenites of Israel*. Boulder, CO: Westview Press.

Liberman, Mark. 1975. The Intonation System of English. Ph.D. diss., Massachusetts Institute of Technology.

————, and Ivan Sag. 1974. Prosodic Form and Discourse Function. *Chicago Linguistic Society* 10:416–27.

Lucy, John A. 1992a. *Grammatical Categories and Cognition: A Case Study of the Linguistic Relativity Hypothesis*. Cambridge: Cambridge University Press.

————. 1992b. *Language Diversity and Thought: A Reformulation of the Linguistic Relativity Hypothesis*. Cambridge: Cambridge University Press.

Lustick, Ian. 1980. *Arabs in the Jewish State: Israel's Control of a National Minority*. Austin: University of Texas Press.

Lutz, Catherine, A. 1988. *Unnatural Emotions: Everyday Sentiments on a Micronesian Atoll*. Chicago: University of Chicago Press.

Macdonald, Sharon. 1997. *Reimagining Culture: Histories, Identities and the Gaelic Renaissance*. Oxford: Berg.

McLemore, Cynthia A. 1991. The Pragmatic Interpretation of English Intonation: Sorority Speech. Ph.D. diss., University of Texas at Austin.

Marcus, George, and Michael M. J. Fischer. 1986. *Anthropology as Cultural Critique: An Experimental Moment in the Human Sciences*. Chicago: University of Chicago Press.

Maschler, Yael. 1994. Iconic Contrasts in Hebrew-English Bilingual Conversation. Paper presented at the 2nd annual Symposium About Language and Society (SALSA), University of Texas at Austin, Austin, TX, April 1994.

Mead, George Herbert. 1962 [1934]. *Mind, Self, and Society from the Standpoint of a Social Behaviorist.* Chicago: University of Chicago Press.

Mendelberg, Tali. 1997. Executing Hortons: Racial Crime in the 1988 Presidential Campaign. *Public Opinion Quarterly* 61:134–157.

Mercer, Kobena. 1994. *Welcome to the Jungle: New Positions in Black Cultural Studies.* New York: Routledge.

Milroy, Lesley. 1980. *Language and Social Networks.* Baltimore: University Park Press.

Morahg, Gilead. 1997. Breaking Silence: Israel's Fantastic Fiction of the Holocaust. In *The Boom in Contemporary Israeli Fiction*, ed. A. Mintz, pp. 143–184. Hanover, NH: University Press of New England.

Myers-Scotton, Carol. 1982. The Possibility of Code-Switching: Motivation for Maintaining Multilingualism. *Anthropological Linguistics* 24:432–444.

———. 1983. The Negotiation of Identities in Conversation: A Theory of Markedness and Code Choice. *International Journal of the Sociology of Language* 44:115–136.

Nairn, Tom. 1977. *The Break-Up of Britain.* London: New Left Books.

Nakhleh, Khalil, and Elia Zureik, eds. 1980. *Sociology of the Palestinians.* London: Croom Helm.

Ochs, Elinor. 1988. *Culture and Language Development: Language Acquisition and Language Socialization in a Samoan Village.* New York: Cambridge University Press.

O'Connor, Joseph D., and G. F. Arnold. 1973. *Intonation of Colloquial English*, 2nd ed. London: Longman.

Ogbu, John. 1978. *Minority Education and Caste: The American System in Cross-Cultural Perspective.* New York: Academic Press.

Omi, Michael, and Howard Winant. 1994. *Racial Formation in the United States: From the 1960s to the 1990s.* New York: Routledge.

Oriard, Michael. 1993. *Reading Football: How the Popular Press Created an American Spectacle.* Chapel Hill: University of North Carolina Press.

Pierrehumbert, Janet B. 1980. The Phonology and Phonetics of English Intonation. Ph.D. diss., Massachusetts Institute of Technology.

———, and Mary E. Beckman. 1988. *Japanese Tone Structure.* Cambridge, MA: MIT Press.

Pitts, Walter Franklin. 1986. Linguistic Variation as a Function of Ritual Frames in the Afro-Baptist Church in Central Texas. Ph.D. diss., University of Texas.

Polanyi, Livia. 1985. *Telling the American Story: A Structural and Cultural Analysis of Conversational Storytelling.* Norwood, NJ: Ablex.

Pope, Steven. 1993. Negotiating the "Folk Highway" of the Nation: Sport, Public Culture and American Identity, 1870–1940. *Journal of Social History* 27:327–340.

Pratt, Mary. 1986. Fieldwork in Common Places. In *Writing Culture: The Poetics and the Politics of Ethnography*, ed. James Clifford and George Marcus, pp. 27–50. Berkeley: University of California Press.

Rabin, Chaim. 1970. Hebrew. *Current Trends in Linguistics* 6:305–46.

Rodriguez, Richard. 1982. *Hunger of Memory: The Education of Richard Rodriguez.* Boston: Godine.

Rosenbaum, Yehudit. 1983. Hebrew Adoption Among New Immigrants to Israel: The First Three Years. *International Journal of the Sociology of Language* 41:115–130.

Rosenfeld, Henry. 1978. Class Situation of the Arab National Minority in Israel. *Comparative Studies in Society and History* 20:374–407.

Sachar, Howard M. 1989 [1979]. *A History of Israel: From the Rise of Zionism to Our Time.* New York: Knopf.

———. 1994. *Farewell Espana: The World of the Sephardim Remembered.* New York: Vintage Books.

Said, Edward W. 1979. *Orientalism.* New York: Vintage Books.

———. 1999. *Out of Place: A Memoir.* New York: Knopf.

Sankoff, Gillian, and Suzanne Laberge. 1980. On the Acquisition of Native Speakers by a Language. In *The Social Life of Language,* pp. 195–209. Philadelphia: University of Pennsylvania Press.

Scheindlin, Raymond P. 1998. *A Short History of the Jewish People: From Legendary Times to Modern Statehood.* New York: Macmillan.

Schely-Newman, Esther. 1991. Self and Community in Historical Narratives. Ph.D. diss., University of Chicago.

Schieffelin, Bambi. 1990. *The Give and Take of Everyday Life: Language Socialization of Kaluli Children.* Cambridge: Cambridge University Press.

———, and Elinor Ochs, eds. 1986. *Language Socialization Across Cultures.* New York: Cambridge University Press.

Schiffrin, Deborah. 1981. Tense Variation in Narrative. *Language* 57:45–62.

Scollon, Ronald, and Suzanne Wong Scollon. 1981. *Narrative, Literacy and Face in Interethnic Communication.* Norwood: Ablex.

———. 1995. *Intercultural Communication: A Discourse Approach.* Oxford: Blackwell.

Scott, James C. 1985. *Weapons of the Weak: Everyday Forms of Peasant Resistance.* New Haven: Yale University Press.

———. 1990. *Domination and the Arts of Resistance: Hidden Transcripts.* New Haven: Yale University Press.

Seidman, Naomi. 1997. *A Marriage Made in Heaven: The Sexual Politics of Hebrew and Yiddish.* Berkeley: University of California Press.

Seton-Watson, Hugh. 1977. *Nations and States: An Enquiry into the Origins of Nations and the Politics of Nationalism.* Boulder, CO: Westview Press.

Shafir, Gershon. 1989. *Land, Labor and the Origins of the Israeli-Palestinian Conflict 1882–1914.* Cambridge: Cambridge University Press.

Sherzer, Joel. 1983. *Kuna Ways of Speaking: An Ethnographic Perspective.* Austin: University of Texas Press.

———. 1987. A Discourse-Centered Approach to Language and Culture. *American Anthropologist* 89:295–309.

———, and Greg Urban. 1986. Introduction. In *Native South American Discourse,* ed. Joel Sherzer and Greg Urban, pp. 1–14. Berlin: de Gruyter.

Shiloah, Amnon, and Erik Cohen. 1983. The Dynamics of Change in Jewish Oriental Ethnic Music in Israel. *Ethnomusicology* 27:227–252.

Shipler, David. 1986. *Arab and Jew: Wounded Spirits in a Promised Land.* New York: Penguin.

Shohat, Ella. 1989. *Israeli Cinema: East/West and the Politics of Representation.* Austin: University of Texas Press.

Shorrab, Ghazi Abed-el-Jabbar. 1981. Models of Socially Significant Linguistic Variation: The Case of Palestinian Arabic. Ph.D. diss., SUNY-Buffalo.

Siegel, Dina. 1998. *The Great Immigration: Russian Jews in Israel.* New York: Berghahn Books.

Slyomovics, Susan. 1998. *The Object of Memory: Arab and Jew Narrate the Palestinian Village.* Philadelphia: University of Pennsylvania Press.

Smooha, Sammy. 1999. The Advances and Limits of the Israelization of Israel's Palestinian Citizens. In *Israeli and Palestinian Identities in History and Literature*, ed. K. Abdel-Malek and D. C. Jacobson, pp. 9–33. New York: St. Martin's Press.

Snow, Catherine. 1977. The Development of Conversation Between Mothers and Babies. *Journal of Child Language* 4:1–22.

Sobel, Zvi. 1986. *Migrants from the Promised Land*. New Brunswick, NJ: Transaction Books.

Spiro, Melford E. 1963 [1956]. *Kibbutz: Venture in Utopia*. New York: Schocken.

Spolsky, Bernard, and Robert L. Cooper. 1991. *The Languages of Jerusalem*. Oxford: Clarendon Press.

———, and Elana Shohamy. 1999. *The Languages of Israel: Policy, Ideology and Practice*. Clevedon, UK: Multilingual Matters.

Swedenburg, Ted. 1995. *Memories of Revolt: The 1936–39 Rebellion and the Palestinian National Past*. Minneapolis: University of Minnesota Press.

Swirski, Shlomo. 1989. *Israel: The Oriental Majority*. London: Zed Books.

Telushkin, Joseph. 1991. *Jewish Literacy: The Most Important Things to Know About the Jewish Religion, Its People, and Its History*. New York: Morrow.

Trudgill, Peter. 1972. Sex, Covert Prestige and Linguistic Change in the Urban British English of Norwich. *Language in Society* 1:179–195.

Tyler, Stephen A. 1986. Post-Modern Ethnography: From Document of the Occult to Occult Document. In *Writing Culture: The Poetics and Politics of Ethnography*, ed. James Clifford and George Marcus, pp. 122–140. Berkeley: University of California Press.

Uldall, Elizabeth. 1964. Dimensions of Meaning in Intonation. In *In Honour of Daniel Jones*, ed. D. Abercrombie, D.B. Fry, P.A.D. MacCarthy, N.C. Scott, and J.L.M. Trim, pp. 271–279. London: Longman.

Urban, Greg. 1991. *A Discourse-Centered Approach to Culture: Native South American Myths and Ritual*. Austin: University of Texas Press.

———, and Joel Sherzer. 1988. The Linguistic Anthropology of Native South America. *Annual Review of Anthropology* 17:283–307.

Vaughn-Cooke, Anna Fay. 1975. The Black Preaching Style: Historical Development and Characteristics. *Georgetown University Working Papers on Languages and Linguistics* 5:28–39.

Vološinov, Valentin N. 1973. *Marxism and the Philosophy of Language*. Translated by Ladislav Matejka and I. R. Titunik. Cambridge, MA: Harvard University Press.

Ward, Gregory, and Julia Hirschberg. 1985. Implicating Uncertainty: The Pragmatics of Fall-Rise Intonation. *Language* 61:747–776.

Webster, Gerald R., and Jonathan I. Leib. 2001. Whose South Is It Anyway? Race and the Confederate Battle Flag in South Carolina. *Political Geography* 20:271–299.

Weedon, Chris. 1987. *Feminist Practice and Poststructuralist Theory*. Oxford: Blackwell.

Weiner, E. Judith, and William Labov. 1983. Constraints on the Agentless Passive. *Journal of Linguistics* 19:29–58.

Weingrod, Alex. 1966. *Reluctant Pioneers: Village Development in Israel*. Ithaca: Cornell University Press.

Weinreich, Uriel. 1953. *Languages in Contact, Findings and Problems*. New York: Linguistic Circle of New York.

———, William Labov, and Marvin Herzog. 1968. Empirical Foundations for a Theory of Language Change. In *Directions for Historical Linguistics*, ed. Winfred Lehman and Yakov Malkiel, pp. 97–195. Austin: University of Texas Press.

White, Hayden. 1980. The Value of Narrativity in the Representation of Reality. *Critical Inquiry* 7:5–27.

Williams, Brackette. 1989. A Class Act: Anthropology and the Race to Nation Across Ethnic Terrain. *Annual Review of Anthropology* 18:401–444.

Williams, Carl E., and Kenneth N. Stevens. 1972. Emotions and Speech: Some Acoustical Correlates. *Journal of the Acoustical Society of America* 52:1238–50.

Williams, Raymond. 1977. *Marxism and Literature*. Oxford: Oxford University Press.

Wilson, William A. 1973. Herder, Folklore and Romantic Nationalism. *Journal of Popular Culture* 6:818–835.

Wollheim, Richard. 1971. *Sigmund Freud*. Cambridge: Cambridge University Press.

Woodbury, Anthony. 1987a. Meaningful Phonological Processes: A Consideration of Central Alaskan Yupik Eskimo Prosody. *Language* 63:685–740.

———. 1987b. Rhetorical Structure in a Central Alaskan Yupik Eskimo Traditional Narrative. In *Native American Discourse: Poetics and Rhetoric*, ed. Joel Sherzer and Anthony Woodbury. Cambridge: Cambridge University Press.

Woolard, Katherine, and Bambi Schieffelin. 1994. Language Ideology. *Annual Review of Anthropology* 23:55–82.

Yaeger-Dror, Malcah. 1988. The Influence of Changing Group Vitality on Convergence Toward a Dominant Linguistic Norm: An Israeli Example. *Language and Communication* 8:285–305.

———. 1991. Linguistic Evidence for Social Psychological Attitudes: Hyperaccommodation or (r) by Singers from a Mizrahi Background. *Language and Communication* 11(4):309–331.

———. 1993. Linguistic Analysis of Dialect "Correction" and Its Interaction with Cognitive Salience. *Language Variation and Change* 5:189–224.

Yehoshua, Abraham B. 1977. *The Lover*. Translated by Philip Simpson. San Diego, CA: Harcourt Brace.

———. 1991. Facing the Forests. Translated by Miriam Arad. In *The Continuing Silence of a Poet: The Collected Stories of A. B. Yehoshua*, pp. 203–236. New York: Penguin Books.

Zerubavel, Yael. 1995. *Recovered Roots: Collective Memory and the Making of Israeli National Tradition*. Chicago: University of Chicago Press.

Index